Jim Harrison

# Jim Harrison

*A Comprehensive Bibliography,
1964–2008*

Gregg Orr and Beef Torrey

FOREWORD BY JIM HARRISON
INTRODUCTION BY ROBERT DEMOTT

UNIVERSITY OF NEBRASKA PRESS | Lincoln and London

Frontispiece: Wood-engraved portrait of
Jim Harrison by Barry Moser from *Portraits*
(North Hatfield MA: Pennyroyal Press, 2007).
Used by permission.

All images with art by Russell Chatham are
used by permission of Russell Chatham.

© 2009 by the Board of Regents of the
University of Nebraska
All rights reserved
Manufactured in the
United States of America
∞
Library of Congress
Cataloging-in-Publication Data

Orr, Gregg.
Jim Harrison: a comprehensive bibliography,
1964–2008 / Gregg Orr and Beef Torrey; foreword by Jim Harrison; introduction
by Robert DeMott.
p. cm.
Includes index.
ISBN 978-0-8032-1614-3 (cl.: alk. paper)
1. Harrison, Jim, 1937—Bibliography.
I. Torrey, Beef. II. Title.
Z8387.92.O77 2009
[PS3558.A67]
016.8185409—dc22
2009000792

Set in Iowan Old Style.
Designed by R. W. Boeche.

# Contents

| | |
|---|---|
| Foreword: Nebraska Redux by Jim Harrison | vii |
| Acknowledgments | xi |
| Introduction by Robert DeMott | xv |
| A Note on Structure | xxxiii |
| Chronology | xxxv |
| Section A: *Books and Broadsides by Jim Harrison* | 1 |
| Section B: *Individually Published Poetry* | 115 |
| Section C: *Individually Published Fiction* | 135 |
| Section D: *Individually Published Nonfiction* | 139 |
| Section E: *Reviews and Criticism by Jim Harrison* | 169 |
| Section F: *Screenplays* | 173 |
| Section G: *Miscellany: Audio Readings, Videotapes, Dust-Jacket Encomiums* | 175 |
| Section H: *Annotated Interviews with Jim Harrison* | 213 |
| Section I: *Critical Articles, Essays, and Studies concerning Jim Harrison's Works* | 265 |
| Section J: *Reviews of Jim Harrison's Works* | 275 |
| Index | 303 |

# Foreword
## *Nebraska Redux*

This book helps fulfill my unrequited affair with Nebraska that began on a late August evening in 1954 when I slept out in a pasture near the Platte River. I was hitchhiking back to Michigan from a summer job in Colorado and was plumb tired when I knelt by the river to wash up. I recall that I was hearing a whip-poor-will, fine night music, and watching a group of Hereford cattle upstream. When I awoke at dawn, there was a circle of young Herefords close around me. I'm still the only environmentalist I know who loves cattle, but I grew up with them as my dad was a county ag agent who judged them at fairs. In any event it was the sweetest night you could have by yourself far from home, perhaps misinformed by my idea that one of my high school favorite authors, Willa Cather, might have visited the very spot where I slept.

I suspect that it was this experience that helped bring me back to Nebraska in the mid-1980s when I was taking very long nondirectional car trips to mentally survive my livelihood at the time, which was commuting between northern Michigan and Hollywood. I quickly became and remain obsessed by the Sandhills and ended up actually dreaming my character Dalva sitting on a balcony in Santa Monica, California, planning her return to the Sandhills. On a strictly rational level I needed a somewhat mythological area that educated readers would know existed but with which they would be unfamiliar. Americans tend to be historically naive, and I wanted to direct their attention to the general area of northwest Nebraska where the last violent collision of two cultures took place.

An old man's memory bank (I'm sixty-eight) is overfull and is, in fact, uncontainable. When I first looked at the manuscript of this bibliography, it was unsettling indeed. Each of the hundreds of items raised memories, pleasant and unpleasant. What precisely was I doing in Africa, Europe, Russia, and South America in a space of a little over a year? Well, I was either writing about these locations or intending to. It was my father who told me that curiosity will carry your life in goodly fashion better than anything else. The French poet Rimbaud wrote about "a child crazed with maps." That was me, and, when you add the essential factor of coming from a reading family, the seven of us sitting the evening all separately reading, you add a great deal of fuel to the life that ensues. In fact bookishness has occasionally reached the disease level in my life, and only through travel have I been able to liberate myself from books as an addiction. My wife, Linda, used to be amused when I'd travel north to our cabin with many cartons of books for a short week. "Only a carton a day?" she'd ask.

Of course, if I hadn't spent a good deal of my life on the move, I wouldn't have written half my novels and novellas. I chafed at my two years in the English Department at Stony Brook University on Long Island not because it was unpleasant but because I'm a claustrophobe and prefer living in remote places. The scholar-novelist Fred Turner wrote a fascinating book, *The Spirit of Place*, and, despite the media telling us that the media has made the world a more uniform place, each location seems to have its geographic and cultural uniqueness. If I hadn't visited Russia in 1972, I certainly wouldn't have written *Letters to Yesenin*, and an early foray into northwest Montana gave me *Legends of the Fall* and a solvency at age forty I had long sought in despair. *Revenge* and its doomed and brooding atmosphere came from a trip to Mexico, and *A Good Day to Die* emerged from fishing trips to Key West. *Sundog* wouldn't have been possible without visits to Costa Rica, Ecuador, and Brazil. You snoop around, read, talk to people, and generally look things over. Your approach is decidedly not scholarly because you are looking for the *feel* of the place, its spirit. For instance, Nebraska had meant inestimably more to me because I had read Willa Cather, Wright Morris, and Mari Sandoz. In addition I was lucky enough to meet and come to know Bill and Anne Quigley up in Valentine, John Carter at the Nebraska State Historical Society, who is a living encyclopedia, the noted poet Ted Kooser, Roger and Linda Welsch, and Beef Torrey. It is fascinating to see in the relatively new academic discipline of human geography that we tend to *become* where we live.

When I tried to answer queries from Gregg Orr for this bibliography, it was, as I've inferred, a not altogether pleasant experience. I suspect that in any writer's life there are things he wished he hadn't written. I have my own private list, and Gregg Orr has helped me add to it. I'm not gifted in the political arena and tend to rant and rave, and many of the critical pieces I wrote for the *New York Times Book Review* smack of the young smartass. There's also the novel *Warlock* I wrote when I was drinking too much, though some people care for the work. The novelist Thomas McGuane and I used to look at Faulkner's work and figure out when he was strictly boozed amid his splendor.

The initial fifteen years of my career were especially hard for a bibliographer because I never kept track of anything, but luckily for the past twenty-seven years I have been partnered with my aide, Joyce Harrington Bahle, who has brought a specific order to my life and work. When I saw that there were over fifteen hundred citations in this bibliography, I recalled humorously a possible gravestone inscription: "He Got His Work Done." This seems a little more typical of the Midwest than our dream coasts. Or, perhaps better yet, as the ancient historian Nonnius said: "I have made a heap of all I have met."

*Jim Harrison*
Patagonia, Arizona

## Acknowledgments

The work before you was born from reading and collecting Jim Harrison's work for over twenty-five years. It is grounded in a profound respect for Harrison's writing and admiration for him as a writer and friend. As Robert DeMott so eloquently states in his fine introduction: "Occasionally . . . a writer comes along who says everything we imagine ourselves being capable of saying if we only had the skill, energy, or talent to do so." This statement strikes at the heart of how this work came into being.

I would like to extend my sincere thanks to the many booksellers and book collectors who've assisted in putting together the information contained in this work. You are too numerous to name individually; however, you know who you are, and I can't begin to express my gratitude for your assistance and support over the years.

My thanks go to Judy Hottensen and Claire Howorth, present and former employees at Grove/Atlantic, who were patient beyond reason with many separate inquiries and requests. To Tony and Pam Delcavo, who in 1999 provided an extraordinary Evil Companions evening in Denver and put me behind the wheel of Ed Abbey's Cadillac. You guys may be responsible for getting this ball rolling. Also, special thanks and appreciation to Barry Moser and Cara Moser, who provided the fine portrait of Jim for our frontispiece. To Karen Dmochowsky of *Sports Illustrated*, a fellow Midwesterner whose help and cheerfulness were a treasure. To Mary Harrison Dumsch, for saving stuff.

Special thanks go to Keith Comer for his work on the "Jim Harrison: A Bibliography" Web site (www.jimharrison.org). Also, to all the members of the Jim Harrison Society (a subchapter of the American Literature Association) and especially to Michael Ryan and William Barillas. Sincere thanks to Bruce Kahn, whose excellent Harrison collection, generosity, knowledge, and fine conversation are a constant aid. To Jeff Maser and Peter Howard, booksellers who go well beyond the call of duty when it comes to the mania of a collector with a bibliographic bent. To Allen Ahearn, whose knowledge and insight into all matters concerning collectable books is vast. To Ladette Randolph and all the helpful folks at the University of Nebraska Press. Many thanks to my sister Amber Felts for her photographs in section A.

My unending thanks and gratitude to Robert DeMott and Patrick Smith, Harrison scholars, academic advisers, and friends who provided a seemingly endless supply of information, time, suggestions, and friendship. To Joseph Bednarik, whose keen insight, energy, and thoughtfulness were pillars of this effort and to whom I am deeply indebted for his encouragement, advice, and experience. To Beef Torrey, whose camaraderie, fine nature, unbelievable generosity, and friendship I have come to rely on. To Grand Valley State University, where the Harrison Papers are archived. GVSU provided support and unlimited access to Harrison's materials. Special thanks to Robert Beasecker, the head of the Special Collections, and Nancy Richard, the university archivist, for their fine hospitality, assistance, and patience.

To Jim Harrison and Joyce Harrington Bahle, who facilitated and provided unwavering support for this project. A work like this could not and would not have been completed without your help and patience. Joyce—your friendship, hospitality, and advice have been and remain remarkable. Jim—I hope this effort is, in some small way, a means to repay the many hours of thought-provoking and entertaining reading you've provided over the years. It has been one of my more rewarding endeavors to catalog your published work. This project has opened doors and led me to places and people I'd never have known had I not embarked on the journey. Many thanks, Jim, for all these gifts.

Last, but not least by any means, I want to thank my wife, Janice, and my children, Jeffrey and Cameryn, whose patient understanding and support allowed for untold hours of library time, travel, and days away from home for this project.

This work is dedicated to Marilynn Orr and Joyce Bahle.

*Gregg Orr*
St. Louis, Missouri

This volume is largely a labor of love and would not have been possible without the sustained assistance, support, and encouragement of numerous individuals, in fact far too many to name individually.

Despite such, for starters, I wish to thank my fellow co-compiler, Gregg Orr. Gregg has been most instrumental in making this publication a reality and assumed the leadership role in its final revision and completion. I value greatly his friendship, generosity, and passion. Moreover, I thank his wife, Janice, and their children, Jeffrey and Cameryn, who have welcomed me into their home and lives with opened arms.

A special thanks to Joseph Bednarik at Copper Canyon Press in Port Townsend, Washington. Joseph did the early groundwork and helped launch the Web site; he cites Garret S. Brunswick for providing amazing work/research at the Library of Congress and on Nexus/Lexus. I vividly recall, over a decade ago, our discussion of compiling a Jim Harrison bibliography and our innumerable parcels and e-mail exchanges through the years. I have tremendous respect and appreciation for you and your steadfast support of this project.

To my cherished friend and hunting companion, Jim Harrison, I thank you way down deep inside my heart, where it really counts. Your words, your company, your friendship—I will never forget. Some of the most enjoyable and treasured times of my life have been in your presence.

To your lovely wife, Linda, your daughter Jamie and son-in-law, Steve Potenberg, their children and your grandchildren, John and Will, your daughter Anna and son-in-law, Max Hjortsberg, and their infant son, also your grandchild, Silas, whose friendships I prize as well.

Joyce Bahle, none of this could have been even attempted without your assistance, insight, and support.

A special tribute of thanks and sincere appreciation to our dear friend and mentor Dr. Bob DeMott at the University of Ohio in Athens, who has been unswerving in his support of this project and has contributed a great deal to its contents and publication, as well as to Dr. Patrick Smith of Tallahassee, Florida.

To the current and former staff at Grove/Atlantic—Judy Hottensen, Amy Hundley, Deb Seager, Daniel Ricciato, Claire Howorth, and Erin Flanigan, among others—who provided prompt responses to our repeated queries.

To our mutual friends who have enriched my life, Guy de la Valdene, Thomas McGuane, Russell Chatham, Doug and Andrea Peacock, Gatz, Elwood Reid, John Fryer, Dan Lahren, Doug Stanton, Bob Dattila, Jim Fergus, the late Richard Brautigan . . . (a long list).

To the special contributions and encouragement of David Harrison, Minneapolis; David Stamm, Denver; Brandon Kelley, New York City; Ted Kooser, Garland, Nebraska; Sy Settell, Firth, Nebraska; Jan Seng, Pittsburgh; Emily C. Hunter, Matfield Green, Kansas; James H. Lee, Northfield, Minnesota;

Bill Kohlhaase, Bozeman; Ana Sedlar, Traverse City, Michigan; Kevin P. Simonson, Omaha, Nebraska; Crystal (Christensen) Richard, the Upper Peninsula; Ron Vogele, Wymore, Nebraska; J. R. Hansen, Lincoln, Nebraska; Keith Abbott, Longmont, Colorado; Evelyn Adams, North Newton, Kansas; Dinah Henderson, Greenwood, Missouri; Robert Bertholf, SUNY Buffalo; and Chicago Steve.

Members past and present of the Jim Harrison Society of the American Literature Association: Patrick Smith, Lilli Ross, Aaron Parrett, Michael Ryan, and William Barillas, among others.

Richard Ardinger of Limberlost Press; Clark City Press in Livingston. Jim Carvalho, publisher of *Border Beat* in Tucson, Arizona; Michael Peich of Aralia Press; Kermit Lynch Wine Merchant and staff in Berkeley, California.

Patty Beutler, Jeff Korbelik, and George Wright of the *Lincoln Journal Star*; Jim Barnes, the managing editor of *Independent Publisher On-line* in Traverse City, Michigan; and Kathryn and Robin Smiley of *Firsts Magazine*.

To University of Nebraska Press staff and former associate director, Ladette Randolph, for accepting the manuscript and ensuring it progressed from start to finish.

In memory of the late Dr. John Harrison and Rose.

*Beef Torrey*
Rural Crete, Nebraska

# Introduction

Yet it is not until the inner-most core is reached that the meaning of the whole is revealed, and, as one penetrates deeper and deeper . . . layer upon layer is seen . . . each with a character of its own but which can be fully understood only in relation to the others. | Herbert Weisinger, *Tragedy and the Paradox of the Fortunate Fall* (1953)

Although I should probably know better, in considering Jim Harrison's writing career, it's difficult for me to separate the man and his words or to sufficiently remove myself from the impact of knowing both the author and his work. But then I've never considered myself academically fashionable or, for that matter, dispassionately or clinically objective, so why start now? And, though my willful confusion of means and ends might be troubling, unsettling, and even embarrassing to Harrison, who has usually insisted on the priority of the written work over the cult of personality, he has himself managed to complicate issues even further by claiming: "We become what we write." The inverse of this is that we write what we become. Either way, the two are joined at the hip. In setting out to introduce Gregg Orr and Beef Torrey's landmark resource book, *Jim Harrison: A Comprehensive Bibliography, 1964–2008*, I am mindful of Rick Bass's statement in his 1998 essay "France" where he tries to explain how much Harrison means to him as both a friend and a writer: "I can't imagine him not ever being here," Bass concludes. In this moment of bibliographic celebration, what follows is a minority report—part confession and part observation—on the curative power of authorial friendship. It is my praiseful story, and I am sticking to it, though I suspect that it speaks for many of Jim's readers, each of whom will have their own twist on the tale.

||||||| ||||||| |||||||

Recently, after taking some knocks on the head from seismic personal upheavals and the allover gravitational pull of geezerdom, which has a tendency to dull even our sharpest edges, I thought life had lost its juice and what remained were only bruised skins and rinds, the kind of dispensable leftovers that exited the back door of Gatsby's mansion after one of his extravagant bashes. At the risk of sounding ridiculous, I knew I was in a grievous slump when, watching a dozen improbably large trout slurping down newly hatched mayfly duns on Montana's Beaverhead River, I felt none of that jangling anticipation that, no matter how skilled or experienced you are, accompanies casting a tiny dry fly on light tippet to a pod of gorging fish. Witnessing trout on the feed, counting heads as they effortlessly pick off floating insects, is usually enough to jazz me because it's a known fact that angling expectations increase exponentially with the size and frequency of rising trout. My funk at being out of step with the rhythms and abundance of life around me seemed to come and go during the next two weeks, as it had all summer, but the fishing—normally effective and reliable therapy for what ails me—seemed to be somehow unfulfilling, monotonous, even— God forbid—trivial and frivolous. Clearly, a fire had banked and some part of me turned to ash. Meanwhile, I muddled along and eventually fished my way to Jim Harrison's in Livingston, where we were meeting for our annual foray after Yellowstone River trout.

In the months before his fourteenth book of fiction, a novel called *Returning to Earth* (not to be confused with his 1977 poetry chapbook of the same name), was set to appear, Jim had started a comic novel called *The English Major*, and he was relatively deep into the handwritten manuscript when I showed up at the Harrison house. He had redefined contractual relations with his publisher (Grove/Atlantic) and had gone through a series of complex negotiations with a new literary agent in New York, and as a result he was working no less intently but certainly less obsessively than he had in the past. ("Got exhausted and extremely enervated by my own novel," he told me a year earlier. "Can't write six days in a row anymore without popping my skull.")

So his new regimen last summer, a routine with which he seemed reasonably comfortable, was to write four days a week (mostly a page a day on the fiction, but with inevitable side trips into poetry and essays), then decompress by fishing on the other three. He had once again arranged his schedule and that of his master trout guide and angling partner, Dan Lahren, to coincide with my visit (and those of about a dozen other visitors who came through Livingston that summer). Fishing sixty days a year (ninety when he was younger) is Harrison's way of combating the rigors of writing and offsetting the incessant demands and numbing effects of what he regularly refers to—ironically and self-deprecatingly, I should add—as the "literary life," especially its potential for suffocating his central drives in a "mud bath" of peripheral seductions, against which he remains as vigilant as possible.

Nowadays, fishing is a Harrison "panic hole," an idea he adapted from Gerald Vizenor's novel *The Trickster of Liberty*: it's that place—literal or metaphoric—"where you flee to get back the present as a wild season rather than a ruse," he claims in his 2001 essay collection, *The Raw and the Cooked: Adventures of a Roving Gourmand*. To put it in more pedestrian terms, as he did in a brief preface to a special issue of *Men's Journal* on "Hideouts, Dream Towns, and Great Escapes," a panic hole is a hiding place "where you can shed the usual accouterments of your attitudes and personality, where you can rid yourself of the banality of your day-to-day perceptions." It can be a locality or a state of mind, or both. So fishing is Harrison's refuge, passion, and antidote. "The only way I can erase everything. . . . I think it's a Taoist thing," he informed the interviewer Lindsay Ahl in a recent issue of *Bliss* magazine. "A river has such an acceptance of mortality and it's such an aesthetically overwhelming thing that you don't think about anything else. . . . [Fishing] erases everything impossible in your life." Angling and water gazing help fill the tank and keep the keel even: "I turned down being on Cannes jury this year because I MUST be on the Big Hole River in May," he wrote me earlier in the season. Perhaps only an angling addict can understand the implacable logic and utter sanity of such a move. Indeed, fly fishing is one of the well-fingered obsessions around which Jim built his 2002 memoir, *Off to the Side*. He is the person, after all, who wrote *the* poetic treatise on rivering, *The Theory and Practice of Rivers*.

What I found out in Livingston—not that I had ever totally forgotten it—is how difficult it is to be depressed or dispirited in Jim's company. He says of Julip Durham, one of his fiercely independent female characters, that in a world of hemophiliacs she's a blood transfusion. Not to put too melodramatic a spin on this, Harrison too can have that kind of effect. He has a way, in his high-calorie, chain-smoking, gravel-voiced, go-for-broke manner, of completely filling the space he inhabits and sweeping you into it, for better or for worse, whether you are ready or not.

So the truth is that three days of float fishing the Yellowstone River in Lahren's Lavro driftboat (always enjoyable even if the fishing is so-so, as it was last summer) is really the least part of our yearly visit. Although fishing is an essential shared bond between us, a kind of bedrock of like-minded interests—especially our partiality to brown trout (*Salmo trutta*) and our dislike of any kind of competitive, one-upmanship air—I'd be lying if I did not say that for me the heart of our visit is elsewhere: in nonstop gabfests and lively banter; running commentary, mostly sardonic and humorous and frequently off-color, on the foibles and fiddle-faddle of the usual suspect male topics, which is to say, food, sex, politics, culture, nature, and dogs. And, because Harrison is a master raconteur and hypnotic talker, there is a barrage of animated reminiscences, anecdotes, yarn spinning, and storytelling, all with his characteristic digressions and looping, multidirectional tangents. (When Patrick Smith and I conducted interviews with Harrison in 1997 and 1998, the typescript of our audiotapes ran to well over 150 pages. Shaping a final version of sixteen thousand words for *Conversations with Jim Harrison* took several months, during which time we learned that, where Jim is concerned, the digressions *are* the story. Though he has a reputation for being gruff, imperious, and elusive, we could not have asked for a more candid, generous, and voluble conversationalist, as the annotated list of interviews included in this bibliography attests.)

But our locker-room banter doesn't paint the whole picture. There are also fabulous meals on which Jim and his wife, Linda, lavish so much attention and care that the course and arc of a whole day might be organized around an evening at their long harvest table. The dining room's ceiling-tall windows frame the Absaroka Mountains on the eastern side of Paradise Valley, across the Yellowstone River. It's what realtors mean when they say: "Location, location, location." (Even claustrophobic Jim admits to a sense of freedom in that breathtaking setting, where it is possible to see for miles.) After a stretch of serious angling, dinner is not just a welcome reward but a symphonic experience. In Jim's case, because he and Dan swap rowing chores, fishing is not only a contemplative Waltonian activity but a strenuously physical one as well. In the grand scheme of things, there is nothing like rowing a driftboat or casting a fly rod a thousand times a day to build a suitably deserving, guilt-free hunger.

And it isn't just eating as a routine feed-your-face activity but dining rightly and gloriously well. Judging from the number of food and wine columns listed in this excellent bibliography, cooking with gusto and imagination and savoring the results is not just a way of life but lifesaving. "I like to think that my eating and drinking comprise a strenuous search for the genuine, that I am a voyager, an explorer, an adventurer in the ordinary activity of what we do every day: eat and drink," he announces in *The Raw and the Cooked*.

Life, according to Harrison's signature mantra, is best approached with "more red wine and garlic." It's all been vividly detailed in Jim's fiction, where many of his protagonists find refuge and diversion in cooking or learning to do so—Nordstrom in "The Man Who Gave Up His Name" comes immediately to mind. In his copious essays his fellow food and wine impresarios Mario Batali, Russell Chatham, Guy de la Valdene, Peter Lewis, Gerard Oberle, and his own culinarily gifted family members (Linda Harrison and daughters Jamie and Anna and their husbands, Steve and Max) appear often, so I can't add much in the face of those intimate experts except a few weak tea impressions. The particularity, the specificity, of meals, with their complex preparation, their collage of tastes, smells, and textures, sets an overarching tone for our visits. Fishing, cooking, writing: they are all of a piece. "You're a dead duck if you don't love the process," he's said on many occasions.

Mornings are a bit rushed so we can get to a launch site ahead of other boats (we despise being crowded or fishing in another boat's wake), but breakfast is always simple and hearty and not exactly low fat in content because it usually involves fresh sausage (from one of Guy's fattened and sweetened feral pigs) or bacon (obtained from an outstanding local butcher shop) and skillet-fried potatoes unearthed from Linda's garden (sometimes in duck or goose confit, sometimes not). Lunches I'll get to shortly. Dinners are off the chart and too elaborate to do justice to here, though, when the house is awash with the tantalizing odors of cooking—fresh chile verde, spicy Thai chicken, sautéed abalone, or roast shoulder of lamb—and bustling with the work of many hands, I sometimes feel that I am inside one of Jim's food essays, and I can't decide whether life imitates art or the other way around. It's a happy dilemma, and, fortunately, I don't really have to choose; being in the moment seems luxury enough. Whatever, it is hard not to smile inwardly, give thanks for such largesse and fellow feeling, and ride the dining car as far as it will go.

Lunches, too, are right up my alley because in the fifty years I've been traipsing through the outdoors (an alternate universe to my academic life) I've never found anything that compares with eating at midday something I've carried to the woods or water. Senses are keener after a morning of trout fishing, appetites sharper after following a zigzagging pointing dog through grouse cover. Jim, too, knows the drill because he might have invented it: fennel and oregano salamis and culatello from Armandino Batali's Salumi in Seattle, crusty artisanal breads and sharp imported cheeses, and the ever-present bottle of Trappy's delectable pepperoncini for our alfresco dining, laid out without fanfare, monogrammed silverware, or hoity-toity Orvis pretentiousness on top of Dan Lahren's well-traveled portable cooler. "We're American sportsmen," Jim jokes, "and need to keep up our strength to battle these great fish." We're in on the joke and fall to.

Anchored at river's edge miles east of Livingston, watching the great (and thankfully as yet undammed) Yellowstone roll by, listening to wind in the cottonwoods carrying the *yucka-yucka-yucka* of a red-shafted flicker or the piercing cry of a circling osprey, I began to feel that life had regained some color and vibrancy—and urgency as well. Not full-fledged healing, but a beneficial shift in attitude and perspective. If I hadn't become the bitter wine, as Rilke councils, at least some of my impossibilities had been erased, and life began to matter again. I resisted being naively optimistic as long as I could, but spending time at the Harrisons'—maybe it's better to call it *hiding out*—is good for the soul if not the liver and waistline.

||||||||  ||||||  ||||||

Among American novelists and poets Jim Harrison is the epic bard of epicureanism, the sweet singer of imbibement, the grand nabob of gustation—in short, he is America's poet laureate of appetite. "The way you eat," he told the *Paris Review* interviewer Jim Fergus, "bespeaks your entire attitude toward life." That's typical of Harrison—he lays what matters right on the table. In fact one of the happiest-looking author photos I have ever seen is on the cover of *The Raw and the Cooked*. Jim Harrison is smiling ear to ear, glass of red wine in hand, bottle of Louisiana hot sauce at the ready, and the entire table in front of him at his beloved Ajax Diner in Oxford, Mississippi, set as far as the eye can see with home-cooked fare. He's being challenged by all that deliciousness, I imagine, by all that's spread before him, and can't wait for the good work of tasting to begin. In the end, for the man who told the interviewer Kay Bonetti in 1984 that his defense against the world was to build a sentence out of it, food equals language, and language equals food, which is, of course, an invitation for us to taste his words and for him to invite another episode of gout or begin another radical diet. "Eat or Die," as his column title puts it: despite what our elders tell us, the path of excess sometimes leads to wisdom.

For the man of appetite, the sybarite of experience, the whole world is a sensory smorgasbord. With Jim Harrison, the good work is far more than mere taste-bud gratification. He's a glutton for experience; everything is grist for his writerly mill. A brief parable that prefaces *The Raw and the Cooked* is entitled "The Man Who Ate Books." There is something especially fitting and arresting in that image because it characterizes Harrison's edible take on the world, his self-confessedly "fatal" appetite, not just for food and unalloyed physical experience, but perhaps more than anything else for language, for the life of the mind, for the sustenance that feeds the soul as well as the body: "There were books in the schools, where our young hero had taken to reading one every day, sometimes two, while totally neglecting his other studies. There were also many books at home but at home he was forbidden to tear out the endpapers and chew on them, which he sneakily did at school. Endpapers were his gum and candy."

The narrator of Harrison's novella "The Beast God Forgot to Invent" says of the wounded Joseph Lacort: "He's literally taking bites out of the sun, moon, and earth." I take that to be a self-referential statement because I know few other people with a more insatiable curiosity for life or a greater hunger to devour life in as many of its varied guises and obsessive forms. Eating, drinking, tasting, become the central somatic metaphors and processes that link all the writer's compelling pursuits, as he reveals in the introduction to *The Raw and the Cooked*:

> I love to cook, hunt, fish, read good books, and not incidentally try to write them. Even the occasional glories of our sexual lives can be drawn into this picture. Not that much is finer than a morning spent at the Metropolitan Museum of Art in New York or the Musee d'Orsay in Paris followed by a good lunch. All of our senses and passions merge because we are one person and it's best not to neglect any of those passions if we wish to fully live our lives.

And yet, for every reference to organic processes, sexual practices, natural places, animal denizens, or bodily functions in Harrison's work (references that have caused some critics and reviewers to brand him as crude, sexist, earthy, brutish), there are equally frequent allusions to the world of art, literature, philosophy, history, cinema, and music. When Philip Caulkins, the narrator of Harrison's novella "The Beige Dolorosa" (included in *Julip*), takes on the task of renaming American birds (he believes that, with the exception of the elegant *trogan*, *whimbrel*, and *Hudsonian godwit*, their names are too pedestrian), he christens the curve-billed thrasher "the 'beige dolorosa,' which is reminiscent of a musical phrase in Mozart, one that makes your heart pulse with mystery, as does the bird." It is nearly impossible to read even two pages of Harrison's edgy prose without bumping up against the aesthetic world, the realm of artistic artifacts and signifiers. Unfortunately, relatively few critics and reviewers outside France (where Harrison has a large, dedicated audience of informed, attentive readers) are clued in to this referential dimension of his work, preferring instead to view him as a rough-and-tumble bully boy of American letters, a writer whose book the barroom cooler Dalton (played by Patrick Swayze) is briefly shown reading in the 1989 cult action film *Road House*. To reduce Harrison's work to a single preoccupation, however, is to distort the integrity and complexity of the whole. "It is what it is," he's said often.

The sweep of Harrison's imagination is wide, and the pulse of mystery can be found everywhere. "I test the thickness of the universe, its resilience / to carry us further than any of us wish to go," he says in "Cabbage," a poem in his 2006 collection *Saving Daylight*. The Huron Mountains of Michigan's Upper Peninsula and James Joyce's *Finnegans Wake*, Nebraska's austere Sandhills and New York's sumptuous MOMA or Guggenheim, Drum Hadley's vast Grey Ranch in Arizona and the poetry of John Clare coexist, not as schizophrenic opposites or self-canceling binaries, as some critics have claimed, but in a mutually enriching, harmonious dance of affinities that defines Harrison's encompassing worldview, his homegrown version of Keatsian negative capability. This all adds up to a portrait of the artist in motion, resolutely lighting out for the territory, but stopping often enough to read the stack of books under his arm.

The two realms—action and reflection, outside and inside, nature and culture—are inseparably linked, and their borders are permeable. Both/and (not either/or) is the Harrisonian equation: the liminal moment, the evening hour, as the French say, *entre chien et loup* (between dog and wolf), where belief and disbelief, domesticity and wildness, reality and dream are necessary components of a fully realized, observant life. Speech and writing fall in this category as well. In his metafictional novel *Sundog*, enticingly subtitled *The Story of an American Foreman, Robert Corvus Strang, as Told to Jim Harrison*, the narrator/interviewer, a jaded author and former journalist named "Jim Harrison," and Robert Corvus Strang, his interviewee, an invalid dam builder, are, despite their strikingly different temperaments, both varyingly fictionalized manifestations of their creator, which is to say that they are a result of Harrison interrogating complementary facets of himself. He confessed to Kay Bonetti that Strang and the narrator are "almost extremities of the right and left lobes of the same head." In *Sundog*, the narrator's abundant indulgence in conversation is allied to his "pleasure in being told a story so directly from someone's life." And yet "Jim Harrison" is compelled to turn Strang's raw story into art. The narrator's desire for imagining a life without dread (a key theme of the novel and one of Harrison's longed-for life goals) realizes itself as the oral tale morphs into a print narrative before our eyes.

To put it another way: even if Harrison, a dyed-in-the-wool nonacademic writer, is considered a "reluctant postmodernist" (David Pichaske's term in *Rooted: Seven Midwest Writers of Place*) who adopts some of the modes and methods he disparages (he isn't the kind of writer who second-guesses himself), his true subject is still the insatiable, perhaps unappeasable, dimensions of individual consciousness pushing against, responding to, the tragic excesses, contradictions, and paradoxes of our cultural, social, and environmental histories and practices. Asked to describe "the core, the spirit" of his work in a 1997 interview in the *Wild Duck Review*, Harrison replied to Casey Walker: "This consciousness, I would say. Otherness. Otherness to remind ourselves of the bedrock of life, and death, and love, and suffering." I have a hunch that's why we read, study, critique, praise, admire, collect, talk back to, argue with, and otherwise pay attention to his texts.

Harrison likes to speak of his capacity to enter into the Zen master Dogen's world of ten thousand things, an egoless place of soulful vulnerability, empathy, and openness where everything speaks if we only learn to listen with our inner ear, see with our inner eye, which requires Zen-like attentiveness. "I do Za Zen for the same reason that I fish and hunt," he confessed to Patrick Smith and me. "They're all confused in my mind, and that's evidently how it started. It's a primitive hunting technique. You know if you sit very still in the woods for two hours you're going to see things. . . . That maybe is the prehistorical origin of what Pound called the 'dimension of stillness.'"

In this scene in Harrison's twelfth book of fiction, *True North*, David Burkett, the unwilling scion of a northern Michigan timber family who has set out, however inexpertly, to right his family's environmental wrongs, finds a vast graveyard of white pine stumps: "I turned around and stood there a full ten minutes, my enervation and fatigue now gone, until I could imagine what this patch of forest looked like. I can't say how but the massive stumps [three men with hands joined could not encircle these trees] now seemed alive." Later, he says: "I thought this was as close as I could come to finding a church for myself in our time." Similar moments recur throughout Harrison's work (David Burkett is again prominent in *Returning to Earth*) and, ultimately, constitute an ennobling vision of human beings, a way we all imagine we might like ourselves to be, even when the "days are stacked against who we think we are," as Harrison claims in *The Theory and Practice of Rivers*—that is, those moments when the world bites back, as it often does to Harrison's comic alter ego, the irrepressible Brown Dog, the protagonist of four novellas (and at least one more to come).

Yet Harrison is generally disinclined to wax mystical or highfalutin about his authorial vocation or revel in exalted notions of egoistic genius. "The dream that I could write a good poem, a good novel, or even a good movie for that matter, has devoured my life," he admits in *Off to the Side*. In short, there is nothing precious or pedantic about his view of his calling, as this modest, workaday autobiographical parable in Will Blythe's 1998 anthology, *Why I Write*, suggests:

> The act of writing is a boy hoeing a field of corn on a hot day, able to see either a woodlot or, more often, an immense forest where he'd rather be. This is uncomplicated, almost banal. He has to hoe corn in order to be allowed to reach his beloved forest. This can easily be extrapolated into the writer as a small god who has forty acres as a birthright in which to reinvent the world. He cultivates this world, but then there is always something vast and unreachable beyond his grasp, whether it's the forest, the ocean, or the implausible ten million citizens of New York or Paris. While he hoes or writes, he whirls toward the future at a rate that with age becomes quite incomprehensible. He leaves a trail of books, but he really marks the passage of time by the series of hunting dogs he's left behind. His negative capability has made the world grow larger rather than shrink, and not a single easy answer has survived the passing of years.

Bird dogs aside, the trail of books Harrison has made is impressive: thirty-eight books and chapbooks of poetry, fiction, and nonfiction (many of which have been translated into more than twenty languages), plus numerous screenplays (the lucrative Hollywood jobs that helped him buy time to write his fiction) and a couple of collections edited by others: *The Sumac Reader* and *Conversations with Jim Harrison*. The former are the items included in section A of this bibliography, the primary imaginative texts that have preoccupied Harrison, summoned nearly every bit of his time, energy, and intelligence for the past four decades. From *Plain Song* to *The English Major*, these books define and shape the main contours of the author's life as a poet and prose writer who trafficked in nothing but his "own sign," as he admitted to Joseph Bednarik in an interview published in 2002 in *Five Points*.

That most of Jim's books (including all his fiction) are in print is a testimony to his artistic importance and international appeal as a writer. "You can't worry about posterity, how history will judge you, because you don't have any control over that. Your only ambition should be that your stuff stays in print," he's told me many times in the past decade. That's as it should be, I think—a major writer's books should be available and accessible to the public, though, of course, that is not always the case, as we know from the frequently dismal record of commercial publishers. In the case of Jim's fiction, however, it's been well served by Seymour Lawrence's imprint at Houghton Mifflin, by the Paris publisher Christian Bourgois (Harrison's French translator is the gifted Brice Matthieussent), and especially in recent years by the Atlantic Monthly Press and the Grove Press imprints of Grove/Atlantic. Now, in a dramatic turnabout from his earliest years as a struggling writer, the appearance of a new Harrison novel is a bankable literary event, one that includes publishing not only the traditional hardcover trade edition but also a limited boxed edition, an audio CD, an audiocassette, and even a CD-ROM text version. Then, too, there are numerous media interviews and a limited (by his own preference) multicity book tour with exclusive stops at his favorite independent booksellers: Elliott Bay Book Company in Seattle, Lemuria Bookstore in Jackson, Mississippi, Tattered Cover in Denver, etc. In recent years we have entered the era of Jim Harrison, Inc.

In fact, the Grove/Atlantic publisher Morgan Entrekin's open letter of endorsement on the back cover of the advanced reading copy of Jim's 2007 novel, *Returning to Earth*, is unabashed testimony to Harrison's status as "one of America's greatest living writers." Entrekin's economic self-interest and Harrison's trademark author status aside, there's still no gainsaying that Harrison's books—in all their current forms—are the most visible proof of his compulsive productivity and his being-in-the-world as a writer. His trail of books is undoubtedly the reason his audience knows him so well and considers him a candidate for greatness, however variously that distinction is defined. (Reacting to Bernard Levin's assessment in the *Sunday Times* of London that "Harrison is a writer with immortality in him," Jim has more than once wondered aloud whether that means he will still have to take out the garbage in two hundred years.)

But, just when we think we have Harrison pegged or understand the nature of his iconic status, he eludes us by doing the unexpected. "Every writer must learn the culture, then unlearn it," he told me last summer, which I took to mean that one shouldn't be tyrannized by monoethical values. The recent appearance of his first-ever published short story in the *New Yorker* is a case in point, as is "Tracking," the omnisciently narrated redaction of his autobiography that concludes *The Summer He Didn't Die*. *Braided Creek*, a collection of unsigned short poems written to and by the former U.S. poet laureate Ted Kooser and published by Copper Canyon Press (arguably the finest independent poetry publisher in the United States), took everyone by surprise, and the last I heard it was in its fourth printing. What this superb bibliography reveals are the staggering number and range of publications that fill out the main contours of Jim's expansive career. I mean the one-of-a-kind, side-alley pieces that some future scholar, bibliophile, collector, or biographer will consider not just fascinating but absolutely essential for a full understanding of his career and life.

Compared to individual books, these items might seem slight, even ephemeral (especially the uncollected pieces and the single-sheet broadside poems), but they add texture, dimension, and relatedness to the overall canvas. I am particularly fond of a number of them that Orr and Torrey include: Harrison's introduction to Donald Walsh's bilingual edition of Pablo Neruda's *Residencia an la Tierra/Residence on Earth* (it is as much an introduction to Harrison's poetics as it is to Neruda's); his moving introduction to Guy Le Querrec's *On the Trail to Wounded Knee* (it resonates deeply with his myriad writings on Native Americans); his *New York Times Magazine* piece "First Person Female" (it is a perfect introduction to Dalva, Julip, Clare of "The Woman Lit by Fireflies," the women of "Republican Wives," and *True North*'s and *Returning to Earth*'s Cynthia); and two *Men's Journal* essays, "Starting Over" (it is one of the best pieces on fishing I've ever read) and "Life on the Border" (it is powerful social commentary on America's illegal worker dilemma). And of his poetry: *Livingston Suite* (with illustrations by Greg Keeler), lovingly letterpress printed at Richard Ardinger's Limberlost Press; and "Night Dharma," my favorite limited-edition broadside, designed and printed by Sam Hamill and Amy Schaus at Copper Canyon. Then there are Jim's generous dust-jacket blurbs for hundreds of other writers' books. The encomiums alone constitute a kind of scorecard of Harrison's readerly interests, and they point the way to a number of writers whose work I might never have otherwise encountered without Jim's enthusiastic endorsement: Jack Turner, Merrill Gilfillan, and Charles Bowden, to name but three. Any person perusing this bibliography will surely find offbeat candidates of his or her own among the entries that strike responsive chords. Finding these out-of-the-way pieces fuels the search, enlivens every enthusiast's bibliographic quest.

All of which leads me to change direction in midstream. My facile interpretation of the smiley-faced Harrison on the dust jacket of *The Raw and the Cooked* is only part of the story, part of the persona, and needs to be balanced with a more recent photo on the cover of *Off to the Side*. Leaning against a barbed-wire fence in a wide-open Southwestern landscape is the wild-haired, grim-faced, steely-eyed Jim Harrison, the Harrison with old-time attitude who challenges us to open his book. After forty years he is still the independent poet resolutely off to the side of our culture looking out from one of his signature out-of-the-way thickets, panic holes, or hide-outs in Michigan, Arizona, Nebraska, or Montana, his beloved flyover places, where with his single good eye, trained on us like a lens, he is watching our every move, taking us in, practicing his discipline of scrutiny. Indeed, I wonder, who is reading whom?

||||||| ||||||| |||||||

Long before I met Jim Harrison, I studied his work—well-thumbed paperbacks of the early novels *Wolf* and *Farmer* (which had their own intriguing back-cover author photos), poems here and there in various literary magazines (I remember vividly the issue of the *American Poetry Review* with yet another of his arresting photo portraits on the cover), the multiauthor poetry anthology *Five Blind Men* (with contributions by Harrison, Dan Gerber, George Quasha, J. D. Reed, and Charles Simic), and his sporting essays in popular magazines such as *Playboy* and *Sports Illustrated*. Early to late 1970s I was coediting *Back Door*, a poetry journal founded by my close friend and compatriot Dave Smith, and I recall in those days looking often at *Sumac*, edited by Jim and Dan Gerber, which was a legend in little-magazine circles in spite of its having been published for only three or four years. In other words I did what most of Jim's audience did who might never have the opportunity to meet him otherwise—I got a jolt of life, an inspiration, a set of orientations, a blood transfusion (the kind he often got as a young writer from reading Henry Miller), from his writing, which is, for many of us outside his immediate family (who see him in very different light), the most accessible legacy of the man.

So if Jim Harrison is a formidable presence in person, he is perhaps even more daunting in print. In short Harrison has left a lot more tracks than most readers—maybe even he—realize. William Faulkner is one of his esteemed forebears (and a novelist whose subject is also the totality and burden of consciousness), and, like Faulkner's fiction, Harrison's writings are not so much discrete, isolated points on a linear trajectory as they are a web of related, overlapping texts. Characters emerge in one novel, disappear, then resurface in a later text, as in *Dalva* and *The Road Home*, the Brown Dog series ("Brown Dog," "The Seven Ounce Man," "Westward Ho," "The Summer He Didn't Die"), and *True North* and *Returning to Earth*.

More than that, however, nearly everything Harrison writes is illuminated by and connected to everything else he's penned. Fiction, poetry, essays, memoir, interviews, journalism—all radiate from a central nexus, and sometimes, but not always, the authorial voices overlap, echo, and merge into each other. His writings are lapidary, and reading through them is like peeling an onion or an artichoke: as layer after layer is exposed, you go deeper and deeper into the meaning of the whole. Though addressing another topic altogether, the words of Herbert Weisinger, Harrison's revered teacher and intellectual mentor, are appropriate here. "It is not until the innermost core is reached," Weisinger states, "that the meaning of the whole is revealed, and, as one penetrates deeper and deeper . . . layer upon layer is seen . . . each with a character of its own but which can be fully understood only in relation to the others." Reason enough to herald the publication of *Jim Harrison: A Comprehensive Bibliography*. Think of it as a Baedeker to the country of Harrison's life work in language, a Michelin Guide to the territory of his consciousness.

Compiling a bibliography of a living writer's work is a confounding, frustrating task at best. When the writer is as prolific and enduring as Harrison has been, the task is nearly overwhelming. Not that the resulting investigative work is futile or thankless or meaningless, but, rather, it enacts a complicated process—certainly passionate and almost fetishistic in its allure. If the process seems endless and impossible, like casting a too-light fly rod into a twenty-knot wind, it is also endlessly fascinating and compelling. The task of compilation seems to stretch out forever toward a horizon that is tantalizingly always out of reach. Just when you think you've got the whole package in hand, some unknown scrap turns up that you never saw before. Immediately, of course, bibliophilic anxiety sets in, and you are haunted by the absent, undetected items you might never find. (The scarcity of the uncorrected proofs of Jim's first novel, *Wolf*, makes them one such item that has reached nearly mythic proportions among bibliophiles and collectors. They are a kind of Holy Grail of the booking quest.) There is some consolation, I suppose, in recognizing that bibliographic lists are always incomplete. It's their nature to be so, for they are always works in progress. They require a slow hand and a fixed gaze. If you are excessively hasty, impatient, or unmethodical, a bibliography's demands might drive you crazy. That's why patient, detail-oriented people compile them. But the hunt has to be carried out because, as most literary historians and biographers agree, a reliable bibliography is indispensable for informed study and serious research.

Over the years a number of eager people, expecting Harrison to cooperate directly in their projects, have made a stab at compiling his bibliography, but the task was so daunting, the sources so scattered, widespread, and fugitive, and the assistance so reluctant that, except for Tom Colonnese, they have thrown up their hands in defeat. All of this points to the fact that, despite the staggering number, range, and quality of his publications and compositions in poetry, fiction, prose, and screenplays, Jim Harrison is unconcerned—almost perversely so—with the niceties of bibliographic decorum and protocol. (He told me recently that an "intended" bibliography ". . . from U of California fell through a decade ago because I had no records.") So, except in a tangential way, he has not been directly involved with keeping track of his output.

That task fell to Jim's beloved late brother, John (the former director of the University of Arkansas Library), and Jim's dedicated assistant, Joyce Bahle, who have done their part—heroic, it should be added—to keep track of his voluminous publications, most of which, along with his manuscripts, correspondence, and all other manner of Harrisoniana, now fortunately reside on 160 linear feet of shelf space in the Special Collections library at Grand Valley State University in Allendale, Michigan. The collection is ably curated by Nancy Richard, whose ninety-four-page catalog of its contents is accessible at www.gvsu.edu/library/specialcollections/index.cfm. The Harrison material at Grand Valley is an especially bounteous and rich authorial archive, made possible by the generosity of the Meijer Foundation. Orr and Torrey have consulted many of its holdings to untie some problematic and tangled bibliographic knots, notably the section on Harrison's Hollywood screenplays and treatments.

Since Michel Foucault's interrogation of the archaeology of knowledge, it's common in some quarters to believe that archives don't—and can't—explain everything. True enough. Yet it is foolhardy to think that private and public archives and collections don't go a long way toward establishing a significant and irreplaceable research resource. Given the choice between nothing and everything, I think that librarians, bibliographers, and collectors will always choose the latter. Mystification or not, original manuscripts seem to possess, even for a brief moment, an air of authenticity, origination, presence: they offer a window into the process of creativity and bring us close to the hand of their maker, which, in an increasingly depersonalized world, strikes me as being a cheerful and worthwhile prospect.

Now, Gregg Orr and Beef Torrey, with the incalculable aid of Copper Canyon Press's Joseph Bednarik ("my poor bibliographers," Harrison quipped recently in an interview with Angela Elam in *New Letters*), have done what no one else before them has been able to accomplish—so far as it is humanly possible, they have created a complete bibliography of Harrison's writings. Most of the entries are drawn directly from the compilers' exceptional personal collections of Harrisoniana. Make no mistake: this compilation is an extreme labor of love, a compulsive record of obsession, homage to one gifted man's life in words. Neither Orr nor Torrey is a professional literary scholar (the former is a communications executive who left college before completing his degree; the latter is a former college football player who became an educational psychologist), yet they strike me as precisely the kind of literate, passionate, engaged audience Jim Harrison most appreciates. No one can predict how Orr and Torrey's book will fare; no one can say how many old items are yet to be discovered by them or other biblio-minded sleuths or how many new ones will have to be added if Jim keeps writing at his current pace. This book should not be considered a gravestone, a capstone monument, to Harrison's career (which shows no signs of slowing down), but, let's face it, with over sixteen hundred separate entries, *Jim Harrison: A Comprehensive Bibliography* will, I believe, be the definitive bibliographic resource for a long time to come.

||||||  |||||  |||||

Occasionally in our reading lives a writer comes along who says everything we imagine ourselves being capable of saying if we only had the skill, energy, or talent to do so. We all have candidates (often more than one) who fill that role and who we swear are telling our own story, speaking directly to us. For untold thousands of readers here and abroad, Harrison is that kind of writer. In his excellent book *The Gift: Imagination and the Erotic Life of Property*, Lewis Hyde names what's at stake:

> The art that matters to us—which moves the heart, or revives the soul, or delights the senses, or offers courage for living, however we choose to describe the experience—that work is received by us as a gift is received. Even if we have paid a fee at the door of the museum or concert hall, when we are touched by a work of art something comes to us which has nothing to do with price. . . . When we are moved by art we are grateful that the artist lived, grateful that he labored in the service of his gifts.

I cannot think of a more appropriate grace note for this project. Jim Harrison has done it all—he's been everywhere we would want to go (and some places we wouldn't), he knows everyone we might wish to know (and some we might not), he's done everything we always wanted to do (no complaint there), and through it all he's done what all of us hope our best writers will always do—write, write, and then write some more because there is no such thing as enough. Jim ended *Off to the Side* this way: "My life could have been otherwise but it wasn't." This bibliography is one proof among many that he made the right choices and left us the right gifts.

*Robert DeMott*
Athens, Ohio

## A Note on Structure

Our intention from the onset of this project was not to produce a full descriptive bibliography but to ultimately end up with a complete list of Jim Harrison's published work to aid librarians, scholars, collectors, booksellers, and anyone interested in Harrison's work. Because Harrison is still actively writing and publishing, this cannot be considered a definitive listing.

Section A goes into some detail concerning the different states of the books and broadsides because it was our intent to have a complete list of these states to aid collectors and booksellers. In some cases there are significant textual changes from an early proof to a finished trade edition that the collector and scholar would be interested in. We also wanted to provide enough detail on the books for collectors to identify first editions and the different states of proof copies. In that regard section A does have some attributes of a descriptive bibliography, but by no means should it be considered such in a classic descriptive sense. A full descriptive bibliography is a project that will, one hopes, be completed sometime in the future. All publications in sections A–F of this bibliography were seen unless otherwise noted.

The more contemporary citations listed often contain information that is sometimes not included in the older citations. Information such as published price, published date, and number of copies printed of a certain title was sometimes not available or lost in the passage of time. If this information was not available or reliable, it was simply not included in the description. The annotations contained in this work are intended to provide the reader or researcher with information pertaining to the publishing history of a citation and, when available, a pertinent or interesting side note. On some of the periodical citations, MLA style does not require the citing of volume or issue numbers; however, these are provided to aid in locating these citations. Although the bibliography does contain some citations of relevant foreign sources, we did not focus on foreign editions of books by or essays by or about Harrison. At last count Harrison's books have been translated into over twenty-five languages, and collecting information on these editions is, indeed, a daunting task. There are numerous essays by and about Harrison in foreign journals and periodicals, especially in France, where Harrison's work is highly regarded and quite popular. Again, translating and gathering the information on these citations will have to be left to others. In all sections of the bibliography, the citations have been arranged chronologically. In a given year, citations will be arranged by the month they appeared. In the case of journals or periodicals that are published by season, the order will run spring, summer, fall, and winter. Priority is given to the year, then season, then month.

**Works Referenced in Preparation of This Book**

The following works were referenced for a correct and consistent listing of citations. In some instances the format and style have been modified somewhat to fit the section needs in describing the work cited.

MLA *Style Manual and Guide to Scholarly Publishing.* By Joseph Gibaldi. 2nd ed. New York: Modern Language Association of America, 1999.

*On Compiling an Annotated Bibliography.* By James L. Harner. 2nd ed. New York: Modern Language Association of America, 2000.

*A New Introduction to Bibliography.* By Philip Gaskell. New York: Oxford University Press, 1972.

*Principles of Bibliographical Description.* By Fredson Bowers. Winchester and New Castle DE: Oak Knoll Press, 2005.

# Chronology

1937     James Thomas Harrison is born 11 December in the northern Michigan town of Grayling, the second of five children of Winfield Sprague Harrison and Norma Olivia (Wahlgren) Harrison. Winfield Harrison works as a government agriculture agent. Both parents are avid readers.

1940     Harrison family moves to Reed City, Michigan.

1945     Harrison is accidentally blinded in his left eye by a playmate with a broken glass laboratory beaker.

1949     Harrison family moves to Haslett, Michigan, in part to be closer to Michigan State University.

1951     Though raised Congregationalist, Harrison experiences a religious conversion at a Baptist revival and becomes a preacher at fundamentalist youth fellowships and president of the Bible Club.

1952–56     Harrison attends Haslett Rural High School, where he plays offensive left guard and defensive middle linebacker on the football team. Father works for the U.S. Soil Conservation Service. English teacher and librarian Bernice Smith encourages Harrison's sophisticated reading interests with the *Nation* and the *Saturday Review*. In 1953, after a summer working as a busboy at the Stanley Hotel in Estes Park, Colorado, Harrison finds that the religious urge fades, and he transfers his fervor to literary pursuits. During his sophomore year, he announces his intention to become a writer: receives his first typewriter as a gift from his father for his seventeenth birthday. In 1954, in the summer before his junior year, Harrison and a friend drive to Greenwich Village in New York for a few days to investigate bohemian life. Elected president of his graduating class and of the student council, but resigns from latter. In September 1956 enrolls at Michigan State University in East Lansing.

1957–59   A period of restlessness, occasional travel, and temporary residence in New York City, San Francisco, and Boston. Drops out of Michigan State toward the end of his freshman year and hitchhikes to New York's Greenwich Village (at different times lives on McDougal Street and Grove Street). Returns to Michigan State in the fall of 1958, but drops out again. Goes to Boston, then hitchhikes to California. Works at various odd jobs, including crop picker. In 1959 he returns to Michigan State. At MSU part-time jobs include working at library and horticulture farm. Marries Linda May King on 10 October 1959.

1960   Earns BA degree, Michigan State University. Daughter Jamie Louise born on 21 May. Fellow students at MSU include poet and novelist Dan Gerber, novelist and screenwriter Thomas McGuane, both of whom later become lifelong friends, and Bob Dattila, who later becomes Harrison's agent.

1962   Father and younger sister Judith killed in a head-on automobile accident in November. Harrison leaves graduate program at Michigan State.

1963–64   Moves to Cambridge, Massachusetts, and lives with his older brother John, a Harvard librarian, in an apartment on Kirkland Street; works for two years as a book salesman at Campbell and Hall, a general wholesaling firm, and is joined by his wife and daughter. Letter to the editor of *Contact*, a California literary journal, is published concerning the poet William Carlos Williams.

1965   Moves to Kingsley, Michigan. Has odd jobs as a laborer, hod carrier, brick layer, and carpenter. Publishes a review (his first published critical writing) in the 15 February issue of the *Nation* and two poems (his first published poetry) in the 5 April issue of the same magazine. Has his first poetry reading on 19 April at the Poetry Center at the 92nd Street Y in New York City, and publishes five poems in the August issue of *Poetry*. On the strength of reading ten of Harrison's poems, Denise Levertov recommends his first book, *Plain Song*, for publication by W. W. Norton. Encouraged by his mentor, Herbert Weisinger, to complete his graduate work, Harrison writes essay about his poems that becomes his master's thesis, "The Natural History of Some Poems."

1966   Harrison earns MA degree in comparative literature at MSU. Turns down a teaching position at Northern Michigan University to follow Herbert Weisinger to the State University of New York at Stony

Brook, where he becomes Weisinger's assistant, then assistant professor of English.

1967    Receives first of three consecutive annual National Endowment for the Arts grants. Publishes limited-edition chapbook, *Walking*. In October Harrison participates in the Writers and Artists' March on the State Department, Washington DC.

1968    Publishes second poetry collection, *Locations*. With Weisinger and Louis Simpson organizes the World Poetry Conference at Stony Brook, 21–23 June. Contributes to the political manifesto titled "Stony Brook Poets' Prophesy—June 23, 1968" (see item G22 below). Contributes "Dreams" to the *Stony Brook Holographs*, a collection of handwritten poetry broadsides. Though listed in the 1968–69 Stony Brook catalog as assistant professor, in June resigns and returns to Michigan. Purchases Lake Leelanau, Michigan, farm. First issue of *Sumac* appears in the fall, edited by Harrison and Dan Gerber. Begins visiting the Florida Keys for winter fishing.

1969–70    Awarded a Guggenheim fellowship. Publishes *5 Blind Men*, a poetry collection with Dan Gerber, J. D. Reed, George Quasha, and Charles Simic. Meets the painter and writer Russell Chatham (beginning in 1979 with *Legends of the Fall*, most of Harrison's books will feature Chatham artwork on their dust jackets and covers), suffers a severe back injury when he falls from a bluff during a grouse-hunting trip. Spends a month in traction at Munson Hospital in Traverse City, Michigan. During a long recovery from his back injury he is urged by McGuane to complete a novel. Publishes "The Real Fun of the Fair Was the Horse Pulling" in *Sports Illustrated*, beginning an association with the magazine that lasts until 1975.

1971    Daughter Anna Severin is born on 6 April. Publishes his first novel, *Wolf: A False Memoir*. Also publishes his collection of poems *Outlyer and Ghazals*. *Sumac* ceases publication after nine issues, but it continues to publish individual books. In October he makes a literary pilgrimage to Moscow and Leningrad with Dan Gerber.

1973    Publishes the novel *A Good Day to Die* and the suite of poems *Letters to Yesenin*, which he considers an "anti-suicide note." In February travels to Africa with Gerber.

1974    With McGuane and Richard Brautigan he contributes to *Tarpon*, a documentary film on saltwater fly fishing filmed in Key West, directed by Christian Odasso and Guy de la Valdene.

1975    Publishes the novel *Farmer*. Writes the screenplay of *A Good Day to*

*Die* for documentary filmmaker Frederick Weisman, but the film is never made. Meets the actor Jack Nicholson on the Montana film set of *Missouri Breaks*.

1976–77　Publishes chapbook poem *Returning to Earth*. Publishes his first of many essays in *Esquire*, "A River Never Sleeps," and in *Playboy*, "A Sporting Life."

1978　Visits his friend Jack Nicholson on the Durango, Mexico, set of *Going South*; Nicholson loans Harrison $30,000 to pay off debts and finance his writing for a year. Meets Seymour ("Sam") Lawrence, who becomes his publisher at Delacorte, Dutton, and Houghton Mifflin. In the winter he checks into the Jolli Lodge in Lake Leelanau, where he writes the novella "The Man Who Gave Up His Name" and, in a concentrated nine-day burst, "Legends of the Fall," a novella based in part on the journals kept by William Ludlow, his wife's great-grandfather, an immigrant Cornish mining engineer who accompanied George Custer on his Black Hills expeditions.

1979–80　Publishes the combined reprint volume *Letters to Yesenin* and *Returning to Earth*. Also publishes his breakthrough novella collection *Legends of the Fall*, which includes "Revenge" and "The Man Who Gave Up His Name." The title novella and "Revenge" both appear in *Esquire* before the collection is released in late May. Begins writing screenplays in Hollywood for Warner Brothers. His work as a contract screenwriter will last until 2000. Employs Joyce Harrington as his administrative assistant. Purchases a cabin on the Sucker River in Michigan's Upper Peninsula.

1981–82　Publishes his novel *Warlock* and the poetry collection *Selected and New Poems 1961–1981*. Publishes his first of four food columns in *Smoke Signals*, a literary journal published in Brooklyn, New York. Publishes the limited-edition *Natural World: A Bestiary*, which features his poetry along with photographs of the sculpture of Diana Guest.

1984　Publishes *Sundog: A Novel: The Story of an American Foreman*.

1986　Publishes a signed, limited edition of poems entitled *The Theory and Practice of Rivers: Poems*. Publishes "History as Torment," a preface for a tribute to Ezra Pound titled *"What Thou Lovest Well Remains": A Hundred Years of Ezra Pound* (Boise ID: Limberlost Press).

1988　Publishes the novel *Dalva*. Beginning with the premiere issue Harrison becomes the contributing food editor of *Smart*, a mass-circulation magazine edited by Terry McDonell. He will go on to publish ten separate food columns in this magazine.

1989   Publishes *The Theory and Practice of Rivers and New Poems*. The film *Cold Feet*, cowritten with Thomas McGuane, is released. In the January/February issue of *Smart* he publishes the novella "The Sunset Limited."

1990   Publishes the novella collection *The Woman Lit by Fireflies*, which includes "Brown Dog," "Sunset Limited," and "The Woman Lit by Fireflies." The film *Revenge*, which is based on the novella of the same name, is released. Publishes the preface to *Russell Chatham: One Hundred Paintings* (Livingston MT: Clark City Press). Receives the Mark Twain Award from the Center for the Study of Midwestern Literature and Culture for distinguished contributions to Midwestern literature. Begins regular winter residence in Patagonia, Arizona.

1991   Publishes *Just Before Dark: Collected Nonfiction*. In February he publishes in *Esquire* the first of twenty-four monthly food columns, "The Raw and the Cooked," which continue through December 1993.

1992   Publishes *The Raw and the Cooked*, a limited-edition chapbook of three *Esquire* food columns. Publishes the introduction ("The Chippewa-Ottawa") to George Weeks, *Mem-ka-weh: Dawning of the Grand Traverse Band of Ottawa and Chippewa Indians* (Traverse City MI: Village Press).

1993   Subject of the documentary film by Georges Luneau and Brice Matthieussent, *Jim Harrison: Entre Chien et Loup* (English version: *Jim Harrison: Half Dog and Half Wolf*). Honored by the Institute Lumiere in Lyon, France. Publishes the novella "Julip: An Entertainment" in the March issue of *Esquire* magazine.

1994   Publishes the novella collection *Julip*, which includes "Julip," "The Seven-Ounce Man," and "The Beige Dolorosa." The film *Wolf* (not based on the Harrison novel of the same name) is released. Harrison is associate producer and shares the screenwriting credit with Wesley Strick. Longtime publisher and friend Seymour Lawrence dies.

1995   The film *Legends of the Fall* is released. Publishes the introduction ("Hunting with a Friend") to Guy de la Valdene's *For a Handful of Feathers* (New York: Atlantic Monthly Press). Begins writing irregular monthly columns for the *Kermit Lynch Wine Merchant Newsletter* that usually deal with wine-related matters. Begins research on a sequel to *Dalva*.

1996   In January Harrison is a featured participant in the fourteenth Key West Literary Seminar, "American Writers and the Natural World." Publishes *After Ikkyu and Other Poems*. *Carried Away*, a feature-film version of *Farmer*, is released. Release of Edward Reilly's *Jim Harrison* (New York: Twayne Publishing), part of the Twayne's "United States Authors" series. Purchases Patagonia, Arizona, casita for winter home.

1997 Publishes the introduction to *The Sumac Reader* (East Lansing: Michigan State University Press), edited by Joseph Bednarik. In May Harrison is a featured participant in the Festival International du Livre in Saint-Malo, France.

1998 Publishes the novel *The Road Home* in France in July and in the United States in October. Publishes *The Shape of the Journey: New and Collected Poems*. Becomes a contributing editor to *Men's Journal* and a consultant to the Orvis sporting goods company.

1999 Receives the Evil Companions Literary Award (given annually by the *Colorado Review*) in Denver. Wins the Michigan State University College of Arts and Letters Distinguished Alumni Award. In May receives honor at the Festival International du Livre in Saint-Malo, France. *The Shape of the Journey* is a finalist for the *Los Angeles Times* Book Prize.

2000 The novella collection *The Beast God Forgot to Invent* is published; it includes "The Beast God Forgot to Invent," "Westward Ho," and "I Forgot to Go to Spain." Publishes the children's book *The Boy Who Ran to the Woods*, illustrated by Tom Pohrt. Awarded the Spirit of the West literary achievement award by the Mountains and Plains Booksellers Association.

2001 Begins writing and publishing short essays that appear in *Men's Journal* and that will turn into a full-length memoir in 2002. Publishes *The Raw and the Cooked: Adventures of a Roving Gourmand*, a collection of food columns (later called by *Saveur* magazine one of the top food memoirs of all time). Publishes *A Conversation*, a limited, letterpress collection of postcard poems written between Harrison and friend and fellow poet Ted Kooser. Harrison's essay "Starting Over" is included in *The Best American Sports Writing 2001* (New York: Houghton Mifflin Co.).

2002 Publishes *Off to the Side*, a memoir. Publication of *Conversations with Jim Harrison* (Jackson: University Press of Mississippi), a collection of interviews edited by Robert DeMott. Publication of *The True Bones of My Life: Essays on the Fiction of Jim Harrison*, by Patrick Smith (East Lansing: Michigan State University Press). Harrison's essay "Soul Food" is selected for inclusion in *The Best American Travel Writing* (New York: Houghton Mifflin Co.). Is the featured writer at the eighteenth annual Spring Literary Festival at Ohio University. Sells longtime home in Lake Leelanau, Michigan, and moves to Livingston, Montana, to be close to his daughters and grandchildren.

2003 Publishes *Braided Creek: A Conversation in Poetry,* a poetry correspondence between Harrison and the U.S. poet laureate Ted Kooser. Begins yet another series of food columns in *Brick,* a Canadian literary journal, entitled "Eat or Die."

2004 Publishes the novel *True North*. On March 29 he publishes his first short story in the *New Yorker* entitled "Father Daughter." Publishes the introduction for a new edition of Pablo Neruda's poetry collection, *Residence on Earth* (New York: New Directions Publishing). Harrison sells his beloved hunting cabin in the Upper Peninsula of Michigan.

2005 Publishes the novella collection *The Summer He Didn't Die,* which contains "The Summer He Didn't Die," "Republican Wives," and the autobiographical essay "Tracking." Harrison's essay "A Really Big Lunch" is selected for *The Best American Travel Writing 2005* (New York: Houghton Mifflin Co.). Publishes *Livingston Suite,* a limited-edition, fine-press poetry chapbook. In September Grand Valley State University holds a reception at Siedman House to announce the acquisition of the Harrison Archive and Papers. *The Summer He Didn't Die* is nominated for the Story Prize.

2006 Publishes the poetry collection *Saving Daylight*. Performs a reading and conversation with Ted Kooser for the Lannan Foundation in Sante Fe, New Mexico. Harrison's poem "On the Way to the Doctor's" is selected for *The Best American Poetry 2006* (New York: Charles Scribner's Sons). Harrison's papers are opened to the public for research at Grand Valley State University Special Collections in Allendale, Michigan.

2007 Publishes the novel *Returning to Earth*. Appears on the cover of the 11 February issue of the *New York Times Book Review*. In May is inducted into the American Academy of Arts and Letters. Copper Canyon Press reissues *Letters to Yesenin*.

2008 Publishes the novel *The English Major*. Provides a new introduction for the Penguin Classics reprint of James Welch's novel *The Death of Jim Loney*. Publishes the short story "Outcast" in the August issue of *Best Life* magazine. In July appears with fellow Michigan State alumni authors Thomas McGuane and Richard Ford in East Lansing for a literary panel sponsored by the Michigan Humanities Council.

**Note:** Thanks to Robert DeMott, whose chronology in *Conversations with Jim Harrison* (Jackson: University Press of Mississippi, 2002) we have drawn on for much of the information. Also thanks to Nancy Richard of Grand Valley State University, archivist for the Jim Harrison Papers.

Jim Harrison

# Section A
## *Books and Broadsides by Jim Harrison*

A1. *Plain Song* (poetry)
A2. *Walking* (poetry)
A3. *Dreams* (poetry broadside)
A4. *Locations* (poetry)
A5. *Ghazal for Christmas* (poetry broadside)
A6. *Outlyer and Ghazals* (poetry)
A7. *Wolf: A False Memoir* (novel)
A8. *Sergei Yesenin 1895–1925* (poetry broadside)
A9. *A Good Day to Die: A Novel* (novel)
A10. *Letters to Yesenin* (poetry)
A11. *Farmer* (novel)
A12. *Returning to Earth* (poetry)
A13. *Letters to Yesenin and Returning to Earth* (poetry)
A14. *Legends of the Fall* (fiction—novellas)
A15. *Warlock* (novel)
A16. *Selected and New Poems* (poetry)
A17. *Natural World: A Bestiary* (poetry)
A18. *Sundog: A Novel: The Story of an American Foreman* (novel)
A19. *The Theory and Practice of Rivers: Poems* (poetry)
A20. *Dalva* (novel)
A21. *The Theory and Practice of Rivers and New Poems* (poetry)
A22. *The Woman Lit by Fireflies* (fiction—novellas)
A23. *Kobun* (poetry broadside)
A24. *Just Before Dark: Collected Nonfiction* (essays)
A25. *Sketch for a Job Application Blank* (poetry broadside)
A26. *The Raw and the Cooked* (essays)

## PLAIN SONG
### JIM HARRISON

Jim Harrison is a natural poet, with an unfailing instinct for where to break his lines, for the image that embodies meanings beyond appearance yet that can, if you will be taken for itself alone; for the sound of words in relation to their meaning. He belongs to a tradition that includes poets as far apart in time as Sappho and Lorca, Li Po and much of William Carlos Williams — a tradition of nonsyllabic, nonphilosophizing poetry in which "form follows function" and symbols are not applied but are deeply inherent in the image itself — the purest lyric tradition, which partakes of the nature of music without imitating it.

In his late twenties, Jim Harrison is a mature person and a poet who has found his own voice. Denise Levertov comments, "I think this is a beautiful book."

After graduating from Michigan State University, Mr. Harrison became a teaching assistant while he worked for his M.A. but he abandoned the academic life because it was in conflict (for him) with the life of poetry. He now lives in Michigan, with his wife and daughter.

$1.50

---

**PLAIN SONG**
JIM HARRISON
*poems*

PLAIN SONG  *poems*  HARRISON
Norton

---

### Other Books of Poetry
#### FROM NORTON

**ALL**, the collected short poems 1923-1958
LOUIS ZUKOFSKY

"Louis Zukofsky is one of the most important poets of my generation. These poems are absolute clarification, crystal cabinets full of air and angels. I very much doubt if any book of verse more important or more moving (or more exemplary and instructive to the young) is likely to be published for some time."
— KENNETH REXROTH

**THE MUSIC**
HELEN WOLFERT

"These poems open into amazing places. The short poems are precise, the long ones apocalyptic. But the reader will discover that they are in the same voice; he will be drawn into the world of blazing creation, of desire that is a desire for the universe as well as for the powers of man, this world of love.... This is one of the books which could speak for the inner genius of our time."
— MURIEL RUKEYSER

---

### love makes the air light
#### raymond roseliep

Raymond Roseliep, who is both poet and Catholic priest, has that exquisite care for language that marks the true poetic gift. He is a poet whose visual sense never outstrips his verbal capacities but complements them. His poems are closely packed and sharp-edged, truly word-music rather than faint imitations of music-music. They are autonomous constructions whose music resides in the interplay of words and meaning. As a poet he has elegance, wit, style, and important things to say.

Now in his forties, Father Roseliep teaches at Loras College in Dubuque, Iowa. Two previous volumes of his poems, *The Linen Bands* and *The Small Rain*, have been published, and many of his poems have appeared in magazines and national quarterlies.

---

Item A1.b, *Plain Song*. © 1965 by Jim Harrison.
Used by permission of W. W. Norton & Company, Inc.

A27. *Coyote No. 1* (poetry broadside)
A28. *Julip* (fiction—novellas)
A29. *After Ikkyu and Other Poems* (poetry)
A30. *The Road Home* (novel)
A31. *From Geo-Bestiary* (poetry broadside)
A32. *The Shape of the Journey: New and Collected Poems* (poetry)
A33. *Older Love* (poetry broadside)
A34. *The Evil Companions Literary Award* (fiction broadside)
A35. *Portal, Arizona* (poetry broadside)
A36. *The Beast God Forgot to Invent* (fiction—novellas)
A37. *The Same Goose Moon* (poetry broadside)
A38. *The Boy Who Ran to the Woods* (children's fiction)
A39. *The Raw and the Cooked: Adventures of a Roving Gourmand* (essays)
A40. *Off to the Side: A Memoir* (memoir)
A41. *Night Dharma* (poetry broadside)
A42. *A Conversation* (poetry)
A43. *Braided Creek: A Conversation in Poetry* (poetry)
A44. *True North: A Novel* (novel)
A45. *I Prefer the Skyline of a Shelf of Books* (poetry broadside)
A46. *The Davenport Lunar Eclipse* (poetry broadside)
A47. *Livingston Suite* (poetry)
A48. *Republican Wives: A Novella* (novella)
A49. *The Summer He Didn't Die* (fiction—novellas)
A50. *Cabbage* (poetry broadside)
A51. *Saving Daylight* (poetry)
A52. *Returning to Earth* (novel)
A53. *Letters to Yesenin* (poetry)
A54. *Old Bird Boy* (poetry broadside)
A55. *The English Major* (novel)

A1.a. *Plain Song*
*First edition, uncorrected proof (1965).*
**Title Page:** Plain Song | James Harrison | [row of 15 small circles] | W. W. Norton & Company Inc. | New York [row of 8 small circles and publisher's device]
**Copyright:** No copyright page.
**Binding:** Light green paper covers printed in black, spiral bound with dark green plastic spiral material. Unnumbered pages and printed on rectos only. Cover states "uncorrected proofs."

# WALKING

*Jim Harrison*

Item A2.a., *Walking*. Used by permission of Jim Harrison.

**Dust Jacket:** Not issued with dust jacket.
**Note:** Uncorrected proof measures 8" × 12". Dedicated to Linda (Linda Harrison). Harrison's first collection of poetry and first published book.

### A1.b. *Plain Song*

*First edition, first printing (1965).*

**Title Page:** Plain Song | James Harrison | [row of 15 small circles] | W. W. Norton & Company Inc. | New York [row of 8 small circles and publisher's device]
**Copyright:** [13 of lines of information] FIRST EDITION, 1 2 3 4 5 6 7 8 9 0
**Binding:** Green cloth over boards. Facsimile signature ("James Harrison") blind-stamped on front board. Gold lettering on spine.
**Dust Jacket:** Off-white dust jacket with black lettering and a charcoal sketch on the front panel. Published price of $4.50.
**Note:** 1,500 copies printed in first edition. Harrison's first collection of poetry is dedicated to Linda (Linda Harrison). The review slip in the advance copies states that the publication date is 24 November 1965.

### A1.c. *Plain Song*

*First edition, first printing, edition in wraps (1965).*

**Title Page:** Plain Song | James Harrison | [row of 15 small circles] | W. W. Norton & Company Inc. | New York [row of 8 small circles and publisher's device]
**Copyright:** [13 of lines of information] FIRST EDITION, 1 2 3 4 5 6 7 8 9 0
**Binding:** Off-white wraps with black lettering and a charcoal sketch on the front panel.
**Dust Jacket:** Not issued with jacket. Priced at $1.95.
**Note:** 1,500 copies issued simultaneously with the hardcover edition. Harrison's first collection of poetry is dedicated to Linda (Linda Harrison).

### A2.a. *Walking*

*First edition, first printing, numbered edition (1967).*

**Title Page:** Walking | Jim Harrison | The Pym Randall Press | 361 Harvard Street | Cambridge, Mass. 02138
**Copyright:** [1 line of information] No statement of printing. See colophon page.
**Binding:** Heavy brown paper with black lettering. Hand-sewn wraps.
**Dust Jacket:** Not issued with dust jacket.
**Note:** Colophon page states 100 numbered and 26 lettered and signed copies. Published April 1967. A single poem.

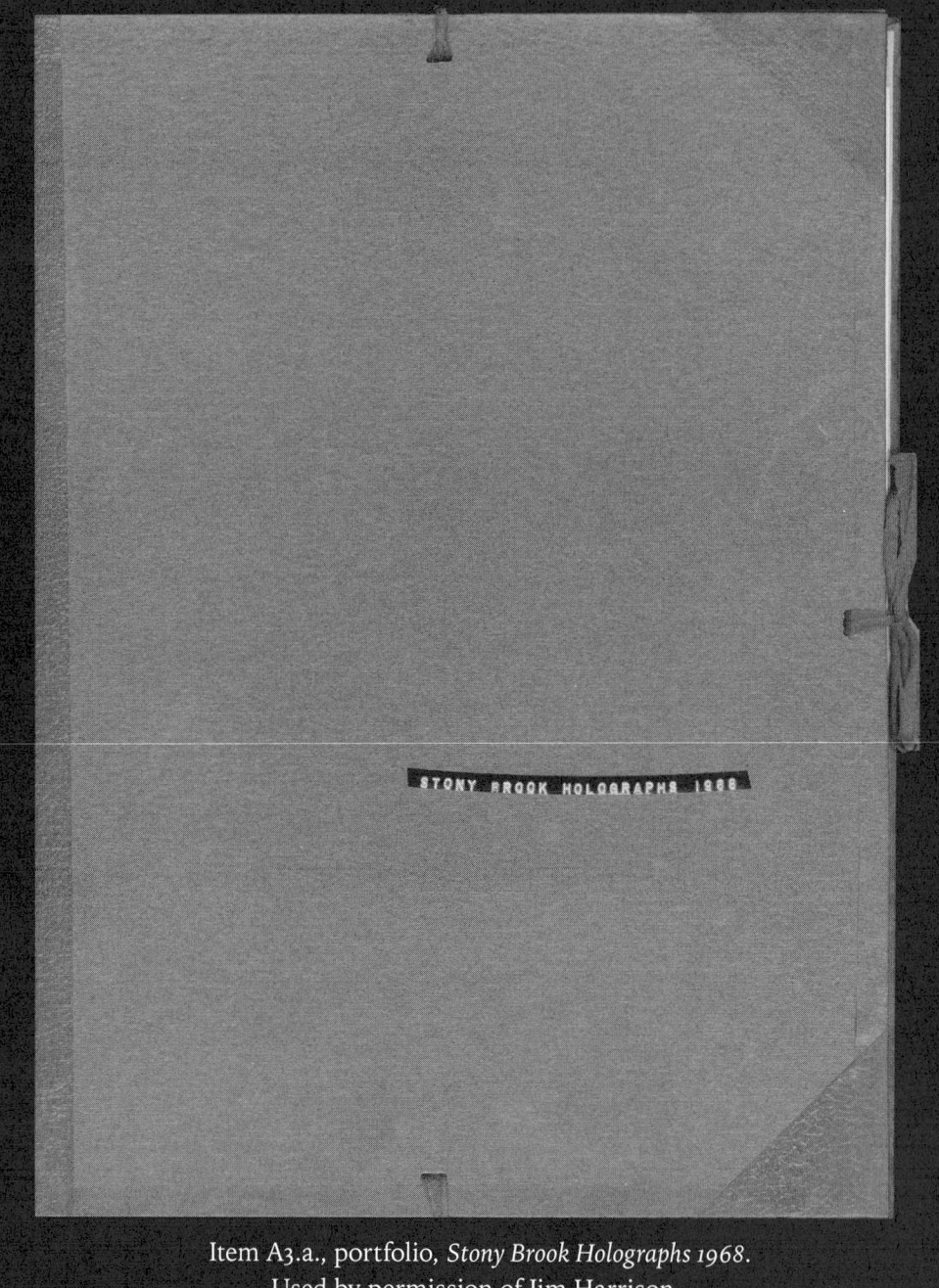

STONY BROOK HOLOGRAPHS 1968

Item A3.a., portfolio, *Stony Brook Holographs 1968*.
Used by permission of Jim Harrison.

**A2.b.** *Walking*

*First edition, first printing, lettered edition (1967).*
**Title Page:** Walking | Jim Harrison | The Pym Randall Press | 361 Harvard Street | Cambridge, Mass. 02138
**Copyright:** [1 line of information] No statement of printing. See colophon page.
**Binding:** Heavy brown paper with black lettering. Hand-sewn wraps.
**Dust Jacket:** Not issued with dust jacket.
**Note:** Colophon page states 100 numbered and 26 lettered and signed copies. Published April 1967. A single poem. This poem was later published in Harrison's collection of poetry entitled *Locations* in 1968.

**A3.a.** *Dreams*

*Broadside, first printing (1968).*
**Note:** Contained in the portfolio *Stony Brook Holographs* (New York: Stony Brook Poetics Foundation, 1968). Seven poets (Robert Duncan, Jim Harrison, Denise Levertov, Jerome Rothenberg, Charles Simic, Louis Simpson, John Wieners) wrote holograph copies of their poems and signed their entries. Only ten copies of these handwritten broadsides were printed. Broadside measures 8½" × 11" and is housed in a publisher's black paper over boards portfolio with leatherette corners and spine. This portfolio has three black cloth ties and a label that reads "Stony Brook Holographs 1968." The portfolio measures 12½" × 16". This broadside represents the only published appearance of this poem. Copies of this portfolio can be found at the following institutions: the State University of New York at Stony Brook, the State University of New York at Buffalo, Michigan State University, Cornell University, Ball State University, Southern Methodist University, and the University of Victoria.

**A4.a.** *Locations*

*First edition, first printing (1968).*
**Title Page:** [4 leaf cluster design] | Locations | [single line] | Jim Harrison | [publisher's device] | W. W. Norton & Company Inc. | New York
**Copyright:** [14 of lines of information] FIRST EDITION 1 2 3 4 5 6 7 8 9 0
**Binding:** Green cloth over boards. Facsimile signature ("Jim Harrison") blind-stamped on front board. Gold lettering on spine.
**Dust Jacket:** Off-white jacket. A bamboo leaf on handmade paper design on front panel with green lettering. Spine and back panel off-white with green lettering. Priced at $4.95.

## Dreams
### to D.H.

In the West the cities of the North
New York cool as a fresh apple
girls who shower and change their underpants
marriage to Lee Remick
my distant love of the moment, dreams
of great power over nothing in particular,
poet dreams of "not since Dante..."
terror dreams that I dream awake
stream flowing through pigfarms
glutted with muck and shit
the largest watersnake on earth
upon its bank.
I dream not to dream
my other who stunned with waking
sees a scythe awake
moving through the dark
make me still, give me an eye
that moves toward earth, some giant
anti-observatory, glistening, huge thick
glass toward ground.

                      Jim Harrison

**Note:** 1,250 copies published. This collection of poetry is dedicated to H.W. (Herbert Weisinger). The review slip that Norton provided in the advance copies of this book states a publication date of 14 October 1968. Norton has stated that it did not print proof copies of this book.

### A4.b. *Locations*

*First edition, first printing, edition in wraps (1968).*
**Title Page:** [4 leaf cluster design] | Locations | [single line] | Jim Harrison | [publisher's device] | W. W. Norton & Company Inc. | New York
**Copyright:** [14 of lines of information] FIRST EDITION 1 2 3 4 5 6 7 8 9 0
**Binding:** Off-white wrappers. A bamboo leaf on handmade paper design on front panel with green lettering. Spine is off-white with green lettering. Back panel is off-white with black lettering and has an uncredited photo of the author.
**Dust Jacket:** Not issued with dust jacket. Priced at $2.45.
**Note:** 1,250 copies in wraps issued simultaneously with the hardcover edition. This collection of poetry is dedicated to H.W. (Herbert Weisinger).

### A5.a. *Ghazal for Christmas*

*Broadside, first printing (1969).*
**Note:** Contained in the portfolio *Four Poems for Christmas 1969* (Fremont MI: Sumac Press, December 1969). In an edition of 25 numbered and signed copies issued in a brown paper portfolio that contains 4 $9^{15}/_{16}$" × 13" hand-printed broadsides by Sequoia Press, each with a poem by Harrison, James Tate, Dan Gerber, and J. D. Reed. Portfolio measures 11" × $13^7/_8$". This Ghazal is actually no. 1 from *Outlyer and Ghazals*. This was the first published appearance of this poem.

### A6.a. *Outlyer and Ghazals*

*First edition, advance uncorrected proof (1971).*
**Title Page:** Outlyer | [small design] And | Ghazals | By | Jim Harrison | Simon and Schuster · New York
**Copyright:** [18 lines of information] FIRST PRINTING
**Binding:** Tall pad-bound brown wrappers with black lettering.
**Dust Jacket:** Not issued with jacket. On the cover of the proof it states that the probable published price will be $4.95 for the cloth edition and $1.95 for the paper edition.
**Note:** The cover of this proof states the probable publication date of the

$4.95

## LOCATIONS
POEMS
By JIM HARRISON

To get the intensity of the lyric into poems whose subjects and lengths tend to resist the lyric mode, Mr. Harrison has moved to longer forms, and particularly to the suite-form. In *Locations*, which represents his work since the publication of *Plain Song* three years ago, Mr. Harrison employs the suite to attain a discursory, circling effect, by which he draws many wedges onto the focal metaphor of the poem. The suite's abrupt tonal shifts and geometric linear development of the poem — a succession of variations on a single theme which stalk rather than present the poem.

Most of the poems in *Locations* are centered on nature, with the natural world although not to the usual manner of the nature poet. The central figure is human, the poems are immersed in a sense of man violently wrestling with the earth and the physical world he has built for himself. Though many of the poems are personal, they reflect a feeling of a nearly exhausted planet.

"My direction," writes Mr. Harrison of this second volume of poems, "seems toward a larger (larger in form) attempt to keep the tension of the construct. My sympathies, which are reasonably humble, run hot and cold to the great imagists: Whitman, Rilke, Neruda, among others."

Mr. Harrison was born in Grayling, Michigan, in 1937. He graduated twice from Michigan State University and now teaches in the English Department at the State University of New York at Stony Brook. He is married, has one daughter, and although born in Michigan now lives in Long Island, New York.

---

**LOCATIONS** Poems by **Jim Harrison** NORTON

---

### Other Books of Poetry

**ALL**
the collected short poems 1923-1958
*Louis Zukofsky*

**ALL**
the collected short poems 1956-1964
*Louis Zukofsky*

**THE MUSIC**
*Helen Wolfert*

**LOVE MAKES THE AIR LIGHT**
*Raymond Roseliep*

**PLAIN SONG**
*Jim Harrison*

**NONSEQUENCES**
*Christopher Middleton*

**A BEGINNING**
*William Burford*

**VIRGIL'S MACHINES**
*Joel Sloman*

**THE DUMBFOUNDING**
*Margaret Avison*

**NECESSITIES OF LIFE**
*Adrienne Rich*

**SNAPSHOTS OF A DAUGHTER-IN-LAW**
*Adrienne Rich*

**THE BOOK OF THE GREEN MAN**
*Ronald Johnson*

**THE PERFECT FICTION**
*Gilbert Sorrentino*

W · W · NORTON · COMPANY · INC ·
55 FIFTH AVENUE, NEW YORK, N.Y. 10003

---

"These are strong, skillful poems, written by a natural poet, who, happily, deals in poems of communication. They are tough poems, at times, with streaks of realities striking through, surprisingly broad at times, but with a penetrating tenderness."
—PHILIP LEVINE

### PLAIN SONG
### JIM HARRISON

Jim Harrison is a natural poet, with an unfailing instinct for where to break his lines, for the image that embodies meaning beyond appearance yet that can, if you will, be taken for itself alone; for the sound of words in relation to their meaning. He belongs to a tradition that includes poets as far apart in time as Sappho and Lorca, Li Po and much of William Carlos Williams — a tradition of nondidactic, nonphilosophizing poetry in which "form follows function" and symbols are not applied but are deeply inherent in the image itself — the purest lyric tradition, which partakes of the nature of music without imitating it.

---

Item A4.a., *Locations*. © 1968 by Jim Harrison.
Used by permission of W. W. Norton & Company, Inc.

### Ghazal For Christmas

Unbind my hair she says. The night is white and warm,
the snow on the mountains absorbing the moon.

We have to get there before the music begins, scattered,
elliptical, needing to be drawn together and sung.

They have dark green voices and listening, there are birds,
coal shovels, the glazed hysteria of the soon-to-be-dead.

I suspect Jesus *will* return and the surprise will be
fatal. I'll ride the equator on a whale, a giraffe on land.

Even stone when inscribed bears the ecstatic. Pressed to
some new wall, ungiving, the screams become thinner.

Let us have the tambourine and guitars and forests, fruit,
and a new sun to guide us, a holy book, tracked in new blood.

*Jim Harrison*
JIM HARRISON

Four Poems for Christmas
1969

Item A5.a., portfolio and poem, "Ghazal for Christmas."
Used by permission of Dan Gerber and Sumac Press.

# Outlyer

## AND Ghazals
### POETRY BY Jim Harrison

"one of the most authentic voices of his time" —DACTUS LASTNAME

SIMON AND SCHUSTER

OUTLYER and Ghazals • Jim Harrison

---

Jim Harrison lives on a farm in Northern Michigan with his wife, daughter, dogs, horses, and a voracious appetite for the pleasures of this world which (fortunately) was funded by a National Endowment of the Arts Fellowship in 1968 and a Guggenheim Fellowship in 1969–1970. He is the author of two previous collections, *Plain Song* and *Locations*, and his work has appeared in dozens of anthologies and little magazines. His first novel, *Wolf*, will be published by Simon and Schuster this fall.

Jacket design by Paul Bacon

---

Harrison's works are so real and are about such real things that at first they sound like something you must have heard someone say out loud, perhaps some tentatively friendly but formidable man in the kind of bar where you lay out your table stakes before you order your shot. And indeed most of us would have to be drinking or would have to be reborn as courageous poets before we could dare speak of our boredom, our love, our fear, our death, as freely as Harrison does. But then as we hear a little more, we realize how much this man knows about these things, and how artfully the wit of his speech works with the deep design of his form and the intelligence of his imagination to help us understand things, too.

—JOHN A. THOMPSON

Jim Harrison grew up in Northern Michigan and shares with the other Michigan poet, Theodore Roethke, not only the longing to be part of the instinctual world, but also the remarkable knowledge of plant and animal life that comes only with long familiarity and close observation. This raises an incidental question: How many more poets of his kind will we see in the United States? It is a melancholy thought that Mr. Harrison may be one of the last of the species.

—*Poetry Magazine*

---

"Of all the books of verse into which man has poured his energy and intelligence, this may be the most noteworthy and overlooked collection of the past quarter of a century," wrote Louis Simpson about Jim Harrison's second book, *Locations*.

Now Harrison, only thirty-two, gives us his third and last collection to date: precise, lucid poems in praise of survival, nature, loves, lost, fantasies of a ragged paradise filled with wine and women where he provides the song—a glorious celebration of everyman's desires, song with a sureness, full-throated voice, jubilant, lyric, superbly controlled.

$5.95

20862

---

Item A6.b., *Outlyer and Ghazals*. Used by permission of Jim Harrison.

$5.95

"This book is a tale told by a poet, full of life and magic, signifying joy."
—William Eastlake

Meet Swanson. Swanson, spinner of tales, winner of tails.

Northern Michigan's prodigal son, down from the farm (typewriter, knapsack and cardboard suitcase in tow), is on the prowl to make his fame and fortune in the citadels of America—with a heart, a libido, an appetite as vast as the rugged country he was born in.

This rawboned, beautiful novel—fast, loose, funny—is his memoir, filled with the natural (and sexual) lore of a rural renegade writer whose penchant for flights of fantasy is as irrepressible as his spirit. The effect is somewhat akin to early Hemingway and middle Henry Miller: recollections of conquest and glory in cities visited, of camping and fishing in backwoods revisited, told from the vantage point of one of the last male chauvinists of his time (see photo on back of jacket for further details), elaborated and embellished with remarkable energy and grace.

Swanson's memoir is "A roaring trek around the madlands of Jim Harrison's brain, and around a homeless America. With memory and invention by Rabelais out of Walter Mitty, this is a rich, sad, sensuous, rereadable book."
—John MacDonald

# Wolf

## A FALSE MEMOIR
## Jim Harrison

Wolf  Jim Harrison

Simon and Schuster

21387

Jim Harrison's rustic lyricism and lusty barroom exuberance have previously combined in three highly acclaimed collections of verse: *Plain Song*, *Locations*, and *Outlyer*. In praise of *Outlyer*, *The New York Times Book Review* wrote: "It just may be that Harrison has a good deal to show us about the psychic landscape of working-class American life.... This is poetry worth loving, hating, and fighting over, a subjective mirror of our American days and needs."

He is also one of the sports who contribute regularly to *Sports Illustrated*. *Wolf* is his first novel.

Jacket design by Paul Bacon
Photograph of author by John Schulz

Item A7.b., *Wolf*. Used by permission of Jim Harrison.

## SERGEI YESENIN 1895-1925

*to D.G.*

This matted and glossy photo of Yesenin
bought at a Leningrad newsstand - permanently
tilted on my desk: he doesn't stare at me
he stares at nothing; the difference between
a plane crash and a noose adds up to nothing.
And what can I do with heroes with my brain fixed
on so few of them? Again nothing. Regard his flat
magazine eyes with my half-cocked own, both
of us seeing nothing. In the vodka was nothing
and Isadora was nothing, the pistol waved
in New York was nothing, and that plank bridge
near your village home in Ryazan covered seven feet
of nothing, the clumsy noose that swung the tilted
body was nothing but a noose, a law of gravity
this seeking for the ground, a few feet of nothing
between shoes and the floor a light year away.
So this is a song of Yesenin's noose which came
to nothing, but did a good job as we say back home
where there's nothing but snow. But I stood under
your balcony in St. Petersburg, yes St. Petersburg!
a crazed tourist with so much nothing in my heart
it wanted to implode. And I walked down to the Neva
embankment with a fine sleet falling and there was
finally something, a great river vastly flowing, flat
as your eyes; something to marry to my nothing heart
other than the poems you hurled into nothing those
years before the articulate noose.

*Jim Harrison*

The Sumac Press

book is April 1971. Proof measures 5⅜" × 8". It also states "advance uncorrected proof" on the front panel. This collection of poetry is dedicated to Pat Paton on the copyright page.

### A6.b. *Outlyer and Ghazals*
*First edition, first printing (1971).*
**Title Page:** Outlyer | [small design] And | Ghazals | By | Jim Harrison | Simon and Schuster · New York
**Copyright:** [14 of lines of information] FIRST PRINTING
**Binding:** Green paper over boards with black lettering on spine.
**Dust Jacket:** Off-white jacket with sunburst design in black with green, blue, yellow, and black lettering on front panel. Priced at $5.95. Jacket design by Paul Bacon. Author photo on inside back flap by Dan Gerber.
**Note:** Review slips in the advance copies state the published date of this book as 26 April 1971. This collection of poetry is dedicated to Pat Paton.

### A6.c. *Outlyer and Ghazals*
*First edition, first printing edition in wraps (1971).*
**Title Page:** Outlyer | [small design] And | Ghazals | By | Jim Harrison | Simon and Schuster · New York
**Copyright:** [14 of lines of information] FIRST PRINTING
**Binding:** Off-white wraps with sunburst design in black with green, blue, yellow, and black lettering on front panel. Wrappers design (same as dust jacket for hardcover edition) by Paul Bacon. Author photo on rear panel by Dan Gerber.
**Dust Jacket:** Not issued with dust jacket. Priced at $2.45.
**Note:** Issued simultaneously with the hardcover edition. This collection of poetry is dedicated to Pat Paton.

### A7.a. *Wolf: A False Memoir*
*First edition, uncorrected proof (1971).*
**Title Page:** Wolf: A False Memoir | Simon and Schuster, New York (1971)
**Copyright:** This proof was not seen by the compilers.
**Binding:** In tall pad-bound yellow wraps.
**Dust Jacket:** Not issued with dust jacket.
**Note:** This proof was not seen by the compilers. The description above is based on those from booksellers who have handled this proof in the past.

Advance uncorrected proofs
from
**SIMON AND SCHUSTER**

# A GOOD DAY TO DIE

A NOVEL BY

**Jim Harrison**

Probable publication: SEPTEMBER 1973

**A7.b.** *Wolf: A False Memoir*
*First edition, first printing (1971).*
**Title Page:** Wolf | A False Memoir | Jim Harrison | [publisher's device] | Simon and Schuster | New York
**Copyright:** [12 of lines of information] FIRST PRINTING
**Binding:** White cloth over boards with black lettering. Black top stain on pages.
**Dust Jacket:** Off-white jacket with black lettering on front panel. Design of a man standing on the earth drinking from a bottle, holding a rifle, on front panel. Lettering on spine in black, blue, and green. Jacket design by Paul Bacon. Author photo on rear panel by John Schulz. Priced at $5.95.
**Note:** This first novel is dedicated to Thomas McGuane and in memoriam Missy 1966–1971. Review slips in the advance copies state that the publication date is 22 November 1971.

**A8.a.** *Sergei Yesenin 1895–1925*
*Broadside, first printing (1971).*
**Note:** Single broadside designed and printed by Dan Gerber (Fremont MI: Sumac Press, ND). For many years it was thought that only 33 copies were produced. This information was based on an inscription that Harrison had written on the back of a copy in 1972. The exact number of copies printed is unknown; however, according to Dan Gerber there were actually between 80 and 100 copies printed. The Harrison Archive has a letter from Gerber to Harrison dated 5 January 1972 that discusses this broadside. The date of that letter and other research points toward a printing date of December 1971. Harrison and Gerber returned from a trip to the former Soviet Union in November 1971. This broadside was not issued signed by the author, though most copies seen have been signed by Harrison and many by Gerber as well. The broadside, which measures 6" × 9", was issued in two states. One is printed in red ink and one in black ink; no priority has been established between the two states; however, the red-ink state is missing a period at the end of the poem and seems to be the scarcer of the two. The black state has the period present. This was the first published appearance of this poem.

**A9.a.** *A Good Day to Die: A Novel*
*First edition, advance uncorrected proofs (1973).*
**Title Page:** A | Good | Day | To | Die | A Novel By | Jim Harrison | Simon and Schuster New York

*(continued from front flap)*

This is Harrison's second novel, and like *Wolf* it is the story of an expedition across a psychic as well as a geographic United States. It is an account of the journey of three young Americans who, no longer able to connect with their world, set out from Florida across the country in order to destroy a dam—they decide is being built in the Grand Canyon—the final, purgative release that will allow them to live as human beings.

...A worn-out Tom Sawyer who can no longer believe in his own romantic fantasies and a Huck Finn who's duped his survival instincts out of existence set out across America ... but disrupting the Sunday School picnic is no longer enough, and there are no Nigger Jims to be rescued, so they decide to rescue the Grand Canyon instead ... this novel speaks with absolute accuracy to and about its generation; the thing that comes through most strongly is the directionlessness, the bankruptcy of even the most recent American dream, the apathy ... though there are sporadic attempts on the part of the central character to struggle through to something better, or at least something that will get him through the next day ... a killer.
—Margaret Atwood

Of the novel, Harry Crews writes:
"*A Good Day to Die* is a brilliant performance, even better I think than his wild lyrical first novel, *Wolf*. His is the language of a poet. But his heart must be the muscle of a red-legged angel of rage, confusion, bitterness, expansiveness of it ... unbounded by a tentative sanity. If he didn't have such a heart, he could not make us feel our own tentative grasp of the world the way he does. I will always be among his most dedicated readers. *A Good Day to Die* is sad, bitter, violent, and at the same time a singular joy to read."

JACKET DESIGN BY PAUL BACON

## A GOOD DAY TO DIE / Jim Harrison

PHOTO BY JILL KREMENTZ

Jim Harrison is a recipient of the country's two most distinguished creative-writing fellowships: The National Endowment for the Arts and the Guggenheim. He is also a contributor to *Sports Illustrated*. When not writing, he lives on Lake Leelanau, in northern Michigan, with his wife and daughters.

Simon and Schuster

21324

## A GOOD DAY TO DIE / Jim Harrison

*A Good Day to Die* should be the thriller of the year—and at last, a new kind of thriller. It is the comic and terrifying adventure of three depraved innocents in a cross-country chase to save our land: a poet who loves only fishing (and girls); a Nam veteran who loves only violence (and drugs); a gorgeous long-legged girl who loves only one of them (at first). And there is the case of dynamite.... Harrison is a wonderful writer.
—John Thompson

Jim Harrison, both a poet and a novelist, is one of our most admired and celebrated younger writers. Of his first novel, *Wolf*, *The New York Times* said: "A funny, swaggering, angry cocksure book... a poignant, handsomely written self explanation", and *The Washington Post* remarked: "like the best of Thoreau."

And Thomas Berger has written:
"Jim Harrison is a fine poet who from time to time demonstrates for those of us condemned to prose how a novel should be written. *A Good Day to Die* is the product of a love of language and a passion for experience."

*(continued on back flap)*

$5.95

Item A9.b., *A Good Day to Die*. Used by permission of Jim Harrison.

**Copyright:** [11 lines of information] 1 2 3 4 5 6 7 8 9 10
**Binding:** Advance uncorrected proofs. In oblong plain yellow wraps with black lettering on front panel.
**Dust Jacket:** Not issued with dust jacket.
**Note:** On front cover of this proof it states that the probable publication date will be September 1973. This novel is dedicated to Dan Gerber.

**A9.b.** *A Good Day to Die: A Novel*
*First edition, first printing (1973).*
**Title Page:** A | Good | Day | To | Die | A Novel By | Jim Harrison | Simon and Schuster New York
**Copyright:** [11 lines of information] 1 2 3 4 5 6 7 8 9 10
**Binding:** Brown cloth spine with yellow lettering. Orange paper over boards.
**Dust Jacket:** White jacket with black and red lettering. Design on front panel has a fly fisherman with Indian headdress over the Grand Canyon. Jacket design by Paul Bacon. Author photo on rear panel by Jill Krementz. Published price of $5.95.
**Note:** This novel is dedicated to Dan Gerber.

**A10.a.** *Letters to Yesenin*
*First edition, first printing, unbound galleys (1973).*
**Title Page:** Letters to Yesenin | Jim Harrison | [publisher's device] | The Sumac Press | Fremont, Michigan
**Copyright:** [8 lines of information] FIRST EDITION. See colophon page.
**Binding:** Four separate unbound signatures measuring $6^{3/16}" \times 9^{1/8}"$. Each signature is unbound and folded only. There are no covers on these signatures.
**Dust Jacket:** Not issued with dust jacket.
**Note:** The number of these unbound signatures printed is unknown. An inscription from Harrison on a copy in the Bruce Kahn collection states that these were "unbound galleys"; however, it may be that these were simply the unbound sheets of the book before trimming and binding. This theory is borne out by the fact that all the sheets in these signatures are exactly the same as the finished book, including the title page, copyright page, page numbers, and colophon page. Colophon page states 26 lettered and 100 numbered copies are hardbound and have been signed by the poet. It is also stated that there are 1,000 softcover copies. This collection of poetry is dedicated to J.D. (J. D. Reed).

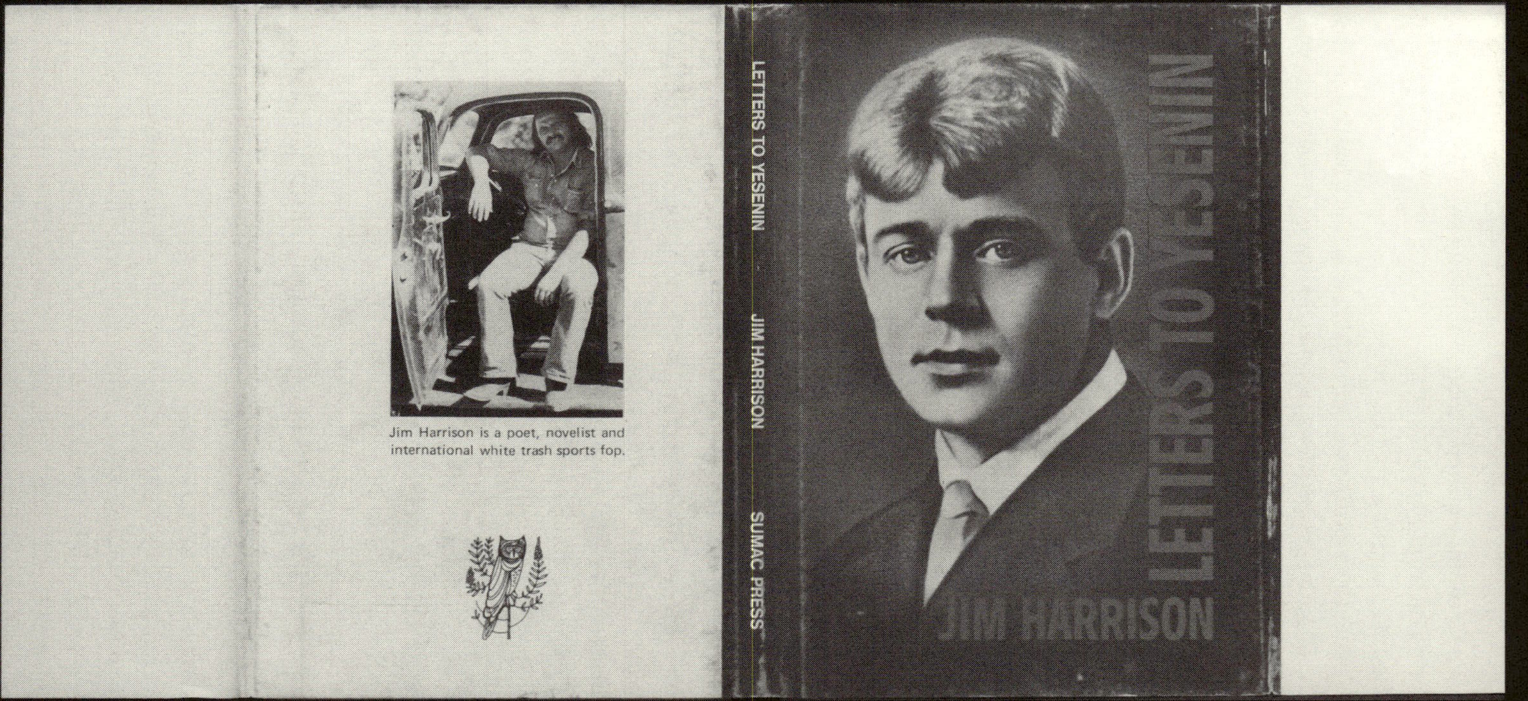

**LETTERS TO YESENIN**     **JIM HARRISON**     **SUMAC PRESS**

Jim Harrison is a poet, novelist and international white trash sports fop.

Item A10.c., *Letters to Yesenin*. Used by permission of Dan Gerber and Sumac Press.

**A10.b.** *Letters to Yesenin*

*First edition, first printing, edition in wraps (1973).*

**Title Page:** Letters to Yesenin | Jim Harrison | [publisher's device] | The Sumac Press | Fremont, Michigan

**Copyright:** [8 lines of information] FIRST EDITION. See colophon page.

**Binding:** Brown wrappers with red lettering on front panel with antique photo of Sergei Yesenin. White lettering on spine. Author photo on back panel (not credited). Priced at $2.45.

**Dust Jacket:** Not issued with dust jacket.

**Note:** Issued simultaneously with the limited edition. Colophon page states 26 lettered and 100 numbered copies are hardbound and have been signed by the poet. It is also stated that there are 1,000 softcover copies. This collection of poetry is dedicated to J.D. (J. D. Reed).

**A10.c.** *Letters to Yesenin*

*First edition, first printing, numbered edition (1973).*

**Title Page:** Letters to Yesenin | Jim Harrison | [publisher's device] | The Sumac Press | Fremont, Michigan

**Copyright:** [8 lines of information] FIRST EDITION. See colophon page.

**Binding:** Black cloth over boards with gold lettering on spine. "Jim Harrison" and "Letters to Yesenin" blind-stamped on front board.

**Dust Jacket:** Brown jacket with red lettering on front panel with antique photo of Sergei Yesenin. White lettering on spine. Author photo on back panel (not credited). Published price of $7.50. Jacket flaps are white and blank.

**Note:** Colophon page states 26 lettered and 100 numbered copies are hardbound and have been signed by the poet. It is also stated that there are 1,000 softcover copies. This collection of poetry is dedicated to J.D. (J. D. Reed).

**A10.d.** *Letters to Yesenin*

*First edition, first printing, lettered edition (1973).*

**Title Page:** Letters to Yesenin | Jim Harrison | [publisher's device] | The Sumac Press | Fremont, Michigan

**Copyright:** [8 lines of information] FIRST EDITION. See colophon page.

**Binding:** Black cloth over boards with gold lettering on spine. "Jim Harrison" and "Letters to Yesenin" blind-stamped on front board.

**Dust Jacket:** Brown jacket with red lettering on front panel with antique photo of Sergei Yesenin. White lettering on spine. Author photo on back panel

# FARMER

## Jim Harrison

Galley no.: ____ Pub. date: 8/76 Price: $7.95

Unrevised proofs. Confidential. Please do not quote for publication until verified with finished book.

THE VIKING PRESS

Item A11.a., unrevised proofs, *Farmer*.
Used by permission of Jim Harrison.

(not credited). Published price of $7.50. Jacket flaps are white and blank.
**Note:** Colophon page states 26 lettered and 100 numbered copies are hardbound and have been signed by the poet. It also states that there are 1,000 softcover copies. This collection of poetry is dedicated to J.D. (J. D. Reed).

A11.a. *Farmer*

*First edition, unrevised proofs (1976).*
**Title Page:** Farmer | Jim Harrison | The Viking Press New York
**Copyright:** No copyright page.
**Binding:** Heavy greenish blue paper with black lettering. Front panel states "unrevised proofs." No printing on spine or rear panel.
**Dust Jacket:** Not issued with dust jacket. On the front panel of the proof it states a price of $7.95 and a publication date of August 1976.
**Note:** Proof measures 5$7/16$" × 8$1/4$".

A11.b. *Farmer*

*First edition, first printing (1976).*
**Title Page:** Farmer | Jim Harrison | [publisher's device] | The Viking Press New York
**Copyright:** [12 lines of information] FIRST PUBLISHED IN 1976 BY THE VIKING PRESS
**Binding:** Black cloth spine with gold and bronze lettering. Brown paper over boards. Yellow top stain on pages.
**Dust Jacket:** White jacket with yellow and black lettering. Pitchfork and barn door illustration on front panel. Jacket design by Janet Halverson. Author photo on rear inside flap by Guy de la Valdene. Priced at $7.95.
**Note:** There is a second-state binding of this title. In a letter dated 3 August 1976 the publisher requests that all booksellers destroy the first issue of the book because of a binding defect. In the first-issue binding the measurement from the edge of the board to the beginning of the cloth on the spine is 5$1/16$". In the second-issue binding the measurement is 4$7/8$". There were 7,500 copies published in each state. Publication date of this book was 25 August 1976. This novel is dedicated to Jamie and Norma (Jamie Harrison and Norma Harrison).

A12.a. *Returning to Earth*

*First edition, first printing (1977).*
**Title Page:** Returning to Earth | Jim Harrison | The Court Street Chapbook Series | An Ithaca House Book

Item A11.b, *Farmer*. Used by permission of Jim Harrison.

**Copyright:** [10 lines of information] No statement of printing.
**Binding:** Orange brown paper wraps with black lettering. Stapled.
**Dust Jacket:** Not issued with dust jacket. Priced at $2.50.
**Note:** 500 copies were printed. This poem is dedicated to Guy and Anna (Guy de la Valdene and Anna Harrison).

A13.a. *Letters to Yesenin and Returning to Earth*
*First edition, first printing (1979).*
**Title Page:** Letters To Yesenin | (and) | Returning to Earth | Poems By Jim Harrison | Sumac Poetry Series | Center Publications | 1979
**Copyright:** [14 lines of information] No statement of printing.
**Binding:** Light tan paper wraps with black and white lettering. Antique photo of Sergei Yesenin on front panel. Photo of Harrison and his daughter Anna on rear panel is not credited.
**Dust Jacket:** Not issued with dust jacket. Priced at $3.95.

A14.a. *Legends of the Fall*
*First edition, uncorrected galley proof (1979).*
**Title Page:** Jim Harrison | [2 ruled lines] | Legends | Of The | Fall | Delacorte Press/Seymour Lawrence | [3]
**Copyright:** [12 lines of information] FIRST PRINTING
**Binding:** White pad-bound binding with black lettering. Cover of this proof is paper and is a photocopy of the title page.
**Dust Jacket:** Not issued with dust jacket.
**Note:** This state of the proof measures 5" × 7¼". Total number of copies printed of this proof is unknown, but it is thought that very few were distributed (probably fewer than 15).

A14.b. *Legends of the Fall*
*First edition, uncorrected proof (1979).*
**Title Page:** Jim Harrison | [2 ruled lines] | Legends | Of The | Fall | Delacorte Press/Seymour Lawrence | [3]
**Copyright:** [12 lines of information] FIRST PRINTING
**Binding:** In red heavy stock wrappers with black lettering.
**Dust Jacket:** Not issued with dust jacket.
**Note:** This state of the proof measures 5⁷⁄₁₆" × 8⁵⁄₁₆".

Item A12.a., *Returning to Earth*.
Used by permission of Jim Harrison.

**A14.c.** *Legends of the Fall*

*First edition, first printing, single volume (1979).*

**Title Page:** Jim Harrison | [2 ruled lines] | Legends | Of The | Fall | Delacorte Press/Seymour Lawrence

**Copyright:** [31 lines of information] FIRST PRINTING

**Binding:** White cloth over boards with facsimile signature ("Jim Harrison") in silver on front board. Silver lettering on spine.

**Dust Jacket:** White jacket with black lettering. Painting on front panel by Russell Chatham. Jacket design by Giorgetta Bell McRee. Author photo on rear panel by Bob Wargo. Priced at $10.95.

**Note:** Review copies state publication date of the book was 30 May 1979. 12,000 copies printed. This is the first of many Harrison books to use a Russell Chatham painting for the dust-jacket art. This first collection of novellas is dedicated to Guy and Jack (Guy de la Valdene and Jack Nicholson). This collection of novellas, Harrison's first such collection, contains the titles "Revenge," "The Man Who Gave Up His Name," and "Legends of the Fall."

**A14.d.** *Legends of the Fall*

*First edition, first printing, 3-volume set (1979).*

**Volume 1 Title Page:** Jim Harrison | [2 ruled lines] | Revenge | Delacorte Press/Seymour Lawrence

**Copyright:** [29 lines of information] FIRST PRINTING

**Binding:** White cloth over boards with silver green lettering on spine.

**Dust Jacket:** Not issued with dust jackets.

**Note:** This is the first volume of a 3-volume set issued in a white paper-covered slipcase with black lettering. The slipcase has a Russell Chatham painting on the front panel. 1,000 copies were published.

**Volume 2 Title Page:** Jim Harrison | [2 ruled lines] | The Man | Who Gave Up | His Name | Delacorte Press/Seymour Lawrence

**Copyright:** [21 lines of information] FIRST PRINTING

**Binding:** White cloth over boards with silver green lettering on spine.

**Dust Jacket:** Not issued with dust jacket.

**Note:** This is the second volume of a 3-volume set issued in a white paper-covered slipcase with black lettering. The slipcase has a Russell Chatham painting on the front panel. 1,000 copies were published.

**Volume 3 Title Page:** Jim Harrison | [2 ruled lines] | Legends | Of The | Fall | Delacorte Press/Seymour Lawrence

**Copyright:** [23 lines of information] FIRST PRINTING

Item A13.a., front panel (*left*), rear panel (*right*), *Letters to Yesenin and Returning to Earth*.
Used by permission of Jim Harrison.

**Binding:** White cloth over boards with silver green lettering on spine.
**Dust Jacket:** Not issued with dust jacket.
**Note:** This is the third volume of a 3-volume set issued in a white paper-covered slipcase with black lettering. The slipcase has a Russell Chatham painting on the front panel. 1,000 copies were published. This first collection of novellas is dedicated to Guy and Jack (Guy de la Valdene and Jack Nicholson).

A14.e. *Legends of the Fall*
*First edition, first printing, 3-volume limited set (1979).*
**Volume 1 Title Page:** Jim Harrison | [2 ruled lines] | Revenge | Delacorte Press/Seymour Lawrence
**Copyright:** [29 lines of information] FIRST PRINTING
**Binding:** Light tan cloth over boards with bronze lettering on spine.
**Dust Jacket:** Not issued with dust jacket.
**Note:** This is the first volume of a 3-volume set issued in a light tan paper-covered slipcase with black lettering. The slipcase has a John Thompson illustration on the front panel. This edition was limited to 250 numbered copies, and all were signed by the author on a limitation page tipped in to the third-volume "Legends of the Fall."
**Volume 2 Title Page:** Jim Harrison | [2 ruled lines] | The Man | Who Gave Up | His Name | Delacorte Press/Seymour Lawrence
**Copyright:** [21 lines of information] FIRST PRINTING
**Binding:** Light tan cloth over boards with bronze lettering on spine.
**Dust Jacket:** Not issued with dust jacket.
**Note:** This is the second volume of a 3-volume set issued in a light tan paper-covered slipcase with black lettering. The slipcase has a John Thompson illustration on the front panel. This edition was limited to 250 numbered copies, and all were signed by the author on a limitation page tipped in to the third-volume "Legends of the Fall."
**Volume 3 Title Page:** Jim Harrison | [2 ruled lines] | Legends | Of The Fall | Delacorte Press/Seymour Lawrence
**Copyright:** [23 lines of information] FIRST PRINTING
**Binding:** Light tan cloth over boards with bronze lettering on spine.
**Dust Jacket:** Not issued with dust jacket.
**Note:** This is the third volume of a 3-volume set issued in a light tan paper-covered slipcase with black lettering. The slipcase has a John Thompson illustration on the front panel. This edition was limited to 250 numbered

Item A14.a. (*left*), item A14.b. (*right*), proof copies, *Legends of the Fall*.
Used by permission of Dell Publishing, a division of Random House, Inc.

copies, and all were signed by the author on a limitation page tipped in to the third-volume "Legends of the Fall." This first collection of novellas is dedicated to Guy and Jack (Guy de la Valdene and Jack Nicholson).

A15.a. *Warlock*

*First edition, uncorrected proof (1981).*
**Title Page:** Jim Harrison | [double rule] | Warlock | [single rule] | Delacorte Press/Seymour Lawrence
**Copyright:** [12 lines of information] FIRST PRINTING
**Binding:** Yellow wraps with black lettering.
**Dust Jacket:** Not issued with dust jacket.
**Note:** Publication date on proof states October 1981. This novel is dedicated to Bob Dattila.

A15.b. *Warlock*

*First edition, first printing (1981).*
**Title Page:** Jim Harrison | [double rule] | Warlock | [single rule] | Delacorte Press/Seymour Lawrence
**Copyright:** [23 lines of information] FIRST PRINTING
**Binding:** Dark blue cloth on spine with silver lettering. Light blue paper over boards with facsimile signature in silver on front board.
**Dust Jacket:** White jacket with black lettering. Russell Chatham painting on front panel. Jacket design by Giorgetta Bell McRee. Author photo on rear panel by Bob Wargo. Priced at $13.95.
**Note:** This novel is dedicated to Bob Dattila. There were reportedly 19,000 copies printed.

A15.c. *Warlock*

*First edition, first printing, limited edition (1981).*
**Title Page:** Jim Harrison | [double rule] | Warlock | [single rule] | Delacorte Press/Seymour Lawrence
**Copyright:** [23 lines of information] FIRST PRINTING
**Binding:** Off-white cloth over boards with gold lettering. Gilt page edges all around. Off-white cloth over boards slipcase with a facsimile signature on front panel in gold.
**Dust Jacket:** Not issued with dust jacket.
**Note:** Colophon page tipped in with a stated limitation of 250 copies and author's signature. This novel is dedicated to Bob Dattila.

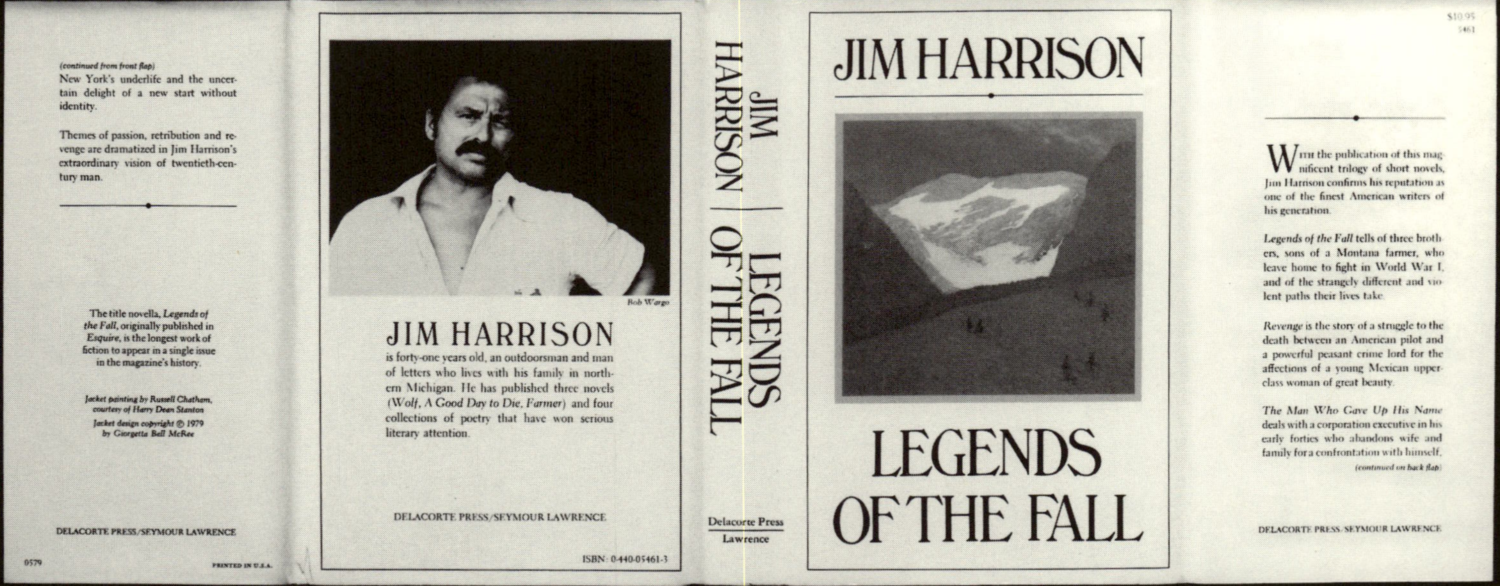

$10.95
1963

(continued from front flap)
New York's underlife and the uncertain delight of a new start without identity.

Themes of passion, retribution and revenge are dramatized in Jim Harrison's extraordinary vision of twentieth-century man.

●

The title novella, *Legends of the Fall*, originally published in *Esquire*, is the longest work of fiction to appear in a single issue in the magazine's history.

Jacket painting by Russell Chatham, courtesy of Harry Dean Stanton
Jacket design copyright © 1979
by Georgetta Bell McRee

DELACORTE PRESS/SEYMOUR LAWRENCE

PRINTED IN U.S.A.

9579

---

# JIM HARRISON

is forty-one years old, an outdoorsman and man of letters who lives with his family in northern Michigan. He has published three novels (*Wolf*, *A Good Day to Die*, *Farmer*) and four collections of poetry that have won serious literary attention.

Bob Wargo

DELACORTE PRESS/SEYMOUR LAWRENCE

ISBN: 0-440-05461-3

---

JIM HARRISON | LEGENDS OF THE FALL

Delacorte Press/Lawrence

# JIM HARRISON
# LEGENDS OF THE FALL

---

With the publication of this magnificent trilogy of short novels, Jim Harrison confirms his reputation as one of the finest American writers of his generation.

*Legends of the Fall* tells of three brothers, sons of a Montana farmer, who leave home to fight in World War I, and of the strangely different and violent paths their lives take.

*Revenge* is the story of a struggle to the death between an American pilot and a powerful peasant crime lord for the affections of a young Mexican upper-class woman of great beauty.

*The Man Who Gave Up His Name* deals with a corporation executive in his early forties who abandons wife and family for a confrontation with himself.

*(continued on back flap)*

DELACORTE PRESS/SEYMOUR LAWRENCE

---

Item A14.c., *Legends of the Fall.*
Used by permission of Dell Publishing, a division of Random House, Inc.

**A16.a.** *Selected and New Poems 1961–1981*

*First edition, uncorrected page proof (1982).*

**Title Page:** Jim Harrison | Selected | & | New Poems | 1961–1981 | Drawings by Russell Chatham | Delacorte Press/Seymour Lawrence

**Copyright:** [14 lines of information] FIRST PRINTING

**Binding:** Light gray wraps with black lettering.

**Dust Jacket:** Not issued with dust jacket.

**Note:** Publication date on proof states August 1982. This collection of poetry is dedicated to John and Rebecca (John and Rebecca Harrison).

**A16.b.** *Selected and New Poems 1961–1981*

*First edition, first printing (1982).*

**Title Page:** Selected & | New Poems | 1961–1981 | Jim Harrison | Drawings by | Russell Chatham | Delacorte Press/Seymour Lawrence

**Copyright:** [28 lines of information] FIRST PRINTING

**Binding:** Beige cloth on spine with silver lettering. Gray paper over boards with facsimile signature in box in silver on front board.

**Dust Jacket:** White jacket with black lettering. Russell Chatham painting on front panel. Jacket design by Giorgetta Bell McRee. Author photo on rear panel by Bob Wargo. Priced at $14.95.

**Note:** This collection of poetry is dedicated to John and Rebecca (John and Rebecca Harrison). Review material states that the publication date is 9 August 1982. 2,500 copies were printed.

**A16.c.** *Selected and New Poems 1961–1981*

*First edition, first printing, edition in wraps (1982).*

**Title Page:** Selected & | New Poems | 1961–1981 | Jim Harrison | Drawings by | Russell Chatham | [publisher's device] | Delta/Seymour Lawrence | [title page information enclosed in box]

**Copyright:** [32 lines of information] FIRST DELTA PRINTING—AUGUST 1982

**Binding:** Off-white paper binding with black lettering. Russell Chatham painting on front panel. Cover design by Giorgetta Bell McRee. Author photo on rear panel by Bob Wargo. Priced at $7.95.

**Dust Jacket:** Not issued with dust jacket.

**Note:** Issued simultaneously with the hardcover edition. This collection of poetry is dedicated to John and Rebecca (John and Rebecca Harrison).

$13.95
9462

"An epic storyteller who feeds in great vistas and vast distances."
—*Sunday Times Book Review*

"A writer with immortality in him."
—*Sunday Times* (London)

*Warlock* is an attempt at a comic novel not ruled by Irony, who drags her tired ass, making us suckers comically rather than laugh out loud, to a certain extent, of course, she is the true Queen of our age, but in recent times not only is the world viewed ironically but so are her slow-witted children—ourselves. *Warlock* aims to draw its energies from more primary colors, say from the dance that is *A Midsummer Night's Dream* to those two artichok Don Quixote and Walter Mitty, with the definite modification of a venal Quixote and a gluttonous, horny Mitty.

The meat and potatoes of the story of Johnny Lundgren, a.k.a. Warlock, not to speak of the gravy, is a grim tale of crime and vengeance set in a framework of mythic simplicity. Johnny Lundgren is an unemployed foundation...
*(continued on back flap)*

DELACORTE PRESS/SEYMOUR LAWRENCE

# JIM HARRISON

# WARLOCK
## A Novel

JIM HARRISON | WARLOCK

Delacorte Press
Lawrence

ISBN 0-440-09462-3

*(continued from front flap)*
tion executive literally hauled off a sleepy northern Michigan farm to confront a foe no less evil than Holmes's Professor Moriarty, a foe who embodies perverted sex, drugs, greed, and the destruction of the social contract. Warlock's wife, the fabled Diana, is less than helpful, finding herself sunk in the evil her husband combats. Warlock pursues his enemies from the haunted wilderness of northern Michigan to the disgusting undersides of Palm Beach and Key West. In a way, he does battle with earth herself, whose vast, globy body has never been known to smile.

An outdoorsman and man of letters, lives with his family in northern Michigan. He has published a collection of novellas, *Legends of the Fall;* three novels: *Wolf, A Good Day to Die,* and *Farmer;* and five collections of poetry.

*Jacket painting by Russell Chatham, courtesy of Jack Nicholson*
*Jacket design copyright © 1981 by Georgetta Bell McRae*

DELACORTE PRESS/SEYMOUR LAWRENCE
PRINTED IN U.S.A.

1981

Item A15.b., *Warlock*. Used by permission of Dell Publishing, a division of Random House, Inc.

Item A16.b., *Selected and New Poems*.

Used by permission of Dell Publishing, a division of Random House, Inc.

Item A17.a., *Natural World*. Used by permission of Open Book/Station Hill Press.

"Set in the heart of America, his stories move with random power and reach, in the manner of Melville and Faulkner."
—*The Boston Globe*

This powerful new novel by the author of *Legends of the Fall* and *Farmer* concerns the life and loves of a foreman named Robert Corvus Strang. Strang worked on giant dam projects in the U.S., South America, and Africa, until he was crippled in a fall down a three-hundred-foot dam. Now as he tries to regain use of his legs, he has a chance to reassess his life, and a blasé journalist who has heard of Strang's reputation in the field arrives to draw him out about his various incarnations. Strang recounts his life, including his childhood in the Midwest, his several marriages and children, dozens of lovers, and his work on projects around the world. Strang has the violently heightened sensibilities of a man who has gone to the limits and back, a man who is passionately and unequivocally committed to life. Harrison captures the foreman's tale with head-on frankness and clarity

*(continued on back flap)*

# JIM HARRISON

# SUNDOG

JIM HARRISON  **SUNDOG**  Dutton / Lawrence

## PRAISE FOR JIM HARRISON'S NOVELS

"A writer with immortality in him."
—BERNARD LEVIN, *The London Sunday Times*

"An epic storyteller who deals in great vistas and vast distances."
—*The New York Times Book Review*

### FARMER

"...a quiet triumph...Joseph is a man sufficated by everything he loves most in the world: the land and its ghosts, love and friendship, integrity. Yes, it is the old story again. Taking it and making it new, as Harrison has done, is a miracle on the order of the loaves and fishes. But then so are all good novels."
—*The Washington Post*

"Superb."
—*Saturday Review*

"In Harrison's hand the story is fresh with a gentle intuition."
—*Houston Chronicle*

### LEGENDS OF THE FALL

"Harrison at the height of his powers...He does honor to the old art of storytelling."
—*Chicago Tribune*

"All three of the novellas have a mythic quality...fine, mature, sensitive, complex fiction."
—*The Washington Star*

*(continued from front flap)*

that needs no elaboration, no embellishment. This is a story as true and gripping as real life, and ultimately as victorious.

JIM HARRISON has been awarded the National Endowment for the Arts (1968–69) and the Guggenheim Fellowship (1969–70). He is the author of *Wolf: A False Memoir*, *A Good Day to Die*, *Farmer*, *Legends of the Fall*, *Warlock*, and *Selected and New Poems*. The author lives in Michigan.

*Jacket painting by Russell Chatham*
*Jacket design by Nancy Etheredge*

E. P. Dutton / Seymour Lawrence
2 Park Avenue, New York, N.Y. 10016

Item A18.b, *Sundog*. Used by permission of Jim Harrison.

Item A19.b., *The Theory and Practice of Rivers*. Used by permission of Winn Books.

**A16.d.** *Selected and New Poems 1961–1981*
*First edition, first printing, limited (1982).*
**Title Page:** Selected & | New Poems | 1961–1981 | Jim Harrison | Drawings by | Russell Chatham | Delacorte Press/Seymour Lawrence
**Copyright:** [28 lines of information] FIRST PRINTING
**Binding:** Tan cloth over boards with bronze lettering. Facsimile signature in box in bronze lettering on front board. Gilt page edges all around. Off-white glossy paper over boards slipcase with a Russell Chatham painting on front panel and a Russell Chatham sketch of the author on the rear panel.
**Dust Jacket:** Not issued with dust jacket.
**Note:** Colophon page tipped in with stated limitation of 250 copies and author's signature. This collection of poetry is dedicated to John and Rebecca (John and Rebecca Harrison). Published price was $100.

**A17.a.** *Natural World: A Bestiary*
*First edition, first printing (1982).*
**Title Page:** Natural World | A Bestiary | [snail sculpture] | Poems By Jim Harrison | Sculpture By Diana Guest | Open Book | [all title page information enclosed in box]
**Copyright:** [11 lines of information] No statement of printing. See colophon page.
**Binding:** Course woven tan cloth over boards with gold lettering on front board and spine.
**Dust Jacket:** Not issued with dust jacket.
**Note:** Colophon page in rear of book states book was limited to 350 copies, of which 250 copies are *hors commerce*. Of the copies for sale, 100 copies were hand-numbered on this colophon page; however, the half-title page at the beginning of the book serves as the signature page ("Jim Harrison and Diana Guest"). The *hors commerce* copies were not numbered. Book designed by Susan Quasha. This book is a collection of Harrison poems (14) and photographs of the sculpture of Diana Guest. Harrison also provided the preface for this book.

**A18.a.** *Sundog*
*First edition, advance uncorrected proof (1984).*
**Title Page:** Jim Harrison | Sundog [contained in large box] | E.P. Dutton, Inc. / Seymour Lawrence New York
**Copyright:** [17 lines of information] 10 9 8 7 6 5 4 3 2 1 FIRST EDITION
**Binding:** Orange wraps with black lettering.

Item A20.b, *Dalva*. Used by permission of Jim Harrison.

**Dust Jacket:** Not issued with dust jacket.
**Note:** This novel is dedicated to Russell Chatham.

### A18.b. *Sundog: A Novel: The Story of an American Foreman*
*First edition, first printing (1984).*
**Title Page:** Sundog | [black and white Russell Chatham painting] | a novel | The Story of an American Foreman, | Robert Corvus Strang, as told to | Jim Harrison | E.P. Dutton, Inc. / Seymour Lawrence New York
**Copyright:** [23 lines of information] 10 9 8 7 6 5 4 3 2 1 FIRST EDITION
**Binding:** Green cloth on spine with gold lettering. Light green paper over boards.
**Dust Jacket:** White jacket with black lettering. Russell Chatham painting on front panel. Jacket design by Nancy Etheredge. Author photo on rear inside flap is credited to W. Patrick Chambers; however, it is by Bob Wargo. Priced at $15.95.
**Note:** This novel is dedicated to Russell Chatham. In a letter included with the review copies of this novel the publication date is stated to be 22 May 1984.

### A18.c. *Sundog: A Novel: The Story of an American Foreman*
*First edition, first printing, limited (1984).*
**Title Page:** Sundog | [black and white Russell Chatham painting] | a novel | The Story of an American Foreman, | Robert Corvus Strang, as told to | Jim Harrison | E.P. Dutton, Inc. / Seymour Lawrence New York
**Copyright:** [23 lines of information] 10 9 8 7 6 5 4 3 2 1 FIRST EDITION
**Binding:** Off-white cloth over boards with gold lettering. Facsimile signature stamped into front board in gold. Gilt page edges all around. Green cloth over boards slipcase.
**Dust Jacket:** Not issued with dust jacket.
**Note:** Colophon page tipped in with stated limitation of 250 copies and author's signature. This novel is dedicated to Russell Chatham.

### A19.a. *The Theory and Practice of Rivers: Poems*
*First edition, first printing, limited (1986).*
**Title Page:** The Theory & Practice | of Rivers | Poems by | Jim Harrison | Illustrated by Russell Chatham | Winn Books | Seattle : 1986
**Copyright:** [10 lines of information] 2 4 6 8 9 7 5 3 FIRST PRINTING. See colophon page.
**Binding:** Green cloth spine with gold lettering. Light tan cloth over boards.

*The* THEORY & PRACTICE
*of* RIVERS
AND
NEW POEMS

JIM HARRISON

I've decided to make up my mind
about nothing, to assume the water mask,
to finish my life disguised as a creek,
an eddy, joining at night the full,
sweet flow, to absorb the sky,
to swallow the heat and cold, the moon
and the stars, to swallow myself
in ceaseless flow.

— from *Cabin Poem*

CLARK CITY PRESS
LIVINGSTON · MONTANA

Item A21.a., *The Theory and Practice of Rivers and New Poems.*
Used by permission of Clark City Press.

Light tan cloth over boards slipcase with a facsimile signature in gold on the front panel.
**Dust Jacket:** Not issued with dust jacket.
**Note:** Book design by Scott Freutel. This edition was done in a limited printing of 350 signed copies. The publisher has stated that none were numbered; however, numbered copies have been seen on the market. The author has signed the book on the half-title page at the front of the book, and the colophon page appears at the rear. The book was illustrated by Russell Chatham, who also did a portfolio of 5 signed and numbered relief prints measuring 14½" × 18" to accompany the book. The numbering on these prints states that there were 175 copies of this portfolio done; however, the relative scarcity of the portfolio would indicate that that number is overstated. There have also been seen sets of artist's proofs of these prints numbered to 40. This collection of poetry is dedicated in memory of Gloria Ellen Harrison 1963–1979.

**A19.b.** *The Theory and Practice of Rivers: Poems*
*First edition, first printing, in wraps (1986).*
**Title Page:** The Theory & Practice | of Rivers | Poems by | Jim Harrison | Illustrated by Russell Chatham | Winn Books | Seattle: 1986
**Copyright:** [10 lines of information] 2 4 6 8 9 7 5 3 FIRST PRINTING. See colophon page.
**Binding:** White paper wraps with black lettering.
**Dust Jacket:** Green jacket with black lettering. Russell Chatham painting on front panel. Author photo on rear panel is by Bob Wargo. Priced at $7.95.
**Note:** Issued simultaneously with the limited edition. There were 3,000 copies printed. This collection of poetry is dedicated in memory of Gloria Ellen Harrison 1963–1979.

**A20.a.** *Dalva*
*First edition, advance uncorrected proof (1988).*
**Title Page:** Dalva | [Dalva portrait] | Jim Harrison | [contained in box] | E.P. Dutton / Seymour Lawrence | New York
**Copyright:** [23 lines of information] 1 3 5 7 9 10 8 6 4 2 FIRST EDITION
**Binding:** Tan wraps with black lettering. Photocopy of "Dalva" dust-jacket art on front panel.
**Dust Jacket:** Not issued with dust jacket; however, on the rear panel of proof copy, it states that the published price of the book will be $18.95.
**Note:** There was also a numbered and signed excerpt taken from the

$39.95

"Set in the heart of America, his stories move with random power and reach, in the manner of Melville and Faulkner."
—*Boston Globe*

The celebrated author of *Dalva* and *Legends of the Fall* has created three stunning novellas:

"Brown Dog" is a comic, near-mythological tale of a Michigan scoundrel, a freewheeling memoir of an ex-Bible student with criminal tendencies who loves to eat, drink, and chase women — and his adventures with a submerged Indian chief.

"Sunset Limited" concerns a forty-one-year-old mother of a teenage daughter who attempts to reconcile her sixties radical politics with growing older.

"The Woman Lit by Fireflies" is about death and transfiguration, baptism, being lost, the dissolution of a marriage, and the discovery of religion. It is the nighttime threnody of a woman's anguish and victory.

# JIM HARRISON

# THE WOMAN LIT BY FIREFLIES

## JIM HARRISON  THE WOMAN LIT BY FIREFLIES

HOUGHTON MIFFLIN
SEYMOUR LAWRENCE

"Jim Harrison is a writer with immortality in him."
— Bernard Levin, *Sunday Times* (London)

"An epic storyteller who deals in great vistas and vast distances."
— *New York Times Book Review*

ISBN 0-395-4884-2

Jim Harrison lives with his family on a farm in northern Michigan. He has written a collection of novellas, *Legends of the Fall*, six novels, *Wolf*, *A Good Day to Die*, *Farmer*, *Warlock*, *Sundog*, and *Dalva*, and eight books of poetry. His work has been translated and published in nine languages.

Jacket painting: *Apple Orchard at Sunset* by Russell Chatham (private collection)

Back jacket photo: © Dennis Grippentrog

HOUGHTON MIFFLIN
SEYMOUR LAWRENCE
2 Park Street
Boston, Massachusetts 02108

Item A22.b., *The Woman Lit by Fireflies*. Used by permission of Jim Harrison.

uncorrected proofs distributed with a letter from Seymour Lawrence and a color photograph of the dust-jacket art. The excerpt is in off-white, stapled paper wraps with black lettering and is 13 pages long. The letter from Lawrence is dated 7 January 1988 and states that the publication date of this novel will be 29 March 1988. This novel is dedicated to Linda King Harrison.

A20.b. *Dalva*
*First edition, first printing (1988).*
**Title Page:** Dalva | [single rule] | Jim Harrison | [portrait of "Dalva"] | [double-ruled open-ended box] | E.P. Dutton / Seymour Lawrence [spacing mark] New York
**Copyright:** [29 lines of information] 1 3 5 7 9 10 8 6 4 2 FIRST EDITION
**Binding:** White cloth spine with gold lettering and black rule. Light green paper over boards with facsimile signature in gold on front board.
**Dust Jacket:** White jacket with black lettering and tan rule. Russell Chatham painting of "Dalva" on front panel. Jacket design by Nancy Etheredge. Author photo on rear panel is credited to David C. Brigham. Priced at $18.95.
**Note:** This novel is dedicated to Linda King Harrison.

A21.a. *The Theory and Practice of Rivers and New Poems*
*First edition, first printing (1989).*
**Title Page:** The Theory & Practice | of Rivers | and | New Poems | by | Jim Harrison | [Chatham sketch] | Illustrated by | Russell Chatham | Clark City Press | Livingston • Montana
**Copyright:** [8 lines of information] FIRST CLARK CITY PRESS EDITION JULY 1989
**Binding:** Tan cloth over boards with gold lettering on spine.
**Dust Jacket:** Gray green jacket with Russell Chatham painting on front panel with black lettering. Black lettering on spine and back panel. Author photo on rear panel credited to Rollie Mckenna. Priced at $17.95.
**Note:** This collection of poetry is dedicated in memory of Gloria Ellen Harrison 1964–1979. It should be noted that, in earlier editions of *The Theory and Practice of Rivers*, her dates are given as 1963–1979.

A21.b. *The Theory and Practice of Rivers and New Poems*
*First edition, first printing, edition in wraps (1989).*
**Title Page:** The Theory & Practice | of Rivers | and | New Poems | by | Jim Harrison | [Chatham sketch] | Illustrated by | Russell Chatham | Clark City Press | Livingston • Montana

# KOBUN

Hotei didn't need a zafu,
saying that his ass was sufficient.
The head's a cloud anchor
that the feet must follow.
Travel light, he said,
or don't travel at all.

Jim Harrison

Dim Gray Bar
Broadside Two
Number 9/100

Center For
Book Arts
New York

Item A23.a., "Kobun." Used by permission of Dim Gray Bar Press.

**Copyright:** [8 lines of information] FIRST CLARK CITY PRESS EDITION JULY 1989

**Binding:** Gray green wrappers with Russell Chatham painting on front panel with black lettering. Black lettering on spine and back panel. Author photo on rear panel credited to Rollie Mckenna.

**Dust Jacket:** Not issued with dust jacket. Priced at $13.95.

**Note:** This collection of poetry is dedicated in memory of Gloria Ellen Harrison 1964–1979. It should be noted that, in earlier editions of *The Theory and Practice of Rivers*, her dates are given as 1963–1979. This edition in wraps was issued simultaneously with the hardcover edition.

### A22.a. *The Woman Lit by Fireflies*

*First edition, uncorrected proof (1990).*

**Title Page:** The | Woman Lit | by Fireflies | Jim Harrison | [publisher's device] | Boston 1990 | Houghton Mifflin / Seymour Lawrence | ISBN 0-395-48884-2 Code 6-87367-7

**Copyright:** [8 lines of information] 000 10 9 8 7 6 5 4 3 2 1

**Binding:** Yellow wraps with black lettering.

**Dust Jacket:** Not issued with dust jacket. On first page of the proof it states that the probable price will be $19.95.

**Note:** Publication date on proof states June 1990. This collection of novellas is dedicated to Anna (Anna Harrison).

### A22.b. *The Woman Lit by Fireflies*

*First edition, first printing (1990).*

**Title Page:** The | Woman Lit | by Fireflies | [single rule] | Jim Harrison | [publisher's device] | Houghton Mifflin / Seymour Lawrence | Boston 1990

**Copyright:** [24 lines of information] FFG 10 9 8 7 6 5 4 3 2 1

**Binding:** Off-white cloth spine with gold lettering. Off-white paper over boards with facsimile signature on front board in gold.

**Dust Jacket:** White jacket with black lettering. Russell Chatham painting on front panel. Author photo on rear panel is credited to Dennis Gripentrog. Priced at $19.95.

**Note:** Publication date June 1990. This collection of novellas is dedicated to Anna (Anna Harrison). This collection of novellas contains the titles "Brown Dog," "Sunset Limited," and "The Woman Lit by Fireflies." 20,000 copies printed.

ISBN 0-944439-30-6

JUST BEFORE DARK
COLLECTED NONFICTION
JIM HARRISON
ILLUSTRATIONS BY RUSSELL CHATHAM

THE TRADITIONAL TALE struggling for a life that's more abundant is here Jim Harrison has declared the thread holding together his six novels, two volumes of novellas and seven collections of poetry. The essays in *Just Before Dark*, organized in sections titled "Food," "Travel and Sport" and "Literary Matters," address this abundance humorously, critically and critically, and range in topic from dreams to bar food, Zen to ice fishing, revenge to *suisse semeuse* to waking at night.

Though known primarily as a writer of fiction, Harrison has freelanced for years, initially for financial survival and later as a means of satisfying an intellectual and sexual curiosity about the world. Collected from a career spanning more than twenty-five years and from sources as diverse as *Esquire*, *Antaeus*, *Sports Illustrated* and *The Psychoanalytic Review*, the essays and articles in *Just Before Dark*, several never before published, chronicle the maturation of one of our finest writers.

$19.95

---

# JUST BEFORE DARK
## COLLECTED NONFICTION
### JIM HARRISON

HARRISON     JUST BEFORE DARK

Clark City Press

ISBN 0-944439-30-6

CLARK CITY PRESS

"Harrison's books aspire [to] an enlarged and generous vision of a troubled but remarkably beautiful world, where a sensuous passion for life may be not just the best but the only revenge. In each new work—and this includes his often hilarious and erudite magazine articles on food and travel—the same distinctively personal voice is present. He is unfailingly entertaining but has much more—a haunting, gifted writer who can't be shoved into any category."

—JUDITH FREEMAN, *THE LOS ANGELES TIMES*

JIM HARRISON is a poet and a novelist whose books include *The Woman Lit by Fireflies*, *Dalva*, *Legends of the Fall*, *Farmer*, *Selected and New Poems* and *The Theory & Practice of Rivers and New Poems*. He lives with his family on a farm in northern Michigan.

Jacket painting, *Just Before Dark*, by Russell Chatham.
Jacket design by Russell Chatham and Anna Larsen.

CLARK CITY PRESS
P.O.B. WEST CALLENDER
LIVINGSTON, MONTANA 59047

Item A24.b., *Just Before Dark*. Used by permission of Clark City Press.

**A22.c.** *The Woman Lit by Fireflies*
*First edition, first printing, limited edition (1990).*
**Title Page:** The | Woman Lit | by Fireflies | [single rule] | Jim Harrison | [publisher's device] | Houghton Mifflin / Seymour Lawrence | Boston 1990
**Copyright:** [24 lines of information] FFG 10 9 8 7 6 5 4 3 2 1
**Binding:** Off-white cloth over boards with gold lettering. There is a facsimile signature on front board in gold. Off-white cloth over boards slipcase.
**Dust Jacket:** Not issued with dust jacket. Priced at $150.
**Note:** Publication date June 1990. Limitation and signature page is tipped in to front of book. 225 copies of the limited edition were printed. This collection of novellas is dedicated to Anna (Anna Harrison).

**A23.a.** *Kobun*
*Broadside, first printing (1990).*
**Note:** Single broadside by Dim Gray Bar Press, Broadside 2. New York: Center for Book Arts, 1990. This broadside was issued in a signed and numbered edition of 100 copies. Broadside measures 11" × 13".

**A24.a.** *Just Before Dark: Collected Nonfiction*
*First edition, advance uncorrected proof (1991).*
**Title Page:** Just Before Dark | [Russell Chatham sketch] | Collected Nonfiction by | Jim Harrison | Clark City Press | Livingston · Montana
**Copyright:** [16 lines of information] FIRST EDITION
**Binding:** White pictorial wrappers with a Russell Chatham painting on front panel with black letters. White spine and back panel with black lettering.
**Dust Jacket:** Not issued with dust jacket. On back panel of the proof it states that the retail price will be $24.95.
**Note:** Publication date on proof states 14 July 1991. This collection of nonfiction essays is dedicated to Steve, Jamie, and Will (Steve, Jamie, and Will Potenberg).

**A24.b.** *Just Before Dark*
*First edition, first printing (1991).*
**Title Page:** Just Before Dark | [Russell Chatham sketch] | Collected Nonfiction by | Jim Harrison | Clark City Press | Livingston · Montana
**Copyright:** [16 lines of information] FIRST EDITION
**Binding:** Light tan cloth over boards with bronze lettering on spine. One-eyed Harrison caricature embossed in cloth on front board.

## SKETCH FOR A JOB APPLICATION BLANK

My left eye is blind and jogs like
a milky sparrow in its socket;
my nose is large and never flares
in anger, the front teeth, bucked,
but not in lechery—I sucked
my thumb until the age of twelve.
O my youth was happy and I was never lonely
though my friends called me "pig eye"
and the teachers thought me loony.

    (When I bruised, my psyche kept intact:
    I fell from horses, and once a cow but never
    pigs—a neighbor lost a hand to a sow.)

But I had some fears:
the salesman of eyes,
his case was full of fishy baubles,
against black velvet, jeweled gore,
the great cocked hoof of a Belgian mare,
a nest of milk snakes by the water trough,
electric fences,
my uncle's hounds,
the pump arm of an oil well,
the chop and whirr of a combine in the sun.

From my ancestors, the Swedes,
I suppose I inherit the love of rainy woods,
kegs of herring and neat whiskey—
I remember long nights of pinochle,
the bulge of Redman in my grandpa's cheek;
the rug smelled of manure and kerosene.
They laughed loudly and didn't speak for days.

    (But on the other side, from the German Mennonites,
    their rag smoke prayers and porky daughters
    I got intolerance, an aimless diligence.)

In '51 during a revival I was saved:
I prayed on a cold register for hours
and woke up lame. I was baptized
by immersion in the tank at Williamston—
the rusty water stung my eyes.
I left off the old things of the flesh
but not for long—one night beside a pond
she dried my feet with her yellow hair.
    O actual event dead quotient
    cross become green
I still love Jubal but pity Hagar.

    (Now self is the first sacrament
    who loves not the misery and taint
    of the present tense is lost.
    I strain for a lunar arrogance.
        Light macerates
        the lamp infects
    warmth, more warmth, I cry.)

JIM HARRISON

From JUST BEFORE DARK: COLLECTED NONFICTION.
Copyright 1991 by Jim Harrison, all rights reserved,
published by arrangement with Clark City Press, 1991.
Houghton Mifflin/Seymour Lawrence, 1992.
Okeanos Press Design.

**Dust Jacket:** Tan jacket with Russell Chatham painting (entitled *Just Before Dark*) on front board with tan lettering. Dark brown lettering on spine and back panel. Author photo on rear panel is credited to Jim Fergus. Jacket design is by Russell Chatham and Anne Garner. Priced at $24.95.
**Note:** This collection of nonfiction essays is dedicated to Steve, Jamie, and Will (Steve, Jamie, and Will Potenberg). This book was designed by Stacy Feldmann and Jamie Potenberg. Review copies list the publication date as 14 July 1991. The colophon page at the rear of the book is the same as in the limited editions.

**A24.c.** *Just Before Dark: Collected Nonfiction*
*First edition, first printing, limited edition of 250 (1991).*
**Title Page:** Just Before Dark | [Russell Chatham sketch] | Collected Nonfiction by | Jim Harrison | Clark City Press | Livingston • Montana
**Copyright:** [16 lines of information] FIRST EDITION See colophon page.
**Binding:** Gray cloth spine with gold lettering on spine. One-eyed Harrison caricature blind-stamped in cloth on front board. Marbled paper over boards. Gray cloth over boards slipcase with one-eyed Harrison caricature embossed on front panel.
**Dust Jacket:** Not issued with dust jacket.
**Note:** This collection of nonfiction essays is dedicated to Steve, Jamie, and Will (Steve, Jamie, and Will Potenberg). This book was designed by Stacy Feldmann and Jamie Potenberg. The colophon page at the rear of the book is hand-numbered in pencil, and Harrison has signed the book on the half-title page.

**A24.d.** *Just Before Dark: Collected Nonfiction*
*First edition, first printing, limited edition of 26 (1991).*
**Title Page:** Just Before Dark | [Russell Chatham sketch] | Collected Nonfiction by | Jim Harrison | Clark City Press | Livingston • Montana
**Copyright:** [16 lines of information] FIRST EDITION See colophon page.
**Binding:** Gray cloth spine with gold lettering on spine. One-eyed Harrison caricature blind-stamped in cloth on front board. Marbled paper over boards. Gray cloth over boards slipcase with one-eyed Harrison caricature embossed on front panel.
**Dust Jacket:** Not issued with dust jacket.
**Note:** This collection of nonfiction essays is dedicated to Steve, Jamie, and Will (Steve, Jamie, and Will Potenberg). This edition of 26 copies came with 2 5" × 8" relief prints by Russell Chatham that are signed and numbered to

Illustrations by
Deborah Nordan

Jim Harrison

# THE RAW
# & THE
# COOKED

DIM GRAY BAR PRESS   NEW YORK 1992

Item A26.a., title page, *The Raw and the Cooked*.
Used by permission of Dim Gray Bar Press.

match the copy of the book. The prints were laid into the book in a handmade tissue envelope wrapped in a ribbon. This book was designed by Stacy Feldmann and Jamie Potenberg. The colophon page at the rear of the book is hand-numbered in pencil, and Harrison has signed the book on the half-title page.

**A25.a.** *Sketch for a Job Application Blank*
*Broadside, first printing (1991).*
**Note:** A single broadside designed by Okeanos Press Design. Published by arrangement with Clark City Press. New York: Houghton Mifflin Co., 1991. Broadside produced to advertise *Just Before Dark*. Number of copies printed is unknown; however, it is believed that a very limited number were done for sales representatives and friends to coincide with the publication of the wrapped edition of *Just Before Dark*. Broadside measures 9" × 13".

**A26.a.** *The Raw and the Cooked*
*First edition, first printing, numbered edition (1992).*
**Title Page:** Jim Harrison | The Raw | & The | Cooked | Dim Gray Bar Press New York 1992 | [all enclosed in decorative box]
**Copyright:** [3 lines of information] No statement of printing. See colophon page.
**Binding:** Red cloth spine with gold lettering. Peach-colored paper over boards.
**Dust Jacket:** Not issued with dust jacket.
**Note:** Colophon page states that there were 126 hand-printed, signed copies. Harrison has signed on the colophon page. These copies are also hand-numbered in pencil on this page. This is a collection of three food essays that first appeared in *Esquire* magazine.

**A26.b.** *The Raw and the Cooked*
*First edition, first printing, lettered edition (1992).*
**Title Page:** Jim Harrison | The Raw | & The | Cooked | Dim Gray Bar Press New York 1992 | [all enclosed in decorative box]
**Copyright:** [3 lines of information] No statement of printing. See colophon page.
**Binding:** Green quarter-morocco over boards covered with handmade paper infused with garlic and herbs. Gold lettering on spine.
**Dust Jacket:** Not issued with dust jacket.
**Note:** Colophon page states there were 126 hand-printed, signed copies.

### Coyote No. 1

Just before dark
watched coyote take a crap
on rock out cropping,
flexing hips (no time off)
swiveled owl-like to see
in all six directions:
sky above
earth below,
points of compass
in two half circles.
There.
And there is no distance.
He knows the dreamer
that dreams his dreams.

Jim Harrison

Item A27.a., "Coyote No. 1."
Used by permission of Alternative Press.

Harrison has signed on the colophon page. These copies are also hand-lettered in pencil on this page. This is a collection of three food essays that first appeared in *Esquire* magazine.

**A27.a.** *Coyote No. 1*
*Broadside, first printing (1993).*
**Note:** Designed and printed by the Alternative Press, Ann Arbor, Michigan, 1993. Illustrated by Ann Mikolowski. A hand-printed, letterpress, postcard poem that was included in issue 18 of the Alternative Press's collection of broadsides, postcard poems, bumper stickers, etc., published in 1993. The publisher (Ken Mikolowski) stated that this postcard poem was probably printed in 1992; however, it was issued to the press's subscribers sometime in 1993. 500 copies were printed. Postcard measures 4" × 6½". This was the first published appearance of this poem. Later published in *After Ikkyu and Other Poems*.

**A28.a.** *Julip*
*First edition, uncorrected proof (1994).*
**Title Page:** Julip | [decorative line] | Jim Harrison | Houghton Mifflin / Seymour Lawrence | Boston New York 1994 | ISBN 0-395-48885-0 Code 6-87377-4
**Copyright:** [11 lines of information] 000 10 9 8 7 6 5 4 3 2 1
**Binding:** Green wraps with black lettering. A facsimile of Harrison's signature is printed on the front cover.
**Dust Jacket:** Not issued with dust jacket. On first page of the proof it states that the probable price will be $21.95.
**Note:** Publication date on proof states April 1994. This collection of novellas is dedicated to Sam Lawrence.

**A28.b.** *Julip*
*First edition, first printing (1994).*
**Title Page:** Julip | [decorative line] | Jim Harrison | [publisher's device] | Houghton Mifflin / Seymour Lawrence | Boston New York 1994
**Copyright:** [18 lines of information] BP 10 9 8 7 6 5 4 3 2 1
**Binding:** Gray cloth spine with silver lettering. Gray blue paper over boards with facsimile signature on front board in silver.
**Dust Jacket:** White jacket with dark blue lettering. Jacket design by Mark Caleb. Russell Chatham painting on front panel. Author photo on rear panel is credited to Thierry Lefebure. Priced at $21.95.

## Front flap

An exciting new work of fiction by the author of *Legends of the Fall* and *Dalva*.

"Julip" is the story of a bright and resourceful young woman of our times and the mixed horror and pleasure of much older lovers. It is about the recovery rather than the loss of innocence.

"The Seven-Ounce Man" continues the adventures of Brown Dog, a Michigan scoundrel and an ex-Bible student with criminal tendencies who knows to eat, drink, and chase women. A dazzling *keepsmith* through the mind and life of a testosterone-ridden North Woods malcontent, this is a picaresque view of a man who sails along in the bottom ten percent.

"The Beige Dolorosa" deals with the regeneration of a man destroyed by one of the latest of our national insanities, political correctness. Phillip Caulkins is communicated from an academic world that resembles the cell structure of political life in Cuba, and finds solace in the discovery of incomprehension and in the discovery of the natural world.

## Back flap

Jim Harrison lives with his family on a farm in northern Michigan. He has written two collections of novellas, *Legends of the Fall* (to be released as a major motion picture in 1994) and *The Woman Lit by Fireflies*; six novels, *Wolf, A Good Day to Die, Farmer, Warlock, Sundog,* and *Dalva*; eight books of poetry; and a collection of nonfiction, *Just Before Dark*. His work has been translated and published in eleven languages.

*Front jacket painting: Russell Chatham*
*Back jacket photograph: © 1990 Thomas Victor*
*Jacket design: Mark Caleb*

Houghton Mifflin/Seymour Lawrence
222 Berkeley Street
Boston, Massachusetts 02116

## Cover

JIM HARRISON

# JULIP

JIM HARRISON

HOUGHTON MIFFLIN
SEYMOUR LAWRENCE

## Back cover

"Jim Harrison is a writer with immortality in him."
— Bernard Levin, *Sunday Times* (London)

Item A28.b, *Julip*. Used by permission of Jim Harrison.

**Note:** Publication date was April 1994. This collection of novellas is dedicated to Sam Lawrence. 21,000 copies were printed. This collection of novellas contains the titles "Julip," "The Seven Ounce Man," and "The Beige Dolorosa."

**A28.c.** *Julip*
*First edition, first printing, limited edition (1994).*
**Title Page:** Julip | [decorative line] | Jim Harrison | [publisher's device] | Houghton Mifflin / Seymour Lawrence | Boston New York 1994
**Copyright:** [18 lines of information] BP 10 9 8 7 6 5 4 3 2 1
**Binding:** Tan cloth over boards with bronze lettering. There is a facsimile signature on front board in bronze. Dark green cloth over boards slipcase.
**Dust Jacket:** Not issued with dust jacket. Priced at $150.
**Note:** Publication date was April 1994. This collection of novellas is dedicated to Sam Lawrence. Limitation and signature page is tipped in to front of book. 200 copies of the limited edition were printed.

**A29.a.** *After Ikkyu and Other Poems*
*First edition, first printing (1996).*
**Title Page:** After Ikkyu | and Other Poems | Jim Harrison | [publisher's device] | Shambhala | Boston & London | 1996
**Copyright:** [24 lines of information] 9 8 7 6 5 4 3 2 1 FIRST EDITION
**Binding:** Dark maroon cloth spine with gold lettering. Gray paper over boards.
**Dust Jacket:** Light green jacket with black and maroon lettering. Russell Chatham painting on front panel with black and maroon lettering. Author photo on rear inside flap is credited to David Brigham. Priced at $20.
**Note:** This collection of poetry is dedicated to Jack Turner. 500 copies were printed.

**A29.b.** *After Ikkyu and Other Poems*
*First edition, first printing, editions in wraps (1996).*
**Title Page:** After Ikkyu | and Other Poems | Jim Harrison | [publisher's device] | Shambhala | Boston & London | 1996
**Copyright:** [24 lines of information] 9 8 7 6 5 4 3 2 1 FIRST EDITION
**Binding:** Light green wraps with black and maroon lettering. Russell Chatham painting on front panel with black and maroon lettering.
**Dust Jacket:** Not issued with dust jacket. Priced at $10.
**Note:** This collection of poetry is dedicated to Jack Turner. 1,000 copies were printed. Issued simultaneously with the hardbound edition.

Item A29.a., *After Ikkyu*. Used by permission of Shambhala Publications Inc.

**A30.a.** *The Road Home*
>  *First edition, uncorrected manuscript (1998).*
> **Title Page:** uncorrected manuscript | The Road Home | Jim Harrison | Atlantic Monthly Press | New York
> **Copyright:** No copyright page.
> **Binding:** Tan wraps with brown lettering.
> **Dust Jacket:** Not issued with dust jacket. On rear panel of the proof it states that the probable published price will be $25.
> **Note:** Publication date on proof states October 1998.

**A30.b.** *The Road Home*
> *First edition, first printing (1998).*
> **Title Page:** The | Road | Home | Jim Harrison | [publisher's device] | Atlantic Monthly Press | New York
> **Copyright:** [21 lines of information] FIRST EDITION 98 99 00 01 10 9 8 7 6 5 4 3 2 1
> **Binding:** Blue cloth spine with silver lettering. Gray paper over boards with publisher's device blind-stamped on front board.
> **Dust Jacket:** Light gray jacket with black and blue lettering. Jacket design by Charles Rue Woods. Russell Chatham painting on front panel. Author photo on rear panel is credited to Jurg Ramseier. Priced at $25.
> **Note:** Publication date was October 1998. This novel is dedicated to Peter and Molly Phinny. 34,655 copies were printed. Besides this regular trade edition, Atlantic Monthly also produced copies with a tipped-in signature and limitation page of 600 copies for promotional uses. In the Washington Square Press edition of *The Road Home*, published in wraps in 1999, there was a brief interview with Harrison printed in the rear of the book that did not appear in this Atlantic Monthly Press edition. The true first edition of this title appeared in France as *La Route du Retour* a few months before the American edition. This edition, published by Christian Bourgois and translated by Brice Matthieussent, was printed in wraps with a Winslow Homer painting on the cover and has no statement of printing on the copyright page.

**A30.c.** *The Road Home*
> *First edition, first printing, limited edition (1998).*
> **Title Page:** The | Road | Home | Jim Harrison | [publisher's device] | Atlantic Monthly Press | New York
> **Copyright:** [21 lines of information] FIRST EDITION 98 99 00 01 10 9 8 7 6 5 4 3 2 1

$25

"A fabric of impressive strength and depth... a deep and nourishing story."
—*Publishers Weekly* (starred review)

Jim Harrison is one of this country's most acclaimed writers, and in *The Road Home*, his first full-length novel since *Dalva* ten years ago, he delivers a majestic and generous story that is no less than a true American epic.

*The Road Home* continues the story of his captivating heroine Dalva and her peculiar and remarkable family. It encompasses the voices of Dalva's grandfather John Northridge, the austere, hard-living half-Sioux patriarch; Naomi, the widow of his favorite son and namesake; Paul, the first Northridge son, who lived in the shadow of his brother; and Nelse, the son taken from Dalva at birth, who now has returned to find her. It is haunted by the towering spirits of the father and the lover Dalva lost to this country's wars. It is a family history drenched in suffering and joy, imbued with fierce independence and love, rooted in the Nebraska soil, and interwoven with the destiny of whites and Native Americans in the American West.

Epic in scope, stretching from the close of the nineteenth century to the present day, *The Road Home* is a stunning and trenchant novel, written with the humor, humanity, and inimitable evocation of the American spirit that have designed Jim Harrison's legion of fans.

# THE ROAD HOME

## JIM HARRISON
author of *Legends of the Fall* and *Dalva*

# THE ROAD HOME
## JIM HARRISON

Atlantic Monthly Press

"Set in the heart of America, his stories move with random power and reach, in the manner of Melville and Faulkner."
—*The Boston Globe*

"Harrison is among the foremost writers of the literary generation that has succeeded Styron, Mailer, Jones and Updike."—Phillip Caputo

"Jim Harrison is a writer with immortality in him."—*The Sunday Times* (London)

Jim Harrison is the author of three volumes of novellas, *Legends of the Fall*, *The Woman Lit by Fireflies*, and *Julip*; six novels, *Wolf*, *A Good Day to Die*, *Farmer*, *Warlock*, *Sundog*, and *Dalva*; seven collections of poetry; and a collection of nonfiction, *Just Before Dark*. He has been awarded a National Endowment for the Arts grant and a Guggenheim Fellowship, and his work has been published in twenty-two languages. He lives in northern Michigan and in Arizona.

Jacket design by Charles Rue Woods
Jacket painting: "Twilight in Eastern Montana" by Russell Chatham
Author photograph by Joy Harrison

ATLANTIC MONTHLY PRESS BOOKS
ARE DISTRIBUTED BY
PUBLISHERS GROUP WEST

PRINTED IN THE U.S.A.    1998

ISBN 0-87113-724-0

Item A30.b., *The Road Home*. © 1998 by Jim Harrison.

**Binding:** Blue cloth over boards with silver lettering on front board and spine. Blue cloth over boards slipcase with a Russell Chatham painting set into the cloth on the front panel.
**Dust Jacket:** Not issued with dust jacket. Published price of $150.
**Note:** Publication date was October 1998. This novel is dedicated to Peter and Molly Phinny. The limitation page is tipped in to the front of the book and states that there were 250 copies numbered and signed. The author's signature is also on this page.

### A31.a. *From Geo-Bestiary*
*Broadside, first printing (1998).*
**Note:** A single broadside designed by Sam Hamill and illustrated by Suzuki Shonen. Port Townsend WA: Copper Canyon Press, 1998. 500 numbered and signed copies were issued. Broadside measures 10¾" × 11¼". This broadside was printed to celebrate the publication of *The Shape of the Journey*.

### A32.a. *The Shape of the Journey: New and Collected Poems*
*First edition, uncorrected page proof (1998).*
**Title Page:** Jim Harrison | [single rule] | The Shape | of the Journey | [single rule] | New and Collected Poems | [publisher's device] | Copper Canyon Press
**Copyright:** [13 lines of information] 9 8 7 6 5 4 3 2 FIRST EDITION
**Binding:** White pictorial wrappers with a reproduction of the finished dust jacket on front panel with black, white, and green lettering. White spine and back panel with black and green lettering.
**Dust Jacket:** Not issued with dust jacket. On back panel of the proof it states that the retail price will be $30.
**Note:** A letter issued with the proof announcing the publication of this collection is dated July 23, 1998. Publication date on rear panel of the proof states November 1998. Copper Canyon Press also published a 32-page advance excerpt in wraps of this title. This collection of poetry is dedicated Lawrence Sullivan. 150 copies of this proof were issued.

### A32.b. *The Shape of the Journey: New and Collected Poems*
*First edition, first printing (1998).*
**Title Page:** Jim Harrison | [single rule] | The Shape | of the Journey | [single rule] | New and Collected Poems | [publisher's device] | Copper Canyon Press
**Copyright:** [31 lines of information] 9 8 7 6 5 4 3 2 FIRST EDITION. See colophon page.

## *from* Geo-Bestiary

I sat on a log fallen over a river and heard
that like people each stretch had a different voice
varying with the current, the nature
of its bed and banks, log jams, boulders,
alder or cedar branches, low slung
and sweeping the current, the hush of eddies.
In a deep pool I saw the traces of last night's moon.

Jim Harrison

Designed & printed by Sam Hamill in an edition of five hundred copies, celebrating publication of *The Shape of the Journey: Collected & New Poems* by Jim Harrison. Illustration by Suzuki Shonen.

COPPER CANYON PRESS 1998

Item A31.a., "From Geo-Bestiary."
Used by permission of Copper Canyon Press.

**Binding:** Black cloth over boards with bronze lettering on spine. Maroon paper over boards with a one-eyed Harrison caricature blind-stamped on front board along with a facsimile signature in bronze.
**Dust Jacket:** Light green jacket with Russell Chatham painting on front board with black and maroon lettering. Black and maroon lettering on spine and back panel. Jacket design is by Valerie Brewster. Author photo on rear inside flap is credited to Robert Turney. Priced at $30.
**Note:** The colophon page at the rear of the book states that 250 numbered and signed copies have been issued as well as a lettered, signed edition of 26 copies that are *hors commerce*. This collection of poetry is dedicated to Lawrence Sullivan. 9,200 copies were printed. Review material states that the book was published in November 1998.

**A32.c.** *The Shape of the Journey: New and Collected Poems*
*First edition, first printing, numbered edition (1998).*
**Title Page:** Jim Harrison | [single rule] | The Shape | of the Journey | [single rule] | New and Collected Poems | [publisher's device] | Copper Canyon Press
**Copyright:** [31 lines of information] 9 8 7 6 5 4 3 2 FIRST EDITION. See colophon page.
**Binding:** Tan cloth spine with brown lettering. Blue paper over boards with a one-eyed Harrison caricature blind-stamped on front board along with a facsimile signature in brown. The slipcase is constructed of blue paper over boards on the front panel, rear panel, and spine. The top and bottom are tan cloth over boards.
**Dust Jacket:** Not issued with dust jacket. Published price of $125.
**Note:** The colophon page at the rear of the book states that 250 numbered and signed copies have been issued as well as a lettered, signed edition of 26 copies that are *hors commerce*. The colophon page is hand-numbered, and Harrison has signed the book on the half-title page. This collection of poetry is dedicated to Lawrence Sullivan.

**A32.d.** *The Shape of the Journey: New and Collected Poems*
*First edition, first printing, lettered edition (1998).*
**Title Page:** Jim Harrison | [single rule] | The Shape | of the Journey | [single rule] | New and Collected Poems | [publisher's device] | Copper Canyon Press
**Copyright:** [31 lines of information] 9 8 7 6 5 4 3 2 FIRST EDITION. See colophon page.

Item A32.b., *The Shape of the Journey*. Used by permission of Copper Canyon Press.

**Binding:** Tan cloth spine with brown lettering. Blue paper over boards with a one-eyed Harrison caricature blind-stamped on front board along with a facsimile signature in brown. The slipcase is constructed of blue paper over boards on the front panel, rear panel, and spine. The top and bottom are tan cloth over boards.

**Dust Jacket:** Not issued with dust jacket. The lettered copies were *hors commerce* and reserved for friends of the author and Copper Canyon Press.

**Note:** The colophon page at the rear of the book states that 250 numbered and signed copies have been issued as well as a lettered, signed edition of 26 copies that are *hors commerce*. The colophon page is hand-lettered, and Harrison has signed the book on the half-title page. This collection of poetry is dedicated to Lawrence Sullivan. The binding and slipcases for the numbered and lettered copies are identical; only the colophon page differs. There were also 24 additional copies that were not numbered or lettered and were marked "press copy" by the press.

### A33.a. *Older Love*

*Broadside, first printing (1999).*

**Note:** A single broadside designed by Sam Hamill and illustrated by Philip Levine. Port Townsend WA: Copper Canyon Press, 1999. Issued in a numbered edition of 200 copies and a lettered edition of 26 copies, all of which were hand-numbered or -lettered in pencil. There were also 50 *hors commerce* copies that have no designation on them. Both issues are signed by the author and the illustrator. Broadside measures 9¼" × 14". This was the first published appearance of this poem. This broadside was produced as a fund-raiser for the Leelanau County (Michigan) Historical Society and museum.

### A34.a. *The Evil Companions Literary Award 1999*

*Broadside, first printing (1999).*

**Note:** A single broadside designed by Susan Goulet for the Center for Literary Publishing. NP: NP, 1999. Printed to commemorate Harrison being awarded the seventh annual Evil Companions Award in Denver at the Oxford Hotel on 8 April 1999. Broadside measures 11" × 17" and reprints an excerpt from *The Road Home* along with artwork depicting the Chicago skyline. 400 copies were printed. Even though the publisher and city are not printed on the broadside, it was published by the *Colorado Review* in Fort Collins, Colorado.

JIM HARRISON

# OLDER LOVE

His wife has asthma
so he only smokes outdoors
or late at night with head
and shoulders well into
the fireplace, the mesquite and oak
heat bright against his face.
Does it replace the heat
that has wandered from love
back into the natural world?
But then the shadow passion casts
is much longer than passion,
stretching with effort from year to year.
Outside tonight hard wind and sleet
from three bald mountains,
and on the hearth before his face
the ashes we'll all become,
soft as the back of a woman's knee.

*Jim Harrison*

COPPER CANYON PRESS

*Levine*
*5/63*

Designed and printed in an edition of two hundred seventy-six, numbered 1-200 and lettered A-Z, fifty copies hors commerce, with Lutetia and Italian Old Style types on Fabriano Rosapina paper by Sam Hamill, and signed by the poet, spring, 1999.
Illustration by Philip Levine.

170/200

Item A33.a., "Older Love." Used by permission of Copper Canyon Press.

# Jim Harrison

> The prairie and the forest on a moonlit night are not threatening to me but Chicago and New York are, with Paris a little less so. In these cities, even among polite company, my skull tightens, and I sweat nervously from the degree of attention required to keep oneself out of a thousand varieties of trouble.
> —*The Road Home*

## THE EVIL COMPANIONS LITERARY AWARD 1999

Item A34.a., *The Evil Companions Literary Award 1999*. Broadside designed by Susan Goulet for the Center for *Literary* Publishing, 1999. Used by permission of the Center for Literary Publishing.

### PRESSED WAFER BROADSIDES for JOHN WIENERS

This collection of broadsides endows the first annual Pressed Wafer Lifetime Achievement Award, which was presented to John Wieners on April 8, 2000 in Boston. The fifty-two writers present here responded because they value John's work and example. All of them save Robert Duncan, represented by a previously unpublished poem, and Ed Dorn, who died while this was a work in progress, signed their broadsides.

Many others helped to make this collection possible. The editors thank Russell Banks, Chase Twichell, Steve Dickison, Linda Norton, Geoffrey Young, Steve Clay, Amber Phillips, and Raymond Foye. Generous contributions to this project were made in the names of Madeline Franco-Kennedy and Thomas Franco. Of the three editors, Michael Gizzi did the lion's share of the work and deserves everyone's thanks for that.

As this collection took shape two of its contributors, Paul Auster and Siarris Havaras suggested that it also be printed as a book. The editors thought this a wise idea because it meant a great many more writers who wished to honor John could be included. That book titled *The Blind See Only This World* after a title from John's pamphlet *Pressed Wafer* has been published by Pressed Wafer and Granary Books. On the book's cover is a photograph of John taken by his old friend Allen Ginsberg.

This broadside collection is in an edition of twenty-six lettered A-Z. Box A includes all the manuscripts and correspondence involved in the project.

William Corbett
for Michael Gizzi and Joseph Torra

Copy U

---

*Portal, Arizona*

I've been apart too long
from this life we have.
They deep fry pork chops locally.
I've never had them that way.
The beautiful girl with bare breasts
comes toward me on the t.v. screen
but from her chest an oozy
creature bursts, rips off the guy's face
luckily not my own.
In the canyon at dawn the cooper's hawk
rose from her nest. Lion's pug marks
a few miles up where the canyon narrowed
and one rock had an eye with sky beyond.
A geezer told me Nabokov wrote here
while his beloved Vera tortured the piano.
He chased butterflies to their pinheaded doom
but Lolita survived. What beauty
can I imagine beyond these vast rock walls
with caves sculpted by wind where perhaps
Geronimo slept quite innocent of television
and when his three-year-old son died
made war these ravens still talk about.

*Jim Harrison*

Item A35.a., colophon page (*left*), poem (*right*), "Portal, Arizona." Used by permission of Pressed Wafer and Granary Books.

Item A36.b., *The Beast God Forgot to Invent*. © 2000 by Jim Harrison.

# JIM HARRISON

### The Same Goose Moon

Peach sky
at sunset,
then (for a god's sake)
one leaf whirled
across the face
of the big October moon.

From *The Shape of the Journey: New and Collected Poems*. Copper Canyon Press, 1998
This broadside was designed and printed letterpress by Grey Spider Press on the occasion
of a reading by the author at Square Books, Oxford, Mississippi, October 31, 2000.

THIS IS ONE OF THREE HUNDRED

Item A37.a., "The Same Goose Moon." Used by permission of
Stern & Faye, Printers (Grey Spider Press).

A35.a. *Portal, Arizona*
*Broadside, first printing (1999).*
**Note:** Contained in the portfolio *The Pressed Wafer Broadsides for John Wieners* (New York: Pressed Wafer and Granary Books, 1999). 26 hand-lettered copies signed by each poet. A set of 52 poems done by individual poets printed as 8½" × 11" broadsides in a plain portfolio. These poems were compiled to honor the work of John Wieners. This was the first published appearance of this poem. There were also a very few copies of the broadside printed as overruns of the lettered edition that have been seen on the market. They are printed on medium-weight, light blue card stock and are identical to the copies in the portfolio.

A36.a. *The Beast God Forgot to Invent*
*First edition, uncorrected manuscript (2000).*
**Title Page:** The Beast God | Forgot to Invent | Jim | Harrison | [publisher's device] | Atlantic Monthly Press | New York
**Copyright:** No copyright page.
**Binding:** White wraps with a Russell Chatham illustration on the front panel with blue and black lettering.
**Dust Jacket:** Not issued with dust jacket. On rear panel of the proof it states that the probable published price will be $24.
**Note:** Publication date on proof copy states October 2000.

A36.b. *The Beast God Forgot to Invent*
*First edition, first printing (2000).*
**Title Page:** Jim Harrison | The Beast | God Forgot | to Invent | [publisher's device] | Atlantic Monthly Press | New York
**Copyright:** [24 lines of information] FIRST EDITION 00 01 02 03 10 9 8 7 6 5 4 3 2 1
**Binding:** Black paper over boards on spine with silver lettering. Brown paper over boards with publisher's device stamped into the front board.
**Dust Jacket:** Dark brown jacket with a Russell Chatham illustration on the front panel with light blue lettering. Spine and rear panel have light blue and white lettering. Jacket design is by Russell Chatham. Author photo on rear panel is credited to Sophie Bassouls. Published price of $24.
**Note:** This collection of novellas is dedicated to Joyce and Bob Bahle. There were 34,655 copies in the first printing. Publication date was October 2000. In this regular trade edition Atlantic Monthly also produced copies with a tipped-in signature and limitation page of 300 copies for promotional

## THE BOY WHO RAN TO THE WOODS

**JIM HARRISON**

ILLUSTRATED BY TOM POHRT

---

THE BOY WHO RAN TO THE WOODS — JIM HARRISON

---

**JIM HARRISON** is best known for his novels and poetry that speak wisdom and illuminate the soul. *The Boy Who Ran to the Woods* is a wonderfully told children's story that recounts a childhood tragedy that ends in redemption.

Jimmy is a young boy who suffers a tragic eye injury and must learn life's many meanings through adversity. Through Jimmy's discovery of nature—animals, birds, and the lovely woods—he is able to overcome the intense hardship and suffering and live a happier and more fulfilled childhood.

Beautifully written with Harrison's quintessential style of writing about the natural world, combined with the unique and exquisite illustrations of Tom Pohrt, a renowned illustrator, the book will delight children of all ages and will appeal to all the devoted fans of Harrison's literature and poetry as well.

---

**JIM HARRISON** is the author of four volumes of novellas, including *Legends of the Fall* and his most recent collection, *The Road Gad Forgot to Invent*, as well as six novels including *The Road Home* and *Dalva*, seven collections of poetry, and a collection of nonfiction *Just Before Dark*. His work has been published in twenty-two languages. He lives in northern Michigan and Arizona.

**TOM POHRT** illustrated the best-seller *Crow and Weasel*, a collaboration with Barry Lopez, as well as *Trickster and the Fainting Birds*, with Howard Norman. He is also the author of many children's books including *Having a Wonderful Time* and *Coyote Goes Walking*. He is a self-taught artist who lives in Ann Arbor, Michigan.

Jacket design by Marita Mazza
Jacket illustration by Tom Pohrt
Author photograph by Jürg Kamerer
Illustrator photograph by Stuart Mccook

Atlantic Monthly Press books are distributed by Publishers Group West

Printed in the U.S.A.   1/00

---

Item A38.b., *The Boy Who Ran to the Woods*. © 2000 by Jim Harrison.

uses. This collection of novellas contains "The Beast God Forgot to Invent," "Westward Ho," and "I Forgot to Go to Spain."

**A36.c.** *The Beast God Forgot to Invent*
*First edition, first printing, limited edition (2000).*
**Title Page:** Jim Harrison | The Beast | God Forgot | to Invent | [publisher's device] | Atlantic Monthly Press | New York
**Copyright:** [24 lines of information] FIRST EDITION 00 01 02 03 10 9 8 7 6 5 4 3 2 1
**Binding:** Green cloth over boards with gold lettering on spine and front board. Top stain in gold. Green cloth over boards slipcase.
**Dust Jacket:** Not issued with dust jacket. Published price of $150.
**Note:** The limitation page is tipped in to the front of the book and states that there were 250 copies numbered and signed. The author's signature is also on this page. This collection of novellas is dedicated to Joyce and Bob Bahle. Publication date was October 2000.

**A37.a.** *The Same Goose Moon*
*Broadside, first printing (2000).*
**Note:** A single broadside designed and printed by Grey Spider Press, Sedro Woolley, Washington, in 2000. Printed in an edition of 300 copies. Broadside measures $8^{13}/_{16}$" × $12^{11}/_{16}$" and was printed to commemorate a reading by the author at Square Books in Oxford, Mississippi, on 31 October 2000. Poem was first printed in *The Shape of the Journey* (Copper Canyon Press, 1998).

**A38.a.** *The Boy Who Ran to the Woods*
*First edition, advance reader's edition (2000).*
**Title Page:** The Boy Who Ran | To The Woods | [Tom Pohrt illustration] | Jim Harrison | Illustrated by Tom Pohrt | [publisher's device] | Atlantic Monthly Press | New York
**Copyright:** [31 lines of information] FIRST EDITION 00 01 02 03 10 9 8 7 6 5 4 3 2 1
**Binding:** Tan wraps with a Tom Pohrt illustration on the front panel with white, tan, orange, and yellow lettering. Black and orange lettering on rear panel.
**Dust Jacket:** Not issued with dust jacket. On the rear panel of the proof it states that the tentative published price of the book will be $18.95.
**Note:** The stated publication date on the proof is October 2000. On the copyright page Harrison has dedicated this children's story to Will and

# JIM HARRISON

## THE RAW AND THE COOKED

### ADVENTURES OF A ROVING GOURMAND

---

**MARIO BATALI ON THE RAW AND THE COOKED:**

"Jim Harrison is the Homer, the Michelangelo, the Lamborghini, the Willie Mays, the Secretary of words, the peak of perfection in all writing, but achieves Jim Hendrix solo perfection when he waxes the gristle about our most primordial need and luxury. His words are not the mere musings of an effete intellectual: these are the lust-filled poems of an expert, a hunter, an eater, a stalker, a rabid mongrel, and a drinker not afraid to get excited about the kind of nuts a particular partridge must have eaten this morning to taste so damned good for lunch. And that the occasional breakfast of sow's heart needs to be anointed with even an off-vintage Bordeaux is not hidden, nay, celebrated in the deeply starving heart of America's greatest living writer. It is with total joy that I share my dinner table with a hero so honest, so erudite, so poetic, so huge in stature and genius, and yet so much himself a cook in the chuckwagon on a moose hunt in British Columbia. Most important, Harrison's words bring me the most guttural, the most thirst quenching, itch scratching, and ultimately satisfying feeling that he really knows and appreciates what makes my job as a cook so filled with joy, the smell and anticipation of a perfect and divine edible and drinkable moment."

---

JIM HARRISON is the author of four volumes of novellas, *The Beast God Forgot to Invent*, *Legends of the Fall*, *The Woman Lit by Fireflies*, and *Julip*; seven novels, *The Road Home*, *Wolf*, *A Good Day to Die*, *Farmer*, *Warlock*, *Sundog*, and *Dalva*; nine collections of poetry, the most recent being *The Shape of the Journey: New and Collected Poems*; a children's book, *The Boy Who Ran to the Woods*; and a collection of nonfiction, *Just Before Dark*. He has been awarded a National Endowment for the Arts grant and a Guggenheim Fellowship, and his work has been published in twenty-two languages. He recently received the Spirit of the West Award from the Mountains & Plains Booksellers Association. Jim Harrison lives in northern Michigan and Arizona.

Jacket design by Gretchen Mergenthaler
Jacket photograph by Maggie Schnauffer Clay

GROVE PRESS BOOKS
are distributed by Publishers Group West

PRINTED IN THE USA 1/01

---

USA $25.00
Can $40.50

JIM HARRISON is one of this country's most beloved writers, a muscular, brilliantly economic stylist with a salty wisdom. For over twenty years, he has also been writing some of the best food criticism around—in fact, *The Plain Dealer*, in a review of Harrison's most recent work of fiction, *The Beast God Forgot to Invent*, praised its "great helpings of Harrison's expert, lush writing on food and wine, reminiscent of the marvelous column he once wrote for *Esquire* magazine." Now, for the first time, all of Harrison's food writing is available in one volume—from his columns for *Smart* and *Esquire* magazines, to recent work for *Men's Journal*, work commissioned for French publications, and a piece (including his meatball recipe!) for Michael Ondaatje's *Toronto* magazine.

Any reader of Harrison's fiction is struck by his love for food, wine, and other sensual pleasures that permeates it—and anyone who has read his essays and journalism has encountered a food critic unlike any other, unpretentious, witty, humane, and unabashedly passionate. Whether cooking pasta puttanesca in the freezing elevations of New Mexico's Animas Mountains, being reminded by a passing black bear of the importance of contact with where his food comes from, or singing the praises of a humble meatball, Harrison's writing warms the stomach and feeds the soul.

"Where is the food book?" is a question that never fails to come up at Harrison's readings. *The Raw and the Cooked* answers that question with a nine-course meal that will satisfy every appetite.

ISBN 0-8021-1698-1

Item A39.b, *The Raw and the Cooked*. © 2001 by Jim Harrison.

John and Georgia (Harrison). Pohrt has dedicated his work to Kara and John. On the rear panel of the proof it states that there was to be a 25,000-copy first printing.

A38.b. *The Boy Who Ran to the Woods*
*First edition, first printing (2000).*
**Title Page:** The Boy Who Ran | To The Woods | [Tom Pohrt illustration] | Jim Harrison | Illustrated by Tom Pohrt | [publisher's device] | Atlantic Monthly Press | New York
**Copyright:** [31 lines of information] FIRST EDITION 00 01 02 03 10 9 8 7 6 5 4 3 2 1
**Binding:** Off-white speckled paper over boards with black lettering.
**Dust Jacket:** Tan wraps with a Tom Pohrt illustration on the front panel with tan, orange, and yellow lettering. Another Pohrt illustration on rear panel. Published price of $18.95.
**Note:** The publication date is October 2000. On the copyright page, Harrison has dedicated this children's story to Will and John and Georgia (Harrison). Pohrt has dedicated his work to Kara and John. Information from the publisher states that there were 15,820 copies in the first printing.

A39.a. *The Raw and the Cooked*
*First edition, uncorrected proof (2001).*
**Title Page:** The Raw | And The | Cooked | Jim Harrison | [publisher's device] | Atlantic Monthly Press | New York
**Copyright:** [29 lines of information] No statement of printing.
**Binding:** Bright orange wraps with black lettering.
**Dust Jacket:** Not issued with dust jacket. Rear panel of proof states that the tentative price will be $26.
**Note:** Harrison has dedicated this collection of food essays to Terry McDonell and Gerard Oberle. Publication date on the proof states November 2001. The front cover has the subtitle "Adventures of a Roving Gourmand" printed; however, the title page does not include the subtitle.

A39.b. *The Raw and the Cooked: Adventures of a Roving Gourmand*
*First edition, first printing (2001).*
**Title Page:** The Raw | And The | Cooked | Adventures of | a Roving Gourmand | Jim Harrison | [publisher's device] | Grove Press | New York
**Copyright:** [42 lines of information] FIRST EDITION 01 02 03 04 10 9 8 7 6 5 4 3 2 1

Item A40.a. (*left*), item A40.b. (*center*), item A40.c. (*right*), proof copies, *Off to the Side*. © 2002 by Jim Harrison.

**Binding:** Mustard yellow paper over boards on spine with red lettering. Orange paper over boards.
**Dust Jacket:** Photograph of Harrison on front panel with red and black lettering. Rear panel of jacket is black and white with black and red lettering. Jacket design by Gretchen Mergenthaler. Author photo credited to Maude Schuyler Clay. Published price is $25.
**Note:** Harrison has dedicated this collection of food essays to Terry McDonell and Gerard Oberle. Publication date was 15 November 2001. There were 17,881 copies in the first printing.

A40.a. *Off to the Side: A Memoir*
*First edition, unedited and uncorrected proof (2002).*
**Title Page:** Off To | The Side | A Memoir | Jim Harrison | [publisher's device] | Atlantic Monthly Press | New York
**Copyright:** [11 lines of information] No statement of printing.
**Binding:** Cream wraps with brown lettering.
**Dust Jacket:** Not issued with dust jacket. On rear panel of the proof it states that the tentative published price will be $25.
**Note:** Publication date on proof states November 2002. There were 150 copies of this proof printed.

A40.b. *Off to the Side: A Memoir*
*First edition, uncorrected proof (2002).*
**Title Page:** Off To | The Side | A Memoir | Jim Harrison | [publisher's device] | Atlantic Monthly Press | New York
**Copyright:** [11 lines of information] No statement of printing.
**Binding:** White wraps with black and rust lettering. Photo of the author on front panel.
**Dust Jacket:** Not issued with dust jacket. On rear panel of the proof it states that the tentative published price will be $25.
**Note:** Publication date on proof states November 2002. There were 300 copies of this proof printed.

A40.c. *Off to the Side: A Memoir*
*First edition, final uncorrected proof (2002).*
**Title Page:** Off To | The Side | A Memoir | Jim Harrison | [publisher's device] | Atlantic Monthly Press | New York
**Copyright:** [29 lines of information] FIRST EDITION 02 03 04 05 06 10 9 8 7 6 5 4 3 2 1

Item A40.d, *Off to the Side*. © 2002 by Jim Harrison.

**Binding:** Light blue wraps with black lettering.
**Dust Jacket:** Not issued with dust jacket. On rear panel of the proof it states that the tentative published price will be $25.
**Note:** Publication date on proof states November 2002. There were 50 copies of this proof printed. In a letter from Grove/Atlantic dated 13 September 2002 the publisher asks reviewers to please use this edition to write any reviews because of extensive copyediting in the earlier proofs. On the copyright page Harrison has dedicated this memoir in memoriam Winfield Sprague Harrison and Norma Olivia Wahlgren.

### A40.d. *Off to the Side: A Memoir*
*First edition, first printing (2002).*
**Title Page:** Off To | The Side | A Memoir | Jim Harrison | [publisher's device] | Atlantic Monthly Press | New York
**Copyright:** [29 lines of information] FIRST EDITION 02 03 04 05 06 10 9 8 7 6 5 4 3 2 1
**Binding:** Yellow tan paper over boards on spine with gold lettering. Tan paper over boards with publisher's device stamped on front board.
**Dust Jacket:** Photograph of author on front panel by Harry Benson with black and rust lettering. Lettering on spine in black and rust. Lettering on back panel is black. Author photo on rear panel by Italo Scanga. Dust-jacket design by Charles Rue Woods. Published price of $25.
**Note:** Review material sent out with book is not dated; however, book was released on 15 October 2002. There were 23,000 copies in the first printing. In this regular trade edition Atlantic Monthly Press also produced copies with a tipped-in signature and limitation page of 300 copies for promotional use. On the copyright page Harrison has dedicated this memoir in memoriam Winfield Sprague Harrison and Norma Olivia Wahlgren.

### A40.e. *Off to the Side: A Memoir*
*First edition, first printing, limited edition (2002).*
**Title Page:** Off To | The Side | A Memoir | Jim Harrison | [publisher's device] | Atlantic Monthly Press | New York
**Copyright:** [29 lines of information] FIRST EDITION 02 03 04 05 06 10 9 8 7 6 5 4 3 2 1
**Binding:** Maroon cloth over boards with gold lettering on spine and front board. Maroon cloth over boards slipcase.
**Dust Jacket:** Not issued with dust jacket. Published price of $150.
**Note:** The limitation page is tipped in to the front of the book and states that

# NIGHT DHARMA

How restlessly the Buddha sleeps
between my ears, dreaming his dreams
of emptiness, writing his verbless poems.
I almost rejected "green tree
white goat red sun blue sea."
Verbs are time's illusion, he says.

In the stillness that surrounds us
we think we have to probe our wounds
but with what? Mind caresses mind
not by saying no or yes but neither.

Turn your watch back to your birth
for a moment, then way ahead beyond
any expectation. There never was a coffin
worth a dime. These words emerge
from the skin as the sweat of gods
who drink only from the Great Mother's breasts.

Buddha sleeps on, disturbed when I disturb
him from his liquid dreams of blood and bone.
Without comment he sees the raven carrying
off the infant snake, the lovers' foggy
gasps, the lion's tongue that skins us.

One day we dozed against a white pine stump
in a world of dogwood and sugar plum blossoms.
An eye for an eye, he said, trading
a left for my right, the air green tea
in the sky's blue cup.

JIM HARRISON

*Jim Harrison*

*Designed and printed by Sam Hamill and Amy Schaus
at Copper Canyon Press in the Year of the Horse,
celebrating the Lannan Foundation
Readings and Conversations Series.*

there were 250 copies numbered and signed. The author's signature is also on this page. On the copyright page Harrison has dedicated this memoir in memoriam Winfield Sprague Harrison and Norma Olivia Walhgren.

### A41.a. *Night Dharma*

*Broadside, first printing (2002).*

**Note:** Single broadside designed by Sam Hamill and Amy Schaus. Port Townsend WA: Copper Canyon Press, 2002. Broadside states "in the year of the horse" and ". . . celebrating the Lannan Foundation Reading and Conversations Series. . . ." The broadside was printed to commemorate the Lannan Foundation honoring the work of Harrison. Printed in an edition of 250 copies. Broadside measures 7½" × 14⅞". This was the first published appearance of this poem.

### A42.a. *A Conversation*

*First edition, first printing, author proofs (2002).*

**Title Page:** No title page; however, the first page of this proof states "Harrison—Kooser proof: 16-viii-01."

**Copyright:** [one line of information] No statement of printing, but dated 2001.

**Binding:** Light green handmade paper wraps. Binding is hand-sewn.

**Dust Jacket:** Not issued with dust jacket.

**Note:** Michael Peich, the publisher and printer, states that he printed 7 copies of this proof to send to the authors to review and to keep in the press archive. These copies are numbered 1–5 on the colophon page with the author copies not bearing any numbers. The colophon page also differs from the regular and lettered editions. The proof colophon page states that there are 150 copies in wrappers and "Thirty copies in boards, twenty-six lettered." Ultimately, there were 38 copies printed in boards, which means 12 *hors commerce* copies printed, as opposed to the original plan of 4 copies. The notation on the first page of this proof refers to the date they were printed (16 August 2001). All copies are hand-printed.

### A42.b. *A Conversation*

*First edition, final imposition proofs (2002).*

**Title Page:** Jim Harrison | A Conversation | Ted Kooser | Aralia Press · 2002

**Copyright:** [1 line of information] No statement of printing, but dated 2001.

Item A42.e. (*left*), item A42.c. (*center*), item A42.d. (*right*), and presentation box, *A Conversation*. Used by permission of Aralia Press.

**Binding:** Light brown handmade paper wraps. Binding is hand-sewn.
**Dust Jacket:** Not issued with jacket.
**Note:** Michael Peich states that there were 5 copies of this final state of the proof printed and that they were meant to be exactly like the trade wrappered editions. On these "final imposition" proofs the first page, which would normally be the first endpaper, has poems mistakenly printed on it. Colophon page states that there were 150 copies in wrappers. 38 signed copies in boards with 26 of these lettered. All copies are hand-printed. This collection of poetry is unaccredited to either poet and was done as a collaboration between Harrison and Kooser.

### A42.c. *A Conversation*

*First edition, first printing (2002).*
**Title Page:** Jim Harrison | A Conversation | Ted Kooser | Aralia Press · 2002
**Copyright:** [1 line of information] No statement of printing, but dated 2002. See colophon page.
**Binding:** Gray handmade paper wraps. Binding is hand-sewn. White label on front panel with black lettering.
**Dust Jacket:** Not issued with dust jacket. Published price of $40.
**Note:** Colophon page states that there were 150 copies in wrappers. 38 signed copies in boards with 26 of these lettered. The 12 remaining copies were *hors commerce* and reserved for the authors and friends of the press. All copies are hand-printed. This collection of poetry is unaccredited to either poet and was done as a collaboration between Harrison and Kooser.

### A42.d. *A Conversation*

*First edition, first printing, lettered edition (2002).*
**Title Page:** Jim Harrison | A Conversation | Ted Kooser | Aralia Press · 2002
**Copyright:** [1 line of information] No statement of printing. See colophon page.
**Binding:** Black cloth over boards with the symbol of the Aralia Press imprint blind-stamped on the front board.
**Dust Jacket:** Not issued with dust jacket. Published price of $175.
**Note:** Colophon page states that there were 150 copies in wrappers. 38 signed copies in boards with 26 of these lettered. The 12 remaining copies were *hors commerce* and reserved as presentation copies for the authors and friends of the press. All copies are hand-printed. This collection of poetry is

# BRAIDED CREEK
*A Conversation in Poetry*

Jim Harrison and Ted Kooser

---

*Under the storyteller's hat
are many beads, all troubled.*

Longtime friends, Jim Harrison and Ted Kooser always exchanged poems in their letter writing. After Kooser was diagnosed with cancer several years ago, Harrison found that his friend's poetry became "overwhelmingly vivid," and they began a correspondence comprised entirely of brief poems, "because that was the essence of what we wanted to say to each other."

In these epigrammatic, aphoristic poems, two accomplished poets explore love and friendship and their passionate search for a little wisdom, pausing to celebrate the natural world, aging, everyday things and scenes, and poetry itself. When asked about attributions for the individual poems, one of them replied, "Everyone gets tired of this continuing cult of the personality... This book is an assertion in favor of poetry and against credentials."

COPPER CANYON PRESS
Cover illustration *Snowygoose Creek*
by Russell Chatham

POETRY / $15.00

ISBN 1-55659-187-X

Item A43.c., *Braided Creek*. Used by permission of Copper Canyon Press.

unaccredited to either poet and was done as a collaboration between Harrison and Kooser. Signed in pencil by both authors on the colophon page.

**A42.e.** *A Conversation*
*First edition, first printing, presentation edition (2002).*
**Title Page:** Jim Harrison | A Conversation | Ted Kooser | Aralia Press · 2002
**Copyright:** [1 line of information] No statement of printing. See colophon page.
**Binding:** Tan half calf on spine with the initials of the poets ("JH" and "TK") stamped onto the spine. Black cloth over boards with the symbol of the Aralia Press imprint blind-stamped on the front board.
**Dust Jacket:** Not issued with dust jacket.
**Note:** Colophon page states that there were 150 copies in wrappers. 38 signed copies in boards with 26 of these lettered. The 12 remaining copies were *hors commerce* and reserved as presentation copies for the authors and friends of the press. Each of these 12 presentation copies states "This copy for [the individual it was printed for]" on the colophon page. Signed in pencil by both authors on the colophon page. All copies are hand-printed. Further, these presentation copies are housed in a custom handmade clamshell box that holds this copy, a lettered copy, and the trade copy (in wrappers). The box is of deep red cloth over boards with the Aralia Press imprint on the front board. A half calf leather title label is set into the cloth on the spine. This collection of poetry is unaccredited to either poet and was done as a collaboration between Harrison and Kooser.

**A43.a.** *Braided Creek: A Conversation in Poetry*
*First edition, uncorrected proof, spiral bound (2003).*
**Title Page:** Jim Harrison & Ted Kooser | Braided | Creek | [small design] | A Conversation in Poetry | [publisher's device] Copper Canyon Press
**Copyright:** [16 lines of information] 9 8 7 6 5 4 3 2 FIRST PRINTING
**Binding:** Comb bound in bright yellow paper wraps. Black and white photocopy of cover art (a Russell Chatham painting) for the trade edition on front panel.
**Dust Jacket:** Not issued with dust jacket. On rear cover it states a published price of $15 for the trade edition in wraps.
**Note:** This collection of poetry is dedicated to Dan Gerber. Hand-copied and comb bound at the press to distribute to a select group of reviewers and sales representatives in December 2002. The publisher states that seven copies were printed and bound. On rear cover it states a publication date of April 2003.

Item A44.a. (*left*), item A44.b. (*right*), proof and advance copies,

**A43.b.** *Braided Creek: A Conversation in Poetry*
*First edition, uncorrected proof (2003).*
**Title Page:** Jim Harrison & Ted Kooser | Braided | Creek | [small design] | A Conversation in Poetry | [Copper Canyon symbol] Copper Canyon Press
**Copyright:** [16 lines of information] 9 8 7 6 5 4 3 2 FIRST PRINTING
**Binding:** Bound in white wraps with black lettering. Black and white scan of cover art (a Russell Chatham painting) for the trade edition on front panel.
**Dust Jacket:** Not issued with dust jacket. On rear cover it states a published price of $15 for the trade edition in wraps.
**Note:** This collection of poetry is dedicated to Dan Gerber. On rear cover it states a publication date of April 2003. 155 copies printed.

**A43.c.** *Braided Creek: A Conversation in Poetry*
*First edition, first printing in wrappers (2003).*
**Title Page:** Jim Harrison & Ted Kooser | Braided | Creek | [small design] | A Conversation in Poetry | [Copper Canyon symbol] Copper Canyon Press
**Copyright:** [26 lines of information] 9 8 7 6 5 4 3 2 FIRST PRINTING
**Binding:** Bound in light tan wrappers with brown, black, and rust lettering. Front panel is a Russell Chatham painting.
**Dust Jacket:** Not issued with dust jacket. Stated on the rear panel is the published price of $15.
**Note:** This collection of poetry is dedicated to Dan Gerber. There were 4,455 copies printed. The colophon page states that 250 numbered and signed copies and 26 lettered and signed copies were printed.

**A43.d.** *Braided Creek: A Conversation in Poetry*
*First edition, numbered edition (2003).*
**Title Page:** Jim Harrison & Ted Kooser | Braided | Creek | [small design] | A Conversation in Poetry | [Copper Canyon symbol] Copper Canyon Press
**Copyright:** [26 lines of information] 9 8 7 6 5 4 3 2 FIRST PRINTING
**Binding:** Bound in dark blue ribbed cloth with an aqua silk cloth at the spine over boards. White paper label with black lettering on spine.
**Dust Jacket:** Not issued with dust jacket. Published price of this numbered edition was $100.
**Note:** This collection of poetry is dedicated to Dan Gerber. The colophon page is hand-numbered and states that 250 copies were printed. Each copy is signed by Harrison and Kooser on the half-title page.

# TRUE NORTH
## Jim Harrison

**Praise for Jim Harrison:**

"No one has advanced and expanded the American literary ethos in the latter part of the twentieth century more cogently, usefully, and just plain brilliantly than Jim Harrison... This is a matter to which all literate Americans should pay serious attention."
—Hayden Carruth

"Reading Jim Harrison is about as close as one can come in contemporary fiction to experiencing the abundant pleasures of living."
—*The Boston Globe*

"Harrison has quietly established one of the deeper canons in modern American letters."
—*The Denver Post*

"There is a singular comfort in knowing, on the first page of a novel, that you are in the hands of a master."
—*The New York Times Book Review*

---

*(continued from front flap)*

In the story of the Burketts, Jim Harrison has given us a family tragedy of betrayal and atonement, joy and grief, and justice for the worst of our sins. *True North* is a bravura performance from one of our finest writers, accomplished with deep humanity, humor, and redemptive soul.

**Jim Harrison**'s most recent book is his memoir, *Off to the Side*. He is also the author of four volumes of novellas, *The Beast God Forgot to Invent*, *Legends of the Fall*, *The Woman Lit by Fireflies*, and *Julip*; seven novels, *The Road Home*, *Wolf*, *A Good Day to Die*, *Farmer*, *Warlock*, *Sundog*, and *Dalva*; two collections of nonfiction, including most recently *Braided Creek*, with Ted Kooser, and *The Shape of the Journey: New and Collected Poems*; and two collections of nonfiction, *Just Before Dark* and *The Raw and the Cooked: Adventures of a Roving Gourmand*. The winner of a National Endowment for the Arts grant, a Guggenheim Fellowship, and the Spirit of the West Award from the Mountain & Plains Booksellers Association, his work has been published in twenty-four languages. Jim Harrison divides his time between Montana, Northern Michigan, and Arizona.

*Jacket painting by Russell Chatham*
*Author photograph by Kathleen Bourgeois*

PRINTED IN THE USA 03/04

---

U.S. $25.00

Michigan has been home to Jim Harrison for most of his life, and with his newest and most extraordinary work, he has written the long-awaited story of his homeland. *True North* is the story of a family torn apart and a man engaged in profound reckoning with the damage scarred into the American soil. An epic tale that pits a son against the legacy of his family's desecration of the earth, and his own father's more personal violations, it is a beautiful and moving novel that speaks to the territory in our hearts that calls us back to our roots.

The scion of a family of wealthy timber barons, David Burkett has grown up with a father who is a malevolent force more than a father, and a mother made vague and numb by alcohol and pills. He and his sister, Cynthia, a firecracker who scandalizes the family at fourteen by taking up with the son of their Finnish-Native American gardener, are mostly left to make their own way, and often to play parent to their desolate elders. As David comes to adulthood—often guided and enlightened by the unforgettable, intractable, courageous women he loves—he realizes he must come to terms with his forefathers' rapacious destruction of the woods of Michigan's Upper Peninsula, as well as the working people who made their wealth possible. In the course of his twenty-year quest for the truth of what his family has done and trying to make amends, David looks closely at the root of his father's evil—and threatens to destroy himself

*(continued on back flap)*

---

Item A44.c., *True North.* © 2004 by Jim Harrison.

**A43.e.** *Braided Creek: A Conversation in Poetry*
*First edition, lettered edition (2003).*
**Title Page:** Jim Harrison & Ted Kooser | Braided | Creek | [small design] | A Conversation in Poetry | [Copper Canyon symbol] Copper Canyon Press
**Copyright:** [26 lines of information] 9 8 7 6 5 4 3 2 FIRST PRINTING
**Binding:** Tan leather on spine with a light beige linen cloth over boards. White paper label with black lettering on spine.
**Dust Jacket:** Not issued with dust jacket. Published price of the lettered copies was $350.
**Note:** This collection of poetry is dedicated to Dan Gerber. The colophon page is hand-lettered and states that there were 26 lettered copies printed. Each copy is signed by Harrison and Kooser on the half-title page. Additionally included in these editions are two holograph poems, one by Harrison and one by Kooser, bound in on separate rear endpapers. Each lettered copy has different holograph poems included, making each copy unique.

**A43.f.** *Braided Creek: A Conversation in Poetry*
*First edition, hors commerce edition (2003).*
**Title Page:** Jim Harrison & Ted Kooser | Braided | Creek | [small design] | A Conversation in Poetry | [Copper Canyon symbol] Copper Canyon Press
**Copyright:** [26 lines of information] 9 8 7 6 5 4 3 2 FIRST PRINTING
**Binding:** Tan leather on spine with a light beige linen cloth over boards. White paper label with black lettering on spine. This binding is identical to that of the lettered editions.
**Dust Jacket:** Not issued with dust jacket. These copies were *hors commerce* and were reserved for the authors and friends of the press.
**Note:** This collection of poetry is dedicated to Dan Gerber. The colophon page is the same as the numbered and lettered copies; however, there is a handwritten notation of *hors commerce*. The number of *hors commerce* copies is not stated, but the publisher has stated that there were 19 of these copies printed and reserved for the authors and friends of the press. Each copy is signed by Harrison and Kooser on the half-title page. Additionally included in these copies are two holograph poems, one by Harrison and one by Kooser, bound in on the same front endpaper. Each *hors commerce* copy has different holograph poems included, making each copy unique.

**A44.a.** *True North: A Novel*
*First edition, uncorrected proof (2004).*
**Title Page:** Jim Harrison | True North | A Novel | [Publisher's Device] | Grove Press | New York

I prefer the skyline
of a shelf of books.

*Jim Harrison* (signature)

From *Braided Creek*, by Jim Harrison and Ted Kooser
Copper Canyon Press, 2003

Reprinted with permission of Jim Harrison
On the Occasion of the Twenty-fifth Anniversary of Square Books
300 copies printed at Red Hydra Press
September 14, 2004

Item A45.a., "I prefer the skyline of a shelf of books."
Used by permission of Square Books and Red Hydra Press.

**Copyright:** [One line of information]. No statement of printing.
**Binding:** Pictorial paper binding with black lettering that re-creates the dust-jacket art on the trade edition. Painting by Russell Chatham. Plain white paper spine with black lettering.
**Dust Jacket:** Not issued with dust jacket. On rear panel of the proof it states that the tentative published price will be $24.
**Note:** This novel is dedicated to Judy Hottensen and Amy Hundley. On the rear of the proof it states that the tentative publication date is May 2004. These proofs, of which 427 copies were printed, were sent out to reviewers in early January 2004. States "uncorrected proof" on front panel.

### A44.b. *True North: A Novel*

*First edition, advance reading copy (2004).*
**Title Page:** Jim Harrison | True North | A Novel | [Publisher's Device] | Grove Press | New York
**Copyright:** [16 lines of information]. No statement of printing.
**Binding:** Pictorial paper binding with black lettering that re-creates the dust-jacket art on the trade edition. Painting by Russell Chatham. Plain white paper spine with black lettering.
**Dust Jacket:** Not issued with dust jacket. On rear panel of the advance reading copy it states that the tentative published price will be $24.
**Note:** This novel is dedicated to Judy Hottensen and Amy Hundley. On the rear of the advance reading copy it states that the tentative publication date is May 2004. These advance reading copies, of which 1,300 copies were printed, were distributed toward the end of January. These copies look very similar to the uncorrected proof copies issued about a month earlier; however, it clearly states "advance reading copy" on the front panel, and these advance reading copies are about ¼" thicker than the proof copies.

### A44.c. *True North: A Novel*

*First edition, first printing (2004).*
**Title Page:** Jim Harrison | True North | A Novel | [Publisher's Device] | Grove Press | New York
**Copyright:** [29 lines of information] FIRST EDITION 04 05 06 07 08 10 9 8 7 6 5 4 3 2 1
**Binding:** Light blue paper–covered boards. Light blue paper spine with lettering in gold.
**Dust Jacket:** Russell Chatham painting on front cover and spine with raised lettering in black. Rear panel in yellow with black lettering. Rear

# The Davenport
# Lunar Eclipse

Overlooking the Mississippi
I never thought I'd get this old.
It was mostly my confusion about time
and the moon, and seeing the lovely way
homely old men treat their homely old women
in Nebraska and Iowa, the lunch time
touch over green Jell-O with pineapple
and fried "fish rectangles" for $2.95.
When I passed Des Moines the radio said
there were long lines to see the entire cow
sculpted out of butter. The earth is right smack
between the sun and the moon, the black waitress
told me at the Salty Pelican on the waterfront,
home from wild Houston to nurse her sick dad.
My good eye is burning up from fatigue
as it squints up above the Mississippi
where the moon is losing its edge to black.
It likely doesn't know what's happening to it,
I thought, pressed down to my meal and wine
by a fresh load of incomprehension.
My grandma lived in Davenport in the 1890s
just after Wounded Knee, a signal event,
the beginning of America's *Sickness Unto Death*.

I'd like to nurse my father back to health
he's been dead thirty years, I said
to the waitress who agreed. That's why she
came home, she said, you only got one.
Now I find myself at fifty-one in Davenport
and drop the issue right into the Mississippi
where it is free to swim with the moon's reflection.
At the bar there are two girls of incomprehensible beauty
for the time being, as Swedish as my Grandma,
speaking in bad grammar as they listen to a band
of middle-aged Swede saxophonists braying
"Bye-Bye Blackbird" over and over, with a clumsy
but specific charm. The girls fail to notice me —
perhaps I should give them the thousand dollars
in my wallet but I've forgot just how.
I feel pleasantly old and stupid, deciding
not to worry about who I am but how I spend
my days, until I tear in the weak places
like a thin, worn sheet. Back in my room
I can't hear the river passing like time,
or the moon emerging from the shadow of earth,
but I can see the water that never repeats itself.
It's very difficult to look at the World
and into your heart at the same time.
In between, a life has passed.

Jim Harrison

from *After Ikkyu and other poems* by Jim Harrison. Copyright 1996 by Jim Harrison. Reprinted by arrangement with Shambhala Publications, Inc. Boston.

Item A46.a., Deluxe edition, "The Davenport Lunar Eclipse."
Used by permission of Fox Run Press.

panel also has four blurbs and a photo of the author by Mathieu Bourgois. Published price of $24.

**Note:** In review material sent out it states that the publication date is 22 May 2004; however, this hardback edition was in bookstores in mid-April 2004. There were 37,000 copies in the first printing. This novel is dedicated to Judy Hottensen and Amy Hundley. The true first edition of this title appeared in France as *De Marquette á Veracruz* a few weeks before the American edition. This edition, published by Christian Bourgois and translated by Brice Matthieussent, was printed in wraps with a John Frederick Kensett painting on the cover and has no statement of printing on the copyright page.

**A44.d.** *True North: A Novel*
*First edition, first printing, limited edition (2004).*
**Title Page:** Jim Harrison | True North | A Novel | [publisher's device] | Grove Press | New York
**Copyright:** [29 lines of information] FIRST EDITION 04 05 06 07 08 10 9 8 7 6 5 4 3 2 1
**Binding:** Light blue to bluish gray cloth over boards with gold lettering on front panel and spine. In same cloth over boards slipcase.
**Dust Jacket:** Not issued with dust jacket. Published price of $150.
**Note:** The limitation page is tipped in to the front of the book and states that there were 250 copies numbered and signed. The author's signature is also on this page. This novel is dedicated to Judy Hottensen and Amy Hundley.

**A45.a.** *I Prefer the Skyline of a Shelf of Books*
*Broadside, first printing (2004).*
**Note:** Single broadside designed by Steve Miller. Tuscaloosa AL: Red Hydra Press, 2004. Broadside was printed "On the occasion of the twenty-fifth anniversary of Square Books" in Jackson, Mississippi. Broadside is dated 14 September 2004 and measures 12" × 17". The single-line poem that makes up the title of the broadside was taken from *Braided Creek* (Port Townsend WA: Copper Canyon Press, 2003). There were two separate issues printed of this broadside. One was a letterpress edition of 300 copies on heavier stock reserved for friends of Square Books, the other a regular edition of 1,000 copies. The letterpress issue contains a colophon stating that 300 copies were printed, and the regular edition does not contain a statement of limitation.

# The Davenport Lunar Eclipse

Overlooking the Mississippi
I never thought I'd get this old.
It was mostly my confusion about time
and the moon, and seeing the lovely way
homely old men treat their homely old women
in Nebraska and Iowa, the lunch time
touch over green Jell-O with pineapple
and fried "fish rectangles" for $3.95.
When I passed Des Moines the radio said
there were foot-long lines to see the entire cow
sculpted out of butter. The earth is right smack
between the sun and the moon, the black waitress
told me at the Salty Pelican on the waterfront,
home from wild Houston to nurse her sick dad.
My good eye is burning up from fatigue
as it squints up above the Mississippi
where the moon is losing its edge to black.
It likely doesn't know what's happening to it,
I thought, pressed down to my meal and wine
by a fresh load of incomprehension.
My grandma lived in Davenport in the 1890s
just after Wounded Knee, a signal event,
the beginning of America's *Sieken unto Death*,
I'd like to nurse my father back to health
he's been dead thirty years, I said
to the waitress who agreed. That's why she
came home, she said, you only got one.
Now I find myself at fifty-one in Davenport
and drop the issue right into the Mississippi
where it is free to swim with the moon's reflection.
At the bar there are two girls of incomprehensible beauty
for the time being, as Swedish as my Grandma,
speaking in bad grammar as they listen to a band
of middle-aged Swede saxophonists braying
"Bye-Bye Blackbird" over and over, with a clumsy
but specific charm. The girls fail to notice me —
perhaps I should give them the thousand dollars
in my wallet but I've forgot just how.
I feel pleasantly old and stupid, deciding
not to worry about who I am but how I spend
my days, until I fear in the weak places
like a thin, worn sheet. Back in my room
I can't hear the river passing like time,
or the moon emerging from the shadow of earth,
but I can see the water that never repeats itself.
It's very difficult to look at the World
and into your heart at the same time.
In between, a life has passed.

Jim Harrison

Item A46.a., Diner edition, "The Davenport Lunar Eclipse."
Used by permission of Fox Run Press.

**A46.a.** *The Davenport Lunar Eclipse*

*Broadside, first printing (2004).*

**Note:** Single broadside designed by Anik See. Madeira Park BC: Fox Run Press, 2004. Broadside is not dated but was printed on 25–26 September 2004 and measures 10" × 14". The illustration is by Joanna See. This sheet was part of a series of broadsides entitled "Words and Revolution" that contains the work of five other poets. There were 50 sets printed. In addition there were two individual editions printed of the Harrison broadside, the "Diner" edition and the "Deluxe" edition. The "Diner" edition, which was produced in two issues, was printed on embossed paper place mat material. The first issue was printed with a line of copyright information at the bottom of the sheet and was done in a print run of 20 copies for individual sale. The copies included in the "Words and Revolution" series do not contain the line of copyright information at the bottom of the sheet. This copyright information is contained in a small pamphlet that was included with the set. The "Deluxe" edition was printed on Zerkall Cream Wove rough paper in an edition of 50 copies. This issue was intended solely for individual distribution and was not included in the "Words and Revolution" set. On the rear of all these broadsides is printed "Illustration by Joanna See | Fox Run Press 04." There were also several proof copies printed of the "Diner" edition. These proofs can be identified by the fact that there is no copyright information on the front of the broadside and no publisher's information printed on the rear. Also the lowercase *s* in the word *Swedish* is reversed. This poem was published in the literary journal *Caliban 7* in August 1989 and later in the collection *After Ikkyu and Other Poems* (Boston: Shambhala Publications, 1996).

**A47.a.** *Livingston Suite*

*First edition, first printing (2005).*

**Title Page:** Livingston Suite | [illustration] | Jim Harrison | Illustration by Greg Keeler | Limberlost Press 2005

**Copyright:** [8 lines of information] First edition. See colophon page.

**Binding:** Heavy cream paper with gray lettering. Color illustration by Greg Keeler on front cover. Hand-sewn wraps.

**Dust Jacket:** Not issued with dust jacket. Published price of $25.

**Note:** Colophon page states a letterpress edition of 750 copies printed. 650 copies in wraps and 100 hand-bound copies in cloth and boards, signed and numbered by the poet and artist. Published March 2005. A single long poem published here for the first time. In memory of T. J. Huth. Harrison dedicated

LIVINGSTON SUITE

Jim Harrison

Item A47.a., *Livingston Suite*. Used by permission
of Richard Ardinger and Limberlost Press.

this poem to Huth, a young man who drowned while swimming in the Yellowstone River, which runs through Livingston, Montana. The wrappered edition of this book was bound using a multitude of differently colored and textured tissue endpapers. There is no priority in these copies.

### A47.b. *Livingston Suite*
*First edition, first printing, limited edition (2005).*
**Title Page:** Livingston Suite | [illustration] | Jim Harrison | Illustration by Greg Keeler | Limberlost Press 2005
**Copyright:** [8 lines of information] First edition. See colophon page.
**Binding:** Light green cloth over boards. Cream paper paste down with color illustration and gray lettering on front board. Spine has cream paper paste label with gray lettering.
**Dust Jacket:** Not issued with dust jacket. Published price of $125.
**Note:** Colophon page states a letterpress edition of 750 copies printed. 650 copies in wraps and 100 numbered and signed copies in boards. These limited-edition copies are signed by both Harrison and Keeler and are hand-numbered 1–100. There were also a dozen or so presentation copies that were bound for the author and friends of the press. There is no designation on the colophon page stating that these are presentation copies; however, they are not numbered. Released in early June 2005. A single long poem published here for the first time. In memory of T. J. Huth.

### A48.a. *Republican Wives: A Novella*
*First edition, first printing (2005).*
**Title Page:** Republican | Wives | A Novella | from the collection | *The Summer He Didn't Die* | Forthcoming in August 2005 | Jim Harrison | [publisher's device] | Atlantic Monthly Press | New York
**Copyright:** [19 lines of information] No statement of printing. Statement on copyright page notes "NOT FOR RESALE."
**Binding:** Bound in red cloth over boards. Lettering on front panel is in gold. No spine lettering.
**Dust Jacket:** Not issued with dust jacket.
**Note:** These books were produced as promotional advance issues to introduce Harrison's forthcoming collection *The Summer He Didn't Die*. The publisher printed 1,000 copies to be given out to industry professionals and reviewers at the Book Expo of America trade show in Washington DC in early June 2005. There were two issues of this title, one issue of 500 copies with a signed, tipped-in page and one without the tipped-in page. No priority has been established between the two states.

# Republican Wives

## A Novella

## Jim Harrison

Item A48.a., *Republican Wives*.
© 2005 by Jim Harrison.

**A49.a.** *The Summer He Didn't Die*
 *First edition, uncorrected proof (2005).*
 **Title Page:** The Summer | He Didn't Die | Jim Harrison | [publisher's device] | Atlantic Monthly Press | New York
 **Copyright:** [16 lines of information]. No statement of printing.
 **Binding:** Pictorial paper binding with black lettering and artwork on front board re-creates the dust-jacket art on the trade edition. Painting by Russell Chatham. Plain white paper spine with black lettering.
 **Dust Jacket:** Not issued with dust jacket. On rear panel of the proof it states that the tentative published price will be $24.
 **Note:** On the rear of the proof it states that the tentative publication date is August 2005. These proofs, of which 182 copies were printed, were sent out to reviewers in early May 2005. States "uncorrected proof" on front panel.

**A49.b.** *The Summer He Didn't Die*
 *First edition, first printing (2005).*
 **Title Page:** The Summer | He Didn't Die | Jim Harrison | [publisher's device] | Atlantic Monthly Press | New York
 **Copyright:** [25 lines of information]. FIRST EDITION 05 06 07 08 09 10 9 8 7 6 5 4 3 2 1
 **Binding:** Cream-colored paper over boards with Atlantic's publisher's device blind-stamped on front board. Cream-colored paper spine with lettering in copper.
 **Dust Jacket:** Russell Chatham painting on front, rear, and spine with raised lettering in yellow on front panel. Rear-panel lettering in yellow and cream. Rear panel has five blurbs for this book, the author, and *The Beast God Forgot to Invent*. The rear flap of the jacket contains a photo of the author by Mathieu Bourgois. Published price of $24.
 **Note:** This collection contains the novellas "The Summer He Didn't Die" and "Republican Wives" and the autobiographical essay "Tracking." In review material sent out it states that the publication date is August 2005; however, this hardback edition was in bookstores in mid-July 2005. There were 27,000 copies in the first printing. There is no dedication in this collection of novellas.

**A50.a.** *Cabbage*
 *Broadside, first printing (2005).*
 **Note:** Single broadside designed by Ander Monson of the New Michigan Press, Grand Rapids, Michigan, and printed by Cascade Printing, also of

Item A49.b., *The Summer He Didn't Die*. © 2004 by Jim Harrison.

Grand Rapids, in 2005. Broadside was printed ". . . in appreciation of the author's contribution to Grand Valley State University and his visit to campus on September 19, 2005." The broadside measures 11" × 16½". This broadside was printed to commemorate a private reception given by Grand Valley State University to announce the acquisition of the Harrison Archive and Papers. The broadside's colophon at the bottom states that 500 copies were printed. All copies were signed by the author prior to the reception and are hand-numbered. This poem was first published in *New Letters* in the summer of 2005 and appears in the poetry collection *Saving Daylight* (Copper Canyon Press, 2006).

### A51.a. *Saving Daylight*

*First edition, uncorrected proof (2006).*

**Title Page:** Jim Harrison | Saving Daylight | [publisher's device] | Copper Canyon Press

**Copyright:** [14 lines of information] 9 8 7 6 5 4 3 2 FIRST PRINTING

**Binding:** Bound in white wraps with black lettering. Color scan of dust-jacket cover art (a Russell Chatham painting) for the trade edition on front panel.

**Dust Jacket:** Not issued with dust jacket. On rear cover it states a published price of $22 for the cloth edition.

**Note:** This collection of poetry is dedicated to Linda "(again)." On rear cover it states a publication date of April 2006. 100 copies printed. Although the copyright date states 2006, these proofs were sent out to reviewers in December 2005.

### A51.b. *Saving Daylight*

*First edition, first printing (2006).*

**Title Page:** Jim Harrison | Saving Daylight | [Copper Canyon pressmark] | Copper Canyon Press

**Copyright:** [24 lines of information] 9 8 7 6 5 4 3 2 FIRST PRINTING

**Binding:** Tan cloth over boards with gold lettering on spine. Harrison's facsimile signature is blind-stamped on the front board, and the Copper Canyon pressmark (the Chinese character for poetry) is blind-stamped on the rear board and spine.

**Dust Jacket:** Russell Chatham lithograph on front panel. Brown spine has beige and dark brown lettering. Rear panel has beige and black lettering with a photograph of the author by Alec Soth taken in the lobby of the Murray Hotel in Livingston, Montana. Dust-jacket design by Valerie Brewster. The published price as stated on the rear panel is $22.

# Jim Harrison
## Cabbage

If only I had the genius of a cabbage
or even an onion to grow myself
in their laminae from the holy core
that bespeaks the final shape. Nothing
is outside of us in this over-interpreted world.
Bruises are only the mouths of our perceptions.
The gods who have died are able to come
to life again. It's their secret that they wish
to share if anyone knows that they exist.
Belief is a mood that weighs nothing on anyone's
scale but nevertheless exists. The moose
down the road wears the black cloak of a god
and the dead bird lifts from a bed of moss
in a shape totally unknown to us.
It's after midnight in Montana in which
I test the thickness of the universe; its resilience
to carry us further than any of us wish to go.
We shed our shapes slowly like moving water
which ends up as it will so utterly far from home.

From *Saving Daylight*, Copper Canyon, 2006. This broadside was printed by the New Michigan Press in appreciation of the author's contribution to Grand Valley State University and his visit to campus on September 19, 2005. This is number 25 of 500.

Item A50.a., "Cabbage." Used by permission of New Michigan Press.

**Note:** This collection of poetry is dedicated to Linda "(again)." 4,500 copies of the hardbound trade edition were printed. Book was released in early April 2006. The colophon page at the rear of the book states that *"Saving Daylight* is also issued in a signed limited edition of 250 numbered copies and twenty-six lettered copies."

A51.c. *Saving Daylight*
*First edition, first printing, numbered edition (2006).*
**Title Page:** Jim Harrison | Saving Daylight | [Copper Canyon pressmark] | Copper Canyon Press
**Copyright:** [24 lines of information] 9 8 7 6 5 4 3 2 FIRST PRINTING
**Binding:** Burgundy cloth over boards with brown cloth at spine. Gold lettering on spine.
**Dust Jacket:** Not issued with dust jacket. The published price of this limited edition is $125.
**Note:** This collection of poetry is dedicated to Linda "(again)." The numbered editions were shipped in August 2006. The colophon page at the rear of the book states that *"Saving Daylight* is also issued in a signed limited edition of 250 numbered copies and twenty-six lettered copies." These copies are hand-numbered on the colophon page at the rear of the book and are signed by Harrison on the title page.

A51.d. *Saving Daylight*
*First edition, first printing, lettered edition (2006).*
**Title Page:** Jim Harrison | Saving Daylight | [Copper Canyon pressmark] | Copper Canyon Press
**Copyright:** [24 lines of information] 9 8 7 6 5 4 3 2 FIRST PRINTING
**Binding:** Dark brown cloth over boards with dark burgundy leather on the spine. Gold lettering on the spine.
**Dust Jacket:** Not issued with dust jacket. The published price of this limited edition is $300.
**Note:** This collection of poetry is dedicated to Linda "(again)." These lettered editions were shipped in August 2006. The colophon page at the rear of the book states that *"Saving Daylight* is also issued in a signed limited edition of 250 numbered copies and twenty-six lettered copies." These lettered copies are hand-lettered on the colophon page at the rear of the book and signed by Harrison on the title page. In addition to these lettered copies there were an additional 14 copies bound as *hors commerce* copies to be given to the author and friends of the press. The copies presented to Harrison

# SAVING DAYLIGHT

*I cut the thickness of the universe, its resilience
to carry us further than any of us wish to go.
We shed our shapes slowly like waning water,
which ends up as it will or utterly far from home.*

Jim Harrison is one of America's most versatile and celebrated writers, and his work as a poet has earned him recognition as an "untrammeled renegade genius." *Saving Daylight* is Harrison's tenth book of poems, and his first full-length poetry collection in a decade.

Against the backdrop of an absurd socio-political world and its "well-oiled gates of hell," *Saving Daylight* is grounded by the physical realism of thickets and rivers, birds and bears, and the solace of dogs. Whether contemplating the ephemerality of ninety billion galaxies or the immediate grace of a waitress, Harrison evokes the art of living, and the mysteries that sustain us: "I'm enrolled in a school without visible teachers," he writes in the title poem, "the divine mumbling just out of ear shot."

"Behind the words one always feels the presence of a passionate, exuberant man who is at the same time possessed of a quick, subtle intelligence and a deeply questioning attitude toward life. Harrison writes so winningly that one is simply content to be in the presence of a writer this vital, this large-spirited."
— *The New York Times Book Review*

---

"Jim Harrison is a writer with immortality in him."
— *Sunday Times* (London)

"Harrison equates writing poetry with praying, painting, or petroglyphs, so intimately human is the urge to express the life of the soul, and his poems do make the compassed mind."
— *Bookless* (starred review)

"Jim Harrison's poems embody the deep sense of self-consciousness, fully engaged in the world around it."
— *Salcken*

"Harrison was a poet before he was a novelist, and he continues to craft poetry using clean, straightforward language and highly sophisticated form."
— *Men's Journal*

"Harrison's poetry is characterized by a unique blend of experience and realism, humor and tenderness, craft and intuition."
— *The Oregonian*

"Its language is lusty, cosmic, and stylistically unclassifiable."
— *Shambhala Sun*

"Here is poetry to read and reread."
— *Dallas Morning News*

"From the beginning his poems evince with an almost animal vigor, brimming themselves against the terrible limitations of suffering, whether it comes from physical repression, distance in love, poverty, alcohol, drugs, or self-contempt. The poems move through a wide range of emotions—from raging despair to joyful celebration to a spiritual, egoless acceptance of what the universe may give."
— *American Book Review*

"Here, abundant humor [and] distilled emotion."
— *Houston Chronicle*

"his book is superb."
— *Kansas City Star*

"A wonderful, rewarding book."
— *Philadelphia Inquirer*

"This lucid poetic vision is compellingly expressed for both newcomers and his most ardent fans."
— *The Plain Dealer* (Cleveland)

---

COPPER CANYON PRESS

POETRY / $22.00

ISBN 1-55659-233-3

Item A51.b., *Saving Daylight*. Used by Permission of Copper Canyon Press.

have no designation on the colophon page, and the other copies are marked "HC" below the colophon.

**A52.a.** *Returning to Earth*

*First edition, uncorrected proof (2007).*

**Title Page:** Jim Harrison | Returning | to Earth | [publisher's device] | Grove Press | New York

**Copyright:** [17 lines of information]. No statement of printing.

**Binding:** Plain mustard yellow paper binding with black lettering on front, spine, and rear panels.

**Dust Jacket:** Not issued with dust jacket. On the rear panel of the proof it states that the tentative published price will be $24.

**Note:** On the rear of the proof it states that the tentative publication date is January 2007. These proofs were sent out to reviewers in early September 2006. States "uncorrected proof" on front and rear panels. There are two states of this proof. One state has an undated letter from the publisher, Morgan Entrekin, bound into the proof as the first page. This issue also has three blank rear endpapers. The other state does not have the letter bound into it and has no blank endpapers. This state was sent out with a different letter with similar text from Entrekin that is dated 7 September 2006, folded, and laid in to it. Both letters begin "Dear Friends." No priority of these two states has been established; however, the state with the letter bound into it appeared first on the market.

**A52.b.** *Returning to Earth*

*First edition, advance reading copy (2007).*

**Title Page:** Jim Harrison | Returning | to Earth | [publisher's device] | Grove Press | New York

**Copyright:** [18 lines of information]. No statement of printing.

**Binding:** Pictorial paper binding (French wrappers) with raised black lettering ("Jim Harrison") and artwork on the front panel that re-creates the dust-jacket art on the trade edition. Painting by Russell Chatham. Artwork continued around plain white paper spine with black lettering. Rough-cut fore edge pages. A letter from the publisher, Morgan Entrekin, is printed on the rear panel that differs slightly from the letters included with the uncorrected proof copies.

**Dust Jacket:** Not issued with dust jacket. On the rear inside flap of the binding it states that the tentative published price will be $24.

**Note:** On the rear inside flap of the binding it states that the tentative

Item A52.a. (*left*), item A52.b. (*right*), proof and advance copies, *Returning to Earth*. © 2007 by Jim Harrison.

publication date is January 2007. These advance reading copies were sent out to reviewers in October 2006. A letter from the Grove/Atlantic publicist was folded and laid in to the advance reading copy. The letter is dated 7 October 2006 and is addressed to reviewers. States "advance reading copy" on front panel. Information that appears on the last page of this advance reading copy states that there will be a 50,000-copy first printing.

A52.c. *Returning to Earth*
*First edition, first printing (2007).*
**Title Page:** Jim Harrison | Returning | to Earth | [publisher's device] | Grove Press | New York
**Copyright:** [29 lines of information]. FIRST EDITION 07 08 09 10 11 10 9 8 7 6 5 4 3 2 1
**Binding:** Light blue paper–covered boards. Light blue paper spine with lettering in gold.
**Dust Jacket:** Dust-jacket art and design by Russell Chatham. Raised lettering on the front panel is in burgundy, and the lettering on the spine is also burgundy. Rear panel of jacket is light blue with black and burgundy lettering. Rear panel also has five blurbs concerning Harrison's work. Rear inside flap has a photo of the author by Mathieu Bourgois. Published price of $24.
**Note:** In review material sent out with the advance copies of the trade edition it states that the publication date is 22 January 2007; however, advance copies of the book were sent out in mid-December 2006, and copies were in retail stores at the end of December. This novel is dedicated to Peter Lewis.

A52.d. *Returning to Earth*
*First edition, limited edition (2007).*
**Title Page:** Jim Harrison | Returning | to Earth | [publisher's device] | Grove Press | New York
**Copyright:** [29 lines of information]. FIRST EDITION 07 08 09 10 11 10 9 8 7 6 5 4 3 2 1
**Binding:** Deep purple cloth over boards with gold lettering on spine. In same cloth over boards slipcase.
**Dust Jacket:** Not issued with dust jacket. Published price of $150.
**Note:** The limitation page is tipped in to the front of the book and states that there were 250 copies numbered and signed by the author. The author's signature is also on this hand-numbered page. This novel is dedicated to Peter Lewis.

$24.00

Jim Harrison is one of our finest, most beloved authors, about whom *The New York Times Book Review* has written, "There is a singular comfort in knowing, on the first page of a novel, that you are in the hands of a master.... Makes the ordinary extraordinary, the unattainable unforgettable." In *Returning to Earth* Harrison has delivered a tender, profound, and magnificent novel about life, death, and finding redemption in sometimes unlikely places.

Donald is a middle-aged Chippewa-Finnish man, married to a white woman who renounced the wealth she was raised with, and father to two grown children.

He is dying of Lou Gehrig's disease and realizes no one alive will be able to pass on to his children their family history once he is gone. He begins dictating to his wife, Cynthia, stories he has never shared with anyone—about how three generations ago his family settled in Michigan at the height of the logging industry; about his own relationship to his unique spiritual heritage. Meanwhile, around him, his family struggles with how to lay him to rest with the same dignity with which he always lived.

Over the course of the year following Donald's death, his loved ones struggle to make sense of their loss. His daughter begins studying Chippewa ideas of death for clues on her father's religion, and her mother, Cynthia, is at loose ends for how to protect or guide her. Bereft of the family she created to escape the malevolent influence of her own father, Cynthia and her eccentric brother, David, find, all these years later, that redeeming the past is not a lost cause.

Jim Harrison writes about the heart of this country like no other writer—about the culture of Native America, the natural world and our place in it, the loss that has shaped our history, and the pleasures that raise life to the sublime. *Returning to Earth* is one of the finest novels of Harrison's long, storied career, and will confirm his standing as one of the most important American writers now working.

# JIM HARRISON
# RETURNING TO EARTH

## JIM HARRISON
### RETURNING TO EARTH

PRAISE FOR THE WORK OF
JIM HARRISON

"The genius of Mr. Harrison, it seems to me, is that his characters possess a uniquely human and endearing clumsiness as well as a gracefulness in the way they inhabit the sharp and sometimes exuberantly felt physical world and the restless (though also at times exuberant) realm of spirit. *True North*, with its reveries, tenderness, wisdom, violence, and salvation, is a truly American novel. There is grace and redemption—sometimes earned, other times merely bestowed or observed—on every page."
—Rick Bass, *The Dallas Morning News*

"An American original ... [Harrison's] writing bears earthy whiffs of wild morels and morals and of booze and boozery, as well as hints of William Faulkner, Louise Erdrich, Herman Melville, and Norman Maclean. There is a robust reflectiveness and sheer delight to Harrison's prose.... A luminous, heartwarming reminder of what literature can achieve."
—*San Francisco Chronicle* on *The Summer He Didn't Die*

"One of our master chroniclers of human hungers, flaws, and frustrations."
—*The Kansas City Star* on *The Summer He Didn't Die*

"Full-toned Harrison, weaving together philosophy, religion, sex, sensuality, a love of animals, poetry, and food, and an elegaic appreciation for the natural world.... One of the finest writers working today."
—*The Seattle Times* on *True North*

"No one has advanced and expanded the American literary ethos in the latter part of the twentieth century more cogently, usefully, and just plain brilliantly than Jim Harrison.... This is a matter to which all literate Americans should pay serious attention."
—Hayden Carruth

Born and raised in Michigan, **JIM HARRISON** is also the author of five volumes of novellas: *The Beast God Forgot to Invent*, *Legends of the Fall*, *The Woman Lit by Fireflies*, *Julip*, and *The Summer He Didn't Die*; eight previous novels: *True North*, *The Road Home*, *Wolf*, *A Good Day to Die*, *Farmer*, *Warlock*, *Sundog*, and *Dalva*; eight collections of poetry, including *Braided Creek*, a collaboration with U.S. Poet Laureate Ted Kooser, *The Shape of the Journey: New and Collected Poems*, and his most recent, *Saving Daylight*; and three works of nonfiction, the memoir *Off to the Side* and the collections *Just Before Dark* and *The Raw and the Cooked: Adventures of a Roving Gourmand*. The recipient of a National Endowment for the Arts grant and a Guggenheim Fellowship, his work has been published in twenty-seven languages. Jim Harrison divides his time between Montana and Arizona.

Jacket art and design by Russell Charlton
Author photograph by Matthew Bourgeois

GROVE PRESS
an imprint of Grove/Atlantic, Inc.
Distributed by Publishers Group West
www.groveatlantic.com

PRINTED IN THE USA 0107

ISBN-13: 978-0-8021-1836-7
ISBN-10: 0-8021-1836-3

Item A52.c., *Returning to Earth*. © 2007 by Jim Harrison.

**A53.a.** *Letters to Yesenin*

*First edition, uncorrected proof (2007).*

**Title Page:** Letters to Yesenin | Jim Harrison | [publisher's device] | Copper Canyon Press | Port Townsend, Washington

**Copyright:** [25 lines of information]. 3 5 7 9 8 6 4 2 FIRST PRINTING

**Binding:** Bound in white wraps with black lettering. Color scan of the front-panel cover art for the trade edition. Photo by Tatiana Sayig.

**Dust Jacket:** Not issued with dust jacket. On the rear panel of the proof it states that the published price will be $12.

**Note:** On the rear of the proof it states that the tentative publication date is November 2007. This collection of poetry is in memory of J. D. Reed. These proofs were sent out to reviewers in late August 2007. States "uncorrected proof" on front and rear panels. This is a reissue of Harrison's 1973 collection of poetry of the same name. This edition launches "Copper Canyon Classics," a series dedicated to re-presenting classic poetry in an inexpensive format. 100 copies of this proof were printed.

**A53.b.** *Letters to Yesenin*

*First edition, first printing (2007).*

**Title Page:** Letters to Yesenin | Jim Harrison | [publisher's device] | Copper Canyon Press | Port Townsend, Washington

**Copyright:** [25 lines of information]. 3 5 7 9 8 6 4 2 FIRST PRINTING

**Binding:** Bound in wraps with white and black lettering. The front panel is black with white lettering and a photograph. The rear panel is a yellow gold color with black lettering. Color photograph on front panel is by Tatiana Sayig.

**Dust Jacket:** Not issued with dust jacket. The price on the rear panel states $12.

**Note:** The publication date stated on the proof of this title was November 2007. This collection of poetry is in memory of J. D. Reed. This is a reissue of Harrison's 1973 collection of poetry of the same name. This edition launches "Copper Canyon Classics," a series dedicated to representing classic poetry in an inexpensive format. 3,000 copies were printed.

**A54.a.** *Old Bird Boy*

*Broadside, first printing (2007).*

**Note:** Single broadside designed by Ander Monson of the New Michigan Press, Grand Rapids, Michigan. The photographer is Andrejs Pidjass. The broadside measures 6⅞" × 10¼" and is printed on heavy cream stock. This

Item A53.a. (*left*), uncorrected proof, item A53.b. (*right*), trade edition, *Letters to Yesenin* (reissue). Used by permission of Copper Canyon Press.

was the first published appearance of this poem. This broadside was printed to commemorate a reading given by Harrison at Grand Valley State University on 10 October 2007. The broadside's colophon at the bottom states that 500 copies were printed "in celebration of the author's visit to Grand Valley State University in October 2007." All copies were signed by the author prior to the reading and are hand-numbered.

A55.a. *The English Major*

*First edition, uncorrected proof (2008).*
**Title Page:** Jim Harrison | The | English | Major | [publisher's device] | Grove Press | New York
**Copyright:** [18 lines of information]. No statement of printing.
**Binding:** Plain mustard yellow paper binding with black lettering on front, spine, and rear panels.
**Dust Jacket:** Not issued with dust jacket. On the rear panel of the proof it states that the tentative published price will be $24.
**Note:** On the rear of the proof it states that the tentative publication date is October 2008. These proofs were sent out to reviewers in March 2008. States "uncorrected proof" on front panel and "advance proof" on the rear panel.

A55.b. *The English Major*

*First edition, first printing (2008).*
**Title Page:** Jim Harrison | The | English | Major | [publisher's device] | Grove Press | New York
**Copyright:** [18 lines of information]. FIRST EDITION 08 09 10 11 12 10 9 8 7 6 5 4 3 2 1
**Binding:** Dark orange paper covered boards. Yellow paper spine with copper lettering.
**Dust Jacket:** Russell Chatham artwork on front panel, spine, and partial rear cover. Lettering in burgundy, light yellow, and black. Author photograph on the inside of the rear flap is by Wyatt McSpadden. Dust-jacket design by Charles Rue Woods. The published price as stated on the rear panel and inside the front flap is $24.
**Note:** According to *Publishers Weekly*, 50,000 copies were printed. The review material sent out with the book states that the publication date is 7 October 2008; however, the book appeared on the market in early September. This novel is dedicated to Steve and Max (Steve Potenberg and Max Hjortsberg).

## Old Bird Boy  Jim Harrison

BIRDS KNOW US AS "THE PEOPLE OF THE FEET." I AM WATCHED AS I WALK around and around my green studio, a man of many beaten paths. Near me a willow flycatcher arcs in its air dance to catch a grasshopper, a swift move that I compare to nothing whatsoever that I do. They own the air we breathe. I've studied the feet of the bridled titmouse for years, how they seem to be made of spiderwebs so precariously attached to perch or ground, also the feet of the golden eagle which are death angels, and then the wings of all birds which on close inspection don't seem possible. Most birds own the ancient clock of north and south, a clock that never had hands, the god-time with which the universe began. As the end draws nearer I've taken to praying to be re-incarnated as a bird, and if not worthy of that, a tree in which they live so I could cradle them as I did our daughters and grandsons. Three times last April down on the border a dozen Chihuahuan ravens accompanied me on walks when I sang the right croaking song. I was finally within them. For the first time in my life I dared to say aloud, "I am blessed."

*Jim Harrison* [signature]

Unpublished poem used by permission of the author. Image © Photographer: Andrejs Pidjass. This broadside was printed by the New Michigan Press in celebration of the author's visit to Grand Valley State University in October 2007. This is number 30 of 500.

Item A54.a., "Old Bird Boy." Used by permission of New Michigan Press.

Item A55.b, *The English Major*. © 2008 by Jim Harrison.
Cover design by Russell Chatham. Use by permission of Grove/Atlantic, Inc.

# Section B
## *Individually Published Poetry*

**1965**

1. "New Liturgy," "Exercise." *Nation* 5 April 1965: 374. vol. 200, no. 14. This was the first published appearance of these poems and Harrison's first published poetry. Reprinted in *Plain Song*.
2. "Poem." *Discovery '65*. The Poetry Center, New York. 19 April 1965. A program for a reading presented by the Poetry Center at the 92nd Street Y, New York. This was the first published appearance of this poem. This program also contains a brief biographical sketch written by Harrison, the last line of which states: "As of yet, I haven't published a word but my work has been accepted by 'Poetry' (Chicago) and the 'Nation.'"
3. "Dead Doe," "Complaint," "Return," "Poem," "David." *Poetry* 106.5 (August 1965): 328–30. This was the first published appearance of these poems. Reprinted in *Plain Song*.
4. "Park at Night." *Move* 4 (September 1965): [17]. Preston, Lancashire, England. Ed. Jim Burns. An unpaginated poetry journal in paper wraps. This was the first published appearance of this poem. Reprinted in *Plain Song*.

**1966**

5. "Night in Boston." *Hika* 28.3 (Spring–Summer 1966): 6. *Hika* is the student literary journal from Kenyon College in Gambier, Ohio. This was the first published appearance of this poem. Reprinted in *Locations*.
6. "Night in Boston." NEW: *American and Canadian Poetry* 2 (December 1966): 23. Ed. John Gill. Reprinted in *Locations*.

**1967**

7. "Natural World." *Out of the War Shadow: The 1968 Peace Calendar and Appointment Book*. Ed. Denise Levertov. New York: War Resisters League, 1967. 16.

1968 peace calendar and appointment book published by War Resisters League. This was the first published appearance of this poem.

8. "From the Notebooks." *Soundings* 4.1 (Spring 1967): 82–85. Ed. Laurence Shea. *Soundings* is the literary journal of the State University of New York at Stony Brook. Also contains a brief biography of Harrison. This is the first and only published appearance of snippets of unfinished poetry from Harrison's notebooks.

9. "Suite to Appleness." *TriQuarterly* 10 (Fall 1967): 169–71. This was the first published appearance of this poem. Reprinted in *Locations*.

10. "War Suite." *New University Thought* 5.4 (Autumn 1967): 53–55. This was the first published appearance of this poem. Reprinted in *Locations*.

11. "War Suite." *Loveletter* 4–6 (Winter 1967). 3 pages of an unpaginated poetry journal. Ed. Al Young. Reprinted in *Locations*.

12. "Suite to Fathers." *Poetry* 109.5 (February 1967): 321–24. This was the first published appearance of this poem. Reprinted in *Locations*.

## 1968

13. "American Girl," "Lullaby for a Daughter." *Fire Exit* 1.1 (1968): 56–60. The magazine of the New Poets Theatre. This was the first published appearance of these poems.

14. "Locations." *Fire Exit* 1.2 (1968): 5–10.

15. "Natural World," "Thin Ice." *Hanging Loose* 5–6 (1968): 20, 22. A collection of unbound sheets contained in a printed envelope.

16. "War Suite." *Soundings* 5.1 (Spring 1968): 1–3. *Soundings* is the literary publication from the State University of New York at Stony Brook.

17. "A Year's Changes." *Sumac* 1.1 (Fall 1968): 95–100. This literary journal was edited by Dan Gerber and Jim Harrison.

18. "Locations." *Stony Brook* 1–2 (Fall 1968): 236–40.

19. "Sequence," "Breakthrough," "After the Anonymous Swedish," "White," "The Sign." *Pony Tail: A Magazine for Always* 1.1 (August 1968). Unpaginated journal. Cover states "Poetry from Stony Brook." Ed. Eliot Weinberger and Geoffrey O'Brien. Port Jefferson NY: Yellow Press. This was the first published appearance of these poems.

## 1969

20. "In Interims: Outlyer." *Five Blind Men*. Fremont MI: Sumac Press, 1969. 19–26. Poems by Dan Gerber, Jim Harrison, George Quasha, J. D. Reed, and Charles Simic. This book was published in a signed, hardback, limited edition of 26 lettered copies and 100 numbered copies. It was also published

simultaneously in a wrappered edition of 1,000 copies. Photo on the wrappered edition of the "five blind men" is by Sandy Gatten.

21. "War Suite," "Night in Boston." *31 New American Poets*. Ed. Ron Schreiber. New York: Hill & Wang, 1969. 86–90. From *Locations*.
22. "Locations," "Natural World." *Michigan Signatures: An Anthology of Current Michigan Poetry*. Ed. Albert Drake. Madison WI: Quixote Press, 1969. 20–26. vol. 4, no. 10. An anthology of current Michigan poetry. Both poems from *Locations*.
23. "Suite to Appleness." *Under 30: Fiction, Poetry and Criticism of the New American Writers*. Ed. Charles Newman and William A. Henkin Jr. Bloomington: Indiana University Press, 1969. 169–71. From *Locations*.
24. "In Interims: Outlyer." *Stony Brook* 3–4 (Fall 1969): 158–61. This was the first published appearance of this poem. Reprinted in *Outlyer and Ghazals*.
25. "War Suite." *The American Literary Anthology 2*. Ed. George Plimpton and Peter Ardery. New York: Random House, 28 February 1969. 110–13. From *Locations*.
26. "Sequence." *Mistletoe*. NP: Mephistopheles Publications, December 1969. 19. This piece is from *Locations*, stanza 3 from "Sequence."

**1970**

27. "Cardinal," "Horse," "Morning." *The Wind Is Round*. Ed. Sara Hannum and John Terry Chase. New York: Athenaeum, 1970. 4, 24, 44. Illustrated by Ronald Bowen. All these poems were first published in *Plain Song*.
28. "Poem," "Returning at Night," "Sound," "After the Anonymous Swedish." *The Voice That Is Great within Us*. Ed. Hayden Carruth. New York: Bantam Books, 1970. 710–11. From *Plain Song* and *Locations*.
29. "Thin Ice." *The American Literary Anthology 3*. Ed. George Plimpton and Peter Ardery. New York: Viking Press, 1970. 182–83. From *Locations*.
30. "Seven Ghazals." *Partisan Review* 37.3 (1970): 378–84. Although unnumbered, the ghazals printed are, in order of their appearance here, nos. 26, 18, 61, 16, 2, 6, and 39. This was the first published appearance of these poems. Reprinted in *Outlyer and Ghazals*.
31. "Some Ghazals." *Lillabulero* 9 (Summer–Fall 1970): 72–77. Although unnumbered, the ghazals printed are, in order of their appearance here, 43, 60, 64, 63, 38, and 19. This was the first published appearance of these poems. Reprinted in *Outlyer and Ghazals*.
32. "Eight Ghazals." *Sumac* 2.4 (Fall 1970): 28–31. Although unnumbered, the ghazals printed are, in order of their appearance here, nos. 52, 51, 50, 36, 47, 46, 4, and 41. This was the first published appearance of these poems.

Reprinted in *Outlyer and Ghazals*. The title page of this issue states that it is vol. 2, no. 4; however, the spine states that it is vol. 3, no. 1.

33. "Awake." *Antioch Review* 30.3–4 (Fall–Winter 1970–71): 342–43. This was the first published appearance of this poem. Reprinted in *Outlyer and Ghazals*. This poem is part of a photographic section titled "36 Birthday Poems for Gordon Cairnie." All photos by Elsa Dorfman.

34. "Ghazal for Christmas," "Cowgirl," "Hospital." *Sumac* 2.2–3 (Winter–Spring 1970): 219–20. "Ghazal for Christmas" is ghazal no. 1 in *Outlyer and Ghazals*. This was the first published appearance of "Cowgirl" and "Hospital." There is also a review from Harrison and a tribute to the poet Charles Olson in this issue.

**1971**

35. "Matrix 1: Home," "Matrix 3: Home." *Spectrum* 8.2 (Spring 1971): 24. This is the literary magazine from the University of California, Santa Barbara, and was printed in an edition of 600 copies in May 1971. This was the first published appearance of these poems. Reprinted in *Letters to Yesenin* as "Four Matrices."

**1972**

36. [excerpt] "A Year's Changes." *A Tan and Sandy Silence*. By John D. MacDonald. Greenwich CT: Fawcett Publications, 1972. [5]. A small portion of the poem "A Year's Changes" appears as an epigraph at the beginning of this novel, no. 13 in the Travis McGee series.

**1973**

37. "Sketch for a Job Application Blank," "Fair/Boy Christian Takes a Break," "Trader," "Ghazals XXI and XLIX." *The Norton Anthology of Modern Poetry*. Ed. Richard Ellman and Robert O'Clair. New York: W. W. Norton & Co., 1973. 1362–65. There is also a brief bio of the author on p. 1362. Reprinted as *Modern Poems: An Introduction to Poetry*. Ed. Richard Ellman and Robert O'Clair. New York: W. W. Norton & Co., 1976. 477–79. The later printing contained only the poem "Sketch for a Job Application Blank" along with a brief bio.

38. "Drinking Song," "Awake." *50 Modern American and British Poets, 1920–1970*. Ed. Louis Untermeyer. New York: David McKay Co., 1973. 214, 215. This anthology also contains a brief biographical sketch of Harrison in the back of the book under the section entitled "The Commentary" where the editor also talks about Harrison's poetry. pp. 348, 349.

39. "Horse," "Traverse City Zoo." *A Book of Animal Poems*. Ed. William Cole. New York: Viking Press, 1973. 69, 202. Illustrated by Robert Andrew Parker. From *Plain Song*.

40. "Cowgirl," "VIII Ghazal," "XXX Ghazal," "V Ghazal." *Shake the Kaleidoscope: A New Anthology of Modern Poetry*. Ed. Milton Klonsky. New York: Pocket Books, February 1973. 290–92. From *Outlyer and Ghazals*.

41. [excerpt] "Outlyer and Ghazals," "Drinking Song," "Awake." *Open Poems: Four Anthologies of Expanded Poems*. Ed. Ronald Gross and George Quasha. New York: Simon and Schuster, 16 April 1973. 91–94.

42. "Letters to Yesenin 1, 2, 3, 4, 5, 6, 7, 8, 9 and 10." *American Poetry Review* 2.3 (May–June 1973): 44–46. This was the first published appearance of these poems. Reprinted in *Letters to Yesenin*. Photo of Harrison by Jill Krementz.

43. "Sergei Yesenin 1895–1925." *Red Cedar Review* 8.2-3 (December 1973): 70. This is the literary magazine from Michigan State University.

## 1975

44. "After Reading Takahashi," "I Was Proud," "Today We Moved." *Heartland II: Poets of the Midwest*. Ed. Lucien Stryk. De Kalb: Northern Illinois University Press, 1975. 100–102. This was the first published appearance of "After Reading Takahashi." "I Was Proud" and "Today We Moved" are taken from *Letters to Yesenin*.

45. "Exercise." *Exercise for Chorus and Tape*. Carl Fischer, New York, 1975. Composed by Lawrence Moss. In 1973, Moss used the poem "Exercise" in a composition he wrote for chorus and tape. The premier of this piece was at the National Gallery in Washington DC on 7 April 1974. Moss later rearranged this piece for soprano and tape, retitling it "Hear This Touch," and recording it in 1980 with Orion Recordings.

46. [excerpt] "Letters to Yesenin." *Great Lakes Review: A Journal of Midwest Life* 2.1 (Summer 1975): 30–31. Ed. Gerald Nemanic. Poem is included in the larger section entitled "Poetry: A Gallery of Midwest Poets." Appearance also includes a photo of Harrison by LaVerne H. Clark.

47. "Sketch for a Job Application Blank," "Suite to Fathers," "Locations." *The American Poetry Anthology*. Ed. Daniel Halpern. New York: Equinox Books, October 1975. 142–53.

48. [untitled]. *Noise Number 4*. Ed. Don McClelland. San Francisco: NP, December 1975. This was the first published appearance of this poem. This poster-size item is folded to make 9 panels and states: "Noise is a poetry poster series collected by photocopy and chain letter methods." Other contributors include Galway Kinnell, Allen Ginsberg, Dan Gerber, and Gary Snyder.

## 1976

49. "Jim–Age 38, 5'10", W. 196, Strapping Goggle-Eyed Nordic Bankrupt." *The Face of Poetry: 101 Poets in Two Significant Decades—the 60's and the 70's.* Ed. LaVerne Harrell. Clark and Mary MacArthur. Arlington VA: Gallimaufry Press, 1976. 114–15. Photographic portraits by LaVerne Harrell. Clark. Harrison photo entitled "Jim Harrison (November 1970)." Limited to 1,000 copies in wraps. This was the first published appearance of this poem. This is actually the third stanza of *Returning to Earth*.

50. "Letters to Yesenin 1, 2, 8, 9, 17, 18, and 19." *The Third Coast: Contemporary Michigan Poetry.* Ed. Conrad Hilberry, Herbert Scott, and James Tipton. Detroit: Wayne State University Press, 1976. 72–78.

51. "After Reading Takahashi," "Hello Walls," "Clear Water 3," "Clear Water 4," "Weeping." *Aisling* 7–8 (Summer 1976): 6–11. LaMarque TX. The Harrison piece is entitled "Five Poems by Jim Harrison." This issue also contains a review of *Letters to Yesenin* by Jim Hubert. This was the first published appearance of all these poems except "After Reading Takahashi." A photo of Harrison by Dan Gerber appears on the cover of this issue. Reprinted in *Selected and New Poems*.

52. "Walking," "The Chatham Ghazal." *Agenda* 13.4/14.1 (Winter–Spring 1976): 44–45. Ed. William Cookson and Grey Gowrie. *Agenda* is published in London, England, and this is the "US Poetry" special issue.

53. "The Chatham Ghazal." *American Poetry Review* 5.2 (March–April 1976): 20. This was the first published appearance of this poem. Reprinted in *Selected and New Poems*.

## 1977

54. [excerpt] "Returning to Earth." *Ploughshares* 4.1 (1977): 43–47. This was the first published appearance of this poem.

55. "The Woman from Spiritwood," "Gathering April." *Poetry Now* 3.4–6 (1977): 66, 67. Ed. E. V. Griffith. This was the first published appearances of these poems. These poems were later published in *Selected and New Poems*. This issue also contains a photo of Harrison that is credited to O. Gerbil. The credit should be to Dan Gerber.

## 1978

56. "Marriage Ghazal." *Poetry Now* 4.1 (1978): 13. Ed. E. V. Griffith. This was the first published appearance of this poem. This poem was later published in *Selected and New Poems*.

## 1979

57. "Horse." *My Mane Catches the Wind: Poems about Horses*. Ed. Lee Bennett Hopkins. New York: Harcourt Brace Jovanovich, 1979. 27. Reprints the Harrison poem that first appeared in *Plain Song*.

58. "Horse." *The Poetry of Horses*. Ed. William Cole. New York: Charles Scribner's Sons, 1979. 63. Reprints the Harrison poem that first appeared in *Plain Song*.

## 1980

59. [excerpt] "Letters to Yesenin." *Smoke Signals* 2.1 (1980–81): 35. Ed. Mike Golden. Stanzas 2 and 19. There is also an additional quote from *Letters to Yesenin* on p. 74.

## 1982

60. "Drinking Song." *Wetting Our Lines Together: An Anthology of Recent North American Fishing Poems*. Ed. Allen Hoey. Syracuse NY: Tamarack Editions, 1982. 60.

61. "Walter of Battersea," "Waiting," "The Woman from Spiritwood," "Not Writing My Name," "Followers," "Rooster," "Epithalamium," "After Reading Takahashi." *American Poetry Review* 11.4 (July–August 1982): 3–4. From *Selected and New Poems*. This issue features Harrison on the cover. Photo by Bob Wargo.

## 1983

62. "Suite to Fathers." *Divided Light: Father and Son Poems: A 20th Century American Anthology*. Ed. Jason Shinder. Riverdale-on-Hudson NY: Sheep Meadow Press, 1983. 217–21.

## 1986

63. "The Theory and Practice of Rivers." *New Letters* 52.2–3 (Winter–Spring 1986): 177–99. *New Letters* is the literary magazine for the University of Missouri—Kansas City. This was the first published appearance of this poem.

64. "The Brand New Statue of Liberty." *Exquisite Corpse* 4.5–8 (May–August 1986): 15. This was the first published appearance of this poem. From *The Theory and Practice of Rivers and New Poems*.

## 1987

65. "Dusk." *This Delicious Day*. Ed. Paul B. Janeczko. New York: Orchard Books, 1987. 68. This poem originally appeared in *Plain Song*.

66. [excerpt] "Returning to Earth." *The Ploughshares Poetry Reader.* Ed. Joyce Peseroff. Watertown NY: Ploughshares Books, 1987. 125–28.

## 1988

67. [excerpt] "From 'The Theory and Practice of Rivers,'" "Looking forward to Age." *Contemporary Michigan Poetry: Poems from the Third Coast.* Ed. Michael Delp, Conrad Hilberry, and Herbert Scott. Detroit: Wayne State University Press, 1988. 120–25. Photo of Harrison by Bob Wargo.
68. "Drinking Song." *Season of the Angler.* Ed. David Seybold. New York: Weidenfeld & Nicolson, 1988. 125. From *Outlyer and Ghazals*.
69. "Northern Michigan." *Literary Michigan—a Sense of Place, a Sense of Time.* NP: Michigan Council for the Humanities, 1988. vi. This book was assembled to discuss the many contributions of Michigan authors to literature. Besides the poem noted above, the book includes several sections discussing Harrison's fiction, nonfiction, and screenplay work.
70. "Cabin Poem." *Lord John Ten.* Ed. Dennis Etchison. Northridge CA: Lord John Press, 1988. 198–99. This book celebrates the tenth anniversary of Lord John Press. From *The Theory and Practice of Rivers*.
71. "Counting Birds." *Caliban* 5 (1988): 12–13. The dedication for this poem reads "for Gerald Vizenor"; this dedication does not appear in *The Theory and Practice of River and New Poems*, where the poem was later published. This was the first published appearance of this poem.
72. [excerpt] "The Theory and Practice of Rivers." *Traverse* 8.6 (November 1988): 39–41. These poems are included in an article entitled "Northern Visions: Poetry from the Third Coast."

## 1989

73. "Porpoise," "Awake," "Letters to Yesenin." *The Key West Reader: The Best of Key West's Writers, 1830–1990.* Ed. George Murphy. Key West: Tortugas, 1989. 94–96. Also contained in this collection is an excerpt from the novel *A Good Day to Die*.
74. "The Davenport Lunar Eclipse, August 16, 1989." *Caliban* 7 (1989): 22–23. This was the first published appearance of this poem. Reprinted in *After Ikkyu and Other Poems*.
75. "The Idea of Balance Is to Be Found in Herons and Loons." *Amicus Journal* 11.2 (Spring 1989): 31. The journal of the Natural Resources Defense Council. This was the first published appearance of this poem. Reprinted in *The Theory and Practice of Rivers and New Poems*.

## 1990

76. "The Same Goose Moon." *Book for Sensei*. Pacifica CA: Big Bridge Press, 1990. This was the first published appearance of this poem. Other poets appearing in this accordion-binding book designed and illustrated by Nancy Davis are Michael Rothenberg, Michael McClure, Philip Whalen, Joanne Kyger, and Andre Codrescu. This book was published in a signed, limited edition of 26 lettered copies. It was also issued in a limited edition of 100 numbered copies.

77. "Northern Michigan." *American Way* 15 September 1990: 106. From *Plain Song*. This issue also contains a lengthy article about Harrison (see item H37) and an excerpt from the novella "Brown Dog" (see item C15), which appeared in the collection *The Woman Lit by Fireflies*. *American Way* is the in-flight magazine of American Airlines.

## 1991

78. "After Reading Takahashi," "Dogen's Dream," "Counting Birds," "Kobun," "Walking," "The Idea of Balance Is to Be Found in Herons and Loons." *Beneath a Single Moon: Buddhism in Contemporary American Poetry*. Ed. Kent Johnson and Criad Paulenich. Boston: Shambhala Publications, 1991. 124–32. These poems are from *Locations*, *The Theory and Practice of Rivers and New Poems*, and *Selected and New Poems*. This collection also contains the essay "Everyday Life."

79. "Walking," "Poem." *The Forgotten Language: Contemporary Poets and Nature*. Ed. Christopher Merrill. Salt Lake City UT: Peregrine Smith Books, 1991. 69–70. From *Selected and New Poems*.

80. [excerpt] "The Theory and Practice of Rivers." *Leelanau Cellars Vis à Vis White Table Wine*. 1991. This excerpt from the above-referenced poem appeared on the label of this locally produced wine from Omena, Michigan, in Leelanau County, where Harrison lived at the time.

81. [excerpt] "The Theory and Practice of Rivers." *Futures* 9.2 (Summer 1991): 2. This is the magazine for the Michigan State University Agricultural Department.

82. "North at Fifty-Three." *The Sun* 189 (August 1991): 29. This is the first published appearance of this poem.

## 1992

83. [excerpt] "The Theory and Practice of Rivers." NP, 1992. Printed on an 18" by 23½" poster that was done for the 1992 Michigan Writers Symposium sponsored by Michigan State University. This poster also reprints excerpts from Dan Gerber, Richard Ford, and Ted Weesner.

84. [excerpt] "The Theory and Practice of Rivers." *Hua Hu Ching: The Teachings of Lao Tzu*. By Brian Walker. Livingston MT: Clark City Press, 1992. x (acknowledgments). Reprinted as *Hua Hu Ching: The Unknown Teachings of Lao Tzu*. New York: HarperCollins, 1994. x.

**1993**

85. "Lullaby for a Daughter." *More Light: Father and Daughter Poems: A Twentieth-Century American Selection*. Ed. Jason Shinder. New York: Harcourt Brace & Co., 1993. 85.
86. "Coyote No. 1." *Cutbank* 39 (Winter 1993): 78. This is the literary magazine from the University of Montana. Reprinted in *After Ikkyu and Other Poems*.
87. [excerpt] "The Theory and Practice of Rivers." *The Riverwatch* January 1993. The quarterly newsletter of the Anglers of the Au Sable, Grayling MI.

**1994**

88. "Frog." *Poetry from A to Z*. Ed. Paul B. Janeczko. New York: Bradbury Press, 1994. 34. Illustrated by Cathy Bobak. From *Selected and New Poems*.
89. "Sonoran Radio." *Antaeus: The Final Issue* 75–76 (Autumn 1994): 265. This was the first published appearance of this poem. Reprinted in *After Ikkyu and Other Poems*.

**1995**

90. "Morning." *Wherever Home Begins: 100 Contemporary Poems*. Selected by Paul B. Janeczko. New York: Orchard Books, 1995. 9. From *Selected and New Poems*.
91. [excerpt] "Letters to Yesenin." *A Year in Poetry: A Treasury of Classic and Modern Verses for Every Date on the Calendar*. Ed. Thomas E. Foster and Elizabeth C. Guthrie. New York: Crown Publishers, 1995. 279–80.
92. "Time Suite." *Northwest Review* 33.2 (May 1995): 100. This was the first published appearance of this poem. Reprinted in *After Ikkyu and Other Poems*.

**1996**

93. "Followers." *Road Trips, Head Trips and Other Car Crazed Writings*. Ed. Jean Lindamood. New York: Atlantic Monthly, 1996. 104–05. From *Selected and New Poems*.
94. "Return to Yesenin." *The Party Train*. Ed. Robert Alexander, Mark Vinz, and C. W. Truesdale. Minneapolis: New Rivers Press, 1996. 168. This was the first published appearance of this poem.
95. "Time Suite." *American Poets Say Goodbye to the 20th Century*. Ed. Andrei

Codrescu and Laura Rosenthal. New York: Four Walls Eight Windows, 1996. 149–54.

96. [excerpt] "After Ikkyu." *Tricycle: The Buddhist Review* 5.3 (Spring 1996): 64–70. Stanzas 1, 2, 3, 8, 10, 11, 13, 15, 17, 19, 21, 23, 24, 25, 26, 28, 30, 31, 32, 34, 35, 37, 39, 40, 41, 42, 43, 44, 45, 46, 48, 49, 50, 51, 52, 53, 54, 55, 56, 57. This was the first published appearance of these poems. Reprinted in *After Ikkyu and Other Poems*.

## 1997

97. "A Year's Changes." *The Sumac Reader*. Ed. Joseph Bednarik. East Lansing: Michigan State University Press, 1997. 38–43. This book was published in a limited edition of 26 lettered copies and 100 numbered copies signed by Harrison, Dan Gerber, and Joseph Bednarik. The trade edition was published in wrappers. A selection of poems and essays from the literary journal *Sumac*, which Harrison and Gerber edited from 1968 to 1971. Harrison also supplies an introduction for this book.

98. "Dogen's Dream." *Dharma Family Treasures: Sharing Mindfulness with Children*. Ed. Sandy Eastoak. Berkeley CA: North Atlantic Books, 1997. 277. From *Selected and New Poems*.

99. "Sonoran Radio." *Border Beat* 3 (January–February 1997): 14–19. Reprinted in *After Ikkyu and Other Poems*.

## 1998

100. "After the Anonymous Swedish." *World Poetry: An Anthology of Verse from Antiquity to Our Time*. Ed. Katharine Washburn and John Major. New York: Quality Paperback Book Club (Norton), 1998. 634–35. The general editor of the anthology is Clifton Fadiman. This is a curious citation in that the editors of this anthology state that this poem is a translation from the Swedish (ca. 1650), that its author is anonymous, and that the title of the poem is "Deep in the Forest." They further state that James Harrison is the translator. This entry is not a translation and was included in his second poetry collection, *Locations*.

101. [excerpt] "After Ikkyu." *Copper Canyon Press Catalog*. Fall–Winter 1998. 1. This poem is contained in a full-page ad for Harrison's then-new poetry retrospective *The Shape of the Journey*, published by Copper Canyon in 1998.

102. [excerpts] "North," "Time Suite," "Poem 19," "Poem 41," "Poem 29." "France." By Rick Bass. *Five Points* 2.2 (Winter 1998): 149–88. Although this essay is not strictly about Harrison, much of it does deal with Harrison's influence on Bass. There is also a short excerpt from *Legends of the Fall*.

## 1999

103. "Missy 1966–1971." *Funeral and Memorial Service Readings: Poems and Tributes*. Ed. Rachel R. Baum. Jefferson NC: McFarland & Co., 1999. 91. Poem first appeared in *Letters to Yesenin*.
104. [excerpt] "Fair/Boy Christian Takes a Break." *Halflives: Reconciling Work and Wildness*. By Brooke Williams. Boulder CO: Johnson Books, 1999. 51. A short except from the above-referenced poem appears as an epigraph at the beginning of pt. 2 of this book.
105. "Gathering April." *Big Sky Journal* 6.2 (Spring 1999): 100. Contained in the "Back Forty" column. From *Selected and New Poems*.

## 2000

106. "Cardinal." *The Truth of the Trees*. Arranged by Dick Bennett. Fayetteville AR, 2000. 36. A Harrison poem was included in this spiral-bound booklet printed to protest the cutting of a stand of trees in Fayetteville, Arkansas, in the summer of 2000.
107. [excerpt] "Geo-Bestiary." *New Poems from the Third Coast: Contemporary Michigan Poetry*. Ed. Michael Delp, Conrad Hilberry, and Josie Kearns. Detroit MI: Wayne State University Press, 2000. 86–91. Stanzas 1, 2, 7, 8, 10, 12, 16, 19, 26, 28, and 34. From *The Shape of the Journey*.
108. "Letters to Yesenin." *The Body Electric: America's Best Poetry from the American Poetry Review*. Ed. Stephen Berg, David Bonano, and Arthur Vogelsang. New York: W. W. Norton & Co., 2000. 241–46. From *Letters to Yesenin*.
109. "My Friend the Bear," "Bear." *Grrrr: A Collection of Poems about Bears*. Ed. C. B. Follett. Sausalito CA: Arctos Press, 2000. 54, 64–65. From *The Theory and Practice of Rivers and New Poems, After Ikkyu,* and *The Shape of the Journey*.
110. "Portal, Arizona." *The Blind See Only This World—Poems for John Wieners*. Ed. William Corbett, Michael Gizzi, and Joseph Torra. New York: Granary Books; Boston: Pressed Wafer, 2000. 54. Book printed in wraps only. The first appearance of this poem was in the *Pressed Wafer Broadsides,* for John Wieners, done in 1999.
111. "Cobra," "Counting Birds." *The Boilerplate Rhino*. By David Quammen. New York: Charles Scribner's Sons, 2000. 63, 181–83, 186.
112. "A Domestic Poem for Portia," "Lullaby for a Daughter." *Teaching the Art of Poetry*. By Baron Wormser and David Cappella. Mahwah NJ: Lawrence Erlbaum Associates, 2000. 53, 221–22.
113. [excerpt] "The Theory and Practice of Rivers." *Fall 2000 Poetry Catalog from Copper Canyon Press*. 2000. 15.
114. "Sergei Yesenin 1895–1925." *Red Cedar Review* 35.2 (Winter–Spring 2000): 20.

This issue also contains a lengthy interview with Harrison conducted by Carrie Preston and Anthony Michel.

**2001**

115. "March Walk." *A Writer's Country: A Collection of Fiction and Poetry.* Ed. Jeff Knorr and Tim Schell. Upper Saddle River NJ: Prentice-Hall, 2001. 289. From *Selected and New Poems*.
116. "Letter Poem to Sam Hamill and Dan Gerber." *Brick* 68 (Fall 2001): 124. This poem was also reprinted in the program for the Lannan Foundation's "Reading and Conversations" series to honor Jim Harrison and Peter Lewis on 27. February 2001. On the program the poem is dated 20 June 2001. Another poem entitled "Older Love" is contained in this program and is dated 29 December 1998.
117. "Old Days." *New York Times Book Review* 21 January 2001: 22. This was the first published appearance of this poem.
118. "Cabin Poem," "The Idea of Balance Is to Be Found in Herons and Loons." *Heron Dance* 30 (April 2001): 1, 72. Both these poems were published in *The Theory and Practice of Rivers and New Poems*.
119. "Older Love." *The Writer's Almanac* 10 December 2001. www.writersalmanac.publicradio.org. Published in an online format only.

**2002**

120. "Birthday." *Birthday Poems: A Celebration.* Ed. Jason Shinder. New York: Thunder's Mouth Press, 2002. 136.
121. "The Bear," "Older Love," "November," "Joe's Poem," "Marquette Beach to Larry Sullivan." *Five Points* 6.2 (2002): 39–66. This is the literary journal for the Georgia State University Press edited by David Bottoms. This was the first published appearance of these poems. This issue also contains an interview with Harrison conducted by Joseph Bednarik.
122. "Bars: A Poem." *Men's Journal* January 2002: 61. Included in the article "The 50 Best Bars." This was the first published appearance of this poem.
123. "Twilight." *Traverse* 21.8 (January 2002): 31. This poem is included in an essay that Harrison wrote as a farewell to Leelanau County, Michigan—his home of 35 years.

**2003**

124. [excerpts] *Braided Creek*, "The Theory and Practice of Rivers." *Spring–Summer 2003 Catalog from Copper Canyon Press*. 2003. 9, 35.
125. [excerpt] *Braided Creek*. Copper Canyon Press, *Report to Friends, Fall 2003*. 2003. 11.

Newsletter and financial statement from Copper Canyon Press for 2003 sent to members of the press. Also mention of Harrison on p. 12 in relation to the thirtieth anniversary of Copper Canyon Press.

126. "Geo-Bestiary #X," "Word Drunk," [excerpt] *Braided Creek*. *This Art: Poems about Poetry*. Ed. Michael Weigers. Port Townsend WA: Copper Canyon Press, 2003. 7, 47, 105.

127. [excerpts] "Geo-Bestiary," *Braided Creek*. *Fall–Winter 2003–2004 Catalog from Copper Canyon Press*. 2003. 18, 19. Excerpted from "Geo-Bestiary" is stanza 12.

128. "Ghazal XXXIX." *Visiting Walt: Poems Inspired by the Life and Work of Walt Whitman*. Ed. Sheila Coghill and Thom Tammaro. Iowa City: University of Iowa Press, 2003. 84. This poem was first published in *The Shape of the Journey*.

129. "Poem of War." *Poets against the War*. Ed. Sam Hamill. New York: Thunder's Mouth Press/Nation Books, 2003. 98–99. Harrison's poem is dated 13 February 2003. This was the first published appearance of this poem. This poem also appears on the Poets against War Web site: www.poetsagainstthewar.org.

130. [excerpt] "Dancing." *Dancer*. By Colum McCann. New York: Metropolitan Books, 2003. 219. A small portion of the poem "Dancing" appears as an epigraph at the beginning of bk. 3 of this novel.

131. "Young Love." *Exquisite Corpse: A Journal of Letters and Life* Online Issue 13 (Winter 2003). Online journal www.corpse.org. Poem is dated September 2002 and was published in an online format only. This is the first published appearance of this poem.

132. "Despond." *The Writer's Almanac* 20 January 2003. www.writersalmanac.publicradio.org. Published in an online format only. This was the first published appearance of this poem. This poem also appeared again in the 20 January 2006 installment of the Web site.

133. "Grumpy Old Men." *Men's Journal* June 2003: 26. Under the heading "Agenda Books." Reprints the poem "I grow older. I still like women, but mostly I like Mexican food." From *Braided Creek*.

## 2004

134. "Northern Michigan." *Literature and Its Writers*. Ed. Ann Charters and Samuel Charters. 3rd ed. Boston: Bedford/St. Martin's Press, 2004. 808. The previous two editions of this textbook did not include this poem.

135. "March Walk." *An Introduction to Poetry: The River Sings*. Ed. Jeff Knorr. Upper Saddle River NJ: Prentice-Hall, 2004. 16. Also has a brief quote from Harrison on p. 10. This poem is from *Selected and New Poems*.

136. [excerpt] *Braided Creek. Spring 2004 Catalog of New and Forthcoming Titles from Copper Canyon Press.* 2004. 21. Four poems from the Harrison/Kooser collection.

137. "Cabin Poem." *Fishing Idaho: An Angler's Guide.* By Joe Evancho. 2nd ed. Boise ID: Cutthroat Press, 2004. 3.

138. "After Ikkyu #51," "After Ikkyu #20," "After Ikkyu #19," "From Time Suite," "After Ikkyu #29," "After Ikkyu #24," "Lullaby for a Daughter." *Time Suite: Poems by Jim Harrison.* NP, 2004. Set to music by Alden Jenks. Also a recorded CD titled *Time Suite* recorded 13 November 2005. Performance by Allen Shearer, baritone, with Timothy Bach, piano, at the San Francisco Conservatory of Music, Hellman Hall.

139. [excerpt] "The Theory and Practice of Rivers." *Grieving God's Way.* By Margaret Brownley. Enumclaw WA: Winepress Publishing, 2004. 167.

140. "After the War." *Exquisite Corpse: A Journal of Letters and Life* Online Issue 14 (Spring 2004). Online journal www.corpse.org. Poem was published in an online format only. This is the first published appearance of this poem.

141. "Time." *Brick* 73 (Summer 2004): 145. This poem was part of Harrison's food essay column "Eat or Die." This was the first published appearance of this poem.

142. "Saving the Daylight," "Adding It Up," "Easter Morning," "Endgames." *Open City* 19 (Summer–Fall 2004): 21–26. This was the first published appearance of these poems, with the exception of "Easter Morning."

143. "A Letter to Ted and Dan." *Dunes Review* 9.2 (Winter 2004): 24. This was the first published appearance of this poem.

144. "Easter Morning." *The Writer's Almanac* 18 May 2004. www.writersalmanac.publicradio.org. Published in an online format only. This was the first published appearance of this poem. This poem appeared again on *The Writer's Almanac* on 18 May 2006.

## 2005

145. [excerpt] *Braided Creek. Fall and Winter 2004–2005 Catalog of New and Forthcoming Titles.* Copper Canyon Press, 2005. 16. Four poems from the Harrison/Kooser collection.

146. [excerpt] *Braided Creek. Spring–Summer 2005 New Titles, Recent Releases, Translations, Broadsides, Complete Titles Listing.* Copper Canyon Press, 2005. 12, 51. Three poems from the Harrison/Kooser collection. Also in this catalog is Harrison's poem "Word Drunk," which was published in the 2003 Copper Canyon collection *This Art: Poems about Poetry.*

147. [excerpt] *Braided Creek. Copper Canyon Press, Fall–Winter 2005–2006.* 2005. 14. Three poems from the Harrison/Kooser collection.

148. "Easter Morning." *Good Poems for Hard Times*. Ed. Garrison Keillor. New York: Viking Press, 2005. 122–23. The first appearance of this poem was on Keillor's online literary journal *The Writer's Almanac* (see item B144).

149. "Alcohol." *Brick* 75 (Summer 2005). Page 17 of an unpaginated pamphlet that was inserted into the above-noted issue. The publication of this handwritten poem was an advertisement for an upcoming fund-raising auction that *Brick* was holding in which a number of authors donated manuscript pages and other autograph ephemera to raise money for the magazine. These auctions were held on the online auction service eBay, and it is interesting to note that the Harrison manuscript sold for over $1,700. This was the first published appearance of this poem.

150. "An Old Man," "Brothers and Sisters." *Midwest Quarterly* 46.4 (Summer 2005): 386–87. The *Midwest Quarterly* is a journal of contemporary thought published by Pittsburg State University in Pittsburg, Kansas. This special issue is a tribute to Ted Kooser, the U.S. poet laureate at the time. This was the first published appearance of these poems.

151. "Angry Women," "Cabbage," "L'Envoi," "Two Girls," "On the Way to the Doctor's," "Alcohol." *New Letters* 71.3 (Summer–Fall 2005): 81–87. *New Letters* is the literary magazine for the University of Missouri–Kansas City. This was the first published appearance of these poems, with the exception of "Alcohol," which appeared in *Brick* a few weeks earlier (see item B149).

152. "Memorial Day," "Effluvia." *TriQuarterly* 121 (August 2005): 154–56. This was the first published appearance of these poems. This is the literary magazine from Northwestern University.

## 2006

153. "Poem of War." *American Protest Literature*. Ed. Zoe Trodd. Cambridge MA: Belknap Press of Harvard University Press, 2006. 504, 505.

154. "On the Way to the Doctor's." *The Best American Poetry 2006*. Ed. Billy Collins and David Lehman. New York: Charles Scribner's Sons, 2006. 53, 54.

155. "Cabbage," [excerpt] *Braided Creek*, [excerpt] "Looking forward to Age." *Copper Canyon Press, Spring–Summer 2006, New and Recent Titles*. 2006. 4, 25, 48.

156. [excerpt] "Mother Night." *Quotes and Reflections for 365 Days*. Vol. 2 of *Daily Spirit Journal*. By John P. Cock. Greensboro NC: Transcribe Books, 2006. 176.

157. [excerpt] "The Theory and Practice of Rivers." *Finding Lily*. By Richard Clewes. Toronto: Key Porter Books, 2006. 73. A short excerpt from the poem appears as an epigraph at the start of chap. 7.

158. [excerpt] "Sketch for a Job Application Blank." *A Dash of Style: The Art and*

*Mastery of Punctuation*. By Noah Lukeman. New York: W. W. Norton & Co., 2006. 197.

159. "Mom and Dad," [excerpt] *Braided Creek*. Copper Canyon Press, Fall–Winter 2006–2007. 2006. 13, 44.

160. [excerpt] "The Theory and Practice of Rivers." An advertisement for a new facility being opened on the campus of the Oregon Health and Science University School of Nursing in January 2007.

161. "To a Meadowlark," "Reading Calasso." *Five Points* 10.1–2 (Spring 2006): 241, 242. Tenth anniversary issue.

162. [excerpt] *Braided Creek*, "Dream Love," "Older Love." *Bliss Santa Fe* 5 (Summer 2006): 4, 51. This issue also contains an interview with Harrison.

163. "Barking." *Brick* 78 (Winter 2006): 57. This was the first published appearance of this poem. This issue also contains a food essay by Harrison.

164. "Modern Times," "Dream Love," "Becoming," "Hakuin and Welch." *American Poetry Review* 35.1 (January–February 2006): 11–13. This was the first published appearance of these poems.

165. [excerpt] *Braided Creek*. *Lannan Readings and Conversations 2005–2006*. Program for the event held in Santa Fe, New Mexico, on 18 January 2006 featuring a reading and conversation with Harrison and Ted Kooser. The program reprints all the poems printed on pp. 6–9 of *Braided Creek*. The Lannan Foundation also printed a small excerpt from *Braided Creek* to use in its 2005–06 "Readings and Conversation" series catalog, which has a full listing of all the writers featured in the series for the fall 2005 and winter–spring 2006 season.

166. "Science." *The Writer's Almanac* 8 May 2006. www.writersalmanac.public radio.org. Published in an online format only.

167. "Mother Night." *The Writer's Almanac* 12 May 2006. www.writersalmanac .publicradio.org. Published in an online format only.

### 2007

168. "Rooster." *A Garden of Forking Paths: An Anthology for Creative Writers*. Ed. Beth Anstandig and Eric Killough. Upper Saddle River NJ: Pearson Education, 2007. 314, 315.

169. [excerpt] *Braided Creek*. *Saints of Hysteria: A Half-Century of Collaborative American Poetry*. Ed. Denise Duhamel, Maureen Seaton, and David Trinidad. Brooklyn NY: Small Skull Press, 2007. 349–50.

170. "Larson's Holstein Bull." *Poems across the Big Sky*. Ed. Lowell Jaeger. Kalispell MT: Many Voice Press of Flathead Valley Community College, 2007. 87.

171. "The Bear," [excerpt] *Braided Creek*. Copper Canyon Press, Spring–Summer 2007. 2007. 22, 37.
172. "Cabbage," "From 23," [excerpt] *Braided Creek*. Copper Canyon Press, Fall–Winter 2007–2008. 2007. 6, 7, 42. Catalog.
173. "Another Old Mariachi." *Open City* 23 (Spring–Summer 2007): 95. This was the first published appearance of this poem. This issue also contains a fiction piece by Harrison.
174. "Larson's Holstein Bull." *Brick* 79 (Summer 2007): 148. This was the first published appearance of this poem. This issue also contains a food essay by Harrison.
175. "Burning the Ditches," "Land Divers." *Narrative Magazine* 1 (Fall 2007): 21, 22. This was the first published appearance of these poems. The title at the beginning of these poems is "Two Poems."
176. "Becoming." *The Writer's Almanac* 24 July 2007. www.writersalmanac.publicradio.org. Published in an online format only. First published in *Saving Daylight*.
177. "Brothers and Sisters." *The Writer's Almanac* 2 August 2007. www.writersalmanac.publicradio.org. Published in an online format only. First published in *Saving Daylight*.

**2008**

178. "To a Meadowlark." *The Wide Open: Prose, Poetry, and Photographs of the Prairie*. Ed. Annick Smith and Susan O'Conner. Lincoln: University of Nebraska Press, 2008. 42. This anthology also contains Harrison's essay "Don't Fence Me In" (see item D274).
179. "Birds Again," "To Rose," [excerpt] "Letters to Yesenin," [excerpt] *Braided Creek*. Copper Canyon Press, Spring–Summer 2008 Catalog. 2008. 30, 31, 52.
180. "Poem of War (I)" [excerpt] "Letters to Yesenin." Copper Canyon Press, Fall 2008/ Winter 2009 Catalog. 2008: 20–21.
181. "Mapman," "Early Fishing," "Fibber," "On Horseback in China," "Sunday Discordancies," "My Leader." *Five Points* 12.2 (2008): 7–15. This was the first appearance of these poems.
182. "Eleven Dawns with Su Tung-p'o." *Brick* 81 (Summer 2008): 52–55. This was the first published appearance of this poem. This issue also contains a food essay by Harrison.
183. "Three Poems in Search of Small Gods," "Hard Times," "Easter 2008," "Larson's Holstein Bull." *Conjunctions* 51 (Fall 2008): 400, 401. The Death Issue. *Conjunctions* is the literary magazine from Bard College. This was the first published appearance of the poems "Hard Times" and "Easter 2008."

184. "The Quarter." *The Writer's Almanac* 2 May 2008. Published in an online format only. This was the first published appearance of this poem. www.writersalmanac.publicradio.org.
185. "Mother Night." *The Writer's Almanac* 12 May 2008. Published in an online format only. www.writersalmanac.publicradio.org.
186. "Easter Morning." *The Writer's Almanac* 18 May 2008. Published in an online format only. www.writersalmanac.publicradio.org.
187. "Barking." *Poetry* 192.5 (September 2008): 464. This poem will appear in Harrison's new collection of poetry from Copper Canyon Press in 2009.
188. "Alien." *Earth First Journal* 28.5 (September–October 2008): 23. This was the first published appearance of this poem.
189. "New World." *Orion* 27.6 (November–December 2008): 70. This was the first published appearance of this poem.

# Section C
## *Individually Published Fiction*

**1971**

1. [excerpt] *Wolf. Works in Progress Number 4.* New York: Literary Guild of America, 1971. 305–20. An excerpt from *Wolf*. This excerpt was the first published appearance of any portion of *Wolf*.

**1979**

2. "Legends of the Fall." *Esquire* 2–16 January 1979: 35–69. This novella was the longest piece of fiction *Esquire* had published up to this point. This was the first published appearance of this novella. Illustrated by John Thompson. Also published in *Great Fiction from the New Esquire Fortnightly*. New York: N. E. Corp., 1979. 66–95. Reprints the entire novella as it appeared in the January 1979 *Esquire*, complete with all the Thompson illustrations.
3. "Revenge." *Esquire* 8 May 1979: 58–80. An edited version of the novella that appeared in *Legends of the Fall*. This was the first published appearance of this novella. Illustrated by John Thompson.

**1980**

4. [excerpt] *Wolf. Smoke Signals* 2.1 (1980): 73.

**1981**

5. [excerpt] *Warlock. Smoke Signals* 2.2–3 (1981): 20–21. This excerpt is in "The White Line Issue." This was the first published appearance of this excerpt from *Warlock*.

**1982**

6. "Dog Hunter." *The Third Coast: Contemporary Michigan Fiction*. Ed. James Tipton and Robert E. Wegner. Detroit MI: Wayne State University Press, 1982.

89–94. An excerpt from *Farmer*. Excerpt also has a picture of Harrison with a brief bio.

### 1984

7. "Sundog: A Leelanau Peninsula Author Begins the Long, Painful Journey Back toward Earth." *Michigan: The Magazine of the Detroit News* 24 June 1984: 22, 24. A short excerpt from Harrison's just-released novel *Sundog*.

### 1987

8. "No Man Is in Iceland." *Caliban* 2 (1987): 70–74. This is the first published appearance of this short story.

### 1988

9. "*Dalva*: How It Happened to Me." *Esquire* April 1988: 185–92.
10. [excerpt] *Dalva*. *The Sun* 189 (August 1988): 40. This very brief quote from *Dalva* is in the "Sunbeams" section at the rear of the magazine. Reprinted later in *Sunbeams: A Book of Quotations*. Ed. Sy Safransky. Berkeley CA: North Atlantic Books, 1990. 140.

### 1989

11. [excerpt] *A Good Day to Die*. *The Key West Reader*. Ed. George Murphy. Key West FL: Tortugas, 1989. 97–109.
12. "How It Happened to Me." *The Best of the West 2: New Short Stories from the Wide Side of the Missouri*. Ed. James Thomas and Denise Thomas. Salt Lake City UT: Peregrine Smith Books, 1989. 223–44. From *Dalva*.

### 1990

13. "The Sunset Limited." *Smart* 2 (January–February 1990): 93–112. A shorter version of the novella that appears in *The Woman Lit by Fireflies*. This was the first published appearance of this novella.
14. "The Woman Lit by Fireflies." *New Yorker* 23 July 1990: 25–26. A slightly different version than the final novella published under the same name. This was the first published appearance of this novella.
15. "The Woman Lit by Fireflies." *American Way* 15 September 1990: 112–15. Although titled as referenced above, the piece is actually an excerpt from the novella "Brown Dog." *American Way* is the American Airlines in-flight magazine. This issue also has an article about Harrison with photos of Lake Leelanau and the Upper Peninsula of Michigan.

## 1991

16. [excerpts] "Legends of the Fall," "Revenge," *Warlock*. *In the Beginning: Great First Lines from Your Favorite Books*. Ed. Hans Bauer. San Francisco: Chronicle Books, 1991. 89, 147, 180. This is a collection of opening sentences from over 500 novels.

## 1993

17. "Julip: An Entertainment." *Esquire* March 1993: 127–50. vol. 119, no. 3. This was the first published appearance of this novella.

## 1996

18. "The Woman Lit by Fireflies." *Changing the Bully Who Rules the World*. Ed. Carol Bly. Minneapolis: Milkweed Editions, 1996. 216–71.

## 1997

19. [excerpt] *Wolf*. *Wolf Walking*. Ed. Edwin Daniels. New York: Stewart, Tamori & Chang, 1997. 46–47. Illustrations by Judi Rideout.
20. [excerpts] "Legends of the Fall," "The Man Who Gave Up His Name." *Elements of the Writing Craft*. By Robert Olmstead. Cincinnati: Story Press, 1997. 142, 171.

## 1998

21. [excerpt] *The Road Home*. Grove Atlantic Catalog. Fall 1998. 8–9.

## 2000

22. "The Beast God Forgot to Invent: A Modern Parable." *Men's Journal* June 2000: 145–56. vol. 9, no. 5. An edited version of the novella that appeared in the fall of 2000. This was the first published appearance of this story.

## 2001

23. "From Farmer." *On Killing: Meditations on the Chase*. Ed. Robert F. Jones. Guilford CT: Lyons Press, 2001. 49–54. Excerpt from *Farmer*. There is a short biography of Harrison on p. 241.

## 2002

24. [excerpt] *The Road Home*. *Three Junes*. By Julia Glass. New York: Pantheon Books, 2002. This sentence appears as an epigraph at the beginning of this novel.
25. [excerpt] *A Good Day to Die*. *Gigantic*. By Marc Nesbitt. New York: Grove

Press, 2002. This sentence appears as an epigraph at the beginning of this novel.

**2004**

26. "Father Daughter." *New Yorker* 29 March 2004: 86–90. This is the first published appearance of this short story.
27. "From Farmer." *Birds in the Hand: Fiction and Poetry about Birds.* Ed. Dylan Nelson and Kent Nelson. New York: North Point Press, 2004. 249–53. Excerpt from *Farmer.*
28. [excerpt] "Revenge." *Write Away: One Novelist's Approach to Fiction and the Writing Life.* By Elizabeth George. New York: HarperCollins, 2004. 130–32.

**2005**

29. [excerpts] "Westward Ho," "The Beast God Forgot to Invent," "Legends of the Fall." *Pacific Dream.* By John Illig. Oakland OR: Elderberry Press, 2005. 16, 25, 174. Excerpts from the above-noted works were used as epigraphs at the beginnings of three chapters for this book on the Pacific Crest Trail.

**2006**

30. [excerpts] "The Woman Lit by Fireflies," "Julip," *The Road Home, Off to the Side, Dalva, Wolf,* and *Farmer. Rooted: Seven Midwest Writers of Place.* Ed. David Pichaske. Iowa City: University of Iowa Press, 2006. 263–96.

**2007**

31. "Arizona II." *Open City* 23 (Spring–Summer 2007): 89–93. This was the first published appearance of this chapter of Harrison's forthcoming novel *The English Major.*
32. [excerpt] "Brown Dog." *Hooked: Write Fiction That Grabs Readers at Page One and Never Lets Them Go.* By Les Edgerton. Cincinnati: Writer's Digest Books, 2007. 197.

**2008**

33. "Arizona II." *Narrative Magazine* 6 (Spring 2008): 34–38. Edited by Kira Petersons. This excerpt from *The English Major* appeared only in the online pages of *Narrative Magazine* in a section entitled "Works in Progress."
34. "Outcast." *Best Life* August 2008: 102–09. vol. 5, no. 6. This is the first published appearance of this short story. A short bio of Harrison appears on p. 14 in the "Contributors" section.

# Section D
## *Individually Published Nonfiction*

**1964**
1. Letter. *Contact* 4.3 (January–February 1964): 3. Ed. Kenneth Lamott, Calvin Kentfield, and Evan S. Connell Jr. A letter to the editor concerning an essay that *Contact* printed on the poet William Carlos Williams. The letter is signed "J. Harrison, Brookline, Mass." It should be noted that this is Harrison's first published work. This is the first and only published appearance of this letter.

**1969**
2. "Editorial Note." *Sumac* 1.3 (Spring 1969): 106. A note from the editors—Jim Harrison and Dan Gerber—concerning the direction of future issues of *Sumac*. This is the first and only published appearance of this short essay.

**1970**
3. "Dear George Hitchcock." Letter. *Kayak* 23 (1970): 26–27. This is a letter published in the "Correspondence" section. This is the first and only published appearance on this letter.
4. "Charles Olson." *Sumac* 2.2–3 (Winter–Spring 1970): 242. An obituary for the poet Charles Olson. This is the first and only published appearance of this essay. Harrison was coeditor with Dan Gerber of *Sumac*.
5. "A Note." *Sumac* 3.1 (Fall 1970): 136. A note from the editors—Jim Harrison and Dan Gerber—concerning the direction of future issues of *Sumac* and announcing the addition of Thomas McGuane as the journal's fiction editor. This is the first and only published appearance of this short essay.
6. "The Real Fun of the Fair Was the Horse Pulling." *Sports Illustrated* 31 August 1970: 55, 56. vol. 33, no. 9. This essay appears in a column titled "Yesterday."

This essay formed the basis for the essay "A Memoir of Horse Pulling" that later appeared in *Just Before Dark*.

**1971**

7. "A Chat with a Novelist." *Sumac* 4.1 (Fall 1971): 121–29. Reprinted in *Just Before Dark*. Also reprinted in *Conversations with Jim Harrison*. Ed. Robert DeMott. Jackson: University Press of Mississippi, 2002. 3–8. Also reprinted in *Conversations with Thomas McGuane*. Ed. Beef Torrey. Jackson: University Press of Press, 2007. 3–9. (Also contained in *Conversations with Thomas McGuane* are many references to Harrison's work and career.) Harrison interviewing author Thomas McGuane. This is the first published appearance of this interview. Harrison was coeditor with Dan Gerber of *Sumac*.

8. "A Plaster Trout in Worm Heaven." *Sports Illustrated* 10 May 1971: 70–72, 77. vol. 36, no. 19. This was the first published appearance of this essay. There is also a short feature on Harrison in the "Letter from the Publisher" section on p. 4 of this issue. Also published in *Silent Seasons: 21 Fishing Adventures by 7 American Experts*. Ed. Russell Chatham. New York: E. P. Dutton, 1978. 139–47. Also published in *Silent Seasons: Twenty-one Fishing Stories*. Ed. Russell Chatham. Livingston MT: Clark City Press, 1988. 147–55. Reprinted in *Just Before Dark*.

9. "Grim Reapers of the Land's Bounty." *Sports Illustrated* 11 October 1971: 38–48. vol. 35, no. 14. This was the first published appearance of this essay. This essay was later reprinted in *Just Before Dark* under the title "The Violators."

**1972**

10. "To Each His Own Chills and Thrills." *Sports Illustrated* 7 February 1972: 30–34. vol. 36, no. 6. This was the first published appearance of this essay. This essay was later reprinted in *Just Before Dark* under the title "Ice Fishing: The Moronic Sport" (see item D29).

11. "Old Faithful and Mysterious." *Sports Illustrated* 14 February 1972: 66–79. vol. 36, no. 7. This was the first published appearance of this essay. The accompanying photographs for this essay are by Ansel Adams.

12. "Where the Chase Is the Song of Hound and Horn." *Sports Illustrated* 20 March 1972: 64–75. vol. 36, no. 12. This was the first published appearance of this essay. This essay was later reprinted in a different format in *Just Before Dark* under the title "La Venerie Francaise."

13. "Only 100 Pounds? Turn Him Loose." *True* April 1972: 69–74. vol. 53, no. 419. A long essay on fly fishing for tarpon with Thomas McGuane off Key West FL. This was the first published appearance of this essay.

14. "The Mad Marlin of Punta Carnero." *True* June 1972: 88–94. vol. 53, no. 421.

A long essay on marlin fishing with Guy de la Valdene off the coast of Ecuador. This was the first published appearance of this essay.

## 1973

15. "A Machine with Two Pistons." *Sports Illustrated* 27 August 1973: 36–41. vol. 39, no. 9. This was the first published appearance of this essay.
16. "Guiding Light in the Keys." *Sports Illustrated* 3 December 1973: 78–87. vol. 39, no. 23. This was the first published appearance of this essay. Reprinted in *Just Before Dark*.
17. "Letters to Yesenin/Jim Harrison." *Publications from Sumac Press.* Fremont MI: Sumac Press, ND. An advertising pamphlet printed by the Sumac Press. A short essay from Harrison concerning the release of his poetry collection *Letters to Yesenin*. In this essay Harrison states that this collection is "my best or most completely realized work." This was the first published appearance of this essay.

## 1974

18. "Sporting Life Recaptured." *Sports Illustrated* 14 October 1974: 98–103. vol. 41, no. 16. Under the column titled "Fishing." This was the first published appearance of this essay.
19. "Marching to a Different Drummer." *Sports Illustrated* 4 November 1974: 38–47. vol. 41, no. 19. This was the first published appearance of this essay.

## 1975

20. "A Sort of Purist-Type Chili." *John Keats's Porridge: Favorite Recipes of American Poets.* Ed. Victoria McCabe. Iowa City: University of Iowa Press, 1975. 48. Harrison provides a recipe for chili in this collection of recipes from American poets. This was the first published appearance of this recipe.

## 1976

21. "The Singular Excitement of Water Sports." *Sports Afloat.* Ed. George Constable. New York: Time-Life Books, 1976. 8–11. This essay serves as an introduction to this single volume in the "Time-Life Library of Boating" series. This was the first and only published appearance of this essay.
22. "A Sporting Life." *Playboy* January 1976: 144–46, 214, 216–17. This was the first published appearance of this essay. Also published in *Silent Seasons: 21 Fishing Adventures by 7 American Experts.* Ed. Russell Chatham. New York: E. P. Dutton, 1978. 148–61. Also published in *Silent Seasons: Twenty-one Fishing Stories.* Ed. Russell Chatham. Livingston MT: Clark City Press, 1988. 157–70. Reprinted in *Just Before Dark*.

23. "Salvation in the Keys." *Esquire* June 1976: 152–53. vol. 85, no. 6. This was the first published appearance of this essay. This essay was later reprinted in *Just Before Dark* under the title "A Day in May."
24. "A River Never Sleeps." *Esquire* August 1976: 6. vol. 86, no. 2. This was the first published appearance of this essay. In the "Outdoors" column. This essay was later reprinted in *Just Before Dark* in a different form and retitled "Night Games."
25. "Not at All Like Up Home in Michigan." *Sports Illustrated* 25 October 1976: 54–58. vol. 45, no. 17. This was the first published appearance of this essay. This essay was later reprinted in *Just Before Dark* under the title "Okeechobee."

**1977**

26. "Letter to the Editor." *American Poetry Review* 6.3 (May–June 1977): 46. This letter deals with a Charles Fair review of a Paul Zwieg poetry piece entitled "Three Journeys." This was the first published appearance of this letter.
27. "Hemingway Fished Here." *Esquire* July 1977: 38, 40. vol. 87, no. 7. This essay is printed in the "Outdoors" column. This was the first published appearance of this essay. This essay was later reprinted in *Just Before Dark* under the title "The Last Good Country."
28. "Safety without Portfolio in Key West." *Outside* October 1977: 41–43. This was the first published appearance of this essay. An excerpt of this essay entitled "In Key West: Safety without Portfolio" was also reprinted in the "Selected Readings" section of the 10-year anniversary issue of the magazine. See *Outside* October 1987: 28.

**1978**

29. "Ice Fishing: The Moronic Sport." *Silent Seasons: 21 Fishing Adventures by 7 American Experts*. Ed. Russell Chatham. New York: E. P. Dutton, 1978. 162–71. Also published in *Silent Seasons: Twenty-one Fishing Stories*. Ed. Russell Chatham. Livingston MT: Clark City Press, 1988. 171–80. Reprinted in *Just Before Dark*. Also published in *Michigan Seasons: Classic Tales of Life Outdoors*. Ed. Ted J. Rulseh. Waukesha WI: Cabin Bookshelf, 1997. 212–23. This essay was originally titled "To Each His Own Chills and Thrills" and was published in the 7 February 1972 issue of *Sports Illustrated* (see item D10).
30. [untitled]. *Silent Seasons: 21 Fishing Adventures by 7 American Experts*. Ed. Russell Chatham. New York: E. P. Dutton, 1978. 137–38. This short essay is at the beginning of the "Jim Harrison" section of this collection of fishing essays and is its first published appearance. This section also features a sketch of Harrison by Chatham. Reprinted again in *Silent Seasons: Twenty-one Fishing Stories*. Livingston MT: Clark City Press, 1988. 144.

## 1981

31. "Eat Your Heart Out." *Smoke Signals* 2.2–3 (1981): 13. "The White Line Issue." This is the first published appearance of this essay and the first essay on food that Harrison wrote for *Smoke Signals*. This short-lived literary journal edited by Mike Golden was published in Brooklyn, New York, as part of the Black Market Press.

32. "Controllers' Strike as Seen from Up North." *Detroit Free Press* 13 August 1981: 11C. Printed in the Bob Talbert column. This was the first published appearance of this essay.

## 1982

33. "Eat Your Heart Out." *Smoke Signals* 2.4 (1982): 72–74. "The Jam Issue." This essay discusses a meal at Ma Maison with Orson Welles. This was the first published appearance of this essay.

34. [untitled]. Introduction. *Annex 21* 4 (1982): 58. Ed. Patrick Worth Gray. A short statement that serves as part of an introduction to poems by Lloyd Davis. *Annex 21* is the journal of the University of Nebraska at Omaha's Community Writer's Workshop. This is the first published appearance of this essay.

35. "I'll Take the Top Half—Cloudy Side Up." *Detroit Free Press* 13 June 1982: 6B. Printed in the feature section of the metro final edition. This was the first published appearance of this essay.

36. "Grand Marais: A Rare Refuge for Anglers." *Detroit Free Press* 4 July 1982: 7E. Printed in the "Outdoors" section of the metro final edition. This was the first published appearance of this essay.

37. "Advertisements." Letter. *New York Times Book Review* 19 September 1982: 35. Letter to the editor protesting an advertisement for Harrison's work referring to the author as a "brawny word slinger from the Michigan backwoods." This was the first published appearance of this letter.

## 1983

38. "Tape One of the First Thirty-Three: The Dead Food Scrolls." *Smoke Signals* 1983: 18–20. "The Unbraining Issue." This was the first published appearance of this essay.

39. [untitled]. *Esquire* May 1983: 88. vol. 99, no. 5. This was the first published appearance of this essay. Harrison's essay is included in a larger essay titled "The Revenge Symposium."

## 1984

40. [untitled]. *Riddles in the Sand*. By Jimmy Buffett. MCA Records, 1984. Harrison provides a brief essay concerning the music on this LP record album.

These liner notes appeared on the rear panel of the album cover and are their only published appearance.

41. "An Appreciation." *Russell Chatham—Deep Creek*. Seattle: Winn Publishing, May 1984. 57. Winn did two editions of this monograph celebrating the work of the artist and author Russell Chatham: a signed, limited edition of 150 copies done in cloth over boards and an edition in wrappers. This was the first published appearance of this essay. Also printed in *Russell Chatham: A Monograph*. Livingston MT: Clark City Press, 1987. 61.

42. "Fording and Dread." *Smoke Signals* 23 August 1984: 20. This is in the New York Book Fair special edition. This was the first published appearance of this essay. Reprinted in *Just Before Dark*.

## 1985

43. [untitled]. *Esquire* August 1985: 81. vol. 104, no. 2. Harrison provides a tribute to the writing of Peter Matthiessen next to a photo of Matthiessen. The photo and comment are part of Matthiessen's short story "On the River Styx." This the first published appearance of this short essay.

## 1986

44. "History as Torment." Preface. *"What Thou Lovest Well Remains": 100 Years of Ezra Pound*. Ed. Richard Ardinger. Boise ID: Limberlost Press, 1986. ix–x. A preface for this tribute to Ezra Pound. This was the first and only published appearance of this essay.

45. "Passacaglia on Getting Lost." *Antaeus* 57 (Autumn 1986): 230–35. This was the first published appearance of this essay. Reprinted in *Just Before Dark*.

46. "Revenge: The American Way of Revenge and How It Compares to the Real Thing." *Playboy* February 1986: 114–15, 126, 134–35, 138. vol. 35, no. 2. This was the first published appearance of this essay. Reprinted in *Just Before Dark*.

47. "Log of the Earthtoy Drifthumper." *Automobile Magazine* July 1986: 84–88. vol. 1, no. 4. This was the first published appearance of this essay. Reprinted in *Just Before Dark*.

48. "Floating Is Better Than Sinking." *Cruising World* October 1986: 46–49. This is the first and only published appearance of this essay.

## 1987

49. "Passacaglia on Getting Lost." *On Nature*. Ed. Daniel Halpern. San Francisco: North Point Press, 1987. 230–35. First published in *Antaeus* (see item D45).

50. "Night Walking." *Rolling Stone* 26 March 1987: 91, 149–50. This was the first published appearance of this essay. Reprinted in *Just Before Dark*.

51. "The Changing Face of Northern Michigan." *Michigan Living* April 1987: 46. vol. 70, no. 10. An essay and a short excerpt from *Wolf* in the official publication of the Automobile Club of Michigan. This was the first published appearance of this essay.
52. "Going Places." *Outside* June 1987: 46–50. This was the first published appearance of this essay. Reprinted in *Just Before Dark*. Also reprinted in *Out of Noosphere*. New York: Simon and Schuster, 1992. 400–404. Also reprinted in *The Best of Outside: The First Twenty Years*. New York: Villard Books, 1997. 392–96.
53. "What Is It about Anjelica Houston? We Asked Nine Men to Comment." *Esquire* September 1987: 184. vol. 108, no. 3. Harrison's three-sentence comment is one of the nine. This was the first published appearance of this essay.

## 1988

54. "Re: life, philosophically—no comment." *The Meaning of Life*. Ed. Hugh S. Moorhead. Chicago: Chicago Review Press, 1988. 83. Moorhead, a professor of philosophy at Eastern Illinois University, asked some of the century's greatest writers and thinkers to inscribe a copy of their latest book and attempt to answer the question, What is the meaning of life? Harrison inscribed a copy of *Legends of the Fall* with the above-noted answer. This is the first published appearance of this sentiment.
55. "From the Dalva Notebooks: 1985–1987." *Antaeus* 61 (Autumn 1988): 208–14. This was the first published appearance of this essay. Reprinted in *Just Before Dark*.
56. "Sporting Food." *Smart* 1.1 (Fall 1988): 68–70. Premier issue of a magazine founded and edited by Terry McDonell. This essay was Harrison's first "Sporting Food" column for *Smart* magazine and its first published appearance. Reprinted in *Just Before Dark*. Also appears in *The Raw and the Cooked: Adventures of a Roving Gourmand* as the essay "Eat or Die."
57. "Roving." *Automobile Magazine* May 1988: 66–70. vol. 3, no. 2. This was the first published appearance of this essay.
58. "Look for Real Issues in This Campaign." Letter. *Detroit Free Press* 15 September 1988. This was the first published appearance of this letter. A letter to the editor concerning the upcoming Bush-Dukakis presidential election.
59. [untitled]. "A Harvest of Riches." *Bloomsbury Review* November–December 1988: 16–17. vol. 8, no. 6. A short essay in which Harrison selects his favorite books for 1988. This was the first published appearance of this essay.

## 1989

60. "Dear Caliban." Letter. *Caliban* 7 (1989): 45. This is a letter published in the "Correspondence" section and is its first published appearance.
61. "Don't Fence Me In." *Condé Nast Traveler* March 1989: 114–25. vol. 24, no. 3. This was the first published appearance of this essay. Reprinted in *Just Before Dark*.
62. "Meals of Peace and Restoration." *Smart* 1.2 (March–April 1989): 41–42. This was the first published appearance of this essay. Harrison's ongoing "Sporting Food" column. Reprinted in *Just Before Dark*. Later reprinted in *The Raw and the Cooked: Adventures of a Roving Gourmand*.
63. "Hunger, Real and Unreal." *Smart* 1.3 (May–June 1989): 47–48. This was the first published appearance of this essay. Harrison's ongoing "Sporting Food" column. Reprinted in *Just Before Dark*. Later reprinted in *The Raw and the Cooked: Adventures of a Roving Gourmand*.
64. "Then and Now." *Smart* 1.4 (July–August 1989): 29–31. This was the first published appearance of this essay. Harrison's ongoing "Sporting Food" column. Reprinted in *Just Before Dark*. Later reprinted in *The Raw and the Cooked: Adventures of a Roving Gourmand*.
65. "Leave Us Alone." Letter. *Detroit News* 20 August 1989: 18A. This was the first published appearance of this letter. A letter to the editor concerning a proposed road in Michigan's Upper Peninsula.
66. "Consciousness Dining." *Smart* 1.5 (September–October 1989): 51–52. This was the first published appearance of this essay. Harrison's ongoing "Sporting Food" column. Reprinted in *Just Before Dark*. Later reprinted in *The Raw and the Cooked: Adventures of a Roving Gourmand*.
67. "The Tugboats of Costa Rica." *Smart* 1.6 (November–December 1989): 32–33. This was the first published appearance of this essay. Harrison's ongoing "Sporting Food" column. Reprinted in *Just Before Dark*. Later reprinted in *The Raw and the Cooked: Adventures of a Roving Gourmand*.

## 1990

68. "From the Dalva Notebooks: 1985–1987." *Our Private Lives*. Ed. Daniel Halpern. New York: Vintage Books, 1990. 208–14.
69. [excerpt] "Ice Fishing: The Moronic Sport." *An Angler's Album: Fishing in Photography and Literature*. Ed. Charles H. Traub. New York: Rizzoli, 1990. 100. An excerpt from the essay originally published in *Sports Illustrated* in 1972.
70. "Preface." *One Hundred Paintings*. By Russell Chatham. Livingston MT: Clark City Press, 1990. 1–3. This book coincided with Chatham's 30-year

retrospective at the Museum of the Rockies at Montana State University. This was the first published appearance of this essay.

71. "Susan Thompson, Cape Split, Maine, 1945." *Paul Strand: Essays on His Life and Work*. Ed. Maren Strange. New York: Aperture, 1990. 136–37. This was the first published appearance of this essay. This essay was reprinted in *Just Before Dark* under the title "Paul Strand."

72. [untitled essay]. *Seymour Lawrence Publisher* NP: Seymour Lawrence, 1990. 37–38. A small book in dark blue cloth done to commemorate 25 years in the publishing business (1965–90). Includes contributions by 50 authors, including one by Bob Dattila (Harrison's literary agent at that time). This was the first and only published appearance of this essay.

73. "Big Women." *Literary Outtakes: False Starts, Loose Lines, Dropped Dialogue and Other Fragments from 101 Renowned Writers*. Ed. Larry Dark. New York: Fawcett Columbine, 1990. 61–62. This was the first published appearance of this essay.

74. "Poetry as Survival." *Antaeus* 64–65 (Spring–Autumn 1990): 370–80. This was the first published appearance of this essay. Reprinted in *Just Before Dark*.

75. "Real Big Brown Truck." *Automobile Magazine* January 1990: 96–97. vol. 4, no. 10. This was the first published appearance of this essay.

76. Letter. *Harper's* February 1990: 10–11. A letter to the editor in response to Tom Wolfe's November 1989 *Harper's* essay "Stalking the Billion Footed Beast: A Literary Manifesto for the New Social Novel." This is the only published appearance of this letter.

77. "Midrange Road Kill." *Smart* 8 (March–April 1990): 22–23. This was the first published appearance of this essay. Harrison's ongoing "Sporting Food" column. Reprinted in *Just Before Dark*. Later reprinted in *The Raw and the Cooked: Adventures of a Roving Gourmand*.

78. "The Panic Hole." *Smart* 9 (May 1990): 17–19. This was the first published appearance of this essay. Harrison's ongoing "Sporting Food" column. Reprinted in *Just Before Dark*. Later reprinted in *The Raw and the Cooked: Adventures of a Roving Gourmand*.

79. "Our Roving Poet/Novelist/Sybarite Almost Buys a Subaru Legacy." *Automobile Magazine* May 1990: 120. vol. 5, no. 2. This was the first published appearance of this essay.

80. "Piggies Come to Market." *Smart* 10 (June 1990): 30–33. This was the first published appearance of this essay. Harrison's ongoing "Sporting Food" column. Reprinted in *Just Before Dark*. Later reprinted in *The Raw and the Cooked: Adventures of a Roving Gourmand*.

81. "Look at Keys." Letter. *The Enterprise* 20 September 1990: sec. 1, p. 5. A letter to the editor of the Leland County MI newspaper in protest of ongoing development in the Lake Leelanau area. This was the first published appearance of this letter.
82. "The Fast." *Smart* 12 (October–November 1990): 23–24. This was the first published appearance of this essay. Harrison's ongoing "Sporting Food" column. Reprinted in *Just Before Dark*. Later reprinted in *The Raw and the Cooked: Adventures of a Roving Gourmand*.

**1991**

83. "Bar Pool." *Just Before Dark*. Livingston MT: Clark City Press, 1991. 104–08. This was the first published appearance of this essay. A note in *Just Before Dark* states that this essay was written in 1973.
84. "Bird Hunting." *Just Before Dark*. Livingston MT: Clark City Press, 1991. 163–70. This was the first published appearance of this essay. A note in *Just Before Dark* states that this essay was written in 1985.
85. "Canada." *Just Before Dark*. Livingston MT: Clark City Press, 1991. 120–23. This essay was originally published in the 14 October 1974 issue of *Sports Illustrated* under the title "Sporting Life Recaptured."
86. "A Day in May." *Just Before Dark*. Livingston MT: Clark City Press, 1991. 136–38. This essay was originally published in the June 1976 issue of *Esquire* magazine under the title "Salvation in the Keys."
87. "Dream as a Metaphor of Survival." *Just Before Dark*. Livingston MT: Clark City Press, 1991. 308–18. This was the first published appearance of this essay. Bibliographic notes in *Just Before Dark* state that this essay was first published in the *Psychoanalytic Review* in 1991; however, the issue of the *Psychoanalytic Review* that this essay actually appeared in was the Spring 1994 issue, vol. 81, no. 1. In the introduction to the *Psychoanalytic Review* by Larry Sullivan it also states that the first publication of this essay was in *Just Before Dark*.
88. "The Last Good Country." *Just Before Dark*. Livingston MT: Clark City Press, 1991. 151–56. This essay originally appeared in the July 1977 issue of *Esquire* magazine under the title "Hemingway Fished Here."
89. "La Venerie Francaise." *Just Before Dark*. Livingston MT: Clark City Press, 1991. 82–96. This was the first published appearance of this essay in this format. This essay was originally published in the 20 March 1972 issue of *Sports Illustrated* in a different form under the title "Where the Chase Is the Song of Hound and Horn."
90. "Night Games." *Just Before Dark*. Livingston MT: Clark City Press, 1991.

124–27. This was the first published appearance of this essay in this format. This essay was first printed in a slightly different format in the August 1976 issue of *Esquire* magazine under the title "A River Never Sleeps."

91. "Okeechobee." *Just Before Dark*. Livingston MT: Clark City Press, 1991. 128–35. This essay was originally published in the 25 October 1976 issue of *Sports Illustrated* under the title "Not at All Like Up Home in Michigan."

92. "The Preparation of Thomas Hearns." *Just Before Dark*. Livingston MT: Clark City Press, 1991. 157–62. This was the first published appearance of this essay. In the bibliography of *Just Before Dark* it states that this essay was written in 1980.

93. "The Violators." *Just Before Dark*. Livingston MT: Clark City Press, 1991. 63–71. This essay was originally published in the 11 October 1971 issue of *Sports Illustrated* under the title "Grim Reapers of the Land's Bounty."

94. "A Memoir of Horse Pulling." *Just Before Dark*. Livingston MT: Clark City Press, 1991. 97–103. This was the first published appearance of this essay. The basis of this essay appeared in the 31 August 1970 issue of *Sports Illustrated* as "The Real Fun of the Fair Was the Horse Pulling" (see item D6). In the bibliography of *Just Before Dark* it states that this essay was written in 1973.

95. "A Natural History of Some Poems." *Just Before Dark*. Livingston MT: Clark City Press, 1991. 195–221. This was the first published appearance of this essay and is a condensed version of Harrison's MA thesis, Michigan State University, 1965.

96. "Everyday Life." *Beneath a Single Moon: Buddhism in Contemporary American Poetry*. Ed. Kent Johnson and Craig Paulenich. Boston: Shambhala Publications, 1991. 124–26. This was the first published appearance of this essay. Reprinted in *Just Before Dark*.

97. "A Revisionist's Walden." *Heaven Is under Our Feet*. Ed. Don Henley and Dave Marsh. Stanford CT: Longmeadow Press, 1991. 64–67. This was the first published appearance of this essay.

98. "What Have We Done with the Thighs." *Esquire* February 1991: 45–47. vol. 115, no. 2. This was the first published appearance of this essay and was the first installment of Harrison's long-running monthly food column entitled "The Raw and the Cooked." Reprinted in *Just Before Dark*. Later reprinted in *The Raw and the Cooked: Adventures of a Roving Gourmand*.

99. "The Days of Wine and Pig Hocks." *Esquire* March 1991: 56, 58. vol. 115, no. 3. This was the first published appearance of this essay. Part of the monthly food column "The Raw and the Cooked." Later reprinted in *The Raw and the Cooked: Adventures of a Roving Gourmand*.

100. "Political Intervention." Letter. *Traverse City MI Record-Eagle* 27 March 1991: 6A. A letter to the editor signed "Jim Harrison, Lake Leelanau." This was the first published appearance of this letter.
101. "One Foot in the Grave." *Esquire* April 1991: 65–67. vol. 115, no. 4. This was the first published appearance of this essay. Part of the monthly food column "The Raw and the Cooked." Later reprinted in *The Raw and the Cooked*. Also reprinted in *The Raw and the Cooked: Adventures of a Roving Gourmand*.
102. "Just Before Dark." *Esquire* May 1991: 46, 48. vol. 115, no. 5. This was the first published appearance of this essay. Part of the monthly food column "The Raw and the Cooked." Later reprinted in *The Raw and the Cooked: Adventures of a Roving Gourmand*.
103. "Cooking Your Life." *Esquire* June 1991: 46–50. vol. 115, no. 6. This was the first published appearance of this essay. Part of the monthly food column "The Raw and the Cooked." Later reprinted in *The Raw and the Cooked: Adventures of a Roving Gourmand*.
104. "Ignoring Columbus." *Esquire* August 1991: 32, 34. vol. 116, no. 2. This was the first published appearance of this essay. Part of the monthly food column "The Raw and the Cooked." Later reprinted in *The Raw and the Cooked: Adventures of a Roving Gourmand*.
105. "Eating Close to the Ground." *Esquire* September 1991: 94, 96. vol. 116, no. 3. This was the first published appearance of this essay. Part of the monthly food column "The Raw and the Cooked." Later reprinted in *The Raw and the Cooked: Adventures of a Roving Gourmand*.
106. "Return of the Native; or, Lighten Up." *Esquire* October 1991: 87, 106. vol. 116, no. 4. This was the first published appearance of this essay. Part of the monthly food column "The Raw and the Cooked." Later reprinted in *The Raw and the Cooked*. Also reprinted in *The Raw and the Cooked: Adventures of a Roving Gourmand*.
107. "Let's Get Lost." *Esquire* November 1991: 79–81. vol. 116, no. 5. This was the first published appearance of this essay. Part of the monthly food column "The Raw and the Cooked." Later reprinted in *The Raw and the Cooked*. Also reprinted in *The Raw and the Cooked: Adventures of a Roving Gourmand*.
108. "Principles." *Esquire* December 1991: 95–97. vol. 116, no. 6. This was the first published appearance of this essay. Part of the monthly food column "The Raw and the Cooked."
109. [untitled]. *Russell Chatham, Kimzey Miller Gallery*. NP, ND. Page 14 of an unpaginated pamphlet. Although there is no date on this small monogram of Chatham's work, the Kimzey Miller Gallery advises that the monogram was done in December 1991 by Clark City Press. Harrison's tribute to Chatham's

work is an edited version of the preface that he did for Chatham's retrospective *One Hundred Paintings* published by Clark City Press in 1990.

## 1992

110. "The Chippewa-Ottawa." Introduction. *Mem-ka-Weh: Dawning of the Grand Traverse Band of Ottawa and Chippewa Indians*. By George Weeks. Traverse City MI: Village Press, 1992. ix–x. Harrison's introduction is dated 1991.
111. [untitled]. *A Light from Within: Paintings by Jack R. Smith*. Muskegon MI: Muskegon Museum of Art, 1992. Unpaginated program for a gallery exhibition of Jack Smith's paintings at the Muskegon Museum of Art from 20 September to 1 November 1992. This was the first published appearance of this essay. Also contained in this program is a short essay from Dan Gerber.
112. "New Map of the Sacred Territory." *Esquire Sportsman* Autumn 1992: 29–32. vol. 1, no. 1. Under the column "Sportsman's Journal." This was the first published appearance of this essay. There are two separate covers for this issue of the magazine. One features Jimmy Buffet holding a shotgun, and the other features a scene with Brad Pitt fly fishing from the film *A River Runs through It*. Other than the covers the magazines are identical in layout and content.
113. "The Last Best Place?" *Esquire* February 1992: 59–60. vol. 117, no. 2. This was the first published appearance of this essay. Part of the monthly food column "The Raw and the Cooked." Later reprinted in *The Raw and the Cooked: Adventures of a Roving Gourmand*.
114. "The Morality of Food." *Esquire* March 1992: 77–78. vol. 117, no. 3. This was the first published appearance of this essay. Part of the monthly food column "The Raw and the Cooked." Later reprinted in *The Raw and the Cooked: Adventures of a Roving Gourmand*.
115. "Contact." *Esquire* April 1992: 65–66. vol. 117, no. 4. This was the first published appearance of this essay. Part of the monthly food column "The Raw and the Cooked." Later reprinted in *The Raw and the Cooked: Adventures of a Roving Gourmand*.
116. "Coming to Our Senses." *Esquire* May 1992: 86–91. vol. 117, no. 5. This was the first published appearance of this essay. Part of the monthly food column "The Raw and the Cooked." Later reprinted in *The Raw and the Cooked: Adventures of a Roving Gourmand*.
117. "The 10,000 Calorie Diet." *Esquire* June 1992: 73–74. vol. 117, no. 6. This was the first published appearance of this essay. Part of the monthly food column "The Raw and the Cooked." Later reprinted in *The Raw and the Cooked: Adventures of a Roving Gourmand*.

118. "Walking the San Pedro." *Esquire* August 1992: 51–52. vol. 118, no. 2. This was the first published appearance of this essay. Part of the monthly food column "The Raw and the Cooked." Later reprinted in *The Raw and the Cooked: Adventures of a Roving Gourmand*.

119. "Women We Love: Madeleine Stowe." *Esquire* August 1992: 88. vol. 118, no. 2. This was the first published appearance of this essay. A brief essay on the actress Madeleine Stowe contained in the larger collection of essays "Women We Love."

120. "Back Home." *Esquire* September 1992: 125–26. vol. 118, no. 3. This was the first published appearance of this essay. Part of the monthly food column "The Raw and the Cooked." Later reprinted in *The Raw and the Cooked: Adventures of a Roving Gourmand*.

121. "Repulsion and Grace." *Esquire* October 1992: 95–96. vol. 118, no. 4. This was the first published appearance of this essay. Part of the monthly food column "The Raw and the Cooked." Later reprinted in *The Raw and the Cooked: Adventures of a Roving Gourmand*.

122. "Outlaw Cook." *Esquire* November 1992: 85–86, 88. vol. 118, no. 5. This was the first published appearance of this essay. Part of the monthly food column "The Raw and the Cooked." Later reprinted in *The Raw and the Cooked: Adventures of a Roving Gourmand*.

123. "Beef, Bread and Iron." *Automobile Magazine* November 1992: 90–91. vol. 7, no. 8. This was the first published appearance of this essay. Photo of Harrison by Ted Kooser.

124. "Unmentionable Cuisine." *Esquire* December 1992: 83–85. vol. 118, no. 6. This was the first published appearance of this essay. Part of the monthly food column "The Raw and the Cooked." Later reprinted in *The Raw and the Cooked: Adventures of a Roving Gourmand*.

## 1993

125. "Bird Hunting." *A Literary Feast: An Anthology*. Ed. Lilly Golden. New York: Atlantic Monthly Press, 1993. 128–35. First published in *Just Before Dark*.

126. [untitled]. *Diana Guest, Stonecarver*. Livingston MT: Clark City Press, 1993. 11. This was the first published appearance of this essay.

127. "Spring Coda." *Esquire Sportsman* Spring–Summer 1993: 27–28. vol. 2, no. 1. Under the column "Sportsman's Journal." This was the first published appearance of this essay.

128. [untitled]. "Essays on Home." *Hungry Mind Review* 26 (Summer 1993): 23. This was the first published appearance of this essay. Harrison's essay is part of a larger piece titled "Essays on Home."

129. "Sitting Around." *Tricycle: The Buddhist Review* 3.1 (Fall 1993): 54–57. This was the first published appearance of this essay.
130. "Pie in the Sky." *Esquire Sportsman* Fall–Winter 1993: 33–34. vol. 2, no. 2. Under the column "Sportsman's Journal." This was the first published appearance of this essay.
131. "Nesting in Air." *Northern Lights* 9.1 (Winter 1993): 11. This was the first published appearance of this essay. This essay also includes a recipe for bear. Also reprinted in *Northern Lights*. Ed. Deborah Clow and Donald Snow. New York: Vintage Books, 1994. 262–64.
132. "Heart Food in L.A." *Esquire* February 1993: 37–38. vol. 119, no. 2. This was the first published appearance of this essay. Part of the monthly food column "The Raw and the Cooked." Later reprinted in *The Raw and the Cooked: Adventures of a Roving Gourmand*.
133. "Fresh Southern Air." *Esquire* April 1993: 75–76. vol. 119, no. 4. This was the first published appearance of this essay. Part of the monthly food column "The Raw and the Cooked." Later reprinted in *The Raw and the Cooked: Adventures of a Roving Gourmand*.
134. "Borderlands." *Esquire* May 1993: 67–68. vol. 119, no. 5. This was the first published appearance of this essay. Part of the monthly food column "The Raw and the Cooked." Later reprinted in *The Raw and the Cooked: Adventures of a Roving Gourmand*.
135. "Great Poems Make Good Prayers." *Esquire* October 1993: 146–47. vol. 120, no. 4. This was the first published appearance of this essay.
136. "A Huge Hunger in Paris." *Esquire* December 1993: 71–72. vol. 120, no. 6. This was the first published appearance of this essay. This was the last essay in the monthly food column "The Raw and the Cooked." Later reprinted in *The Raw and the Cooked: Adventures of a Roving Gourmand*.

## 1994

137. "The Beginner's Mind." *Heart of the Land: Essays on Last Great Places*. Ed. Joseph Barbato and Lisa Weinerman. New York: Pantheon, 1994. 136–50. This was the first published appearance of this essay.
138. [excerpt] "Hunger, Real and Unreal." *Travelers' Tales Mexico*. Ed. James O'Reilly and Larry Habegger. San Francisco: Travelers' Tales, 1994. 98, 99.
139. "Dream as a Metaphor of Survival." *Psychoanalytic Review* 81.1 (Spring 1994): 5–14. First published in *Just Before Dark*.
140. "A Spring Sermon . . . or Siberia." *Sports Afield* June 1994: 106. vol. 211, no. 6. In the "Backcountry" column. This was the first published appearance of this essay. Reprinted in *The Best of Sports Afield—the Greatest Outdoor Writing*

*of the 20th Century*. Ed. Jay Cassell. New York: Atlantic Monthly Press, 1996. 326–28.

**1995**

141. "From the Dalva Notebooks: 1985–1987." *Imagining Worlds*. Ed. Marjorie Ford and Jon Ford. New York: McGraw-Hill, 1995. 109–15.

142. "Hunting with a Friend." Introduction. *For a Handful of Feathers*. By Guy de la Valdene. New York: Atlantic Monthly Press, 1995. xi–xvi. (See item D147.)

143. "Squaw Gulch." *Who's Writing This: Notations on the Authorial I with Self Portraits*. Ed. Daniel Halpern. Hopewell NJ: Ecco Press, 1995. 76–78. This was the first published appearance of this essay.

144. "Hunter's Journal." *Simple Cooking* 41 (Winter 1995): 1, 2. This was the first published appearance of this essay.

145. "Sergei Yesenin." *Paris Review* 137 (Winter 1995): 144–45. This short essay, together with a previously unpublished photo of Yesenin, was part of a larger collection entitled "Russian Portraits." This was the first published appearance of this essay.

146. "Sacred Territory." *Sports Afield* Winter 1995–96: 101–05. vol. 214, no. 6. This was the first published appearance of this essay.

147. "A Hunting Pal." *Sports Afield* October 1995: 79–81, 122, 123. vol. 214, no. 4. This was the first published appearance of this essay. This is a modified version of the introduction that would appear later this year in Guy de la Valdene's book *For a Handful of Feathers* (see item D142).

148. "Father-in-Law." *Kermit Lynch Wine Merchant Newsletter*. Berkeley CA, December 1995. This was the first published appearance of this essay.

**1996**

149. "A Day in May." *West of Key West: Adventures and Reflections: Fishing the Flats from the Contents to the Marquesas*. Ed. John Cole and Hawk Pollard. Mechanicsburg PA: Stackpole Books, 1996. 124–26. This essay was also reprinted in a limited and signed edition entitled simply *West of Key West*. Far Hills NJ: Meadow Run Press, 1997. 124–26. 75 signed and numbered copies hardbound in a custom clamshell box. This is a collection of essays on flats fishing from authors such as Russell Chatham, Thomas McGuane, Peter Matthiessen, Guy De la Valdene, and Dan Gerber. "A Day in May" was first published in *Just Before Dark*.

150. "The Violators." *A Hunter's Heart: Honest Essays on Blood Sport*. Collected by David Peterson. New York: Henry Holt & Co., 1996. 210–19. This essay first appeared in *Just Before Dark*.

151. "Passacaglia on Getting Lost," [untitled]. *The Nature Reader*. Ed. Daniel Halpern and Dan Frank. Hopewell NJ: Ecco Press, 1996. 214–19, 336–38. This is an expanded edition of the book *On Nature* published in 1987. Harrison's untitled essay is at the end of the book, in the section "Natural History: An Annotated Booklist," compiled by the book's advisory editors. The other advisory editors include Annie Dillard, Gretel Ehrlich, Edward Hoagland, Barry Lopez, and David Quammen. This is the first appearance of this essay.

152. "The Man in the Back Row Has a Question II." *Paris Review* 138 (Spring 1996): 309–32. The responses in this essay are answers to questions posed to screenwriters regarding the art of screenwriting. This was the first published appearance of this essay.

## 1997

153. [untitled]. Introduction. *The Sumac Reader*. Ed. Joseph Bednarik. East Lansing: Michigan State University Press, 1997. xviii–xx. This was the first published appearance of this essay. This book was published in a limited edition of 26 lettered copies and 100 numbered copies signed by Harrison, Dan Gerber, and Joseph Bednarik. The trade edition was published in wrappers. A selection of poems and essays from the literary journal *Sumac*, which Harrison and Gerber edited from 1968 to 1971.

154. "Germinating Work," "From the Dalva Notebooks: 1985–1987." *The Writer's Journal*. Ed. Sheila Bender. New York: Dell, 1997. 95–103. This was the first published appearance of the essay "Germinating Work" on p. 103.

155. "High on the Hog." Foreword. *Diggin' in and Piggin' Out: The Truth about Men and Food*. By Roger Welsch. New York: HarperCollins, 1997. xi–xvi. This was the first published appearance of this essay. There is also an epigraph from Harrison on p. 45 from private communications with the author that states: "Embrace winter with pork products; lard is the fuel of conquest."

156. [excerpts]. *Poetic Medicine*. By John Fox. New York: Tarcher/Putnam, 1997. 47, 99. Two short statements from Harrison form epigraphs on the pages noted above in this book on poetry and the healing arts.

157. "Dan Lahren." *Big Sky Journal* 4.1 (1997): 71–72. The fly fishing issue for the year. This was the first published appearance of this essay.

## 1998

158. "Night Walking," "Passacaglia on Getting Lost." *The Sacred Earth: Writers on Nature and Spirit*. Ed. Jason Gardner. Novato CA: New World Library, 1998. 21, 28.

159. "Why I Write, or Not." *Why I Write: Thoughts on the Craft of Fiction*. Ed. Will Blythe. Boston: Little, Brown & Co., 1998. 146–54. This was the first published appearance of this essay.
160. [untitled]. *Hooked: Witty Quotes from Serious Anglers*. Ed. Raye Carrington. Kansas City MO: Andrews McMeel Publishing, 1998. 11, 82. Two short quotes from Harrison regarding fishing.
161. "Why I Write, or Not." *Neon: Artcetera* Summer 1998. The newsletter of the Nevada Arts Council. Also appeared later in the year in *Zoetrope* 2.1 (Winter 1998): 41–43.

## 1999

162. [miscellaneous statements]. *Bookstore: The Life and Times of Jeannette Watson and Books & Co*. By Lynne Tillman. New York: Harcourt Brace & Co., 1999. 145–48, 205. Harrison contributes several statements about Watson and her landmark bookstore. Also included is Watson's reminiscence about Harrison's visits and his work.
163. "The Raw and the Cooked." *The Adventure of Food: True Stories of Eating Everything*. Ed. Richard Sterling. San Francisco: Travelers' Tales, 1999. 85–89.
164. [excerpt] "Dream as a Metaphor of Survival." *Brown Dog of the Yaak: Essays on Art and Activism*. Ed. Rick Bass. Minneapolis: Milkweed Editions, 1999. 99–109. Also printed in this anthology is an excerpt from the introduction to *Just Before Dark* as well as the essay "Poetry as Survival" from the same collection.
165. "Going Places." *America: True Stories of Life on the Road*. Ed. Fred Setterberg. San Francisco: Travelers' Tales, 1999. 61–66.
166. "The Situation of American Writing 1999." *American Literary History* 11.2 (Summer 1999): 274–76. A panel of American writers were given a set of 8 questions concerning the status of American writing. Harrison was a member of the panel. This was the first published appearance of this essay.
167. "First Person Female." *New York Times Magazine* 16 May 1999: 98–99, 101. This essay includes a full-page color photograph of Harrison by Catherine Opie. This essay's original title was "Finding Sister." This was the first published appearance of this essay.
168. "Eating French: Time for Some Deep Thinking about Real Food." *Men's Journal* November 1999: 72, 74, 76, 78. vol. 8, no. 9. This was the first published appearance of this essay. Reprinted as "Thirty-three Angles on Eating French" in *The Raw and the Cooked: Adventures of a Roving Gourmand*. 193–208. Photos by Mary Ellen Mark.

## 2000

169. "The Question of Zen." *A Man's Journey to Simple Abundance.* By Sarah Ban Breathnach. Ed. Michael Segell. New York: Charles Scribner's Sons, 2000. 140–44.

170. "Night Walking." *Peninsula: Essays and Memoirs from Michigan.* Ed. Michael Steinberg. East Lansing: Michigan State University Press, 2000. 46–50.

171. [letters]. *Chatter and Feathers: Little Ornithophagic Correspondence: November 1999–April 2000.* Manior de Pron, 2000. This small book, published in France, contains nine letters between Harrison and his friend Gerard Oberle. The first half of the book has the letters in French and the second half the letters in English. It was printed in wraps in an edition of 350 copies. These letters first appeared in the September 2000 issue of the French magazine *Beaux Arts* and appear here in English for the first time. This correspondence was later reprinted in *The Raw and the Cooked: Adventures of a Roving Gourmand.*

172. "Going Places." *Patterns of Exposition 16th Edition.* Ed. Robert A. Schwegler. White Plains NY: Addison Wesley Longman, 2000. 262–68.

173. [excerpt] "Hunting with a Friend." *Heartsblood, Hunting, Spirituality and Wildness in America.* Ed. David Peterson. Washington DC: Island Press, 2000. 170.

174. "Correspondence from Jim Harrison," "Gentle Reader." *Border Beat* 11 (Spring 2000): 8, 9, rear cover. This was the first published appearance of these essays and the poem. The first piece is a letter from Harrison to the editor discussing an unpublished Pablo Neruda poem entitled "In Veracruz in 1941" that is printed on the next page. The second piece is an advertisement of sorts printed on the back cover recommending several upcoming books. The "Neruda" poem was actually written by Harrison, and the letter discussing Neruda is a hoax.

175. [untitled]. "A Symposium on Secret Places." *Michigan Quarterly Review* 39.3 (Summer 2000): 456–57. Ed. Elizabeth Goodenough. The Harrison essay was untitled and was included in pt. 2 of the larger essay. This was the first published appearance of this essay. This essay was later reprinted in the book *Secret Spaces of Childhood.* Ed. Elizabeth Goodenough. Ann Arbor: University of Michigan Press, 2003. 36–37.

176. "The Political Scene." *Ruminator Review* 3.55 (Fall 2000): 13. This was the first published appearance of this essay.

177. "Starting Over." *Men's Journal* February 2000: 100–102, 115–16. vol. 9, no. 2. This was the first published appearance of this essay. This issue also contains a small portrait of Harrison painted by Russell Chatham on p. 21 in

the "Contributors" section. Reprinted in *Wild Stories: The Best of Men's Journal*. Ed. Sid Evans and Staff. New York: Crown Publishers, 2002. 132–40.

178. "Wine." *Kermit Lynch Wine Merchant Newsletter*. Berkeley CA, July 2000. First English publication of an essay that originally appeared in the 28 October 1999 *Revue des Deux Mondes* (Paris). Reprinted in *The Raw and the Cooked: Adventures of a Roving Gourmand*.

179. "Versions of Childhood." *Inside Borders* October 2000: 12–13. This was the first published appearance of this essay. This short essay is accompanied by a photo of Harrison with his brother John and his sister Judith when they were children, ca. 1945.

180. "The Beauty of the Jump." *Men's Journal* November 2000: 91–97. vol. 9, no. 10. This was the first published appearance of this essay.

181. "Through Thicket and Thin." *Utne Reader* November–December 2000: 52. no. 102. This essay was first published as part of a larger collection of essays entitled "A Symposium on Secret Places." *Michigan Quarterly Review* 39.3 (Summer 2000): 456–57. (See item D175.)

**2001**

182. "Jim Harrison on D. T. Suzuki." *Grove Press, Atlantic Press and Canongate Books Fall 2001 Catalog*. 2001. 50. This catalog also contains an excerpt from Harrison's essay "The 10,000 Calorie Diet," which was reprinted in *The Raw and the Cooked: Adventures of a Roving Gourmand*.

183. "Starting Over." *The Best American Sports Writing 2001*. Ed. Bud Collins. New York: Houghton Mifflin Co., 2001. 338–49.

184. "Versions of Reality." *The Raw and the Cooked: Adventures of a Roving Gourmand*. New York: Grove Press, 2001. 186–90. This is the first published appearance this essay.

185. "Wild Creatures: A Correspondence with Gerard Oberle." *The Raw and the Cooked: Adventures of a Roving Gourmand*. New York: Grove Press, 2001. 210–41. This was the first U.S. printing of these letters.

186. "Everyday Life: The Question of Zen." *Brick* 67 (Spring 2001): 52–54.

187. "Meatballs." *Brick* 67 (Spring 2001): 49–51. Short essay with a recipe for spaghetti Bolognese. This was the first published appearance of this essay. Also reprinted in *The Raw and the Cooked: Adventures of a Roving Gourmand*.

188. "The Man in the Back Row Has a Question VII." *Paris Review* 158 (Spring–Summer 2001): 286–307. The "New Writers Issue." These short essays are part of a larger collection of essays from authors concerning their beginnings as writers. This was the first published appearance of this essay.

189. "Soul Food." *Men's Journal* March 2001: 100–108, 136. vol. 10, no. 2. Photos

of Harrison in this article are by Harry Benson. This was the first published appearance of this essay. Also published in Harrison's collection of food essays *The Raw and the Cooked: Adventures of a Roving Gourmand* as "American Food Journal."

190. "Life on the Border." *Men's Journal* July 2001: 52–57, 98–99. vol. 10, no. 6. This was the first published appearance of this essay.

191. "A Man's Guide to Drinking." *Men's Journal* October 2001: 79–83. vol. 10, no. 9. This was the first published appearance of this essay.

192. "Naked Women Dancing." *Men's Journal* December 2001: 114–18, 123, 125. vol. 10, no. 11. This was the first published appearance of this essay.

**2002**

193. "The Beginner's Mind." *Nature Writing: The Tradition in English*. Ed. Robert Finch and John Elder. New York: W. W. Norton & Co., 2002. 759–66. This essay was also published the same year in a revised paperbound edition of this book entitled *The Norton Book of Nature Writing*.

194. "Dear J. D. Salinger." *Letters to J. D. Salinger*. Ed. Chris Kubica and Will Hochman. Madison WI: University of Wisconsin Press, 2002. 48. This was the first published appearance of this essay.

195. "Wine." *Adventures in Wine: True Stories of Vineyards and Vintages around the World*. Ed. Thom Elkjer. San Francisco: Travelers' Tales, 2002. 233–37. First published in the 28 October 1999 *Revue des Deux Mondes* (Paris) and then again in the July 2000 *Kermit Lynch Wine Merchant Newsletter*.

196. [untitled]. Introduction. *On the Trail to Wounded Knee: The Bigfoot Memorial Ride*. By Guy Le Querrec. Guilford CT: Lyons Press, 2002. Unpaginated. This book was first published in France under the title *Sur la Piste de Bigfoot*. Paris: Les Editions Textuel, 2000. This was the first published appearance of this essay.

197. [untitled]. *John Steinbeck: Centennial Reflections by American Writers*. Ed. Susan Shillinglaw. San Jose CA: Center for Steinbeck Studies, 2002. 39–40. The editor of this collection asked prominent American writers to submit essays on the influence of Steinbeck on their work and American letters in general. This was the first published appearance of this essay.

198. "Soul Food." *The Best American Travel Writing 2002*. Ed. Frances Mayes. Boston: Houghton Mifflin Co., 2002. 131–44. Also published in Harrison's collection of food essays *The Raw and the Cooked: Adventures of a Roving Gourmand* as "American Food Journal."

199. [excerpts] *Just Before Dark*. *Travelers' Tales France*. Ed. James O'Reilly, Larry

Habegger, and Sean O'Reilly. San Francisco: Travelers' Tales, 2002. 111, 311, 388.

200. "Jim Harrison, Writer." *Take My Advice: Letters to the Next Generation from People Who Know a Thing or Two*. Ed. James L. Harmon. New York: Simon and Schuster, 2002. 152. This was the first published appearance of this essay. Harrison contributes a 10-point presentation of advice on life in general. This anthology also contains a brief biographical sketch of Harrison at the end of the book.

201. "Jim Harrison's First Car." *Midnight Mind Magazine* 3 (2002): 72. A short paragraph concerning Harrison's first two cars. This was the first published appearance of this essay.

202. "Fishing is the most wonderful thing I do in my life, barring some equally delightful unmentionables, and not counting gluttony and booze. It's in the top five." *The Drake* (Spring 2002): 6–7. This is a small quote from Harrison over a full-page fishing photo. This quote was first published in a slightly different form in Russell Chatham's *Silent Seasons: 21 Fishing Adventures by 7 American Experts*. New York: E. P. Dutton, 1978. This same quote also appeared in the summer 2004 issue of *Outside Bozeman* on p. 40.

203. "Leaving Home." *Traverse* 21.8 (January 2002): 29, 31. Harrison wrote this essay as a farewell to Leelanau County MI—his home of 35 years. This was the first published appearance of this essay. There is also a short essay on Harrison by Deborah Wyatt Fellows in the "Editor's Note" section of the same issue on p. 7.

204. "Wine Notes." *Kermit Lynch Wine Merchant Newsletter*. Berkeley CA, January 2002. 2-page essay from an unpaginated newsletter. This was the first published appearance of this essay.

205. "How Men Pray." *Men's Journal* February 2002: 60–63, 89. vol. 11, no. 1. This was the first published appearance of this essay.

206. "Is Winemaking an Art?" *Kermit Lynch Wine Merchant Newsletter*. Berkeley CA, March 2002. 2-page essay from an unpaginated newsletter. This was the first published appearance of this essay.

207. "Wine from the Heart." *Kermit Lynch Wine Merchant Newsletter*. Berkeley CA, April 2002. 1-page essay from an unpaginated newsletter. This was the first published appearance of this essay.

208. "The Road: A Love Story." *Men's Journal* May 2002: 91–96, 123. vol. 11, no. 4. This was the first published appearance of this essay.

209. "Just Before Dark." *Santa Fean* May 2002: 58–65. vol. 30, no. 4. Illustrations by Steven Noble.

210. "The End of Nature." *Men's Journal* August 2002: 60–63. vol. 11, no. 7. This was the first published appearance of this essay.

211. "My Problems with White Wines." *Kermit Lynch Wine Merchant Newsletter*. Berkeley CA, August 2002. 3-page essay from an unpaginated newsletter. This was the first published appearance of this essay.
212. "A Great Novelist Howls at Hollywood Scripts." *Red Streak* 30 October 2002: 20–21. Premier issue. *Red Streak* is published by the *Chicago Tribune* newspaper. This was the first published appearance of this essay.

**2003**
213. "Grim Reapers of the Land's Bounty." *Sports Illustrated: Fifty Years of Great Writing, 1954–2004*. Ed. Rob Fleder. New York: Sports Illustrated Books, 2003. 224–31.
214. "Posole from Sonora." *The New Great American Writers Cookbook*. Ed. Dean Faulkner Wells. Jackson: University Press of Mississippi, 2003. 66. A single-page recipe from Harrison. This was the first published appearance of this essay.
215. "Michigan: Not Quite Leaving Michigan." *These United States*. Ed. John Leonard. New York: Thunder's Mouth Press/Nation Books, 2003. 198–205. American writers on their state within the Union. This was the first published appearance of this essay.
216. "Painting with a Turtle Hair Paintbrush." *Tricycle: The Buddhist Review* 12.3 (Spring 2003): 19–20. In the "Insights and Outtakes" section. Taken from Harrison's memoir *Off to the Side*.
217. "Eat or Die." *Brick* 71 (Summer 2003): 87–89. In the last paragraph of this essay, Harrison mentions his new position as food editor for *Brick*. This was the first published appearance of this essay.
218. [untitled]. "(Woman Reading) by Balthus, 1996." *Paris Review* 167 (Fall 2003): 122–23. 50th anniversary issue. This short essay is part of a larger collection entitled "Readers and Reading" in which writers were asked to look at portraits of people engaged in reading and submit their comments. All portraits featured in this collection of essays are part of the Oresman collection. This was the first published appearance of this essay.
219. "Good Art Does Not Specialize in Cheap Solutions." *Neon* (Winter 2002–03). Page 10 of an unpaginated newspaper. A 1-line quote in the "Out of Context" section of the Nevada Arts Council publication.
220. "Paris Rebellion." *Brick* 72 (Winter 2003): 8–11. Harrison's second installment of his ongoing "Eat or Die" food column in *Brick*. This was the first published appearance of this essay.
221. "Field Days: A Lifetime of Hunting, Fishing, and Dogs." *Field and Stream* February 2003: 66–69, 94, 96. vol. 107, no. 9. Taken from Harrison's memoir *Off to the Side*.

222. "Going Places." *Literary Cavalcade* 55.8 (May 2003): 22–25. *Literary Cavalcade* is a catalog publication for the publisher Scholastic.

223. [untitled]. Introduction. *Kermit Lynch Wine Merchant Newsletter*. Berkeley CA, June 2003. 2 pages from an unpaginated newsletter. Introduction for *Adventures on the Wine Route* by Kermit Lynch. This is an introduction to the French edition of Lynch's book. *Mes aventures sur les routes du vin*. Paris: Payot, 2004. This was the first published appearance of this essay.

**2004**

224. [untitled]. *The Quotable Writer*. Ed. Lamar Underwood. Guilford CT: Lyons Press, 2004. 221, 224. Harrison contributes two quotes about the art of screenwriting taken from his memoir *Off to the Side* and his essay "Why I Write: Thoughts on the Craft of Fiction."

225. [untitled]. Introduction. *Residence on Earth*. By Pablo Neruda. Trans. Donald D. Walsh. New York: New Directions Publishing, 2004. xi–xvi. A reissue of Neruda's classic poetry collection. This is the first published appearance of this introduction.

226. "Charles Cleland . . . on the occasion of his retirement." Dedication. *An Upper Great Lakes Archaeological Odyssey: Essays in Honor of Charles E. Cleland*. Ed. William A. Lovis. Detroit MI: Wayne State University Press, 2004. Harrison contributes this dedication to Charles Cleland, emeritus professor and curator of anthropology, Michigan State University. This is the first published appearance of this essay.

227. "Father-in-Law," "Richard Olney's Final Book, *Reflexions*," "My Problems with White Wine," "Introduction." *Inspiring Thirst: Vintage Selections from the Kermit Lynch Wine Brochure*. Berkeley CA: Ten Speed Press, 2004. 271–72, 344–45, 365–67, 382–84. All these essays were previously published in the *Kermit Lynch Wine Merchant Newsletter* from 1995 to 2003.

228. [excerpt] "Just Before Dark." *The Retreat*. By Patrick Rambaud. New York: Grove Press, 2004. 199. This short sentence appears as an epigraph to chap. 5 of this novel.

229. [excerpt] "Starting Over." *Wild on the Fly* 2.2 (Spring 2004): cover. Quote from Harrison's essay titled "Starting Over" first published in the February 2000 issue of *Men's Journal*. This quote appears on the cover of this issue of *Wild on the Fly*.

230. "Food, Sex and Death." *Brick* 73 (Summer 2004): 142–45. An entry in Harrison's ongoing food column "Eat or Die." Also contains a new Harrison poem, "Time." This was the first published appearance of this essay and the poem.

231. "Tongue." *Brick* 74 (Winter 2004): 167–70. An entry in Harrison's ongoing food column titled "Eat or Die." This was the first published appearance of this essay.
232. "Odious Comparisons." *Kermit Lynch Wine Merchant Newsletter.* Berkeley CA, January 2004. 3-page essay in this monthly unpaginated newsletter. This was the first published appearance of this essay.
233. "Fifty Days on the Water." *Field and Stream* May 2004: 80–82, 134, 135. vol. 109, no. 1. This was the first published appearance of this essay.
234. "Wine Criticism and Literary Criticism (Part II)." *Kermit Lynch Wine Merchant Newsletter.* Berkeley CA, May 2004. 4-page essay in this monthly unpaginated newsletter. This was the first published appearance of this essay.
235. "Hideouts, Dream Towns and Great Escapes." *Men's Journal* May 2004: 20. vol. 13, no. 4. Harrison writes an introduction for the above-titled collection of essays in the cover story of this issue. This was the first published appearance of this essay.
236. "Dog Years." *Field and Stream* September 2004: 78–82, 131. vol. 109, no. 5. This was the first published appearance of this essay.
237. "A Really Big Lunch." *New Yorker* 6 September 2004: 78–82. This was the first published appearance of this essay. Describes a thirty-seven-course lunch in France.
238. [untitled]. "The Poetry Symposium." *New York Times Book Review* 21 November 2004: 13. Harrison contributes a short essay with eight other poets concerning books that have meant the most to them in the last 25 years. This is the first appearance of this essay.

## 2005

239. "Ducks." *Molto Italiano: 327 Simple Italian Recipes to Cook at Home.* By Mario Batali. New York: Ecco Press/HarperCollins, 2005. 329. Harrison contributes a short essay on the cooking of ducks. This was the first published appearance of this essay.
240. "A Really Big Lunch." *The Best American Travel Writing 2005.* Ed. Jamaica Kincaid. New York: Houghton Mifflin Co., 2005. 92–101. This essay first appeared in the 6 September 2004 issue of the *New Yorker*.
241. "Bear Posole." *Montana Writer's Cookbook: Eat Our Words.* Helena MT: Farcountry Press, 2005. 140. Forward by Mark A. Sherouse, introduction by Kim Anderson. Compiled by the Montana Center for the Book. Also contains a brief excerpt from *The Raw and the Cooked: Adventures of a Roving Gourmand*.
242. [untitled]. *Legends of the Fall.* Dir. Edward Zwick. DVD. Sony, 2005. Harrison provides a short essay in the booklet that accompanies the deluxe edition

re-release of *Legends of the Fall* concerning the film. The essay is dated 15 September 2005 and is its first published appearance. This booklet also contains a 2-page essay concerning Harrison's screenwriting career entitled "The Cinematic World of Jim Harrison."

243. [excerpt] "A Really Big Lunch." *Ennui to Go.* By Jon Winokur. Seattle WA: Sasquatch Books, 2005. 141. A short excerpt from an essay that first appeared in the *New Yorker*.

244. [excerpt] "The Raw and the Cooked." *Out of Range.* By C. J. Box. New York: G. P. Putnam's Sons, 2005. 67. A sentence from the above-referenced essay was used as an epigraph at the beginning of pt. 2 of this novel.

245. "Snake-Eating." *Brick* 75 (Summer 2005): 157–60. An entry in Harrison's ongoing food column titled "Eat or Die." This was the first published appearance of this essay. This issue also contained an unpaginated pamphlet that contained the Harrison poem "Alcohol" (see item B149).

246. "Food, Fitness, and Death." *Brick* 76 (Winter 2005): 9–13. An entry in Harrison's ongoing food column titled "Eat or Die." This was the first published appearance of this essay. Also a brief quote from the column adorns the spine of this issue.

247. "Wine Strategies." *Kermit Lynch Wine Merchant Newsletter.* Berkeley CA, January 2005. 3-page essay in this monthly unpaginated newsletter. This was the first published appearance of this essay.

248. "Memories of Meals with Lulu." *Saveur* 85 (June–July 2005): 86. Harrison contributes a brief reminiscence of a meal with Lulu Peyraud in an essay entitled "Lunch Chez Lulu." This was the first published appearance of this essay.

249. [excerpt] *Off to the Side. Heron Dance* 48 (August 2005): 10. A short quote from the memoir *Off to the Side*.

250. "Resuming the Pleasure." *Kermit Lynch Wine Merchant Newsletter.* Berkeley CA, September 2005. 3-page essay in this monthly unpaginated newsletter. This was the first published appearance of this essay.

**2006**

251. "The Fisherman Gourmand." *Big Sky Cooking.* By Meredith Brokaw and Ellen Wright. New York: Artisan, 2006. 154–55. This was the first published appearance of this essay.

252. [excerpt] *Legends of the Fall*, "Scrubbing the Floor the Night a Great Lady Died." *Eros and Equus: A Passion for the Horse.* Ed. Laura Chester. Minocqua WI: Willow Creek Press, 2006. 79, 189. Photographs by Donna DeMari.

253. "Jim Harrison to Henry Rago." *Letters between the Lines: A History of Poetry in*

*Letters, 1962–2002*. Ed. Joseph Parisi and Stephen Young. Chicago: Ivan R. Dee, 2006. 66, 76. This anthology prints two letters that Harrison wrote, to the then editor of *Poetry* magazine, Henry Rago, regarding publishing early poems and reviews that Harrison had submitted. The earliest letter is dated 6 December 1964, and the second is dated October 1965. This is the first published appearance of these letters.

254. [excerpt] *Off to the Side*. *The Story Factor*. By Annette Simmons. Cambridge MA: Basic Books, 2006. 83. A single sentence serves as an epigraph for chap. 4 in this book on the art of storytelling.
255. "Food and Mood." *Brick* 77 (Summer 2006): 146–50. An entry in Harrison's ongoing food column titled "Eat or Die." This was the first published appearance of this essay.
256. "Eternity and Food." *Brick* 78 (Winter 2006): 153–57. An entry in Harrison's ongoing food column titled "Eat or Die." This was the first appearance of this essay.
257. [untitled]. "Save These Books." *New York Times Book Review* 28 May 2006: 14. A short essay on favorite out-of-print cookbooks featuring chefs, writers, restaurateurs, and foodies. This was the first published appearance of this essay.
258. [excerpt] "Tracking." *Writer's Chronicle* 38.6 (May–Summer 2006): 25. This issue also includes an interview with Harrison.
259. "Vin Blanc." *Kermit Lynch Wine Merchant Newsletter*. Berkeley CA, August 2006. 4-page essay in this monthly unpaginated newsletter. This was the first published appearance of this essay.

**2007**

260. "Eat or Die." *A Garden of Forking Paths: An Anthology for Creative Writers*. Ed. Beth Anstandig and Eric Killough. Upper Saddle River NJ: Pearson Education, 2007. 57–60.
261. [excerpt] *Off to the Side*. *Eight Dogs Named Jack*. By Joe Borri. Troy MI: Momentum Books, 2007. 300. A short sentence serves as an epigraph at the beginning of the afterword to this collection of short stories.
262. "Grand Raptures." *Thin Ice: Coming of Age in Grand Rapids*. Ed. Reinder Van Til and Gordon Olson. Grand Rapids MI: William B. Eerdmans Publishing Co., 2007. 155–58. Harrison's essay deals with his growing up in the Grand Rapids area. This was the first published appearance of this essay.
263. [untitled]. *The Top Ten: Writers Pick Their Favorite Books*. Ed. J. Peder Zane. New York: W. W. Norton & Co., 2007. 72. Authors were asked to submit their list of 10 favorite books. Harrison's list appears on p. 72.

264. "A Really Big Lunch." *Secret Ingredients: The New Yorker Book of Food and Drink.* Ed. David Remnick. New York: Random House, 2007. 90–98. This essay first appeared in the 6 September 2004 issue of the *New Yorker* magazine.
265. "Foreword by Jim Harrison." Foreword. *The Tree of Meaning: Language, Mind and Ecology.* By Robert Bringhurst. Berkeley CA: Counterpoint Press, 2007. 1–5. This was the first published appearance of this essay.
266. "Here I Stand for a Few Minutes." *Brick* 79 (Summer 2007): 8–12. An entry in Harrison's ongoing food column titled "Eat or Die." This was the first appearance of this essay. Also a brief quote from the column adorns the spine of this issue.
267. "Don't Go out over Your Head." *Brick* 80 (Winter 2007): 165–69. An entry in Harrison's ongoing food column titled "Eat or Die." This was the first appearance of this essay.
268. "Don't Feed the Poets." *New York Times Book Review* 28 January 2007: 27. An essay from Harrison regarding the poet Karl Shapiro and his 1964 collection of prose poems, *The Bourgeois Poet*, in the "Essay" section. This was the first appearance of this essay.
269. "The Spirit of Wine." *Kermit Lynch Wine Merchant Newsletter.* Berkeley CA, March 2007. A 4-page essay in this monthly unpaginated newsletter. This was the first published appearance of this essay. There is also an advertisement for the new Harrison novel, *Returning to Earth*, at the end of the essay that also reprints a small portion of the Will Blythe review from the *New York Times Book Review*.
270. "About a Poem: Jim Harrison on 'A Primer on Parallel Lives.'" *Shambhala Sun* March 2007: 120. vol. 15, no. 4. This was the first appearance of this essay. A tribute to Dan Gerber's poem "A Primer on Parallel Lives."
271. "Lauren Hutton's ABC's." *Playboy* December 2007: 152–54, 180. vol. 54, no. 12. This was the first published appearance of this essay. Part of a collection of essays titled "Truly, Madly, Deeply (Mostly Madly)" in which four novelists "express their devotion to the singular icons who inspire love and lust, disorientation and deliverance." Harrison's piece concerns his crush on Lauren Hutton.
272. "One Good Thing Leads to Another." *Kermit Lynch Wine Merchant Newsletter.* Berkeley CA, December 2007. A 3-page essay in this monthly unpaginated newsletter. This was the first published appearance of this essay.

## 2008

273. "Introduction." *The Death of Jim Loney.* By James Welch. New York: Penguin Books, 2008. ix–xiv. This was the first published appearance of this introduction to James Welch's Penguin Classics reprint of his 1979 novel.

274. "Don't Fence Me In." *The Wide Open: Prose, Poetry, and Photographs of the Prairie*. Ed. Annick Smith and Susan O'Conner. Lincoln: University of Nebraska Press, 2008. 111–16. This anthology also contains Harrison's poem "To a Meadowlark" (see item B178).

275. "Rage and Appetite." *Brick* 81 (Summer 2008): 142–48. An entry in Harrison's ongoing food column titled "Eat or Die". This was the first appearance of this essay. There is also a photo of Harrison on p. 144 by Jean-Luc Bertini. A Bertini photo of Harrison also graces the cover of this issue of *Brick*.

276. "Close to the Bone." *Martha Stewart Living* October 2008: 144–51. no. 179. This was the first published appearance of this essay. Recipes and photos of bone in meat dishes. Harrison provided the essay and the text for the photographs.

277. "The Misadventure Journals." *Field and Stream* December 2008, January 2009: 105–08. vol. 113, no. 8. This was the first published appearance of this essay. Excerpts from Harrison's sporting journals. Portrait of Harrison by Riccardo Vecchio. Photos in essay by Terry W. Phipps.

278. "Food, Finance, and Spirit." *Brick* 82 (Winter 2009): 164–68. An entry in Harrison's ongoing food column titled "Eat or Die." This was the first appearance of this essay.

**General Notes**

*Just Before Dark* contains six essays that were previously unpublished. They are "Bar Pool," "The Preparation of Thomas Hearns," "Bird Hunting," "A Natural History of Some Poems," and "Dream as a Metaphor of Survival." The essay "A Memoir of Horse Pulling" appeared in a very different form as "The Real Fun of the Fair was the Horse Pulling" in the 31 August 1970 issue of *Sports Illustrated* (see item D6).

*The Raw and the Cooked: Adventures of a Roving Gourmand* contains two essays that were previously unpublished. They are "Versions of Reality" and "Wild Creatures: A Correspondence with Gerard Oberle."

# Section E
## *Reviews and Criticism by Jim Harrison*

**1965**
1. "The Northness of North." Rev. of *North Winter*, by Hayden Carruth. *Nation* 15 February 1965: 180. vol. 200, no. 7. This was Harrison's first published critical writing.

**1966**
2. "Muse and Hearth." Rev. of *Tape for the Turn of the Year* and *Corson's Inlet*, by A. R. Ammons. *Poetry* February 1966: 330–31. vol. 107, no. 5.
3. "California Hybrid." Rev. of *The Fork*, by Richard Duerden, *Against the Silences to Come*, by Ron Loewinshon, *The Process*, by David Meltzer, and *On Out* and *Hermit Poems*, by Lew Welch. *Poetry* June 1966: 198–201. vol. 108, no. 3.

**1968**
4. "Gnomic Verse." Rev. of *Amulet*, by Carl Rakosi. *New York Times Book Review* 28 January 1968: 10.
5. "Fresh Usual Words." Rev. of *After Experience*, by W. D. Snodgrass, *The Harvester's Vase*, by Ned O'Gorman, *Dying: An Introduction*, by L. E. Sissman, *So Long at the Fair*, by Miller Williams, and *Figure in the Door*, by Arthur Gregor. *New York Times Book Review* 28 April 1968: 6.

**1969**
6. "Some Recent Books." Rev. of *The Naomi Poems: Corpse and Beans*, by Saint Geraud [Bill Knott], *Gunslinger*, by Ed Dorn, and *Poets on Street Corners*, by Olga Carlisle. *Sumac* 1.3 (Spring 1969): 102–03.
7. "A Note on J. D. Reed's Expressways." Rev. of *Expressways*, by J. D. Reed. *Sumac* 2.1 (Fall 1969): 143–46.

8. "Pure Poetry." Rev. of *Bending the Bow*, by Robert Duncan. *New York Times Book Review* 29 September 1969: 24. Reprinted in *Just Before Dark*.

**1970**

9. "Eshleman's Indiana." Rev. of *Indiana*, by Clayton Eshleman. *Sumac* 2.2–3 (Winter–Spring 1970): 231–33.

**1972**

10. "Women Impossible Not to Love and Impossible to Love Right." Rev. of *All My Friends Are Going to Be Strangers*, by Larry McMurtry. *New York Times Book Review* 19 March 1972: 5, 26.
11. "Three Novels: Comic, Cute, Cool." Rev. of *Geronimo Rex*, by Barry Hannah, *The Bride Wore the Traditional Gold*, by Talbot Spivak, and *Tangier Buzzless Flies*, by John Hopkins. *New York Times Book Review* 14 May 1972: 4, 22.
12. "The Importance of Being Young—and Ernest." Rev. of *The Nick Adams Stories*, by Ernest Hemingway. *Washington Post* 4 June 1972: BW6. Reprinted in *Just Before Dark*.

**1974**

13. "Note on Shinkichi Takahashi." Rev. of *Afterimages: Zen Poems*, by Shinkichi Takahashi. *American Poetry Review* 3.2 (March–April 1974): 48–49. Reprinted in *Just Before Dark*.

**1975**

14. "The Dreadful Lemon Sky." Rev. of *The Dreadful Lemon Sky*, by John D. MacDonald. *New York Times Book Review* 23 February 1975: 32–35. Reprinted in *Just Before Dark*.
15. "Of Arms, the Man and the Whale They Sing: Dirges and Flutes in the Fog." Rev. of *Mine in the Waters*, by Joan McIntyre. *Sports Illustrated* 10 March 1975: 10. This review was printed in the "Booktalk" section. Karen Dmochowsky of *Sports Illustrated* says that the column "Booktalk" did not appear in all issues of the magazine. Regional issues carried this column depending on how much ad space was sold in any given region.
16. "A Writer Loses His Way in Clouds of Theory about the Bermuda Triangle." Rev. of *The Bermuda Triangle*, by Charles Berlitz. *Sports Illustrated* 31 March 1975: 15. This review was printed in the "Booktalk" section. Karen Dmochowsky of *Sports Illustrated* says that the column "Booktalk" did not appear in all issues of the magazine. Regional issues carried this column depending on how much ad space was sold in any given region.
17. "A Zoologist Shares the Joys and Woes of Life among the Elephants." Rev.

of *Among the Elephants,* by Iain Douglas-Hamilton and Oria Douglas-Hamilton. *Sports Illustrated* 1 September 1975: 6. This review was printed in the "Booktalk" section. Karen Dmochowsky of *Sports Illustrated* says that the column "Booktalk" did not appear in all issues of the magazine. Regional issues carried this column depending on how much ad space was sold in any given region.

18. "Nashville's Grand Ole Opry." Rev. of *Nashville's Grand Ole Opry,* by Jack Hurst. *New York Times Book Review* 30 November 1975: 286.

19. [untitled]. Rev. of *The Secret Life of Animals,* by Lorus and Margery Milne and Franklin Russell. *Sports Illustrated* 22–29 December 1975: 11, 15. In the "Wrap-Up" section.

**1976**

20. "The Main Character Is the Cold and the Snow." Rev. of *The Snow Walker,* by Farley Mowat. *New York Times Book Review* 26 February 1976: 4–5. Reprinted in *Just Before Dark*.

21. "The Monkey Wrench Gang." Rev. of *The Monkey Wrench Gang,* by Edward Abbey. *New York Times Book Review* 14 November 1976: 59.

22. "Nature." Rev. of *The Audubon Society Book of Wild Birds,* by Les Line and Franklin Russell, *The Worlds of Ernest Thompson Seton,* by John G. Samson, *The Book of Sharks,* by Richard Ellis, *The Swamp,* by Bill Thomas, *Butterflies,* by Kjell Sandman and Jo Brewer, *Sensitive Chaos,* by Theodor Schwenk, *The Audubon Wildlife Treasury,* by Les Line, *Audubon Animals,* by Robert Elman, *Dwellers in the Sea,* by Douglas Faulkner and Barry Fell, and *Birds of the West Coast,* by J. F. Lansdowne. *New York Times Book Review* 5 December 1976: 7, 95, 101.

**1978**

23. "10,000 Successive Octobers." Rev. of *The Snow Leopard,* by Peter Matthiessen. *Nation* 16 September 1978: 250–51. vol. 227, no. 8. Reprinted in *Just Before Dark* retitled as "The Snow Leopard."

**1981**

24. "Voice of the Wilderness." Rev. of *Sand Rivers,* by Peter Matthiessen. *New York Times Book Review* 17 May 1981: 1, 26.

**1995**

25. "Books for Young Adults: Writer's Recommendations." *Hungry Mind Review* 35 (Fall 1995): 55. Harrison's recommendation is *Practice of the Wild,* by Gary Snyder.

**2000**

26. "Richard Olney's Final Book: *Reflexions.*" *Kermit Lynch Wine Merchant Newsletter.* Berkeley CA, March 2000. First English publication of an essay that originally appeared in the 28 October 1999 *Revue des Deux Mondes* (Paris).

**2007**

27. "King of Pain." Rev. of *The Pleasures of the Damned,* by Charles Bukowski, ed. John Martin. *New York Times Book Review* 25 November 2007: 17. This issue of the *New York Times Book Review* also has a brief essay regarding Harrison in the "Up Front" section on p. 8.

# Section F
## *Screenplays*

**Produced Screenplays**
1. *Cold Feet*. Dir. Robert Dornhelm. Avenue Pictures, 1989. Written with Thomas McGuane. Released 19 May 1989. "A comic fable about greed, lust, and high-fashion footwear." Originally titled *Razorback*.
2. *Revenge*. Dir. Tony Scott. Columbia Pictures, 1990. Written with Jeffrey Fiskin. Released 16 February 1990. Also an undated draft by Walter Hill and David Giler. Also another draft by John and Tony Houston dated April 1987. Five different known drafts.
3. *Wolf*. Dir. Mike Nichols. Sony Pictures, 1994. Written with Wesley Strick. Released 17 June 1994. Harrison is also listed as an associate producer for this film.
4. *Legends of the Fall*. Dir. Edward Zwick. Tristar Pictures, 1994. Final screenplay credits to Susan Shilliday and Bill Wittliff. Released 13 January 1995.
5. *Carried Away*. Dir. Bruno Barreto. New Line Cinema, 1996. Final screenplay credits to Ed Jones. Movie stars Dennis Hopper and Amy Irving in this film rendition of *Farmer*. Released 29 March 1996.

**Unproduced Screenplays**
   **Note:** The titles below represent screenplay projects that Harrison was involved with during his Hollywood years. Some of the titles included in this list are ideas or proposals to various studios, directors, or producers and are merely notes or a rough outline. These are identified as treatments. Others represent projects that were relatively far along in the writing process and had gone through significant rewrites and a number of different drafts. These are identified as screenplays. This information was provided by Harrison and taken from his archive at Grand Valley State University.

6. *Prince of Los Angeles*. 1975. Screenplay.
7. *A Good Day to Die*. 1975. Screenplay. A Frederick Weisman project.
8. *Iron Locusts*. 1975–76. Treatment.
9. *Aqua Prieta*. ca. 1976. Treatment.
10. *Wendigo*. 1977. Renamed *Manitou* in 1978. Treatment.
11. *Far Tortuga*. 1978. Treatment for television series based on Peter Matthiessen's book.
12. *Dress Her in Indigo*. 1979. Screenplay. Harrison also worked on a proposal to write a series based on the Travis McGee character of the John D. McDonald novels.
13. *Dead Calm*. 1979. Screenplay.
14. *Charlie Boy*. 1980. Screenplay based on the novel by Peter Feibleman.
15. *Piece of Resistance*. ca. 1981. Treatment.
16. *Revenant*. ca. 1981. Treatment.
17. *Working Horses*. ca. 1981. Treatment.
18. *Man in the Green Suit*. ca. 1981. Treatment.
19. *Blue Moon in Kentucky*. 1982. Screenplay.
20. *Warlock*. 1982. Treatment.
21. *Samba (Brazil)*. 1983–84. Screenplay.
22. *Edward Curtis Project*. 1984–85. Screenplay.
23. *Stanley Jaffee Project*. 1985–86. Screenplay.
24. *Later in Life*. 1985. Treatment.
25. *David Milch Project*. 1987. Screenplay. This appears to be a proposal for an episode of *Miami Vice*.
26. *Sydney Pollack Project*. 1985–87. Screenplay.
27. *Miami Vice TV Project*. 1987. Screenplay.
28. *Between Wars*. 1988–97. Screenplay. Renamed *The Last Posse* (1991–93) in the process. A screenplay Harrison was working on with the producer Doug Wick and Harrison Ford. The final drafts of this project were entitled *Catledge*.
29. *Dalva*. 1993. Treatment. This title was eventually produced for ABC television in 1996; however, Harrison was not involved in the television movie.
30. *Captive*. 1993–95. Screenplay.
31. *The Irish Thing*. 1996. Treatment.
32. *The Way We Are*. 1996. Treatment. A Doug Wick project.
33. *Crockett*. 1996. Treatment. A Doug Wick project.
34. *The Man Who Loved Music*. 1996–99. Treatment.
35. *Julip*. 1997–99. Treatment.
36. *The Raw and the Cooked*. 1998. Treatment with Jamie Harrison.
37. *Flora Montagu*. 1999. Treatment with Jamie Harrison.
38. *Scythian Women*. 2000. Treatment with Jamie Harrison.
39. *The Beast God Forgot to Invent*. 2000. Treatment with Jamie Harrison.

# Section G
## *Miscellany: Audio Readings, Videotapes, Dust-Jacket Encomiums*

**Audio Readings and Presentations**
1. Poetry Reading. Poetry Center at the 92nd Street Y, New York. 19 April 1965. An audiotaped poetry reading of the following poems: "Sketch for a Job Application Blank," "David," "Complaint," "Exercise," "She," "Hitchhiking," "Malediction," "Park at Night," "Dead Doe," "Nightmare," "New Liturgy," "Kinship," "Sequence of Women." All poems read by Jim Harrison are from *Plain Song*.
2. Poetry Reading. Coolidge Hall at the Library of Congress, Washington DC. 3 March 1975. Harrison reads poetry excerpts from the following titles: *Plain Song, Locations, Outlyer and Ghazals,* and *Letters to Yesenin*. Catalog T8333. LC control no. 94838930. Call no. LWO 8333.
3. Audiotape. The Academy of American Poets, New York. 26, 27 January 1978. "Jim Harrison: A Conversation." Three tapes recorded at the Donnell Library Center.
4. Audiotape. American Audio Prose Library, Columbia MO. 1984. "An Interview with Jim Harrison." An interview conducted by Kay Bonetti for the American Prose Library series.
5. Audiotape. American Audio Prose Library, Columbia MO. May 1984. Harrison reads excerpts from *Wolf, Farmer,* "Legends of the Fall," *Sundog,* and "Revenge."
6. Audiotape. *Revenge*. Los Angeles: Book of the Road, 1985. Read by Denis Arndt.
7. Audiotape. *Dalva*. New York: Recorded Books, 1994. Unabridged. Read by Alyssa Bressnahan and Frank Muller. This audiobook was distributed only to libraries.

8. Audiotape. *Legends of the Fall*. Novato CA: Soundelux Audio Publishing, 1994. Read by Jacob Witkin.
9. Audiotape. *Julip*. New York: Pocket Books, 1995. Harrison reads an excerpt from *Julip* on this first annual audio sampler from Pocket Books, a promotional tape sent out to reviewers.
10. Audiotape. *After Ikkyu*. Boston: Shambhala Publications, 1996. Read by Jim Harrison. Unabridged.
11. Audiotape. "The Key West Literary Seminar." Key West Literary Seminar, Key West FL. 11–14 January 1996. 12 tapes recording all the discussion groups at the Key West Literary Seminar. Other writers who attended this seminar included Thomas McGuane, James Welch, Gretel Ehrlich, Terry Tempest Williams, and Doug Peacock. The theme of this seminar was "American Writers and the Natural World."
12. Audiotape. "Voices and Visions." Seattle Arts and Lectures Series, Seattle WA. 3 March 1997. Reading and discussion with question-and-answer session.
13. Audiotape. [untitled]. Portland Arts and Lectures Series, Portland OR. 5 March 1997. Reading and discussion with question-and-answer session.
14. Audiotape and CD. *True North*. Blackstone Audiobooks, 2004. Read by Christopher Lane. Unabridged.
15. Audiotape and CD. "Interview." New Letters on the Air, Kansas City MO. 2005. Interview conducted by Angela Elam in 2004 but not broadcast or released until July 2005. Parts 1 and 2 released separately in 2005. New Letters on the Air is part of the University of Missouri–Kansas City.
16. Audiotape and CD. *The Summer He Didn't Die*. Blackstone Audiobooks, 2005. Read by Lloyd James and Marguerite Gavin. Unabridged.
17. Audiotape and CD. *Returning to Earth*. Blackstone Audiobooks, 2007. Read by Traci Svendsgaard, Ray Porter, Tom Weiner, and Paul Michael Garcia.
18. Audio CD. Interview. *On Point—WBUR Boston*. Interview conducted by host Tom Ashbrook that aired 6 March 2007.

**Videotaped Documentaries**
19. *Tarpon*. Dir. Guy de la Valdene. ca. 1977. Video documentary on tarpon fishing in the waters off Key West FL. Includes appearances by Harrison, Thomas McGuane, and Richard Brautigan, among others, and contains comments and dialogue by them all. Music by Jimmy Buffett.
20. *Jim Harrison: Half Dog and Half Wolf*. Dir. Brice Matthieussent and Georges Luneau. Plante Cable/Cine Cinema Cable/Gedeon, 1993. French video documentary on Harrison's writing and life. French title is *Jim Harrison: Entre Chien et Loup*.

21. *Through Lakota Eyes: A Film about Human Rights*. Dir. Jim Cortez and Eli Tail Sr. Redheart Films, 2008. A film perspective of the Lakota Sioux. Harrison reads his introduction from *On the Trail to Wounded Knee* as a special feature of this film.

## Miscellany

22. "Stony Brook Poets' Prophesy—June 23, 1968." NP, 23 June 1968. 8½" × 11" typed sheet assembled by 23 poets with 12 holographic signatures. The number of copies printed is unknown. Harrison's is one of the signatures that appear on this sheet. This essay was published 2 months later in a slightly different form in the August 1968 issue of *Pony Tail: A Magazine for Always* 1.1 (August 1968). Unpaginated journal. Cover states "Poetry from Stony Brook." Ed. Eliot Weinberger and Geoffrey O'Brien. Port Jefferson NY: Yellow Press. By the time this essay appeared in *Pony Tail* the number of signatories had grown to 36.
23. "Poet Power." *New York Review of Books* 22 August 1968: 38. vol. 11, no. 3. Published in the "Letters" section. Harrison, as a member of the 36 assembled poets, has signed this letter in protest of bad poetry, "ecological disruption of the planet," state-sponsored violence, and the war in Vietnam and in support of Black Power and the academies returning to wisdom study in tree groves. The original title of this essay was "Stony Brook Poets' Prophesy—23 June 1968"; it was first published in *Pony Tail* in a slightly different form (see item G22).
24. "Ford's Better Idea." *New York Review of Books* 25 January 1973: 45, 46. vol. 19, nos. 11–12. Published in the "Letters" section. Harrison, as the editor of *Sumac*, has signed this letter along with the editors of 20 other literary publications in protest of a grant made by the Ford Foundation to the International Association for Cultural Freedom in Paris.
25. *The 1990 Western Wilderness Calendar*. Ed. Ken Sanders. Salt Lake City UT: Dream Garden Press, 1989. Quote from Harrison's first novel, *Wolf*, is included under a photo for the month of July.
26. *Lord John Signatures*. Northridge CA: Lord John Press, 1990. This is a book of autographs, photographs, photostats, etc. Harrison is represented.
27. *Images from the Great West*. Ed. Marnie Walker Gaede. La Canada CA: Chaco Press, 1990. Photographs by Marc Gaede of Western landscapes and Western authors. Harrison is represented on p. 78.
28. "The Montana Suite Convenes: Richard Ford, Annick Smith, Jim Harrison, Beverly Lowry, William Kittredge, and Thomas McGuane. Absent: Rick Bass." *New Yorker* 24 June, 1 July 1996: 105. Full-page color painting by Bruce McCall of the above authors in a spacious Montana setting.

29. *Gone to Sanctuary, from the Sins of Confusion.* Santa Barbara CA: Capra Press, 1997. Photographs by John S. Kiewit. A collection of photographs of the American West matched with quotes from authors, from naturalists, and from the photographer's journal. Harrison has provided quotes from his essay "Going Places" and from *Just Before Dark*. 138, 244.
30. [excerpt] *Just Before Dark. Orvis Catalog—the Sporting Tradition.* Fall 1997. 94. There is also a brief bio and a photograph of Harrison.
31. Author Trading Card, no. 404. San Francisco: Booksmith, 2000. Part of the Booksmith author trading card series; printed to commemorate a reading by Harrison from *The Beast God Forgot to Invent* on 26 October 2000. Photo of Harrison on front of card, which measures 2½" × 3½", and author information on reverse.
32. "Battenkill Magnum Rolladuffle." *Orvis Catalog—Fly Fishing 2001.* 2001. 137. Ad includes a photograph of Harrison.
33. "The Smoker Knocked My Socks Off." *2002 Fall Orvis Catalog.* Fall 2002. 45. Harrison recommends the Orvis electric stainless smoker. Ad includes a photograph of Harrison. This same quote and ad have appeared in several catalogs since this first appearance.
34. "Zingerman's is the ne plus ultra of delicatessens." *Zingerman's Thanksgiving Catalog, 2003.* 2003. 41. Harrison putting in a good word for one of his favorite delis in Ann Arbor MI.
35. *The Book of Fictional Days.* Windsor CT: Tide-Mark Press, 2003. Illustrated by Barry Moser, text by Bob Gordon. A 2004 weekly engagement calendar, spiral bound. Includes 53 woodcut engravings by Moser of different authors. Harrison's portrait is included opposite the week of 21 November 2004. Unpaginated.
36. "Jim Harrison on the Orvis T3." *2004 Volume 1 Fly Fishing Catalog.* 2004. 10. Harrison recommends the new Orvis T3 fly rod. Ad includes a photograph of Harrison. Quote is attributed to Harrison and Dan Lahren.
37. *Shadow and Light.* Northampton MA: Pennyroyal Press, 2004. A portfolio of wood and relief engravings by Barry Moser. Introduction by Ann Patchett with an afterword by Moser. Harrison's portrait is among those presented in this portfolio of "Artists, Architects, Writers, Composers and Friends."
38. *Jim Harrison.* Livingston MT: Clark City Press, 2004. A poster designed by Russell Chatham and printed by his press to announce a reading at the Ezra Pound house in Hailey ID on 9 May 2004. Sponsored by the Idaho Humanities Council. Chatham's painting on this poster is *A Late Afternoon in Chileno Valley*. There was also a program printed for this event with the same painting on the front.

39. "University Acquires Harrison's Manuscripts, Materials." *Grand Valley Magazine* 5.1 (Fall 2005): 8. Quarterly publication from Grand Valley State University. A short article announcing the acquisition of the Harrison Papers by the university's special collections.
40. Author Trading Card, no. 899. San Francisco: Booksmith, 2007. Part of the Booksmith author trading card series; printed to commemorate a reading by Harrison from *Returning to Earth* on 7 February 2007. Photo of Harrison on front of card, which measures 2½" × 3½", and author information on reverse.
41. [untitled]. *Waking Owl Books*. Undated bookmark from Waking Owl Books, an independent bookstore in Salt Lake City UT. The quote attributed to Harrison reads: "My hands are clumsy. I typed five novels with a single forefinger. Frankly, this limited my interest in revision."

**Dust-Jacket Encomiums by Harrison**

Note: A collation of lists by Robert DeMott, Joseph Bednarik, Beef Torrey, Patrick Smith, Gregg Orr, Brandon Kelley, and David Harrison.

42. Carruth, Hayden. *For You: Poems by Hayden Carruth*. New York: New Directions Publishing, 1970.

    "Carruth has become a substantial poet, one of the finest. In 'North Winter' we have a unified sequence forming a single long poem. In itself this is a rare thing in our time: that the poem is completely successful is nothing short of a triumph."

43. Gerber, Dan. *The Revenant*. Fremont MI: Sumac Press, 1971.

    "*The Revenant* is a striking first collection: compact, full of explosive control. Dan Gerber's book transmits a lucid sense of wonderment and pure song, finely honed poetry, pure and unadorned."

44. Hannah, Barry. *Geronimo Rex*. New York: Viking Press, 1972.

    A section of Harrison's *New York Times Book Review* review of *Geronimo Rex* appears on the back cover of Hannah's *Nightwatchman* (New York: Viking Press, 1973) under the heading: "Critics delighted in Barry Hannah's first novel, *Geronimo Rex*."

    "*Geronimo Rex* is a stunning piece of entertainment. . . . Hannah is one of those young writers who is brilliantly drunk with words and could at gunpoint write a life story on a telephone pole. . . . The novel competes with James Whitehead's recent *Joiner* for being the most satisfactory novel to come out of the South by a young writer since Reynolds Price published *A Long and Happy Life* in 1962."

45. McMurtry, Larry. *All My Friends Are Going to Be Strangers*. New York: Simon and Schuster, 1972.

"It is difficult to characterize a talent as outsized as McMurtry's. Often his work seems disproportionately sensual and violent, but these qualities in *All My Friends Are Going to Be Strangers* are tempered by his comic genius, his ability to render a sense of landscape and place, and an interior intellectual tension that resembles in intensity that of Saul Bellow's *Mr. Sammler's Planet*." This blurb was also listed on the dust jacket of McMurtry's *Terms of Endearment* (New York: Simon and Schuster, 1975) under "Praise for Larry McMurtry's *All My Friends Are Going to Be Strangers*."

46. Hjortsberg, William. *Symbiography*. Fremont MI: Sumac Press, 1973.

"*Symbiography* represents a remarkable advance over Hjortsberg's previous novels, *Alp* and *Gray Matters*. This novel puts Hjorstberg among the forefront of our young experimental novelists."

47. Gerber, Dan. *American Atlas*. Englewood Cliffs NJ: Prentice-Hall, 1973.

"*American Atlas* is a splendid first novel. You are immediately engrossed in the charm and general craziness of the hero who, counter to the trend nowadays, isn't a whiner. It's a finely written comic novel with a sure sense of velocity and moral insight."

48. Gerber, Dan. *Out of Control*. Englewood Cliffs NJ: Prentice-Hall, 1974.

"A fascinating novel, ostensibly centered in the racing world, though its true concern is the dome of its driver-hero. Deftly and naturally written, often comic, playing off its interlocking themes of sexuality and the inevitable violence of the conclusion."

49. Jones, Robert F. *Blood Sport: A Journey Up the Hassayampa*. New York: Lyons & Burford, 1974.

"Brilliant. It reads like Henry Miller writing for an outdoor magazine."

50. Welch, James. *Winter in the Blood*. New York: Harper & Row, 1974.

"*Winter in the Blood* is a wonderful novel. The dialog is marvelously apt, and the contrast between traditional and contemporary qualities very powerful. As an 'Indian' novel, it doesn't bow to any other sort of novel. It is deeply and strangely 'American' in a way that very few of our novels are."

51. McIntyre, Joan. *Mind in the Water*. San Francisco: Sierra Club, 1974.

"A magnificent gathering of scientific studies, stories of personal encounters, lore from the whaling days, poems, Greek and Eskimo myths, photographs, all put together for the pleasure and sorrow of those who love or are interested in our brother and sister mammals in the sea."

52. Hubert, Jim. *Hearts of the Tattooed: Poems*. Sunnyvale CA: Impact, 1978.

"I've been reading Jim Hubert's poetry for 5–6 years now and must attribute the slowness of his public recognition to the uniqueness of this voice: steady, utterly idiosyncratic, informed by the sort of talent that will inevitably find a worthy audience."

53. Brautigan, Richard. *June 30th, June 30th*. New York: Delacorte Press/Seymour Lawrence, 1978.

    "What can I say? It is your work that has touched me the most deeply, the least mannered and most exact in its insistent nakedness. It is not a succession of lyrics but finally ONE BOOK. A long poem that offers us its bounty in fragments. It is saturated with the 'otherness' we know to be our most honest state and the true state of poetry. It offers itself in perhaps the unconscious but ancient fabled form of the voyage. It is about the stately courage and loneliness of this voyage into a strange land which is both Japan and the true self of the poet, where there are no barriers to admitting and singing all. It is about love and exhaustion and permanent transition, so fatal that it is beyond the poet's comprehension. I love the book because it is a true song, owning no auspices other than its own; owning the purity we think we aim at on this bloody journey."

54. Reed, J. D. *Freefall*. New York: Delacorte Press, 1980.

    "J. D. Reed's *Freefall* is a wonderful novel about a particularly dangerous subject. I read it compulsively in four hours, waking with the notion that I was lost in a cold, wet forest in the middle of the night. Reed is a first-rate storyteller who should gather a huge audience for his obsession."

55. Gifford, Barry. *Port Tropique*. Berkeley CA: Black Lizard Books, 1980.

    "A wonderful piece of writing."

56. Martin, David. *The Crying Heart Tattoo*. New York: Holt, Rinehart, Winston, 1982.

    "The most truly original novel I've read in some years, plus being a wonderfully poignant love story, a kind of Midwestern gothic."

57. Newth, Rebecca. *Finding the Lamb*. Tarrytown NY: Open Book Publications, 1983.

    "*Finding the Lamb* is a splendid book of poems. There is a quiet, luminescent purity to it, in an age when quietness is likely to go unnoticed. A prose excerpt is first rate; and Newth's poems don't even vaguely resemble anyone else's."

58. Torgersen, Eric. *Ethiopia*. Brooklyn NY: Hanging Loose Press, 1983.

    "I thought the writing in *Ethiopia* to be wonderfully harsh and deft, often brilliant."

59. Russell, Franklin. *The Hunting Animal*. New York: Harper & Row, 1983.

    "Caramba! *The Hunting Animal* is the emotional equivalent of a cyclone.

Russell is well into an area here usually inhabited only by Peter Matthiessen. The book is a stupefying tone poem, with a kind of rare, specific density that signals returns to the volume. The prose and observations are those found rarely outside a major novel. Simply put, *The Hunting Animal* is a delight to the senses and the soul."

60. Barich, Bill. *Traveling Light*. New York: Viking Press, 1984.

    "I had a fine time with *Traveling Light*. Barich is a splendid prose stylist . . . I will continue to look forward to anything he writes."

61. Ford, Richard. *A Piece of My Heart*. New York: Vintage Books, 1985.

    "Superb . . . brutally real and at the same time haunting . . . one of those rare surprises that come along every few years."

62. Carroll, E. Jeanne. *Female Difficulties: Sorority Sisters, Rodeo Queens, Frigid Women, Smut Stars, and Other Modern Girls*. New York: Bantam Books, 1985.

    "E. Jean Carroll has the shock and snazz value that Tom Wolfe had years ago. She is one of a kind."

63. Williams, Joy. *Taking Care*. New York: Random House, 1985.

    "These stories are so chillingly astute about the question of love that one wonders if one has really ever thought about love before, much less been in love before."

64. Welch, James. *Fools Crow*. New York: Viking Press, 1986.

    "James Welch with this novel is indisputably one of the finest writers of his generation."

65. Takahashi, Shinkichi. *The Triumph of the Sparrow: Zen Poems of Shinkichi Takahashi*. Trans. Lucien Stryk, with the assistance of Takahashi Ikemoto. New York: Grove Press, 1986.

    "We visit places in Takahashi that we once may have visited in a dream or in a moment too startling to record the perception. . . . You need know nothing of Zen to become immersed in his work. You will inevitably know something of Zen when you emerge."

66. Gerber, Dan. *Snow on the Backs of Animals*. Seattle: Winn Books, 1986.

    "*Snow on the Backs of Animals* is singularly fine, the kind of book it would not be impertinent to read sitting on a stump in a forest clearing or beside a river. The poems are full of the kind of attention to animal and human life, and to the natural world, that is generally lost in the sump of ego. . . . [The poems] transmit a lucid sense of wonderment and pure song, finely honed poetry, pure and unadorned."

67. Caddy, John. *Eating the Sting*. Minneapolis: Milkweed Editions, 1986.

    "This is an improbably strong book. John Caddy is a piper at the gates of dawn, which is what a poet is supposed to be."

68. Ardinger, Richard. *"What Thou Lovest Well Remains": 100 Years of Ezra Pound*. Boise ID: Limberlost Press, 1986.

    "This anthology is a lovely and appropriate book for a man dead in body only."

69. Groom, Winston. *Forrest Gump*. New York: Doubleday & Co., 1986.

    "*Forrest Gump* is line bred out of Voltaire and Huck Finn; its humor is wild and coarse, a satire right on the money. It is not the less honest for being so funny, for bringing the woebegone archangels of our culture and history to judgment. Anyone who doesn't read this book deserves to spend the winter in North Dakota."

70. Reed, J. D., and Christine Reed. *Exposure*. New York: Soho Press, 1987.

    "A fascinating, engrossing mystery about the world of soccer. The writing transcends the genre."

71. Barich, Bill. *Hard to Be Good*. New York: Farrar Straus Giroux, 1987.

    "He is a splendid stylist and . . . captures the soul of a place in the manner of the travel writings of Norman Douglas and D. H. Laurence."

72. Queffelec, Yann. *The Wedding*. New York: Macmillan, 1987.

    "*The Wedding* is a tremendous novel, fiction of the purest sort and an unqualified act of genius. It's wildly inventive in the terms that we demand from first-rate fiction and its derivations are as mysterious as those that surround all first-rate work. I don't remember reading so striking a piece of European literature since *The Tin Drum* by Gunther Grass."

73. O'Brien, Dan. *The Rites of Autumn: A Falconer's Journey across the American West*. New York: Lyons Press, 1988.

    "A quiet but breathtaking dignity. . . . I would insist that anyone who cares about birds and the natural world read *The Rites of Autumn*."

74. Reinhard, John. *Burning the Prairie*. St. Paul MN: New Rivers Press, 1988.

    "Another test of poetry might be that which you can read when you first get up in the morning in a cabin in the woods. John Reinhard's *Burning the Prairie* is this rare sort of work—not that it's devotional in nature, but that nearly all of the poems give us something we knew but never thought of before. Reinhard seems to live and write between the lines of what is accepted as life, thus the poems surprise and delight us, adding in measure that homely old word, wisdom."

75. Delp, Michael. *Over the Graves of Horses*. Detroit MI: Wayne State University Press, 1988.

    "In *Over the Graves of Horses*, Michael Delp mines an area owned by Rilke and Lorca, and later worked quite successfully by James Wright and Robert Bly. In his best poems, Delp approaches the success of the latter two:

there is the dimension of stillness, a familiarity with beasts, the land, forest and water that is rarely seen in American poetry. This is a wonderful collection of poems for those who are curious about a state of mind that comes before poetry."

76. Quammen, David. *The Flight of the Iguana*. New York: Delacorte Press, 1988.

    "I've been wandering around in the outdoors for 40 years and in recent times have come to depend on David Quammen to tell me what I'm looking at. He has an extraordinary eye and is a truly extraordinary writer. I now place him up there with my favorites, Matthiessen, Hoagland, and Lopez, and will read everything he writes."

77. Currey, Richard. *Fatal Light*. New York: E. P. Dutton/Seymour Lawrence, 1988.

    "Richard Currey's *Fatal Light* is an exquisite, heartrending book. I was reminded of something said by another warrior, Rene Char, 'Lucidity is the wound closest to the sun.' What draws me most to Richard Currey is the beauty and economy of his prose which is, after all, the signal quality that can carry a writer on through a great career."

78. Williams, Joy. *Breaking and Entering*. New York: Vintage Contemporaries, 1988.

    "An ominous and enthralling novel . . . truly significant fiction, of which there is not very much around. *Breaking and Entering* reminds me again that life is short; it is also very wide."

79. Baxter, Charles. *Imaginary Paintings and Other Poems*. Latham NY: Paris Review Editions, 1989.

    "I read Charles Baxter's *Imaginary Paintings* with intense pleasure. This is poetry of the first order, characterized by an anguished, almost inconsolable lyricism, utterly immersed in the life that is, a life that tends to be ignored in our art, whatever the form."

80. Driscoll, Jack. *Building the Cold from Memory*. Greenfield Center NY: Ithaca House/Greenfield Press, 1989.

    "Like all very good poetry *Building the Cold from Memory* confuses and makes our attention gain its own balance. There are many superb pieces (which) snapped me alert as if a ghost was pulling on my ear."

81. Nelson, Richard. *The Island Within*. New York: Random House, 1989.

    "On the borders of consciousness as in Matthiessen and Lopez. Along with very few others, this is a holy book . . . a text to help us understand ourselves within the natural world."

82. Bass, Rick. *Oil Notes*. Boston: Houghton Mifflin Co., 1989.

"Rick Bass' *Oil Notes* is a singular book, perhaps a classic in a brand new form. Bass is a short story writer with a poet's eye who is also, of all things, an oil geologist who loves his work. *Oil Notes* is an exuberant book, written with care and beauty out of the lineage of Annie Dillard, Gretel Ehrlich and Peter Matthiessen. It celebrates life from an absolutely fresh angle and leaves one wishing it were five times as long."

83. Garfunkel, Art. *Still Water*. New York: E. P. Dutton, 1989.

"*Still Water* is an intensely impressive first book of poems. There is a lovely and intricate facility of language coupled with themes, however painful, that show Art Garfunkel has mastered another art form."

84. Gerber, Dan. *Grass Fires*. Livingston MT: Clark City Press, 1989.

"Far from the *au courant* mechanics of minimalism, the stories in *Grass Fires* are strong, visceral, poignant, out of the lineage of Willa Cather and Sherwood Anderson, perhaps the Irish Frank O'Connor and Edna O'Brien. The collection carries a substantial weight, but flies, a night and day bird with a unique and peculiar vision of soul and landscape."

85. Bowden, Charles. *Red Line*. New York: W. W. Norton & Co., 1989.

"Charles Bowden's *Red Line* is a look at America through the window of the southwest. His vision is as nasty, peculiar, brutal, as it is intriguing and, perhaps, accurate. Bowden offers consciousness rather than consolation, but in order to do anything about our nightmares we must take a cold look and *Red Line* casts the coldest eye in recent memory."

86. Bass, Rick. *The Watch*. New York: Washington Square Press, 1990.

"Rick Bass owns a durable and authentic voice. I read *The Watch* with intense pleasure, wondering at the skill of a young writer who can both frighten and amaze. This is a superb debut."

87. Gerber, Dan. *A Voice from the River*. Livingston MT: Clark City Press, 1990.

"Dan Gerber has followed up his wonderful collection of stories, *Grass Fires*, with a first rate novel. It is a mature work of fiction and an engrossing reading experience."

88. de la Valdene, Guy. *Making Game: An Essay on Woodcock*. Livingston MT: Clark City Press, 1990.

"*Making Game* is an elegant tale of the American woodcock. It will be a permanent part of anyone's sporting library."

89. Matthiessen, Peter. *Killing Mister Watson*. New York: Random House, 1990.

"When all the faddish smoke clears, Peter Matthiessen's work will stand revealed as that of an artist of immense talent, grandeur, and genius."

90. Gifford, Barry. *Wild at Heart*. New York: Grove Press, 1990.

"Barry Gifford is a stylist in the manner of Thomas McGuane and Joy Williams, with the heart of Raymond Carver. Gifford's sense of life takes him back to life itself as it is lived now. *Wild at Heart* is a totally engrossing novel, and I will tell that to everyone I know."

91. Adler, John Morel. *The Hunt out of the Thicket*. Chapel Hill NC: Algonquin Books, 1990.

    "*The Hunt out of the Thicket* reminds one again how wonderful and rare it can be when a first-rate writer turns to the most common literary pursuits."

92. Peacock, Doug. *Grizzly Years*. New York: Henry Holt & Co., 1990.

    "Doug Peacock has written about his grizzly bears with a passionate and unguarded heart. *Grizzly Years* is ultimately a love story about a man who returns from war shorn of his soul, and recovers his soul through his efforts to study and protect the grandest predator on earth. . . . I cannot imagine that a more worthwhile book will be printed this year."

93. Block, Ron. *Dismal River*. Minneapolis: New Rivers Press, 1990.

    "Ron Block sent me his manuscript *Dismal River*. I put it at the bottom of a stack of fifty-seven galleys, then changed my mind and took it to my cabin, mostly because I love the actual Dismal River. I'm not sure what to say except that it is a wonderful and totally successful long poem. I was absolutely engrossed by the texture and sense of detail and for Mr. Block's informed passion for the landscape."

94. Chatham, Russell. *One Hundred Paintings*. Livingston MT: Clark City Press, 1990.

    "In Russell Chatham's best work the painting is so inconsolably austere and authoritative that we have a choice of turning away or temporarily losing our personalities, the latter of which, I propose, is the main reason for an enduring work of art."

95. Williams, Joy. *Escapes*. New York: Atlantic Monthly Press, 1990.

    "Ominous and enthralling . . . truly significant fiction."

96. Hall, James. *Paper Products*. New York: W. W. Norton & Co., 1990.

    "I can't think of a writer more poignantly aware of the details and idiosyncrasies of our culture than Jim Hall. . . . He stands high in the ranks of fiction writers. *Paper Products* is a wonderful read."

97. Malan, Rian. *My Traitor's Heart: A South African Exile Returns to Face His Country, His Tribe, and His Conscience*. New York: Atlantic Monthly Press, 1990.

    "Malan is an Afrikaner Diogenes, a brilliant writer, and his story fills us with an almost unbearable amount of terror, beauty and awe."

98. Finkelstein, Dave. *Greater Nowheres*. New York: Fireside, 1990.

    "A classic of travel literature. It's unthinkable that anyone would go to Australia without first reading this book."

99. Ellis, Jerry. *Walking the Trail: One Man's Journey along the Cherokee Trail of Tears.* New York: Delacorte Press, 1991.

    "A wonderful book which should be read by anyone interested in our history or Native Americans or very good writing."

100. Bass, Rick. *Winter: Notes from Montana.* Boston: Houghton Mifflin Co., 1991.

    "Rick Bass writes with care and beauty out of the lineage of Annie Dillard and Peter Matthiessen."

101. Hamper, Ben. *Rivethead: Tales from the Assembly Line.* New York: Warner Books, 1991.

    "Right on the cutting edge, Hamper is a marvelous writer."

102. Mitchell, Stephen. *Parables and Portraits.* New York: Harper Perennial, 1991.

    "It is Stephen Mitchell's peculiar genius to find himself alone and quite naked on the earth. He doesn't remind one of anyone else, whether in his masterful translations of Rilke, Job, or the Tao Te Ching, or now in his own poetry, where there is the breathless quality of creation as a primal act. In *Parables and Portraits* we find work of the first order, poems of improbable directness and integrity that everyone who reads poetry will want to own."

103. Williams, Terry Tempest. *Refuge: An Unnatural History of Place.* New York: Pantheon, 1991.

    "*Refuge* is an almost unbearably intense and skillful essay on mortality, our own and that of the creative world. It is isolated from nearly all others of the genre by Ms. Williams's 'greatness of soul'—there is no other way to express the dense beauty and grace of this book."

104. Corbett, Jim. *Goatwalking: A Guide to Wildland Living.* New York: Penguin, 1991.

    "Cranky, brilliant, unlovable, and true."

105. Nelson, Richard. *The Island Within.* New York: Vintage Books, 1991.

    "On the borders of consciousness as in Matthiessen and Lopez . . . a holy book . . . a text to help us understand ourselves within the natural world."

106. Vizenor, Gerald. *The Heirs of Columbus.* Hanover NH: University Press of New England for Wesleyan University Press, 1991.

    "Gerald Vizenor is high among the dozen American writers I read faithfully. His work demonstrates a tremendous ingenuity and fire, a survival through wit and grace. Vizenor is unique in the sense that he does not vaguely remind you of anyone else nor does he share any of the common, banal assumptions that disfigure modern letters."

107. Blake, Michael. *Airman Mortensen*. Los Angeles: Seven Wolves Publishing, 1991.

"*Airman Mortensen* is by turns comic, melancholy, and strangely jubilant. It is wonderful that Blake could follow up *Dances with Wolves* with such a fine work."

108. O'Brien, Dan. *In the Center of the Nation*. New York: Atlantic Monthly Press, 1991.

"Dan O'Brien's *In the Center of the Nation* is a wonderful and engrossing read. He has a magnificent eye for that high plains landscape."

109. Burroughs, Franklin. *Billy Watson's Croker Sack*. New York: Houghton Mifflin Co., 1991. Trade paperback edition.

"An exquisitely wrought and unerringly graceful book."

110. Gerber, Dan. *A Last Bridge Home: New and Selected Poems*. Livingston MT: Clark City Press, 1992.

"The poems are full of the kind of attention to animal and human life, and to the natural world, that is generally lost in the sump of ego."

111. Baca, Jimmy Santiago. *Working in the Dark: Reflections of a Poet of the Barrio*. Santa Fe NM: Red Crane Books, 1992.

"*Working in the Dark*, a splendid, though painful memoir by the Chicano poet."

112. Kittredge, William. *Hole in the Sky*. New York: Alfred A. Knopf, 1992.

"*Hole in the Sky* is a courageous and engrossing book, full of the very rare winces and shudders of a man truly owning up to his life. Kittredge writes a bountiful, wise, and lucid prose that befits a story of the lineage of Stegner, Guthrie, and that great unknown, John Graves." For 1993 Vintage paperback reprint, Harrison's statement appears in the interior as: "A courageous and engrossing book . . . Kittredge writes a bountiful, wise, and lucid prose."

113. Galvin, James. *The Meadow*. New York: Henry Holt & Co., 1992.

"*The Meadow* is a unique and extraordinary book, a mixture of novel and natural history wherein Galvin reinvents the form, the true mark of genuine artist. . . . I can't recommend it too highly."

114. Nunn, Kem. *Pomona Queen*. New York: Pocket Books, 1992.

"Kem Nunn writes directly out of the lineage of James Cain and Raymond Chandler. If there is a contemporary with a deeper sense of evil, I don't know who it would be. *Pomona Queen* is utterly first rate."

115. Hogan, Linda. *Mean Spirit*. New York: Ivy Books, 1992.

"Linda Hogan's *Mean Spirit* is a marvel. It is interesting to see how gracefully she, like a number of Native American poets—Momaday, Erdrich, Silko—has made a very natural move from poetry to the novel."

116. Cleary, Thomas. *Rational Zen: The Mind of Dogen Zenji*. Boston: Shambhala Publications Inc., 1992.

"My reverence for both Dogen and Cleary is virtually unbounded.... It is becoming hard, in fact to read anyone's transactions but Cleary's."

117. McCarthy, Cormac. *All the Pretty Horses*. New York: Alfred A. Knopf, 1992.

"*All the Pretty Horses* is a superb book, touching on matters that are never allowed access to serious (literary) novels. The prose is both raw and transcendentally lyric, and should gather Cormac McCarthy the attention he has long deserved."

118. Welsch, Roger. *Touching the Fire*. New York: Villard Books, 1992.

"*Touching the Fire* is a remarkable collection of Native stories written by Roger Welsch who is line bred out of Will Rogers and Mark Twain. The book is engrossing, wonderful, and belongs with anyone who cares about our unwritten American history."

119. Ortiz, Simon J. *Woven Stone*. Tucson: University of Arizona Press, 1992.

"It is the kind of poetry that reaffirms your decision to stay alive."

120. Offutt, Chris. *Kentucky Straight*. New York: Vintage Books, 1993.

"An extraordinary debut."

121. Alexander, Robert. *White Pine Sucker River: Poems 1970–1990*. Minneapolis: New Rivers Press, 1993.

"*White Pine Sucker River* is a strange marriage of modesty and authority. I found it to be a lucid and totally engrossing book of poems."

122. Iyer, Pico. *Falling off the Map: Some Lonely Places of the World*. New York: Alfred A. Knopf, 1993.

"A classic travel book in the old sense, not having anything to do with the questionable habits of tourism. Iyer is pungent, witty, often brilliant on his far-flung destinations."

123. Jackson, Jon. *Hit on the House*. New York: Atlantic Monthly Press, 1993.

"*Hit on the House* is an unqualifiedly brilliant novel."

124. Guest, Diana. *Diana Guest, Stonecarver*. Livingston MT: Clark City Press, 1993.

"Her sculpture is nearly Native American in its simplicity, stopping the world for a moment, as all good art does."

125. Middleton, Harry. *Rivers of Memory*. Boulder CO: Pruett Publishing, 1993.

"Harry Middleton's book is a specific tonic in an over-scrutinized sport. He brings to fishing the lyric reverence of Roderick Haig-Brown, a McGuane or Chatham."

126. Porter, Bill. *Road to Heaven: Encounters with Chinese Hermits*. San Francisco: Mercury House, 1993.

"Bill Porter's *Road to Heaven* is a brilliant essay on the traditions of Chinese hermits, a startling reminder of how far we have gone astray. It should be part of any serious Zen or Taoist library. A stupendous corrective to modern Zen practice."

127. Sloan, Bob. *Dad's Own Cook Book*. New York: Workman Publishing Co., 1993.

"The other day I came across an extraordinary cookbook, *Dad's Own Cookbook*. . . . Beginning cookbooks usually contain nothing you might want to eat. But Bob Sloan covers all the basics . . . in admirable recipes that are a pleasure to eat. . . . If I had [had] this book twenty years ago, I could have saved myself a river of frustration in the kitchen."

128. Moore, Susanna. *Sleeping Beauties*. New York: Alfred A. Knopf, 1993.

"What a strange and lovely book with none of the muddy shabbiness that one finds in lesser prolonged rituals of growth. Moore reinvents the form and makes the old voyage new again. She writes like an angel who has taken a lifelong course in demonology."

129. Gallagher, Winifred. *The Power of Place: How Our Surroundings Shape Our Thoughts, Emotions, and Actions*. New York: Poseidon, 1993; paperback, New York: Harper Perennial, 1994.

"*The Power of Place* is first-rate and alarmingly fresh. So far as I know, it is a brand new vision of how we are affected by how and where we live. A wonderful book."

130. Gifford, Barry. *Arise and Walk*. New York: Hyperion, 1994.

"Barry Gifford is a stylist in the manner of Thomas McGuane and Joy Williams, with the heart of Raymond Carver. Gifford's sense of life takes him back to life as it is lived now."

131. McNamee, Gregory. *Gila: The Life and Death of an American River*. New York: Orion Books, 1994.

"Greg McNamee's *Gila* is a splendid book, an extraordinary tale of an American river, absolutely essential to anyone's environmental library."

132. Kilgo, James. *An Inheritance of Horses*. Athens: University of Georgia Press, 1994.

"A remarkable book. The prose has a deep and abiding grace married to a strikingly original candor, more classic than confessional, more mainstream than *au courant*."

133. Gilb, Dagoberto. *The Magic of Blood*. New York: Grove Press, 1994.

"These are lovely, heartbreaking, finely crafted stories dealing with a portion of society literature scarcely ever reaches."

134. Starck, Clemens. *Journeyman's Wages*. Brownsville OR: Story Line Press, 1995.

"Some truly extraordinary poems in here. Easily, gracefully, right up there with the best work being done today."

135. McCumber, David. *Playing off the Rail: A Pool Hustler's Journey*. New York: Random House, 1995.

"The most extraordinary book about pool that I've ever read, with a dimension far beyond the game."

136. Bowden, Charles. *Blood Orchid: An Unnatural History of America*. New York: Random House, 1995.

"*Blood Orchid* is gritty in the extreme. Occasionally infuriating, often heartbreaking, finally a first-rate eye opener to our soul history, the germinal material, vast and brooding, that is always left out of more orthodox (all of them) books about America."

137. de la Valdene, Guy. *For a Handful of Feathers*. New York: Atlantic Monthly Press, 1995.

"Herein we have an exhaustive sporting coda that doesn't presume that we hunt in a vacuum, as if we could separate the land from the creatures that live there. The death of hunting will come not from the largely imagined forces of anti-hunting but by the death of habitat, the continuing disregard for the land in the manner of a psychopath burning down a house and wondering why he still can't live there."

138. D'Ambrosio, Charles. *The Point*. New York: Little, Brown & Co., 1995.

"An extraordinary writer, certainly fated to be well known to those with a serious interest in the literature of our time."

139. Hogan, Linda. *Dwellings*. New York: W. W. Norton & Co., 1995.

"Linda Hogan's *Mean Spirit* is a marvel. It is interesting to see how gracefully she, like a number of Native American poets—Momaday, Erdrich, Silko–has made a very natural move from poetry to the novel."

140. Clark, Robert. *River of the West*. New York: HarperCollins, 1995.

"I began [reading] and had no interest in stopping. *River of the West* is a wonderful and durable book with a dense richness of storytelling fabric."

141. Turner, Jack. *The Abstract Wild*. Tucson: University of Arizona Press, 1996.

"A deep and darkly provocative book, a soul wringer and chaser, written with the resonant authority of a Bach fugue. . . . You need a firm hold on your chair for this one."

142. Cowan, James. *A Mapmaker's Dream*. Boston: Shambhala Publications, 1996.

"I must say *A Mapmaker's Dream* threw me into a speechless whirl. This is a book that cannot be read without red wine; one of those rare works that requires underlining. It's quite extraordinary when a book successfully questions the shape of the world."

143. Quammen, David. *The Song of the Dodo: Island Biogeography in an Age of Extinction*. New York: Charles Scribner's Sons, 1996.

"Since I *was* very young I've always wanted to go to Mauritius and visit the ghost of the Dodo, that vast and fabulous bird we expunged three centuries ago. David Quammen's *The Song of the Dodo*, if properly read, and that's up to us, could radically change the way we perceive the natural world, which also includes us. It is, quite simply, a monumental work of monumental importance."

144. Harvey, John. *Easy Meat*. New York: Henry Holt & Co., 1996.

"There's an improbable technical grace to Harvey's work, in addition to its being an electric page-turner for the high-end reader."

145. Rawlins, C. L. *Broken Country: Mountains and Memory*. New York: Henry Holt & Co., 1996.

"Truly wonderful—I admired its specificity in a maundering time, and also the spaciousness of its thought and the antic wit of its style."

146. Miller, Tom. *Trading with the Enemy*. New York: Basic Books, 1996.

"Written with wit and grace . . . A wonderful book."

147. Ackerman, Jennifer. *Notes from the Shore*. New York: Penguin Books, 1996.

"What an extraordinary book drawn from the grand lineage of Peter Matthiessen, Barry Lopez and Annie Dillard. The great weight of Ackerman's knowledge is delivered so lightly she makes us feel that we know more than we do. . . . She admits that we are nature, too, which most avoid, nearly all, in fact. I can't imagine that one with an interest in natural history will not want a copy both on their nightstands and in the bookshelves."

148. Smith, Lawrence R. *The Map of Who We Are*. Norman: University of Oklahoma Press, 1997.

"An extraordinary novel, unique in its knowledge of the invisible landscape that controls our lives."

149. Burke, James Lee. *Cimarron Rose*. New York: Hyperion, 1997.

"It has become apparent that not since Raymond Chandler has anyone so thoroughly reinvented the crime and mystery genre as James Lee Burke."

150. Erdrich, Heide. *Fishing for Myth*. Minneapolis: New Rivers Press, 1997.

"Heide Erdrich's *Fishing for Myth* is as genuine as a meadowlark. These poems have the fresh astonishment of the violent change of weather."

151. Vizenor, Gerald. *Hotline Healers*. Hanover NH: University Press of New England for Wesleyan University Press, 1997.

"Gerald Vizenor is high among the dozen American writers I read faithfully. His work demonstrates a tremendous ingenuity and fire, a survival through wit and grace. Vizenor is unique in the sense that he does not vaguely remind you of anyone else nor does he share any of the common, banal assumptions that disfigure modem letters."

152. Matthiessen, Peter. *Lost Man's River.* New York: Random House, 1997.

"When all the faddish smoke clears, Peter Matthiessen's work will stand revealed as that of an artist of immense talent, grandeur, and genius."

153. Corbett, William. *Furthering My Education: A Memoir.* Cambridge MA: Zoland Books, 1997.

"William Corbett's *Furthering My Education* is a harrowing, beautiful written memoir of the anguish, and generally the understanding, between father and son."

154. Hennen, Tom. *Crawling out the Window.* Goodhue MN: Black Hat Press, 1997.

"I don't recall when I've read a new book of poems that struck me so deeply. Tom Hennen's *Crawling out the Window* reveals work of the highest order. It's as if he turned his Hubbell brain toward Earth and we are led to see things we've never seen before. This is saying a great deal and I mean a great deal. It is quite simply a work of genius. A goodly number of the poems are permanent. If there were such a thing as literary justice, which of course there isn't, this book would bring Tom Hennen an immense reputation."

155. Lethem, Jonathan. *As She Climbed across the Table.* New York: Doubleday & Co., 1997.

"Jonathan Letham's *As She Climbed across the Table* is an extraordinary, fresh piece of fiction. I was most of all struck by the grace and liveliness of his prose in an age where all sorts of crimes are committed in the name of sincerity."

156. O'Brien, Dan. *Equinox.* New York: Lyons & Buford, 1997.

"Dan O'Brien's *Equinox* is an improbably beautiful book about the life of a falconer. By comparison, it makes nearly all other sporting books look childishly simple. I can't recommend it too highly."

157. Strand, Clark. *Seeds from a Birch Tree: Writing Haiku and the Spiritual Journey.* New York: Hyperion, 1997.

"A brilliant and engaging book on haiku, and on the state of the body and mind required in the million to one shot against producing a good one."

158. Foster, Nelson. *The Roaring Stream.* New York: Harper Perennial, 1997.

"I have used *The Roaring Stream* for a year now as a daily missal. I can think of no more seminal Zen book published in our time."

159. Twichell, Chase. *The Snow Catcher.* Princeton NJ: Ontario Review Press, 1998.

"Chase Twichell's *The Snow Watcher* is raw, fresh, and lucidly harsh. These poems often enter a not quite familiar terrain, talking us on an admirable but not quite comfortable journey into ourselves."

160. Williams, Ben O. *Western Wings: Hunting Upland Birds on the Northern Plains*. Foreword by Thomas McGuane. Gallatin Gateway MT: Wilderness Adventures Press, 1998.

"I must say that I was utterly swept away by Ben Williams' *Western Wings*. It's as if he owns the northern plains and has a rather godlike knowledge of every square foot. *Western Wings* is a must read for any bird hunter, whether he lives in the east or west."

161. Fergus, Jim. *One Thousand White Women: The Journals of May Dodd*. New York: St. Martin's Press, 1998.

"Jim Fergus' *One Thousand White Women* is a splendid, fresh, and engaging novel. If there were any justice . . . it would be a surefire bestseller. Strikingly original."

162. Stroud, Joseph. *Below Cold Mountain*. Port Townsend WA: Copper Canyon Press, 1998.

"At the first onset of surprise I read it carefully twice, the second time as if reliving a grand feast, course by course, seeing the food re-enlivened by the infusion of imagination into memory. I must say I was dumbfounded. I don't recall when a poet unknown to me has struck me so deeply. I had the terribly inaccurate sensation that I was quite young again and reading one of history's good poets for the first time. The book made nearly all the manuscripts and galleys that pass my way seem like thin gruel indeed. What an achievement. There is a range and amplitude here found among only the very best. There aren't a few high points but dozens. We don't have here a few isolated mountains but a whole range, a cordillera. Like all of the best poets, Stroud makes the earth again consolable."

163. McMillion, Scott. *Mark of the Grizzly—True Stories of Bear Attacks and the Hard Lessons Learned*. Helena MT: Falcon Press, 1998.

"This book should be obligatory for back country travelers who wander in the land of grizzlies, for it must be considered theirs or they will vanish."

164. Hamill, Sam, and J. P. Seaton, trans. *The Essential Chuang Tzu*. Boston: Shambhala Publications, 1998.

"*The Essential Chuang Tzu*, newly translated by Sam Hamill and J. P. Seaton, is a stunning achievement. On the surface it is so elegant and witty, so vividly imaginative, that it is breathtaking, but then the book wrings the heart and soul with the reality we have shared for thousands of years. This rendering of the *Chuang Tzu* should be used as a morning missal, a lunchtime rejuvenator, an evening's study, and a night-table reminder—and it also offers serenity for the insomniac."

165. Corcoran, Tom. *The Mango Opera*. New York: St. Martin's Press, 1998.

"*The Mango Opera* is a very engrossing novel. Corcoran deftly evokes the spirit and physicality of the place, the low tide jubilance and enlivening fetor of its pleasures and instinctive criminality, as if the sun and ocean had blasted all the flowers of evil into its very genes."

166. Schneider, Bart. *Blue Bossa: A Novel*. New York: Viking Press, 1998.

"*Blue Bossa* is an improbably lovely novel about a jazz musician on the skids, where they frequently are, and his recovery as an artist. There hasn't been anything like it since John Clellon Holmes. The prose is so graceful that you also hear the actual music in your mind."

167. Hogan, Linda. *Power: A Novel*. New York: W. W. Norton Co., 1998.

"Linda Hogan's *Mean Spirit* is a marvel. It is interesting to see how gracefully she, like a number of Native American poets—Momaday, Erdrich, Silko—has made a very natural move from poetry to the novel."

168. Bass, Rick. *The New Wolves*. New York: Lyons Press, 1998.

"*The New Wolves* is an enthralling and brilliant book on the reintroduction of wolves in the American Southwest . . . written out of the activist lineage of Ed Abbey and Doug Peacock, it is especially passionate, but with the novelist's eye for vivid details."

169. McDonald, Roger. *Mr. Darwin's Shooter*. New York: Atlantic Monthly Press, 1998.

"I began reading *Mr. Darwin's Shooter* at the usual brisk speed but then slowed myself to a scant fifty pages per day, the better to experience the exquisite prose that so ably encompasses the faux war between God and the range of the human mind. I cannot recommend a book more highly."

170. Gilfillan, Merrill. *Chokecherry Places*. Boulder CO: Johnson Books, 1998.

"Last night I read *Chokecherry Places* by Merrill Gilfillan and was quite swept away as I had been with *Magpie Rising*, *Sworn Before Cranes* and *Burnt House to Paw Paw*. If anyone writes better prose in America I am unaware of it. He is an improbably acute student of natural history and his prose frequently passes Matthew Arnold's test of poetry: Does it raise the hair on the back of your neck?"

171. Gerber, Dan. *Trying to Catch the Horses*. East Lansing: Michigan State University Press, 1999.

"Dan Gerber is a unique poet. More than any of his contemporaries he immediately makes the relatively ordinary a transcendent state. His work is completely untarnished by fad or fashion and I enter it again and again with a sense of wonderment. When our age passes, this work will remain."

172. Ortiz, Simon. *Men on the Moon*. Tucson: University of Arizona Press, 1999.

"*Men on the Moon* is a strongly engaging book that does great honor to the art of storytelling."

173. Golden, Mike. *The Buddhist Third Class Junkmail Oracle*. New York: Seven Stories Press, 1999.

    "*The Buddhist Third Class Junkmail Oracle* is a fascinating text reminding us yet again that the sixties were a somber time and that aspects of fascism have always thrived in America. Mike Golden's work on d. a. levy is brilliant."

174. Williams, Brooke. *Halflives: Reconciling Work and Wildness*. Washington DC: Island Press, 1999.

    "In *Halflives* Brooke Williams tells the engrossing story, his own, of a divided man trying to knit his two parts back together within a culture where the economic is considered to be the only appreciable reality. The ideal of 'meaningful work' butchers nearly all of us and it is intriguing indeed to read how Brooke Williams struggled his way free."

175. McCumber, David. *The Cowboy Way*. New York: Random House, 1999.

    "A splendid book that should permanently blow the lid off nearly everyone's absurd preconception of how a cowboy actually spends his time."

176. Barich, Bill. *Crazy for Rivers*. New York: Lyons Press, 1999.

    "A splendid prose stylist. . . . I will continue to look forward to anything he writes."

177. O'Brien, Dan. *The Contract Surgeon*. New York: Lyons Press, 1999.

    "*The Contract Surgeon* is an eerie, harrowing novel with terrifying implications. There is the aura the ghosts of the Sioux made him write this book, [which] should bring O'Brien to the wide audience he deserves. It is lucid and harsh, and deftly avoids the sentimentality that mars novels that deal with our first citizens."

178. Red Pine, trans. *The Zen Works of Stonehouse: Poems and Talks of a Fourteenth Century Chinese Hermit*. San Francisco: Mercury House Press, 1999.

    "*The Zen Works of Stonehouse* drew strongly on all my senses. . . . It is a splendid book, and I imagine that every Zen student will wish to own a copy."

179. Sloan, Bob. *Bliss Jumps the Gun*. New York: Foul Play Press/W. W. Norton & Co., 1999.

    "Though I liked the first *Bliss* very much, *Bliss Jumps the Gun* is a considerable leap forward. I don't hesitate to call it a brilliant mystery, exposing us to a New York City that the faint of heart might not wish to see."

180. Canty, Kevin. *Nine Below Zero*. New York: Nan A. Talese, 1999.

    "Kevin Canty writes beautifully and with style—*Nine Below Zero* is a raw and skin-peeling tale."

181. McGuane, Thomas. *Some Horses*. New York: Lyons Press, 1999.

"In *Some Horses*, Thomas McGuane virtually recreates the animal with his usual magnificent prose so that you'll be incapable of looking at them the same way again."

182. Brautigan, Richard. *An Unfortunate Woman*. New York: St. Martin's Press, 2000.

"Richard Brautigan's *An Unfortunate Woman* is not only vintage Brautigan but is among his best, filled with breathtaking insights about our life now."

183. Brautigan, Ianthe. *You Can't Catch Death*. New York: St. Martin's Press, 2000.

"Ianthe Brautigan has written a lovely memoir of her father. Despite the melancholy and pain, it is an altogether admirable account of a daughter who has not only survived but prevailed."

184. Turner, Jack. *Teewinot: A Year in the Teton Range*. New York: St. Martin's Press, 2000.

"When I first received *Teewinot: A Year in the Teton Range*, I was anxious because as a flatlander I find mountains higher than my head to be intimidating. My hesitation was allayed by the splendor of the book and Turner's absolutely unique insights on why anyone might wish to climb mountains in the first place. This is, simply stated, a wonderful and utterly engaging book."

185. Lindsay, Charles, and Thomas McGuane. *Upstream: Fly Fishing in the American West*. New York: Aperture, 2000.

"The book marriage of Charles Lindsay and Thomas McGuane was a splendid idea indeed. After seeing literally hundreds of books of trout photos, we have an overwhelming one that returns us to the essence of the river itself. And no one writes better about fishing than Thomas McGuane."

186. Mindy, Judith. *Walking with the Bear*. East Lansing: Michigan State University Press, 2000.

"*Walking with the Bear* is an extraordinary collection. I was especially drawn to the new poems, which seem to lift Judith into the very front rank of American Poetry."

187. Nickels, Mark. *Cicada*. New York: Rattapallax, 2000.

"In most ways *Cicada* is an astounding book, nearly a new species of poetry. Often the poems poach gracefully in the territory of the novel. I was poignantly taken by the astute fluidity of the language, the facility of looking at ordinary things in a radical new way. This book should be widely read because it announces the arrival of a poet who has a good shot at being major."

188. Hamill, Sam. *Crossing the Yellow River: 300 Chinese Poems*. Rochester NY: BOA Editions, 2000.

"In *Crossing the Yellow River*, Sam Hamill remaps Chinese poetry for our time. Anyone who writes poetry, or who cares about it, must have this book. It is one of the essential works of our time."

189. Lent, Jeffrey. *In the Fall*. New York: Atlantic Monthly Press, 2000.

"Jeffrey Lent's *In the Fall* is an extraordinary first novel which bears no resemblance to a first novel. Lent has the absolute mastery to create his own reality. It is a fulsome and harrowing tale and I cannot recommend it highly enough."

190. Gifford, Barry. *Wyoming*. New York: Arcade Publishing, 2000.

"A stylist in the manner of Thomas McGuane and Joy Williams, with the heart of Raymond Carver, Gifford's new sense of life takes him back to life itself as it is now lived."

191. Weigl, Bruce. *The Circle of Hahn*. New York: Grove Press, 2000.

"In the arc of human life, salvation and regeneration are rare items indeed. In Bruce Weigl's *The Circle of Hahn* we learn again that on the surface there's nothing worse than war and underneath, within the human psyche, there's nothing worse than the aftereffects of war. With this memoir Weigl joins Caputo and Herr in raising Vietnam to the level of literature."

192. Welch, James. *The Heartsong of Charging Elk*. New York: Doubleday & Co., 2000.

"An utterly harrowing novel but resonant and deeply rewarding."

193. Shaffer, Eric Paul. *Portable Planet*. Chantilly VA: Leaping Dog Press, 2000.

"*Portable Planet* is a marvelous book. I've been following Shaffer's work for years and he's on a definitive upward spiral."

194. Millman, Lawrence. *Northern Latitudes: Prose Poems*. Minneapolis: New Rivers Press, 2000.

"*Northern Latitudes* take us far from our ordinary geographical concerns and is resonantly individual. It is a beautiful voyage into relative 'terra incognito.'"

195. Butson, Denver. *Mechanical Birds*. Laurinburg NC: St. Andrews College Press, 2000.

"Denver Butson's work is splendid and quite remote from the MFA-sodden factories."

196. Quarrington, Paul. *The Spirit Cabinet*. New York: Atlantic Monthly Press, 2000.

"*The Spirit Cabinet* is quite simply a brilliant novel. It recalls the possibility of a more expansive Kafka. It is that very rare novel that is both bizarre and profound."

197. Thorne, John. *Pot on the Fire*. New York: North Point Press, 2000.

"Thorne's best book yet . . . I admire greatly his culinary restlessness, his insistence that there be an organic connection between the theory and practice of food and the life that encompasses it. Thorne's work has spiraled upward into the category of the 'must read,' far above the frivolity of nearly all of the food world."

198. Bayless, Rick. *Mexico: One Plate at a Time*. New York: Charles Scribner's Sons, 2000.

"I have long admired the work of Rick Bayless. In *Mexico: One Plate at a Time* he continues his passionate attempt to introduce us to a long-ignored cuisine. It is a splendid book and anyone who cares about world cuisine will want it in their library."

199. Johnson, Jonathan. *Mastadon: 80% Complete*. Pittsburgh: Carnegie Mellon University Press, 2001.

"Johnson's *Mastodon: 80% Complete* is fresh, tough and stimulating, full of 'thinginess,' textural concretia, a specific density that carries the reader along as a participant, whether willing or not. It is fascinating and original work."

200. Duncan, David James. *My Story as Told by Water*. Los Angeles: University of California Press, 2001.

"This book is the *Desert Solitaire* of water."

201. Baca, Jimmy Santiago. *A Place to Stand: The Making of a Poet*. New York: Grove Press, 2001.

"Jimmy Santiago Baca's *A Place to Stand* is the finest memoir I've read in I don't know how long. It reminded me of the rawness of George Orwell combined with the human exuberance of Neruda's memoirs. For most readers this will be utterly fresh material. Those with Baca's experience usually don't live long enough to write. This book will have a permanent place in American letters."

202. McGookey, Kathleen. *Whatever Shines: Volume I*. New York: White Pine Press, 2001.

"*Whatever Shines* is an admirable and dazzling first collection. The voice is indisputably unique and haunting, and one looks forward to anything the poet writes in the future."

203. Smolens, John. *Cold*. New York: Flame Books, 2001.

"*Cold* is a finely crafted, wild yarn set in the great North. John Smolens gives us a suspenseful tale in a style somewhere between Jack London and Raymond Chandler. A fine read."

204. Gerber, Dan. *A Second Life: A Collected Nonfiction*. East Lansing: Michigan State University Press, 2001.

"It is a great pleasure to re-read Dan Gerber's nonfiction collection in *A Second Life*. Many of these essays are wonderful indeed, journeys we gladly take without getting on a plane. The 'Introduction' alone is worth the price of the book. I am amazed again at the lucidity and deep humanness of Gerber's prose."

205. Gaston, Bill. *The Good Body*. New York: Regan Books, 2001.

"Unpredictable, harrowing and engrossing . . . Bill Gaston is one of Canada's finest young writers."

206. Enger, Leif. *Peace Like a River*. New York: Atlantic Monthly, 2001.

"Once you begin Leif Enger's *Peace Like a River,* you are carried away by the elemental surge of its story, the sheer eagerness to see what happens to the engrossing characters who exist far from the intrusions of the media in the timeless arena of family love and anguish over a lost member. It is Enger's gift that he has made their extraordinary world credible."

207. O'Brien, Dan. *Buffalo for the Broken Heart: Restoring Life to the Black Hills Ranch*. New York: Random House, 2001.

"Dan O'Brien's *Buffalo for the Broken Heart* at first appears to be an agrarian fable on the high order of James Galvin's *The Meadow*. But then O'Brien picks up the energy, and his urgent, desperate attempts to save his ranch explode on the page."

208. Weatherford, Joyce. *The Heart of the Beast*. New York: Charles Scribner's Sons, 2001.

"Alarmingly beautiful."

209. McGuane, Thomas. *The Longest Silence*. New York: Alfred A. Knopf, 2001. Paperback edition.

"Thomas McGuane writes better about fishing than anyone else in the history of mankind."

210. Styron, Alexandra. *All the Finest Girls: A Novel*. New York: Little, Brown & Co., 2001.

"Alexandra Styron's *All the Finest Girls* is exquisitely written. The novel enters deeply into the mystery of how we invent ourselves, often despite our families. It subtly forces itself through the various codas of privilege and out the other side so that we see the fullness of the young woman without the suffocation of cultural accouterments. It is at the same time lyrical and harsh, and the heroine becomes someone we really know, like a friend who makes us sleepless with worry."

211. Nabhan, Gary Paul. *Coming Home to Eat: The Pleasures and Politics of Local Foods*. New York: W. W. Norton & Co., 2002.

"A profound and engaging book, a passionate call to us to re-think our food industry and to return when possible to our own locale for the sources of what we cook and eat."

212. Caputo, Philip. *Ghosts of Tsavo: Stalking the Mystery Lions of East Africa*. Washington DC: Adventure Press/National Geographic Society, 2002.

"Phil Caputo's *Ghosts of Tsavo* is a superb read, engaging our imagination (not to speak of our fears) from start to finish. I think I've read every book Caputo has written and the intensity and range of his curiosity is impressive indeed. *Ghosts of Tsavo* is a natural history mystery story full of very human cads, kings, and heroines. The book will give you a very different feeling the next time you see a zoo lion."

213. Bowden, Charles. *Blues for Cannibals: The Notes from Underground*. New York: North Point Press, 2002.

"To say that *Blues for Cannibals* is trenchant is a record-breaking euphemism. This book scoured my brain pan. I think of Bowden as among the best of our essayists and it is difficult to think of others quite in his league in terms of emotional range. A fine though harrowing book. Superb!"

214. Adams, Christina. *Any Small Thing Can Save You: A Bestiary*. New York: Blue Hen Press, 2002.

"A book of surpassing grace and beauty."

215. Crawford, Max. *Wamba*. Norman: University of Oklahoma Press, 2002.

"A startling and beautiful novel written with a lucid density of character and style rarely seen nowadays."

216. Byler, Stephen Raleigh. *Searching for Intruders*. New York: William Morrow, 2002.

"*Searching for Intruders* is an alarmingly fresh entry into fictive reality. Stephen Byler has managed an intriguing new voice that directly engages us."

217. Kooser, Ted. *Local Wonders: Seasons in the Bohemian Alps*. Lincoln: University of Nebraska Press, 2002.

"Ted Kooser's *Local Wonders* is the quietest magnificent book I've ever read."

218. Davis, Todd. *Ripe: Poems*. Huron OH: Bottom Dog Press, 2002.

"Lovely and lush. Todd Davis's poems gave me quite the boost on a down evening, reaffirming what Codrescu said about poems being the only reliable source of information. At least the information that is vital to me. Davis is a good poet which makes him a rare bird indeed."

219. Reece, Parks. *Call of the Wild: The Art of Parks Reece*. Helena MT: Riverbend Publishers, 2002.

"A truly extraordinary artist."

220. Rosenbauer, Tom. *The Orvis Pocket Guide to Nymphing Techniques.* Guilford CT: Lyons Press, 2002.

"Tom Rosenbauer's *Nymphing Techniques* is splendidly engrossing. There is simply no other work that so lucidly and incisively reveals all the aspects of this form of fishing. This book is a 'must read' for all trout fishermen."

221. Kubica, Chris, and Will Hochman. *Letters to J. D. Salinger.* Madison: University of Wisconsin Press, 2002.

"Meanwhile I hope you keep writing. Tu Fu, perhaps the greatest Chinese poet, published no books in his lifetime but did quite well afterwards."

222. Batali, Mario. *The Babbo Cookbook.* Photographs by Christopher Hirsheimer. New York: Clarkson Potter Publishers, 2002.

"Historically, when we adapt an ethnic cuisine to our own uses we start with the most ordinary and work our way up, frequently making a mess along the way. In our lifelong search for the genuine we need a guidebook to get close to the pinnacle and, in the case of Italian cuisine, it has been delivered in the shape of Mario Batali's *Babbo Cookbook*, which is a new standard of excellence. Babbo is my favorite American restaurant and this book allows me to bring its grace to my home kitchen."

223. Lent, Jeffrey. *Lost Nation.* New York: Atlantic Monthly Press, 2002.

"My real problem with Jeffrey Lent's *Lost Nation* is figuring out whether it is a masterpiece or simply an American classic. This is an age of obtuse hyperbole but I don't recall a recent novel more worthy of the traditional nine bows, a novel that more ruthlessly examines the nearly ancient roots of what we are today."

224. Haight, Robert. *Emergences and Spinner Falls.* Kalamazoo: New Issues/Western Michigan University Press, 2002.

"Robert Haight's *Emergences and Spinner Falls* is an extraordinary collection. This is poetry with teeth that both nibbles and bites hard. It is full of the things of this world, scarcely noticed even by most poets, without which we are the living dead. There is the marvelous sense of the grace and wit of a good poet at the top of his form."

225. Stanton, Doug. *In Harm's Way: The Sinking of the USS* Indianapolis *and the Extraordinary Story of Its Survivors.* New York: St. Martin's Press, 2002.

"*In Harm's Way* is a pungent corrective to Navy injustice and much more. The book is an improbably fatal adventure story, unfortunately true, that leaves you gasping at the sacrifice some men made for the rest of us."

226. Weinzwieg, Ari. *Zingerman's Guide to Good Parmigiano-Reggiano.* Ann Arbor MI, 2002.

"[Zingerman's is] . . . the ne plus ultra of delicatessens . . ."

227. Chaudhuri, Amit. *Real Time: Stories and a Reminiscence*. New York: Farrar Straus Giroux, 2002.

"With Amit Chaudhuri we are in the sparsely populated country of the utterly first rate. *Real Time* is written with starkness, clarity and authority, but still has the lyrical heart. In the current smudgy literary Diaspora, reading Chaudhuri is like drinking fresh cold water on the hottest of days."

228. Roper, Martin. *Gone*. New York: Henry Holt & Co., 2002.

"Martin Roper's *Gone* is a marvelously nasty novel about love in our time. I often shuddered while reading it and was quite happy that I am not obligated to fall in love again. There's a great deal of exquisite prose and one wonders again if this capacity isn't genetic among the Irish. If you are actually a human being this novel will pull strongly at your heart and despite its emotional brutality it is well worth the trip."

229. Gilfillan, Merrill. *Rivers and Birds*. Boulder CO: Johnson Books, 2002.

"If anyone writes better prose in America I am unaware of it. He is an improbably acute student of natural history."

230. Alexander, Robert. *Five Forks: Waterloo of the Confederacy*. East Lansing: Michigan State University Press, 2003.

"Robert Alexander's *Five Forks* is a splendid and intriguing study of the South's Waterloo. I can't recommend too highly this book that so clearly belongs in anyone's permanent Civil War collection. The prose is improbably lucid and lovely."

231. de la Valdene, Guy. *Red Stag*. Guilford CT: Lyons Press, 2003.

"Guy de la Valdene's *Red Stag* is beautifully written: it is both a fine sporting novel and literature."

232. Smith, Lawrence R. *Annie's Soup Kitchen*. Norman: University of Oklahoma Press, 2003.

"I 'bought' the world story in all of its amplitude. Smith is a fine weaver."

233. Peacock, Andrea. *Libby, Montana: Asbestos and the Deadly Silence of an American Corporation*. Boulder CO: Johnson Books, 2003.

"What an extraordinary, meticulous, and heartfelt book. I read it in a single long sitting, which is a tribute to its writerly grace. Andrea Peacock skillfully exposes a true axis of evil and its dire human effects. This is a must read for people of conscience."

234. Matthiessen, Peter. *End of the Earth: Voyages to Antarctica*. Washington DC: National Geographic, 2003.

"No one in our time has voyaged farther or written better about the natural world."

235. Delp, Michael. *The Last Good Water: Prose and Poetry 1988–2003*. Detroit: Wayne State University Press, 2003.

"Michael Delp must be proclaimed the King of moving water. I have long been an ardent fan of both his poetry and prose and in *The Last Good Water* we have a marvelous collection of his best work."

236. *Copper Canyon Catalog, Fall–Winter 2003–2004*. Port Townsend WA: Copper Canyon Press, 2003.

On reader comment card, signed "B. D. Harrison," for *This Art: Poems about Poetry*: "As an ex-military cryptographer I know what you're up to sending these embittered little coded messages. Keep up the good work."

237. Corcoran, Tom. *Octopus Alibi*. New York: St. Martin's Press/Minotaur, 2003.

"I made at least twenty fishing trips to Key West beginning in the late sixties until the early nineties when this hyper-energetic little city plumb wore me out. Naturally I explored fully the soft underbelly of the town, but then gradually realized Key West was all underbelly. Tom Corcoran's *Octopus Alibi* is a true marvel of a mystery, a deeply engrossing guidebook to the *Mango Opera* that is life in Key West."

238. Hartley, Aidan. *The Zanzibar Chest: The Story of Life, Love, and Death in Foreign Lands*. New York: Atlantic Monthly Press, 2003.

"A stunning piece of work. There is an amazing depth, breadth and grace of fine writing in this book. It will reside permanently in my memory. No one should dare say the word 'Africa' without reading it."

239. Turner, Frederick. *1929*. New York: Counterpoint Press, 2003.

"The writing is beautifully controlled and elegant, giving ever greater tension to the often lurid and violent contents. Historically, I can think of no finer portrait of an American artist and his times."

240. Henderson, Fergus. *The Whole Beast: Nose to Tail Eating*. Hopewell NJ: Ecco Press, 2004.

"*Nose to Tail Eating* is an astounding cookbook. This is food that might very well restore our plaintive spirits during a difficult time in world history. Like the work of Mario Batali, Henderson both transcends and exemplifies the best of his genre. Anyone who loves cooking and doesn't buy this book should seek expensive therapy."

241. Codrescu, Andrei. *Wakefield*. Chapel Hill NC: Algonquin Books of Chapel Hill, 2004.

"Andrei Codrescu's *Wakefield* is unremittingly coruscating and immensely submissive, in short, a brilliant comic novel that will give you a fresh look at the homeland."

242. Reid, Elwood. *D.B.* New York: Doubleday & Co., 2004.

"Elwood Reid's *D.B.* is raunchy, seamy, cocksure, perversely juicy, so surprising in its vivid convolution of plot and character that you keep turning back a few pages to see how the author is getting away with it. There's a dose of Raymond Chandler in Elwood Reid's lineage, but his voice is fresh and unique."

243. Shumate, David. *High Water Mark*. Pittsburgh: University of Pittsburgh Press, 2004.

"David Shumate's *High Water Mark* is absolutely fresh and unpredictable. I hope it gathers the attention of everyone who truly cares for poetry in our time. You will be surprised by your confrontation with the utterly first rate."

244. Jackson, Jon. *No Man's Dog*. New York: Atlantic Monthly Press, 2004.

"*No Man's Dog* is an exhilarating tour of the potentialities of domestic terrorism where you begin to understand Homeland Security as a Ping-Pong ball of dread and paranoia. Jackson writes beautifully and introduces us to so much we didn't know."

245. Hemingway, Valerie. *Running with the Bulls: My Life with the Hemingways*. New York: Random House, 2004.

"*Running with the Bulls* is hot to the touch. I was not a little dumbfounded that Valerie Hemingway endured and survived the events of her life to write this improbably skillful memoir that frequently made me wish to climb a mountain and sit on a friendly glacier. The author's life with the Hemingways is utterly compelling, and we must praise her for her gifts in giving us the most lucid look yet written at this haunted family."

246. Spragg, Mark. *An Unfinished Life*. New York: Alfred A. Knopf, 2004.

"I can't get more than a few pages into a novel unless the prose is good. In Mark Spragg's *An Unfinished Life* the writing is of considerable grace and beauty, plus there's a compelling tale of the New West which at times is an uncomfortable page turner where you are standing on the sidelines rooting for your heartbreaking favorites."

247. Turner, Frederick. *In the Land of the Temple Caves*. New York: Counterpoint Press, 2004.

"Frederick Turner's *In the Land of the Temple Caves* examines the first roots of western art in the caves of the Dordogne which may fairly be called the birthplace of the Occident. Turner's prose often reaches sublimity as he castes the wide arc of his profound knowledge and wisdom from Cro-Magnon splendors to the problematical present where the gods die suffocated by our strenuous banality. This book is permanent."

248. Redhill, Michael. *Fidelity*. New York: Little, Brown & Co., 2004.

"Michael Redhill's book of stories, *Fidelity* reminds us again that ordinary life isn't very ordinary, and that most of our presumptions about reality sink gracelessly beneath the waves of the kind of truly penetrating look that only good fiction offers us."

249. Graves, John. *Myself and Strangers: A Memoir of Apprenticeship*. New York: Alfred A. Knopf, 2004.

"A shrewd, lucid and uncomfortable adventure story of a writer's apprenticeship."

250. Osborne, Lawrence. *The Accidental Connoisseur*. New York: North Star Press, 2004.

"Lawrence Osborne's *The Accidental Connoisseur* is shrewd, apt, acerbic and often quite crazy. We are carried on equally by the honed criticism and the fine writing."

251. La Farge, Oliver. *Laughing Boy*. New York: Mariner Books, 2004.

"A seminal book . . . Most of us read *Laughing Boy* when we were young and were awakened to the splendor of a new material for the American novel."

252. Johnson, Jonathan. *Hannah and the Mountain: Notes toward a Wilderness Fatherhood*. Lincoln: University of Nebraska Press, 2005.

"This is a book you don't have a chance of forgetting."

253. Fergus, Jim. *The Wild Girl: The Notebooks of Ned Giles, 1932*. New York: Hyperion, 2005.

"*The Wild Girl* is a wonderfully engrossing novel, a spellbinder and page turner. This is fresh material from a virtually unknown quarter of the continent. Not only is Fergus a fine literary writer but also a master at the ancient art of storytelling."

254. Smoker, Mandy. *Another Attempt at Rescue*. New York: Hanging Loose Press, 2005.

"Mandy Smoker's *Another Attempt at Rescue* is an impressive first book though, in truth, there is nothing here that reminds me of a first book. This is the work of an accomplished and mature poet with a rare and first-rate mind. There are some stunning and memorable poems here."

255. Clark, Patricia. *My Father on a Bicycle*. East Lansing: Michigan State University Press, 2005.

"The reading of Patricia Clark's *My Father on a Bicycle* gave me a great deal of pleasure. I was impressed by the obvious range of her talent and the uniqueness of her voice."

256. Peacock, Doug. *Walking It Off*. Cheney: Eastern Washington University Press, 2005.

"Doug Peacock's *Walking It Off* is an extraordinary and durable book. Frankly, Peacock's life makes nearly all the environmental movement look like an upper class bridge tournament. In *Walking It Off* you have the heart and soul, more exactly the blood and guts, of a man who has given his life in defense of nature, intermixed with the story of his dearest friend and mentor, Ed Abbey."

257. Bowden, Charles. *A Shadow in the City*. New York: Harcourt, 2005.

"I was only a dozen pages into *A Shadow in the City* before I sensed the book was growing ice cubes in my stomach and brain. No writer casts a colder and more perceptive eye on our culture than Charles Bowden. This is a look at drug enforcement that leaves you wishing it was a novel so it wouldn't be true. The hero, Joey O'Shay, is an artist in his own genre and has to be one of the hardest men in our history."

258. Butz, Bob. *Beast of Never, Cat of God*. New York: Lyons Press, 2005.

"A wonderfully engaging book."

259. Hadley, Drum. *Voice of the Borderlands*. Tucson AZ: Rio Nuevo Publishers, 2005.

"Drum Hadley's work is absolutely fresh as a mountain stream. This book does honor to the ancient art of storytelling."

260. Boyden, Joseph. *Three Day Road*. New York: Viking Press, 2005.

"Joseph Boyden's *Three Day Road* is a brilliant novel. You will suffer a bit but, it's overwhelmingly worth the voyage."

261. Winegar, Karin. *Rescuers: Rescued Animals and the People They Help*. Minneapolis: Nodin Press, 2006.

"*Rescuers* is an extraordinarily poignant book. Unfortunately, we tend to treat animals even worse than we treat ourselves or others socially, emotionally, and politically. Redemption comes from changing our behavior toward animals which then spreads to the rest of our lives. They try their best to help us in this process. This book is a roadmap for our possible redemption."

262. Nabokov, Peter. *Where the Lightning Strikes*. New York: Viking Press, 2006.

"As a boy I was addicted to wondering around the countryside and forests of northern Michigan looking for lightning trees because clumsy reading of Indian lore told me that these were powerful places. Sixty years and hundreds of books later I now have in my hands the book I have devoutly wished for. Peter Nabokov is not only a great scholar but also a fine writer so that this exhaustive study of sixteen places reads with uncommon grace. Anyone with an interest in our first citizens or the nature of true reverence will wish to know *Where the Lightning Strikes*."

263. Rinella, Steven. *The Scavenger's Guide to Haute Cuisine*. New York: Miramax, 2006.

"Gary Snyder has pointed out that in America there is a presumed virtue in staying remote from the sources of food. Steven Rinella's *The Scavenger's Guide to Haute Cuisine* is a walk on the wild side of hunting and gathering. It's sure to repel a few professional food sissies but attract many more with its sheer in-your-face energy and fine storytelling."

264. Falconer, Delia. *The Lost Thoughts of Soldiers*. Brooklyn NY: Soft Skull Press, 2006.

"A splendid and absorbing novel."

265. Meek, James. *The People's Act of Love*. New York: Cannongate, 2006.

"In *The People's Act of Love* there is a great suppressed heat, the feeling that James Meek's fine aesthetic sense just barely contains the story. This is a novel of the first order and perhaps that is an understatement. It quickly becomes unimaginable that this story didn't happen exactly as Meek tells it, which is the grand and steadfast illusion of art without which we fail to understand life."

266. Standridge, Dana. *Lessons in Essence*. Emeryville CA: Shoemaker & Hoard, 2006.

"*Lessons in Essence* is a meticulously elegant novel. I was instantly and deeply enmeshed in the grace of the story. I would think that Dana Standridge has a brilliant future as a novelist. She takes us to another world and holds us prisoner until the last page and after that the story lingers like a powerful dream."

267. Clewes, Richard. *Finding Lily*. Toronto: Key Porter Books, 2006.

"*Finding Lily* is an engrossing book. It is one thing when a mate dies and quite another when the reason is suicide, which calls existence into severe question. Clewes struggles and, I think, succeeds, which means he finally understands. This is the most anyone can hope for."

268. Barnstone, Willis. *Sweetbitter Love: Poems of Shappo*. Boston: Shambhala Publications, 2006.

"If there is any justice, which there probably isn't, the world of letters would erect a monument of Willis Barnstone and strew is with fresh wildflowers every day. I think of this Shappo collection as the finest among Barnstone's prodigious achievements."

269. Salter, John. *A Trout in the Sea of Cortez*. New York: Counterpoint Press, 2006.

"John Salter's *A Trout in the Sea of Cortez* is an excellent novel that crisscrosses genres with daring abandon. The perennial theme of male collapse is very fresh, as is the absolutely fresh setting of North Dakota. I like the book very much."

270. Pawlcyn, Cindy. *Big Small Plates*. Berkeley CA: Ten Speed Press, 2006.

"For decades, Cindy Pawlcyn has helped lead the West Coast contingent in revolutionizing our concept of fine food in America. This is, simply enough, a brilliant cookbook and one that every serious cook will want to keep handy in the kitchen."

271. Steinberg, Michael, and Larry Rothe. *For the Love of Music: Invitations to Listening*. New York: Oxford University Press, 2006.

"*For the Love of Music* is simply enough a fabulous work. As an avid listener of classical music for fifty years, it was splendid indeed to have so many doors to the world of musical genius opened for me."

272. Chavez, Denise. *A Taco Testimony: Meditations on Family, Food and Culture*. Tucson AZ: Rio Nuevo Press, 2006.

"Denise Chavez has been a significant and widely acknowledged writer for quite some time and *A Taco Testimony* will add greatly to her reputation. The book is by turns comic and melancholy, graceful and acerbic. It is a fine read."

273. Kain, John. *A Rare and Precious Thing: The Possibilities and Pitfalls of Working with a Spiritual Teacher*. New York: Harmony/Bell Tower Books, 2006.

"Ever since we arrived in the New World in bulk four centuries ago Americans have tried to beat their spiritual paths. John Kain's fascinating *A Rare and Precious Thing* is fine guide to the spiritual possibilities of our time."

274. Turner, Frederick. *Redemption*. New York: Harcourt, 2006.

"Fred Turner's *Redemption* is an implacable stew of sex and love, vice and violence. Turner is a prose master, and also a bear of very large brain. Rarely do we see a novel on this grand scale of historical perceptiveness, with our country's bruised soul a backstory to the finely drawn ordinary characters who become mythic in the progress of the tale. This is an important novel."

275. Davis, Todd F. *Some Heaven*. Lansing: Michigan State University Press, 2007.

"*Some Heaven* is a considerable book of poems. Many poets feel that they know the natural world, but Todd Davis has absorbed this world fully into his heart and mind. He is a fine, rare poet."

276. Lent, Jeffrey. *A Peculiar Grace*. New York: Grove/Atlantic, 2007.

"Unlike nearly everyone else who practices the art, Jeffrey Lent was never a 'beginning novelist.' He arrived, as it were, at the height of his talent and *A Peculiar Grace* increases his reach. It is an uncomfortably brilliant novel both in the human dimensions of the story and the intense grace of the writing."

277. Brown, Larry. *A Miracle of Catfish*. Chapel Hill NC: Algonquin Books of Chapel Hill, 2007.

"Larry Brown's posthumous *A Miracle of Catfish* is simply enough a triumph of the sort of visceral intensity that we have learned to expect from Brown. It is certainly a must-read for all of those concerned with American Literature in our time."

278. Graves, John. *My Dogs and Guns*. New York: Skyhouse Publishing, 2007.

"Over the decades I've developed the impression that John Graves is the most honest writer in America, and also one of the best. Here is further evidence."

279. Otterbacher, John. *Sailing Grace*. Grand Rapids MI: Samadhi Press, 2007.

"*Sailing Grace* is a thoroughly engaging book. Wise people have known forever that life is a near death experience. The costumes of our lives can be suffocating and Otterbacher and his family shed theirs going to sea, a foolhardy venture because of his health, but they win big and we win along with them by reading the engrossing and perilous adventure story they made of their lives."

280. McNamee, Thomas. *Alice Waters and Chez Panisse: The Romantic, Impractical, Often Eccentric, Ultimately Brilliant Making of a Food Revolution*. New York: Penguin Books, 2007.

"Thomas McNamee's *Alice Waters and Chez Panisse* is a fascinating book. Over and above Waters' obvious leadership in the food revolution McNamee's work is as compelling as a very good novel."

281. Rosenbauer, Tom. *The Orvis Fly-Fishing Guide 2007*. Guilford CT: Lyons Press, 2007.

"A splendid guide including everything an angler needs."

282. Kalish, Mildred Armstrong. *Little Heathens: Hard Times and High Spirits on an Iowa Farm during the Great Depression*. New York: Bantam Books, 2007.

"*Little Heathens* is an enchanting but thoroughly unsentimental look at rural life in the Great Depression. In clear clean prose we are offered the grit, struggle, and also the joy of hard work on a farm. I cherish this book for its quite naked honesty and quiet lyricism about a time which makes our current problems nearly childish. This is a fine book."

283. Stegner, Lynn. *Because a Fire Was in My Head*. Lincoln: University of Nebraska Press/Bison Books, 2007.

"A brilliant book, more solid than the ground we stand on. This novel does honor to the best in the tradition of storytelling, even though you occasionally want to shove the heroine off the highest possible cliff. In other words, you are drawn into the story, and when you have finished you have added amplitude to your knowledge of the human condition."

284. McNamer, Deidre. *Red Rover*. New York: Viking Press, 2007.

"*Red Rover* by Deidre McNamer is a rare and considerable achievement, stunning actually. This is a truly impressive novel. She is a master weaver of prose."

285. Erdrich, Lise. *Night Train*. Minneapolis: Coffee House Press, 2008.

"*Night Train* is abrasive, lucid, almost cruel but still very engaging. I admired the open mastery of language. It reminded me how wonderfully rejuvenating it can be to read prose of this quality."

286. Bowden, Charles. *Exodus/Exodo*. Austin: University of Texas Press, 2008.

"Charles Bowden's *Exodus/Exodo* is likely a great book. Since reading it I have that silly fantasy that if the members of the United States Congress and also the media would read this book a new day would be possible, but then both seem convinced that talking is thinking and so the long nightmare will continue. At this moment I'll construct another fantasy and hope that a million intelligent Americans will read this book. They are the source of all effective changes and the victims of the low rent chiselers of politics and the media who must rise to the level of consciousness they will find in *Exodus/Exodo*. The photos of Julius Cardona are marvelous."

287. Sunee, Kim. *Trail of Crumbs*. New York: Grand Central Books, 2008.

"Kim Sunee tells us so much about the French that I never learned in 25 trips to Paris, but mostly about the terrors and pleasure of that infinite octopus, love. A fine book."

288. Parks, Cecily. *Field Folly Snow*. Athens: University of Georgia Press, 2008.

"What an intriguing book. Parks isn't trying to close the coffin lid on language. This is fresh work with a surpassingly delicate sense of language."

289. Adamson, Gil. *The Outlander*. New York: HarperCollins, 2008.

"*The Outlander* is a superb novel, and one senses in the fine writing the potential of a major writer. . . . Suspenseful to a degree that you are often in a state of physical unrest, a condition only occasioned by first-rate fiction."

290. Miles, Jonathan. *Dear American Airlines: A Novel*. New York: Houghton Mifflin, 2008.

"A rough and wild ride . . . I loved this novel, which is strong medicine indeed."

291. See, Anik. *Saudade*. Toronto: Coach House Books, 2008.

"Anik See's *Saudade* is often disturbingly brilliant. It reassures me that much of our experience of the world is still undescribed. *Saudade* is fresh and utterly original."

292. MacFarlane, Robert. *The Wild Places*. New York: Penguin Books, 2008.

"Macfarlane writes about the wild in the language of the wild . . . a uniquely powerful book with a guaranteed destiny unfolding in front of it."

293. Hogan, Linda. *Rounding the Human Corners*. Minneapolis: Coffee House Press, 2008.

"I have long been a fan of Linda Hogan's work. In *Rounding the Human Corners* I quickly found the lines, 'the green floor of the world that so / makes us want to live.' She is a significant figure in our literature."

294. Lent, Jeffrey. *After You've Gone*. New York: Grove/Atlantic, 2009.

"I had a curious and fascinating experience with Jeffrey Lent's *After You've Gone*. I read it three months ago and then let it slip in and out of my consciousness without beckoning it. Like all good novels *After You've Gone* will become part of your life. The triumph is the quality of Lent's prose."

# Section H
## *Annotated Interviews with Jim Harrison*

This list of interviews with Jim Harrison is a composite that includes formal interviews during book promotion tours, formal interviews conducted both at Harrison's residences and at other locations, telephone interviews, interviews transcribed for online venues (such as amazon.com and borders.com), question-and-answer sessions with audiences, and even an online "chat" discussion. All annotations are by Robert DeMott and Gregg Orr.

*Interview* is used in a broad sense. Not all the following pieces are traditional, formal question-and-answer interviews; included are varying-length newspaper sketches, author profiles, informal literary discussions, and edited conversations, all of which rely on or employ direct quotations from Harrison. And, though much effort has been made to track down as many print, oral, and electronic media interviews with Jim Harrison as possible, the following compilation is not complete. However, it should prove useful in suggesting the depth and range of Harrison's intellectual preoccupations, his personal interests, and his consistent conversational voice and discursive style as well as his candor and sense of humor, even when presented with the same questions over and over. For a writer who has a reputation for being reclusive, and who has said often that he is not comfortable giving interviews because they focus on his personality rather than on his work, Harrison has been quite generous with his time, energy, and opinions (up to a certain point). This selection should also indicate the degree (if not always the quality) of attention and coverage he has received during the past three decades. Foreign-language interviews, particularly those exclusively in French, which are legion, are not always included here. The compilation of this list was aided by Patrick Smith, Joseph Bednarik, Gregg Orr, Beef Torrey, and Nancy Richard; the list itself was compiled and annotated with the help of Rae Greiner and Anne Langendorfer.

**1971**

1. Interview. "Jim Harrison: A New Voice from Hemingway's Hills." By Dennis C. Knickerbocker. *Grand Rapids* (MI) *Press* 26 December 1971: 6–7.

    As nearly as can be determined, this is the first published biographical profile on Harrison and provides glimpses (accompanied by several photographs) into his early life and career as poet, novelist, and journalist for *Sports Illustrated*. Information on his travels to New York City and California, youthful religious conversion, deaths of his father and sister in a car accident, penchant for the outdoor life, career at Michigan State University, and preference for country living: "The city brings out all of my neuroses. A lot of poets are trying to get out in the country." Provides background on his first novel, the recently published *Wolf*, already in its second printing. "I think of myself mostly as a poet." Claims to be half finished with a new novel that "will be less autobiographical than *Wolf*" and will be a "comedy involving sabotage."

**1972**

2. Interview. "A New Voice from the North Country: A Portrait of the Prodigal Poet Who Came Home to Michigan." By Eric Siegel. *Detroit Free Press* 16 April 1972: 18–20.

    Siegel describes Harrison's physical appearance and his home "on a nine-acre farm with his wife and two daughters near the tiny town of Lake Leelanau." Notes: "A shed will become his new writing room when the weather clears and he finds time to make renovations." Harrison expresses his fondness for Lake Leelanau: "When you're a writer at a university you're a freak, sort of town clown. I feel much less isolated from people here than at a university." General statements about Harrison's interests. "If you want to be a grown up professional novelist," he advises, "you write five days a week for at least three hours." Talks about his "super-alive" mental state when writing poetry, and that his poetry is written in cycles. "I write a lot for six months and then I can't write for a year. It's very hard on me—the idea that I'm a poet and I can't write a poem for a year." Siegel says Harrison wanted to be a writer since age 12, as an escape from meaningless middle-class life. Talks about his growing up, his family, school, traveling. "I was sure you couldn't be an artist in Michigan," he says. "I was at the age when you think all your problems are geographical." Talks about poets but his dislike for the "poetry scene." Siegel and Harrison go to Dick's Pour House; Harrison wins third place in a pool tournament. Siegel states: "He also knows he doesn't want to earn more than the $9,000 to $10,000 a year he makes now." Admits to being "white sheep" of the family now: "Everybody likes a writer who's successful, but before you're successful, you're a pain in the ass."

## 1976

3. Interview. "Jim Harrison: A Good Day for Talking: An Interview with the Author of *Wolf* and *Farmer*." By Ira Eliott and Marty Sommerness. *October Chronicle* 1.1 (29 October 1976): 16–23. East Lansing MI. Reprinted in *Conversations with Jim Harrison*. Ed. Robert DeMott. Jackson: University Press of Mississippi, 2002. 9–22.

Question-and-answer format interview conducted in Lake Leelanau. Harrison says his MA thesis was an essay explaining how his first poetry got published. Introduction states Harrison "prefers Wakoski over Plath, Chandler over Hammett, Hunter Thompson over James Reston." Discusses the limits of academic life for the writer: "The worst thing about academic writers and people who teach writing or live within an academic atmosphere is that it shears them of a base. People think after they teach a while that academic life is a microcosm of the rest of the world, which it very clearly isn't." Discusses the writing process: he thinks about the subject for years, then writes the first draft "in about six weeks." Discusses contemporary writers he admires (Thomas McGuane, Edward Hoagland, Norman Mailer), calls Hemingway "a pompous wretched human being in that macho sense," but also says that he "was an unquestionably brilliant writer." Discusses Faulkner, Henry Miller, James Joyce, Melville, and Clint Eastwood. Claims that *Wolf* was "probably eighty-five, ninety percent autobiographical." Discusses peyote and women's liberation ("since I've freed my own self, I don't want to be blamed for anybody else's bondage"). Discusses Robert Altman and Stanley Kubrick films. When making characters, writing novels, he says, you don't want to withhold the evidence, which Hemingway does to excess, unlike Faulkner. Discusses the postmodern writers Barth, Pynchon, Gass.

## 1977

4. Interview. "Writer Jim Harrison: Work, Booze, the Outdoor Life—and an Absolute Rage for Order." By Kathleen Stocking. *Detroit Free Press* 5 June 1977: 21–22, 24–26.

## 1978

5. Roundtable Conversation series, Academy of American Poets Audio Archive. By Elizabeth Kray. New York, 26 January 1978. Unpublished.

A lengthy, wide-ranging, energetic, and often humorous and gossipy interview/discussion with Harrison conducted the day before he gave a reading of his fiction and poetry at the Donnell Library in New York City. He begins by discussing three of his favorite books—Knut Hamsun's *Victoria* and Henry Miller's *In the Time of the Assassins* and *A Study of Rimbaud*—with a small audience gathered in the academy offices in New York City. Emphasizes the appeal of the two different kinds of writing temperament—Hamsun is cool and omniscient; Miller is hot and engaged. Claims that discipline is a "false issue." The "world doesn't care if you write," so the real issue is "the degree of your obsession." Quotes approvingly D. H. Lawrence's statement that "the only aristocracy is that of consciousness." In writing a novel "you don't want to withhold . . . evidence," which was Hemingway's weakness at times. Asserts: "I would rather have a young poet read *Popular Mechanics* than the *American Poetry Review*." Complains about "hybridization" of contemporary poetry caused by excessive MFA programs. Praises Howard Norman's translations of Cree poetry and Robert Lowell's *Imitations*. Speaks of his early interest in wanting to be a writer: "And I read James Joyce's *Portrait of the Artist as a Young Man* in chemistry class, and I'd been reading a lot of Byron and Keats. And I thought—I was fifteen—what a grand way to live, which of course is a real false assumption." Tells story of sending poems to Denise Levertov and her role in getting his first book published at W. W. Norton. Discusses professional elements of scriptwriting, and praises William Goldman—"I don't think he's ever written a turkey." Suggests that some books are almost too powerful to bear: "Sort of that feeling of being swept away . . . in one form or another that you can't almost bear the book. Like if you read Hamsun's *Hunger* it's just physically the most unpleasant book you're ever going to read." Quotes Rene Char's line "Lucidity is the wound closest to the sun," and claims to have taken a decade to understand it. Discusses "quadra-schizoid" feeling in writing poetry, fiction, screenplays, journalism. Further discussion of film scriptwriting. Praises poetry contemporaries Galway Kinnell, Charles Olson, Jack Spicer, Gary Snyder, and Charles Simic. Claims to have "quit giving readings about five years ago, because I just couldn't bear going around and all these assistant professors would tell you about their problems in the department. You know, there's a banality in going around to universities and reading your poems which just will drive you nuts." Remembers Thomas McGuane writing *Bushwacked Piano* in a turbulent time, yet he was "writing eighteen hours a day, right at the kitchen table. Nothing could bother him." Humorous story about Richard Brautigan as a screenwriter. Ends with satirizing chic people who move to the country and invite him to their houses for "din-din," which he turns down in favor of going to Dick's Tavern.

**1979**

6. Clark, LaVerne Harrell. *Focus 101: An Illustrated Biography of 101 Poets of the 60's and 70's*. Chico CA: Heidelberg Graphics, 1979. 47, 48.

   Discusses influences: Denise Levertov, Robert Duncan, Louis Simpson, Neruda, Rilke, Yeats, Bunting, Lorca, Whitman, Hart Crane, Pound. Says he "write[s] 'free verse,' which is absurdly indefinite as a name for what any poet writes"; also considers himself to be an "internationalist." Says his "poems seem rural, vaguely surrealistic though after the Spanish rather than the French. My sympathies run hotly to the impure, the inclusive, as the realm of poetry." Short comment from Richard Ellman and Robert O'Clair on his early poems.

7. Interview. "The Wolves Are Howling at Jim Harrison's Door." By Paul Magnusson. *Detroit Free Press* 16 September 1979: 1E, 4ES.

   Interviewer catches up with Harrison, self-proclaimed "intentional white trash sports fop," at his Lake Leelanau home just after publication of *Legends of the Fall*. Its initial print run was 12,000 copies, and it was chosen as a Book-of-the-Month Club alternate. "Success," Magnusson writes, "threatens at every turn." Profile chronicles changes in Harrison's life, career, and financial situation, which for the previous ten years averaged about $11,000 a year. Recounts how the actor Jack Nicholson loaned Harrison money to finish *Legends*, which Harrison's agent, Bob Datilla, considers his "breakthrough" book. Warner Brothers bought "Revenge," and Harrison has accepted a three-screenplay deal with Warner's as well. "Nobody wants to piss away their life on nonsense," Harrison says.

**1980**

8. Interview. "Hard Cases: Conversation with Jim Harrison and Thomas McGuane, Riders of the Purple Rage." By Kathleen Stocking. *Michigan: The Magazine of the Detroit News* 12 August 1980: 14–15.

**1982**

9. Interview. "Jim Harrison." By J. A. Trachtenberg. *The West's New Writers* 12.1 (January 1982): 10.

   *Warlock* was just published in a run of 20,000 copies. Harrison praises "pelvic mysteries of swamps." Recalls initial meeting with Jack Nicholson on movie set of *Missouri Breaks*, success of screenwriting contracts and sale of film rights, and refusal to fit into Hollywood system. "I'm a bit of a recluse. I don't like other people to know what I'm doing." Some coverage of his eating habits and food preferences.

10. Interview. "Legends of the North." By Marc Dettman. *Grand Rapids* 19.8 (August 1982): 30–34.

## 1983

11. Interview. "CA Interview." By Jean W. Ross. *Contemporary Authors: New Revision Series*. Ed. Ann Evory and Deborah A. Straub. Detroit MI: Gale Research, 1983. 227–29. vol. 8. Reprinted in *Conversations with Jim Harrison*. Ed. Robert DeMott. Jackson: University Press of Mississippi, 2002. 23–28.

    Telephone interview conducted on 7 October 1981. Discussion of the oral tradition of his family: "You know, when people spend a lot of their lives based in some kind of oral tradition, they're much more careful about the words and they make a much greater attempt to make what they say interesting." Discusses writing poems and how he got an F in a graduate course; for Harrison, the MA was "not at all" worthwhile for his writing, with the exception of one teacher who made the class mimic the style of Henry James. Much talk about feminism and women ("Most women are still like Tibet to me; though I've studied Tantric Buddhism at some length, I still don't feel I comprehend it"). Explains why he is not active in organized conservationist movements, which are "very busy with language" but have no power. Says: "I don't understand writers who want to be in some publicity-oriented limelight, because it is never based on people who are actually interested in the work."

12. Interview. "An Interview with Jim Harrison." By Jean W. Ross. *Dictionary of Literary Biography Yearbook*. Ed. Richard Ziegfeld. Detroit MI: Gale Research/Bruccoli Clark, 1983. 275–76.

    Harrison doesn't like to think of himself in categories, he says, because it makes him "too schizoid." Since he wants to "make a living as a writer, [he] usually ends up doing a lot of things" to support the writer's life. On the difference between poetry and prose, Harrison says: "I never think of the obvious formal differences, which are almost artificial." When writing, Harrison says that he "never starts with an idea," but rather "with a collection of sensations and images." Further, he states: "A form is a convenience that emerges out of what I have to say rather than something I impose on the material." Discusses writing ghazals, "a kind of lyric explosion," and the uselessness of book reviews and critics. He has started working on a film project with Jeanne Moreau, the French actress (he saw her in *Jules and Jim* "a dozen times"); expresses disdain for colleges, where "all the people are the same." Poetry and fiction are "thoroughly balkanized," located on the coasts; the rest in between are "flyovers." Feels that the Midwest is ignored artistically by the "fungoid, self-congratulatory nature of the Eastern literary Establishment."

13. Interview. "Author's 'Hot, Hopeless' Life Mixes with Success." By Karin Winegar. *Minneapolis Star and Tribune* 8 March 1983. 2 pp., unpaginated.

    Harrison, in Minneapolis to conduct writing workshops at Hamline University and at the Loft, talks about family, dislike for college teaching, European interest in his books, his checkered past with drugs, his screenplay writing, his disinterest in Hemingway. "What's important to me? My family. Bird hunting." Also says: "I never was that interested in Hemingway. My brain tends to be sort of hot and hopeless and his heroes were always cool and collected and knew what they were doing. Have never been able for long to behave on that presumption, although I can carry it off for a while when it's really necessary." Also comments on feminist criticism of his macho style: "I get terribly exhausted about this macho thing. Christ, here I am a nice person who's never hit a woman, never raped anybody, been relatively happily married, so I get hung with this. So I say, no, you've got it wrong, it's 'nacho,' not 'macho.'"

# 1984

14. Interview. "Words from the Woods." By Gregory Skwira. *Detroit* 25 March 1984: 8–9, 11, 13–15, 16, 18–19.

    In this profile, conducted at Lake Leelanau, Harrison reflects on his experience of being disoriented by success. "I lost my equilibrium," he says about a period in the late 1970s and early 1980s. Success was "too abrupt," but having been through the subsequent "mudbath" he is "forgiving" with himself. Claims to have written *Sundog* in 7 weeks, and gives account of writing process: "The first 50 pages are excruciating, and after that it starts to take over. And after you pass 100 it seems to really take over, so you can't *not* do it all the time. . . . Toward the end I did it 40 days in a row, which is why I wasn't in such neat shape when I finished. It seizes you and pulls you along." *Sundog*, he claims, completes a "spiritual autobiography" that includes *Wolf, Farmer*, and "The Man Who Gave Up His Name."

15. Interview. "An Interview with Jim Harrison." By Kay Bonetti. Audiotape. American Audio Prose Library, May 1984.

## 1985

16. Interview. "An Interview with Jim Harrison." By Kay Bonetti. *Missouri Review* 8.3 (1985): 65–86. Reprinted in *Conversations with American Novelists: The Best Interviews from the Missouri Review and the American Audio Prose Library.* Ed. Kay Bonetti et al. Columbia: University of Missouri Press, 1997. 39–55. Also reprinted in *Conversations with Jim Harrison*. Ed. Robert DeMott. Jackson: University Press of Mississippi, 2002. 29–44.

    This is a highly informative and intelligent interview, conducted in May 1984 at Harrison's home in Lake Leelanau MI. Harrison begins by discussing his publishing history and the reason why he is interested in the novella form. He discusses going to a "Mexican fat farm" because he was so exhausted from writing and felt "grotesque." Explains that cooking has replaced excessive drinking and that his marriage of 25 years has been a stabilizing force; nevertheless, he cites McGuane's saying that "alcoholism is a writer's black lung disease." Explains the doubleness in *Sundog*, noting that Strang is a kind of "alter ego"; a comparison is made to Conrad's *The Secret Sharer* and "whether or not it's one person or two," a comment that gives Harrison goosebumps. Harrison notes that "dread and irony have gotten to be literary addictions," but Strang is a metaphor for the artist who is "free from dread." States that "textual concretia, the 'thinginess' of life," is "an old rule I have on the wall. Make it vivid." On the influence of writing poetry on his fiction: "Trying to bear down on the singularity of images. Movement. Those suites were good training for moving from image to mood to mood." Has never taken a writing course "of any sort." Names Alfred Kazin as the critic who told him his characters in *A Good Day to Die* didn't exist. Wants to bring writing and moviemaking to the common characters in Topeka. Discussions of moviemaking, screenplays, San Francisco, and jazz. Talk of his reputation as a macho writer leads him to say: "I'm not trying to get out the vote when I write a novel. A novel's a novel. . . . And I don't like to be attacked for reasons anterior to my work." He berates didactic novels and novelists. Relates seeing a person commit suicide a week earlier by jumping off the Golden Gate Bridge, and notes: "I immediately started making sentences. That's my only defense against this world is to build a sentence."

17. Interview. "The Man Whose Soul Is Not for Sale: Jim Harrison." By Hank Nuwer. *Rendezvous: Idaho State University Journal of Arts and Letters* 21.1 (Fall 1985). 26–42. This interview was also published in *Rendezvousing with Contemporary Writers*. Pocatello: Idaho State University Press, 1988. 26–42. And reprinted in *Conversations with Jim Harrison*. Ed. Robert DeMott. Jackson: University Press of Mississippi, 2002. 45–62.

Harrison talks about meaninglessness of MFA programs, how "eventually [poets from them] all live in Ohio and each one will be given a Xerox machine." Talks about wanting the anonymity of a janitor, about Strang's character in *Sundog*, how he doesn't read novels while he's writing his own, his affinity for travel, his dismissal of critical commentary on his work (especially from the media/literary establishment). Harrison says that, if NASA were to send any writer into space, it should be Mailer, although "certainly Bellow is the bear with the largest brain, as Pooh would say—there is no question." Talks about writers and alcoholism, writers he knows and likes, food and cooking, his macho image, how he doesn't like to think about his novels once they're completed. An explanation of "the theory and practice of rivers" in *Sundog* that later becomes a title of a book of poetry: "The theory and practice of rivers that this man [Strang] has given his life to is almost an Oriental idea about the nature of water, and how humans—you—at your best, live like the river does. All water on earth moves." Says no one reads his work before it's sent out—only typed by his secretary and copyedited by a woman in Kalamazoo. Says he doesn't believe in a lot of revision, explains use of commas in *Sundog*, talks about writing process. Ends by commenting on "scar tissue" and getting over things that are in the past: "I have to constantly forgive myself for not being as good as I'd hoped to be. Even though I couldn't work any harder than I have, I still think somehow it should have been better."

18. Interview. "Jim Harrison: Today's Hemingway?" By Jim Fergus. *MD* magazine May 1985: 116, 118–19, 244–46.
19. "How Writers Live Today." By Tom Jenks. *Esquire* August 1985: 126. Brief entry under the topic "Local Color."

## 1986

20. Interview. "Jim Harrison: The Mad Poet Cools Off (a Little)." By Ric Bohy. *Michigan: The Magazine of the Detroit News* 9 February 1986: 8–10, 14, 16–18.

    Profile/interview with Harrison conducted in Lake Leelanau. The subtitle of the piece, "The Mad Poet of the North, Cools Off (a Little)," provides the angle of approach. Harrison considered by many to be the "New Hemingway" whose masculine writing style and anarchistic escapades with high-profile pals like Nicholson, Thomas McGuane, and Russell Chatham have attracted much media attention. But Harrison could never be called lazy. Since 1965 he has published over a dozen books of poetry and prose and has been translated into eight languages. He has also completed 13 screenplays, mostly original or adaptations of his own work, though none have been produced. Harrison, the Mogul of Macho, has been changing. Reported to be at work on a long novel set in the Midwest in the 19th century, the first third of which is told in a woman's voice. He does not care what reviewers think of it; he's doing it for himself: "They are always telling us that everyone has their feminine side to cover. And this is different in the sense that she's a monster. She's one of those inordinately vital people in every way." Speaks of the financial rewards that followed success of *Legends of the Fall* and a three-screenplay contract with Warner Brothers that boosted his income to middle-six-figure range. Admits difficulties of being unaccustomed to making that kind of money: "I thought of myself as the Leon Spinks of American literature. . . . You have the dollars, but you're so stupid you don't know what to do with it. You had less fun than you did when you were poor." Claims to have started a short story the previous summer called "I Forgot to Go to Spain": "All my life I wanted to go to Spain, and then when I made lots of money I forgot. See, that's the danger of it all." Acknowledges past depressions and excesses and disruptive behavior and need to go on from there: "I would hope I'd see something new tomorrow, but you generally don't 'cause you're banal. You're only vaguely less banal than everybody else. The edge of the artist isn't that big, I don't think."

## 1988

21. Interview. "The Art of Fiction 104: Jim Harrison." By Jim Fergus. *Paris Review* 30.107 (Summer 1988): 52–97. Excerpts from this interview also appear in *The Writer's Chapbook: A Compendium of Fact, Opinion, Wit and Advice from the 20th Century's Preeminent Writers*. Ed. George Plimpton. New York: Viking Press, 1989. 251, 225. New York: Modern Library, 1999. 246, 272. Excerpts also reprinted in "Jim Harrison." *Contemporary Literary Criticism*. 66 (1991): 157–61. Ed. Robert Matus. Also reprinted in *Conversations with Jim Harrison*. Ed. Robert DeMott. Jackson: University Press of Mississippi, 2002. 63–92.

One of the longest and most comprehensive and influential interviews with Harrison, one that was edited down from a much longer transcript that was itself created from almost 15 hours of taped conversation. Fergus's interview was conducted in October 1986 but was published just after the publication of *Dalva*. Major themes and topics include: Harrison's river metaphor, a "life properly lived"; his early interest in the church and his belief that "all [his] religious passions adapted themselves to art as religion." Calls *Wolf* a "poet's book" that he arrived at backward "because poets practice an overall scrutiny habitually, and what's good later for their novels is that they practice it pointillistically." He says that "there's no such thing as regional literature." On academic writers he argues against the notion of "the writer as some kind of hysterical Ichabod Crane—the oddball on campus," a portrait he "loathes." He notes that he "said a nasty thing in an interview once [*Rendezvous* interview (see item H17)] and quotes his comment: 'I'm always being lectured on integrity by professors who've spent a lifetime slobbering at the public trough.'" Recalls aftermath of "absolute failure" of *Farmer*: "That was something I couldn't handle because it just slipped beneath the waters. . . . That was a difficult period and I couldn't maintain my sanity. I had a series of crack-ups." Discusses *Letters to Yesenin*, friendship with Jack Nicholson, financial success that resulted from scriptwriting and *Legends of the Fall*, and his two years as "the Leon Spinks of the literary world." Names 17 contemporary women writers he admires. Discusses James Hillman's idea (actually Jung's) that men give up the feminine, the "twin sister who we abandoned at birth." Claims to have written *Legends of the Fall* in about 10 days and "Revenge" in about 10 days. Says there is "no such thing as discipline. You write it when it is ready to be written." Calls rewriting and revision "an artificiality" for people who "haven't thought about it for three years." Indicates importance of Keats's "negative capability . . . just to be able to hold at bay hundreds of conflicting emotions and ideas." Notes: "Your best weapon is your vertigo." Advises writers to "keep distant from religious, political, and social obligations." Discusses *Sundog* as a "philosophical novel" and the protagonist Strang's need for "meaningful work." Extended statement on awful treatment of Native Americans: "Our doom as a nation will be unveiled in the way we have treated the blacks an Indians, the entire Third World. Washington is a flunked Passion Play." Says that a writer should be a "hero of consciousness." When asked if it is necessary for the writer to "enter into the world and then be able to get out of it unscathed," Harrison responds: "Intact. It's the Zen metaphor of the ox, the ten stages of the ox, to finally have no fences and to be able to return to the city. The whole point is not to need any strictures and to still maintain balance and grace, and if you can't the danger is a life-and-death thing." Ends with account of his "little attack of lycanthropy."

22. Interview. "Of Bears, Bars and Books: Author Jim Harrison Looks Down the Road at Writing." By David Hacker. *Detroit Free Press* 2 March 1988: 3B.

Harrison, interviewed at Art's Tavern, in Glen Arbor MI, says he is planning "to write a couple of pieces on emptiness for *Outside* magazine. I'm going down to Sonora, Mexico, looking for grizzly bears . . . then I'm going to do a piece on western Montana." A film version of his novella "Revenge" is scheduled to come out in February. Harrison indicates that he "buys up land whenever he can, just to keep the developers from getting their hands on it." Notes he wanted to be a painter, "wanted to be Gauguin," but was "no good at it. All I can do is write. I've failed at everything except immediate acts of the imagination. That's what I do well, so that's what I do." Believes that every artist has a duty to regularly throw himself off the edge of the world. Now working on short novels, a "semi–*Big Chill* thing about aging radicals" called "The Sunset" [sic; "Sunset Limited"], a piece called "Brown Dog," and a novel that continues the story told in *Dalva*. Doing "some" speechwriting for the New Jersey senator Bill Bradley.

23. Interview. "The Softer Side of a Macho Man." By Tom BeVier. *Michigan: The Magazine of the Detroit News* 6 March 1988: 14–19.

    Harrison profiled at Leelanau Peninsula home ground prior to publication of *Dalva*, which his publisher, Seymour Lawrence, claims is "the greatest thing he has ever done." First print run by Delacorte/Seymour Lawrence will be 25,000 copies. In the future Harrison will be writing a "sporting food" column for a new magazine and has agreed to write a libretto for an opera by Nick Thorne. "I guess my interest in classical music is something most people don't know about." Discusses *Dalva* the book and Dalva the character: "I got to write all this stuff I had noticed in my life but didn't know I knew. I wanted to write something new. To cross the Rockies. On foot. At night." He adds that *Dalva* is drawn from various literary sources, including Lawrence Durell's Justine and the adventures[s]/author Beryl Markham with smattering of the actress Lauren Hutton. Interview ends at Art's Tavern in Glen Arbor: "People to whom I used to be a hopeless drunk . . . now see me as only a problem drinker."

24. Interview. "Interview with Jim Harrison." By Lynn Neary. *All Things Considered*, National Public Radio, 3 April 1988. Radio broadcast.

    About the title character of *Dalva* Harrison says: "I'm not sure that I would want to know her in real life. I think she's rather frightening, but certainly she includes all the dimensions of women that I have actually perceived. . . . It's hard to imagine anyone more strongly individuated." Says he knows what he knows about "women's emotions" from his family (his mother and her five sisters; his wife; his two daughters). Notes that in this novel he was "trying to get at some of what [he] think[s] of as the soul history of our continent." In order to do so he needed for the second section of the novel "in terms of Shakespearean tragedy . . . a buffoon—a fool. So I needed this kind of academic [Michael] who would be aware, that much aware, of

19th century history." Contextualizes the events of the American Indian "holocaust," a story that "can't be done by textbooks," and notes that the Sand Creek massacre took place when "Henry Ford was . . . dealing with the problem of spare parts in Akron," yet "people choose to forget this."

25. Interview. "Literary Voice in the Wilderness: Jim Harrison, a Novelist and Outdoorsman, Writes from Woman's Point of View in *Dalva*." By Keith Love. *Los Angeles Times* 12 April 1988: 1, 4–5.

    Takes place in Lake Leelanau, just after Harrison has returned from a quail hunt in Georgia. Writer calls *Dalva*'s title character "just another experiment for Harrison, who has defied easy labels in his more than 20 years of writing." Harrison says, "I make everything up," when asked if the Northridge journals (and the man himself) are real. On the significance of Santa Monica CA, Harrison says: "Edward Curtis, the great photographer of the Indians, died there. So one day I thought what if he had had a granddaughter who grew up there, and that was the beginning of the Dalva character. But of course she became the great-granddaughter of Northridge." On the landscape and writing: "You ride down the road and look at things. All of this stuff enters my mind as images rather than as knowledge." Harrison drove around Nebraska, the Dakotas, Arizona, and Mexico to prepare for the book. "I think about the sentence a long time and then I write it. I don't revise it once it's set down." Harrison likes "extremes" but "nothing in between." If he can't be "fishing or hunting," then he wants to be "in the Museum of Modern Art in New York." Ends by quoting Yeats as saying: "The hearth is more dangerous to poets than alcohol."

26. Interview. "Heart and Soul." By Kathleen Stocking. *Detroit Monthly* September 1988: 178, 180.

    Stocking visits Harrison at Lake Leelanau, where he has just returned from a national book tour for *Dalva* that he describes as "idiocy, the cult of personality and gossips . . . I'm basically no good at anything except writing." Stocking sums him up as a "complicated man" with "paradoxical qualities" of sensitivity and roughness. Harrison claims *Dalva*'s underlying theme is the nation's "soul history"—"desecration of the Indians" and "importation of slaves." He continues: "Without a moral vision, there is no future. Without vision, you die." Yet he disclaims having a political purpose; as a writer he is a "perceiver." Speaks of "abnegating" his own personality to become Dalva as he wrote the novel. "The emotional energy I put into this book was enormous." Profile ends with humorous account of Stocking trying to translate an Italian inscription, allegedly from Dante, that Harrison inscribed in a first edition of *Dalva*. The nearest translation is "Today for sure will be like great sex." No one believes it is from Dante, but it is quintessential Harrison.

## 1989

27. Interview. "The Sporting Club." By Jim Fergus. *Outside* March 1989: 40–44, 112–17.

    A group profile article with some interview material. Follows Harrison, Thomas McGuane, Russell Chatham, and Guy de la Valdene during a Key West fishing trip in the spring. Provides history of the men's friendship and details their shared love of art, food, and sport. Notes that, "though Harrison once described himself as a 'monk to art,' none of them have exactly lived cloistered lives." Discusses conservation and ethics, and argues that these men practice a "very different consciousness from the old hook-and-buffet style of outdoor writing." The overview of Harrison comments on his friendship with McGuane, Michigan landscape, his predilection for driving around the country, and his Hollywood connections. "It's just that I'm not an academic writer.... What would one write about growing up the way I did? I can't pretend I didn't grow up hunting and fishing. I write about what I know ... I know about loons and coyotes and crows.... I know about men and women, too." On male relationships: "[They] are full of this very strange and sort of remote pecking order, ever since grade school athletics. Novelists and poets can get fantastically fucked up in that sort of thing, and I don't get involved. Maybe there used to be a competition between Tom and me a long time ago, but I don't sense that anymore." Notes Harrison has called the U.S. government's treatment of the Sioux Indians "our curse on the House of Atreus." At the end of the article, McGuane and Harrison have just received a phone call announcing the sale of the screenplay they coauthored 10 years earlier.

28. Interview. "Jim Harrison: Le Sorcier du Michigan" (Jim Harrison: The Sorcerer of Michigan). By Patrick Raynal. *Telerama* 8 March 1989: 10–13. no. 2043.

    French journalist, admitted fan of Harrison's writing, visits Lake Leelanau to observe Harrison in what Raynal calls his "perfectly bourgeois home." In this very quirky and self-conscious profile, fueled by the two drinking a bottle of tequila, Raynal finds Harrison contradictory—open and guarded—and imagines him to be more like "a farmer, a mechanic, a truck driver, suddenly seized by the demon and grace of writing." The interview moves to Harrison's granary, "an incredible shambles of objects." Harrison says Gauguin and Rimbaud are "the two men I admire most in the world." Harrison takes Raynal around to his local watering spots: "Most people around here don't know I'm a writer, and those who do don't care about it. I think they believe I'm a hunter, a fisherman who talks about his passions in magazines." Back at the house, a sumptuous meal of grouse and venison is prepared and eaten. Harrison responds to critical attacks: "I have finally stopped worrying about that. A critic is just like a sports journalist, he must talk at length about things he does not know intimately." Raynal concludes Harrison is a "fascinating personality, as subtly padlocked as his house is opened."

29. Interview. "A Peek at Jim Harrison's World: Flamboyant, Controversial Novelist Mellows—Just a Little." By Mike Norton. *Traverse City MI Record-Eagle* 23 July 1989: 1D–2D.

    Conducted in Lake Leelanau, beginning with description of Harrison's "totems" above his writing desk in his granary studio.

30. Interview. "After Seven Acclaimed Novels, Jim Harrison Is Finding It Harder to Elude Fame." By Julia Reed. *Vogue* September 1989: 502, 506, 510.

    "In this era of the literary starlet," Reed writes, "when publicity has become a stand-in for talent, Harrison's relentlessly low profile seems suspect, almost perverse." Covers list of publications and screenplays, also mentioning that Patrick Swayze reads a Harrison novel in the movie *Road House*, which Reed calls a "dubious honor." Interviewer writes that Harrison is often "mistakenly considered a member of this macho bunch" (McGuane and Chatham), a confusion he attributes to the fact that both Michigan and Montana "are M words. Our dream coasts are not conscious of the geography of the interior." Discussion of his writing process—longhand and with images collected in a box. Notes that "virtually everything of consequence in *Dalva* got done on solo driving trips." Interviewer states that there is "no formal relationship between any of the books: *Wolf* is a 'false memoir.' Sundog a novel presented as nonfiction. *A Good Day to Die* a thriller. *Legends of the Fall* is a collection of three novellas. . . . *Dalva* is a novel told in three first-person voices: 'a woman, an old man, and a dipshit,'" according to Chatham. Harrison says of *Dalva*: "I invented the woman I wanted to be in love with." Favorite poets are Rilke, Lorca, and Neruda because "they lived life and wrote anything they wanted to." His characters, according to one of the narrators in *Dalva*, live their lives "at an uncommon level of attentiveness." Critics sometimes find Harrison's characters unbelievable. Says that he no longer hunts mammals but still eats them. Notes: "Any habitual pattern distracts you, whether it's in love or work habits or vices, you're a train more than a human being." Ends with a visitor asking, "Don't you wish you could play the sax?" to which Harrison responds, "That's what I try to do in my novels."

## 1990

31. Interview. "Jim Harrison." *Letters from the Leelanau: Essays of People and Place.* Ed. Kathleen Stocking. Ann Arbor: University of Michigan Press, 1990. 72–77.

    A profile in which Stocking details a personal visit with Harrison. Stocking and Harrison discuss *Dalva*, and Harrison addresses the book's "underlying moral theme," saying: "This nation has a history, but it also has a soul history and that's what I was interested in. Our original sin in this country was desecration of the Indians, followed by the importation of the slaves. Underlying this is greed. But if you think a BMW is what works for you, just go look at L.A. Those people are living and dying in a shit monsoon. Because without moral vision there is no future. Without vision, you die." Stocking relates a disturbing anecdote about Harrison at a party, telling a woman recovering from an operation that she should have "her tits cut off." Describes Harrison's granary studio, its contents and impressions. Harrison states that, in order to create the character of *Dalva*, he had to "totally abnegate [his] own personality, to become her." More discussion of the "Indians" and of Dalva's Michael as a "Falstaffian character—loud, smart, mordant, a bottompincher—who can get away with saying things that more serious and sympathetic characters couldn't say." Ends with Harrison autographing Stocking's copy of *Dalva* with an Italian phrase he claims is from Dante: *o chi sigura coglioni*. Stocking can find no translation (and no connection to Dante), and "the nearest anyone can come" is the phrase: "Today for sure will be like great sex." This, she claims, is "quintessential" Harrison.

32. "Media Bail out from Tackling S&L Mess." By Bob Talbert. *Detroit Free Press* 26 June 1990: 5B. Column with interview comments from Harrison.

    First part of longer column is devoted to Harrison ("who checks in from time to time, reporting on something in his craw, usually something stuck sideways and barbed") and his reaction to the national savings-and-loan scandal, which Harrison calls the "biggest swindle of the century." Also notes that publication of *The Woman Lit by Fireflies* is delayed until August by Houghton Mifflin "because *New Yorker* magazine is running the entire [title] novella . . . in its July 23rd issue. That's great for me."

33. Interview. "PW Interviews Jim Harrison." By Wendy Smith. *Publishers Weekly* 3 August 1990: 59–60. This interview was also published in *Writing for Your Life: Ninety-Two Contemporary Authors Talk about the Art of Writing and the Job of Publishing.* Ed. Sybil Steinberg. Wainscott NY: Pushcart, 1992. 236–41. Also reprinted in *Conversations with Jim Harrison.* Ed. Robert DeMott. Jackson: University Press of Mississippi, 2002. 98–104.

On his return to his homeland of northern Michigan, Harrison notes: "Ever since I was seven and had my eye put out, I'd turn for solace to rivers, rain, trees, birds, lakes, animals.... If things are terrible beyond conception and I walk for 25 miles in the forest, they tend to go away for a while. Whereas if I lived in Manhattan I couldn't escape them." Article explains that this is also why Harrison has avoided the academic life: "I had this whole heroic notion of being a novelist.... I wanted to be a writer in the old sense of staying on the outside. I can live for about a year on the proceeds from the first draft of a screenplay ... and I think that's more fun than hanging around some fucking college town for 10 months waiting for summer vacation." Includes frequent Harrison references to Yeats, Camus, and Wallace Stevens, who said "that images tend to collect in pools in your brain." Harrison continues by saying: "When it's no longer bearable not to start to write it down, I start writing." Says that these images "emerge from dreams," and notes that in order to "concentrate" characters you must "try not to figure out what they mean at that point, because what you're trying to do in fiction is reinvent the form."

34. Interview. "The Man Who Likes Empty Spaces." By Ruth Pollack Coughlin. *Detroit News* 14 August 1990: C1.

    Profiler interview conducted around the time of publication of *A Woman Lit by Fireflies*. "Just who Harrison is gets to be a complicated issue, but in the end, it all comes down to passion." Discusses his passions and philosophies of life: "A poet and novelist, that's all you get to be, you have to use your energy for your calling"; "the only magic we get in life, I think, comes out of the ultimate degree of attention we pay"; "what kind of resourcefulness can you summon to avoid a living death?" Admits to having had a sort of crack up in the spring: "I wrote two novellas and six versions of two screenplays—nobody in his right mind does that. But I wasn't in my right mind. I was getting out of debt." Provides anecdotes about his life when writing *Dalva*: "I was only doing two pages a day. At one point I looked in the mirror and I said, 'I'm gonna start bleeding through the eyes.'" Session ends with discussion of his "dark period" after having written *Legends*, when he says: "I didn't know how to handle it; I behaved badly." Describes his current self as much better "mentally," referring to "an epiphany he had when he was sitting on a couch next to his wife: I looked at her knee, and I thought, that's not my knee, it's her knee. The otherness of life got to me. ... I feel quite comfortable now, I don't feel any anxiety anymore—If you publish a book, you've got to be well beyond hope and despair because it's out of your hands. Maybe it's because I hiked those thousand miles this spring with no people. You get detoxed. . . . Maybe it'll go away next week, but I don't think so."

35. Interview. "A Vulnerable Predator, Jim Harrison Writes with a Keen, Compassionate Eye." By Judy Gerstel. *Detroit Free Press* 15 August 1990: 1D.

    Harrison, interviewed in Lake Leelanau prior to starting a 7-city book tour, says: "The only way I want to be strong now is I want to be strong as water. Even dams are a temporary measure. You can't stop it. And it flows, rather than being geometric." Interviewer describes him as sounding like his friend the actor Jack Nicholson, "nasal, laconic, mischievous." Harrison describes his own "sort of Zenist" spirituality and "attitude." Some discussion of food, preference for "good olive oil," family, book publicity tours. "Harrison is generous with his ideas and thoughts and wide-ranging and erudite in his conversation."

36. Interview with Jim Harrison. By Sedge Thompson. *Fresh Air,* National Public Radio, 23 August 1990. Radio broadcast.

    Begins by reading opening of "The Woman Lit by Fireflies." Recounts experience of talking to middle-aged women at a spa/clinic in Mexico about migraine headaches. When Clare's voice arrived, he was receptive. "I was thinking of those . . . ladies at the spa and I was out in the barnyard of my farm and it was a particularly strange summer night and the swamp and the marsh near the barnyard was almost dense with fireflies . . . so that's when I thought of a woman . . . who has left her husband . . . and run off in a cornfield. . . . Somehow that whole beginning came to me right at that point." Comments on Clare's "ritualized" experience. Harrison realizes he is more fragile than he thought. Walking alone is part of his ritual aspect of self-survival. "Brown Dog" reflects rural cultural background. Defines *macho* as "gratuitous cruelty." Explains "bondage of the appropriate" (narrator's description of Strang in *Sundog*): the "free man has absolutely no habits of any sort and aims to be free of all constraints of any sort": "But the way you free yourself from all constraints is through the extremist form of discipline." Elaborates on erotics of writing: "An intoxication with the ordinary in life. I think writers get lost by being very brilliant about perimeters and being very brilliant about edges, and then they forget the core. Food and Sex are at the core." Advises young writers: "Don't forget red wine and garlic!" Riff on garlic and wine. His wife, Linda, and oldest daughter, Jamie, are his "first readers" who make sure he hasn't done something "ill-advised." His daughter—"perhaps my best editor"—encouraged him to amplify certain sex scenes in *Dalva* he was squeamish about. Ends with story of glass eye salesman visiting him in hospital when he was 7 years old.

37. Interview. "Tough Guy, Mad Poet." By Bill Beuttler. *American Way* September 1990: 104–10, 134–40.
38. Interview. "The Writer as Naturalist: Michigan Poet/Novelist Jim Harrison Talks about Food, Buddhism, Politics, Censorship and the Art of Writing." By Marc J. Sheehan. *Lansing* MI *Capital Times* 7 September 1990: 1, 18–19.

    Question-and-answer format. Asked about the mood of censorship in the country, Harrison replies that he doesn't believe First Amendment rights should be infringed on by anyone. Notes: "It's usually religious groups who want an unlimited amount of freedom and prerogative for themselves, but don't want anybody else to have that kind of freedom and it has to be met on every basis. It's just stupidity." Says this atmosphere began with "that dingbat Reagan," and, when asked about his novella *The Woman Lit by Fireflies*, Harrison responds that "every novel is implicitly political." For Harrison, the "single preoccupation" of American society of the last 10 years has been greed. On writing: "I think every time you pick up the pen as a novelist you've got to try to reinvent the form or you're just dog-paddling. You've got to do something different, because a conscious attempt to imitate one's earlier successes is death for the writer." Discusses his view that poetry and prose are not separate enterprises, and relates story of "Archibald McLeish [sic]" asking his graduate students to imitate Andrew Marvell. Interviewer cites Harrison's essay "Poetry as Survival": "I am not going to spend my increasingly precious days stuffing leaks in an educational system as perverse and sodden as the mercantile society for which it supplies faithful and ignorant fodder." Interviewer then asks: "Do you really think it's that bad?" Harrison responds: "Yeah, I think it's worse than that." Talk about Faulkner's screenwriting and lack of competition he feels as a writer: "The great Chinese Buddhist thing is that if you don't worry about being first, you don't have to worry about being second." Believes that "a lot of artists doom themselves by accessibility," and thus he has "a real talent for avoiding things." Discusses the "death" of the environmental movement, which for Harrison was "squashed by that fatuous, inane actor Reagan and the crew of slime that just about crushed the country"; isn't involved in environmental activism because "there's no fresh garlic in jail." Though he isn't tied to Michigan, Harrison says, he is "tied to the landscape," be it Wisconsin, Minnesota, or Michigan. Does like the idea of bioregionalism (from Gary Snyder), but claims to not have understood that term for a while. Of his religion: "I have my own . . . unreconstructed Zen practice" with Snyder and Peter Matthiessen that is "less a religion than an attitude" of consciousness and attentiveness. Writes about suffering, death, and food.

39. Interview. "The *Diddy Wah Diddy* Interview: Jim Harrison." By Aloysius Sisyphus. *Diddy Wah Diddy* (Jackson MS) 6.5 (October 1990): 6–7. Reprinted in *Conversations with Jim Harrison*. Ed. Robert DeMott. Jackson: University Press of Mississippi, 2002. 98–104.

   Describes his finicky nature in regard to publishing his work in periodicals (calls a former editor of *Esquire* "a swine"), and says he's "gotten old and cranky." Says current American poetry is "miserable," especially in terms of MFA program work. "Never has so much rancor been raised over so little, the poetry world." Says his beginning work in poetry was due not so much to his interest in poetry (he wanted to write novels) as to his attention span: "I started in high school, I wanted to be a novelist, and then all I could write was poems because I had the attention span something like Richard Nixon's, very brief, poetry is a young man's form in a sense." Talks about oral tradition—storytelling. Refers to jobs as foreman on horticulture farms and as bricklayer; relates story of how Denise Levertov helped publish his first book. Talks about how time in the wilderness makes you less able to handle the world: "Everybody says if you go on a retreat, then you're fresh for the world, well, bullshit. You just see it, you see that everyone's suffocating in lint." Discusses being able to inhabit different perspectives of different characters as a writer. Says his daughter is his best editor and has been since she was eighteen. Remarks again that Saul Bellow is a "bear with a very large brain, as Pooh would say. Certainly he has the best equipment, mentally, of any American novelist." Also says he likes Nabokov, McGuane, Kundera, Grass, and Marquez (says Mailer "isn't in the same league").

40. Interview. "A Man Lit by Passion: Jim Harrison." By Tom Auer. *Bloomsbury Review* November–December 1990: 1, 16. vol. 10, no. 6. Reprinted in *Conversations with Jim Harrison*. Ed. Robert DeMott. Jackson: University Press of Mississippi, 2002. 105–11.

   Harrison describes what he gets out of writing screenplays: It's "just a downshift. And I only will write originals, so then I get to have the fun of making them up. And I can't write novellas all the time. It seems soporific." Harrison discusses the collection of novellas that make up *A Woman Lit by Fireflies*. He says "Brown Dog" comes from his own experience growing up: "I haven't tried to write anything comic for a long while, and the character Brown Dog, that's sort of the way I grew up. I liked that somewhat opportunistic scoundrel." And then relates an experience of his own: "When I was fifteen I wanted to be a preacher. . . . I did some preaching at Youth for Christ. And then a terrible thing happened. I ran off to Estes

Park, Colorado, and worked as a busboy at the Stanley Hotel and met a girl—I was only sixteen, but I was a fibber. She was a senior at the University of Kansas and she took me way up in a fire tower, and she started taking off her Levi's. It was wonderful, I'll tell you, but I lost my religion. And then my mind started to broaden." Also talks about "Sunset Limited," saying it started as a screenplay. Discusses his poetry, also the novella form. Talks about the difficulty of assuming a woman's voice in *Dalva* and how his wife and daughter said he couldn't "chicken out" on a sex scene in the book, a scene from which he said he knew he was "backing away." Discusses French perception of his work and other American writers as exceptionally positive, "really something." For Harrison publishing a book is "like giving a kid up for adoption or something, and that's a terrifying feeling." His future in writing includes a *Dalva* sequel, new novellas, collected prose. Also: "Now that my youngest daughter is nineteen, I feel I'm going to write a tremendously sexy story. I haven't for years."

## 1991

41. Interview. "On Becoming a Tree." By Joseph Bednarik. *Silverfish Review* 20 (Spring 1991): 24–37.

Bednarik begins this significant formal question-and-answer piece by discussing a critical article, "F. M. Cioran and 'The Man Who Gave Up His Name' by Jim Harrison." The interviewer asks Harrison to respond to the comparison and claims this "precipitated a discussion about how creatures of literature can sometimes lead unique lives in a reader's imagination." Discusses the title character of *Dalva* and the fact that she quotes another Harrison work, *The Theory and Practice of Rivers*, then runs into "two flycasters," one with "a single eye and a brown moonface," which is, of course, the author himself. Harrison describes his "green janitor's suit" and a key ring "with thirty-three keys that don't open any doors" that work as Harrison's disguise: "Like . . . some Zen training, to not leave a trace. Why I drive about 20,000 random miles a year, at least, is the loveliness of Best Westerns and complete anonymity and just seeing the world." Harrison cites Robert Graves and states: "When I said to study the self is to forget the self, and then you get to be anything you want. . . . It's a drifting procedure. You forget the self to have more freedom because then you're not bound by a thousand neurotic knots and hackings in your head all the time. It doesn't take much, the less ego you have that day the more likely you can become a creek." They discuss *Letters to Yesenin* and Harrison's interest in Yesenin himself as well as Native American concerns. Harrison's conservationist inclinations are revealed, and he discusses the deaths of his father and sister, noting that "the world kills our beloveds." Bedarnik asks Harrison about his stereotypical black characters. They discuss the foundation of "Poetry as Survival," and Harrison states: "It's such a musical form, where you have wedges into reality here and there, rather than to pretend that reality presents a coherent narrative, which if it does, I don't know what it is. Life lacks symmetry you know." Calls *A Good Day to Die* the "first ecotage novel"; discusses Ed Abbey and Earth First. Harrison says that he will not "do that many" screenplays in the coming year. Conversation includes discussions of geography, Eastern philosophies, Gary Snyder, and Jungian symbolism. Harrison admits an interest in "walking meditation," which is how it is that "you get to become a tree . . . you disappear totally and you don't know where you left off and the natural world begins, because you're nature too."

42. Interview. "A Drink with Jim Harrison." By Jeff Potter. *Out Your Backdoor* 5 (Spring 1991): 12–13.

    Gushy piece in magazine of "informal adventure" that details an impromptu meeting between the author of the article and Harrison, who ran into each other in "a little lonely bar," during which a wide range of topics was addressed: "We talked about food, garlic, gout, Bushwacker skis, Wilderness State Park, and the Soo locks . . . the unnaturalness of helicopters, I-Ching inventions, and trigger fingers, [etc.]." They discuss women and sex, and Harrison indicates that models "all have seven personalities" and that "dealing with women requires a certain cynicism and cruelty, which I'm sure you know now." Much further discussion of food.

43. "Jim Harrison Screenplay Could Be 'Sues with Wolves.'" By Bob Talbert. *Detroit Free Press* 24 February 1991: 5F. Column with interview comments from Harrison.

    Brief section on Harrison in Talbert's regular entertainment/gossip column; includes a discussion of the screenplay for *Wolf*, though it is described here as "an untitled movie Columbia Pictures is excited about." Interviewer reports that Harrison tells him, probably by phone, that writing the screenplay was easier than editing 700 pages of his nonfiction essays, magazine pieces, cooking columns, etc., down to the 300 pages for *Just Before Dark*, a collection Clark City Press will publish this spring. Notes that Harrison's April *Esquire* column will be "unusual for this meat-eating man's man: all about his battle with gout and how he almost became a vegetarian. 'Two months without eating meat and I never once had to take anything for indigestion,' he admits." Harrison says that he received letters from women readers of *A Woman Lit by Fireflies* "who said they'd done the same thing" as Clare, that novella's frustrated protagonist.

44. "Thinking Small." By David Streitfeld. *Washington Post Book World* 16 June 1991: 15. "Book Report" page.

    Short profile begins with a discussion of Clark City Press, run by Harrison's eldest daughter, Jamie Potenberg, which has published *Just Before Dark*, the author's collected nonfiction. Clark City is 3 years old at this point and began with a republication of Russell Chatham's work. The Press aims to publish 8 works each year. Harrison says: "Naturally, you'd sometimes get more interested in books where somebody's not trying to beat you over the head."

45. Interview. "One-on-One Iron Person Can Hold His Center." By Jim Ricci. *Detroit Free Press* 1 August 1991: 1F.

    A purportedly humorous account of reporter's fanciful one-on-one showdown of egos between himself and Jim Harrison ("notorious macho and celebrated literary carnivore") at his Upper Peninsula cabin and at the Dunes Saloon in Grand Marais. Harrison presented as name-dropper and gun-toting lout but is seen preparing exotic Thai duck soup. "The secret," Harrison says, is "fresh cilantro . . . and Italian parsley." Encounter as a boxing match continues until Ricci finishes quoting a Yeats poem Harrison had started, pulls out a last-minute "come-from-behind win," and defeats Harrison 136–134. The absurdity and willful misrepresentation in this piece is best judged by Ricci's repentant follow-up a week later in his 8 August 1991 *Detroit Free Press* column, "Thoughtful Talk, Thoughtless Writing," in which he confesses to wrenching Harrison's words and actions out of context. "In a brief, correct note, Harrison registered his disappointment. I hadn't dealt at all, he wrote, with what had taken up nearly all of our time together, namely thoughtful talk about art, writing and life." Ricci apologizes to Harrison ("a warm, open and compassionate man") and "to readers who took away from my column a false impression of the man."

46. "Thoughtful Talk, Thoughtless Writing." By Jim Ricci. *Detroit Free Press* 8 August 1991. (See item H45.)

47. Interview. "The Loneliness and the Silence at the Heart of America." By Patrick Raynal. *Manchester Guardian Weekly* 27 October 1991: 15.

    Harrison interviewed at home in Lake Leelanau, where Raynal claims he is better known as a hunter and fisherman than a writer. Shares with Richard Brautigan, Thomas McGuane, James Crumley, and Tony Hillerman "a desire to write about the center of the United States. Most writers and artists fly from one coast to the other without caring about what they're flying over. They really think America is like Steinberg's ironical poster, which consists of the New York skyline, the vast expanse of the Mississippi and, just beyond it, Hollywood."

## 1992

48. Interview. "Siren Song: Will Success Lure Poet/Novelist Jim Harrison out of his Midwestern Lair?" By Robert Cross. *Chicago Tribune Magazine* 30 August 1992: 14–18, 24. Reprinted in *Conversations with Jim Harrison*. Ed. Robert DeMott. Jackson: University Press of Mississippi, 2002. 112–22.

Interview conducted in a New York hotel room. Describes Harrison and a Columbia Pictures producer eating caviar and drinking vodka. Harrison notes that the novella "Legends of the Fall" may be made into a film, and the interviewer gives descriptive background of Harrison and his work's major themes: "woods, water, plains, desert, mountains, and the serio/comic twists of the human psyche." Notes Harrison's popularity in France. On *Just Before Dark* Harrison states: "Walking at twilight owns the same eeriness of dawn. The world belongs again to its former prime tenants, the creatures, and within the dimming light and crisp shadows, you return to your own creature life that is so easily and ordinarily discarded." Harrison had just begrudgingly published his MA thesis, "A Natural History of Some Poems," noting that he "view[s] this as juvenilia, of interest only to assistant professors, should my work prove durable." Discusses the novella "Brown Dog" and the advice given him by a Sioux friend to "do everything backwards to feel better, to reverse your boredom. You get up and cook a big meal, eat it, have two shots of whiskey, take a nap, have a little lunch, eat breakfast and go to bed at 9. Or you go for walks where you've never been before." Takes the idea for the *Wolf* screenplay from the fact that "an Inuit, an Eskimo, believe that if you're very sick physically or mentally—which they look at as the same—the only way you can have a chance of getting better is to go into the body of an animal. And you either come out the other side or you don't." Piece includes some discussion of "a remarkable essay" written last year for the *Psychoanalytic Review* and reprinted in *Just Before Dark* that is unnamed in this interview ("Dream as a Metaphor of Survival" [see items D87 and D139]). On the subject of psychoanalysis, Harrison says: "Some people warned me against it, said that sort of thing might untie my psychic knots and take away my imagination. But I don't think a person's knots are part of his energy." Ends with Harrison noting: "We don't write out of sickness, we write out of health."

49. Interview. "'People with Curiosity Are Always Right out There': Interview

with Jim Harrison." By Nancy Bunge. 7 November 1992. First published in *Master Class: Lessons from Leading Writers*. By Nancy Bunge. Iowa City: University of Iowa Press, 2005. 143–52. This interview was also reprinted in *Writer's Chronicle* 38.6 (May–Summer 2006): 21–25.

Traditional question-and-answer-format interview begins with Harrison asking interviewer a question. Harrison talks about why he dislikes writing with computers, the mystique of writing. Interviewer asks him to clarify his idea of "writer as hero of consciousness." Harrison discusses dreams and notebooks in relation to his writing. Says he cannot write fiction or poetry all the time—certain times of day and certain amount of time between writing of novels is needed. Discusses form. Talks about wanting to have been a painter first. Says screenplay writing has been destructive to his poetry. "A poem is just much more fragile." Also, screenplay writing is a collaborative effort, he says, and this can lead to negative results in terms of Harrison's intent and the final product—the film. Talks about "flow" in his writing. Says reading Neruda's memoirs made him "dysfunctional." Talks about his poem "Acting" and its connections to Zen Buddhism: "When you're released from your obsessions with banality and you get to be a tree or a creek or a bird or a woman . . . That's how you enter into character, by giving yourself up. You can't enter into character if you're carrying yourself along with you." Says it's "fascinating to [him] . . . to let go of everything." Talks often about writing in a woman's voice, especially in *Dalva*, and how he has come to believe that "writers are essentially androgynous." Also talks about doing research for *Dalva*, something he had not done much of before. Talks about curiosity "getting people through life" and the "power" of reading. Explains why he likes Alain Fournier's *The Wanderer*. "That's what I said about *Dalva*. The subject is the character of longing in American fiction; longing is everywhere."

# 1993

50. Film Interview. *Jim Harrison: Half Dog and Half Wolf*. By Brice Matthieussent. English-language version of Georges Luneau and Matthieussent's film portrait, *Jim Harrison: Entre Chien et Loup*. Paris: Plante Cable/Cine Cinema Cable/Gedeon, 1993. (See item G20 as well.)

26-minute on-camera interview with Harrison at his Grand Marais cabin in Michigan's Upper Peninsula. Discusses his Swedish ancestral background, a great-grandfather on his mother's side who went out west "before Wounded Knee." There are farmers on both sides, "not very prosperous farmers." Says that he "got the background for *Farmer*, from [his] mother's family."

Importance of nature and other cultures for self-education and escaping from limits of ego, "dissolving your personality," and, thus, getting rid of vanity. Being in nature opens you for the best parts of the New York or Los Angeles experience once in a while: "The more [time] I spend in the natural world the more I like Mozart . . . Shakespeare . . . Stravinsky. Because it opens you up, now you're listening better, you're hearing what they say to you so it is just unburdening. You don't lose your aesthetic sense." Recalls experiences as teacher at the State University of New York at Stony Brook. Praises Seattle as a "beautiful interesting city." Explains importance and necessity of "full dress" nap each day. *Discipline* is an "ugly word." It's "a false word" that means you are "making yourself work" rather than following creative energy. Quotes Rene Char and Wang Wei on being receptive and present at the right moment of inspiration. Aptness of river as metaphor for continuousness, process. Discusses doing things backward as a way of combating boredom, predictability. Quotes Rimbaud on "deranging the senses." Reads the work of his friends—Peter Matthiessen, Thomas McGuane, Richard Ford—but "can't read fiction" when he is writing a novel. "I suppose I revere Faulkner like I revere Melville or Whitman." Mentions Alain-Fournier's *The Wanderer*, and explains "the real subject of *Dalva* is yearning, longing." Amused by literalness and limited imagination of some aspects of American culture. Discusses reading Henry Miller as a "blood transfusion" for a young writer, "like animals are now, like nature is now" in providing a jolt of energy.

51. Interview. "Le Sel de la Terre" (The Salt of the Earth). By Samuel Blumenfield. *Les Inrockuptibles* 48 (Summer 1993): 103–06.

    Wide-ranging question-and-answer interview includes comments on Harrison's growing up in Michigan, his move from poems to novels, the character of Dalva, Native Americans and the photographer Edward Curtis, and Harrison's ability to "absorb the landscape" of the American countryside, often by driving slowly along back roads.

52. "Jim Harrison's Wolf Movie Will Star Nicholson, Pfeiffer." By Bob Talbert. *Detroit Free Press* 18 April 1993: 6F. Column with interview comments from Harrison.

    First third of column devoted to news that Harrison has several film projects going on, including big-budget *Wolf* directed by Mike Nichols and starring Jack Nicholson and a western script for Columbia Pictures written for Harrison Ford to star in. About *Wolf* he says: "It's something I concocted. I did five drafts of it. It's about Nicholson playing—you'll like this—a New York editor who in 30 days turns into a wolf and gets shipped off to

Labrador. Michelle [Pfeiffer]'s the one who gets to sleep with this animal." Of the western script Harrison says: "It's a western in the style of *The Searchers*, *Shane*, and *High Noon*. Ford's perfect for a classic western. I look at him as the closest thing we have to Gary Cooper."

53. "Jim Harrison: Cigarettes, Whiskey et P'tites Pepees" (Jim Harrison: Cigarettes, Whiskey and Women). By Francois Granon. *Telerama* 28 July 1993: 121.

    A quirky and often antagonistic and pessimistic profile by a somewhat literal-minded French reporter sent to Lake Leelanau, then to Grand Marais, to observe Harrison, whom he finds torn between artifice and sincerity. Granon also records his changing personal feelings about Harrison, and, ultimately, the profile seems as much about his inability to "frame" the "two sided" Harrison and the fact that Harrison has manipulated his entire visit as it is about Harrison's contradictions: "It is . . . useless to ask whether Jim Harrison isn't the first character of his work. It does not take long with him to uncover the alcoholic beneath the gourmet, the greedy pig beneath the gourmand, the obsessed beneath the sensual man. At times, the anxiety is such that the man and the novelist trip together. The autobiography benefits from it, but what about literature?" Granon makes unflattering descriptions (he "moves with the precision and rigidity of a tank"), debatable critical assessments (he "wastes his energy describing a continent that no longer exists"), and erroneous statements (he "can live by himself for an entire month in the middle of the woods"). Claims Harrison "protects himself by wearing successive shells" that are difficult to penetrate. After much drinking Granon can't read the scribbles in his own notebook and decides that interviews with Harrison belong to "oral literature."

54. Interview. "Interview with Jim Harrison." By Thierry Jousse and Vincent Ostria. *Cahiers du Cinema* 470 (July–August 1993): 2430. Prefaced by 1-page statement, "USA: Literature Is Putting on a Great Act," and photo of Harrison at the bar of the Lenox Hotel, Paris. Reprinted in *Conversations with Jim Harrison*. Ed. Robert DeMott. Jackson: University Press of Mississippi, 2002. 123–32.

    Interview focuses primarily on Harrison's interest in film, his experience as Hollywood screenwriter, and his reactions to films made from his books. Discusses his Carte Blanche choices for Institut Lumiere in Lyon, and indicates he prefers Bergman's *Persona* to *Wild Strawberries* and Fellini's *La Strada* to *8½*. He "adores" Orson Welles's *Othello* but admits "nobody likes it." Discusses a western called "The Last Posse" that he is writing for Harrison Ford and his experience writing a screenplay about the life of the photographer Edward Curtis. Praises Sean Penn's *The Indian Runner*; calls *Insatiable* with Marilyn Chambers "the most extraordinary porn film ever made."

55. Interview. "Strong but Never Silent or Macho." By Stephen McGinty. *The Herald* (Glasgow, Scotland) 4 September 1993: 7.

    Transoceanic telephone interview with Harrison, who explains that the *macho* label is "nonsense" and a kind of name-calling. Reveals witnessing incidents of violence in his life. "I have a strange feeling about violence because I have seen a lot of it in my life and usually in books and movies it's done all wrong . . . what I want to do is write it the way I've seen it." Provides recent news about the Montana novelist James Crumley.

## 1994

56. Interview with Jim Harrison. Appended to audio recording of *Legends of the Fall*. Novato CA: Soundelux Audio Publishing, 1994. Untranscribed. 8 minutes.

    Revealing commentary on background and inspirations for *Legends of the Fall* and characterization of Tristan, who is incapable of compromise. "I was trying within a hundred pages to untie all of those permanent knots in my brain at once. I don't know if I succeeded. . . . Lorca said the only stories to be told are about love, suffering, and death, so I had to try to get it all down in one place." Relates episodes of learning that whiskey was smuggled into Montana from Canada on horseback and his wife, Linda's, discovery of the diaries of her great-grandfather Ludlow, who leads expeditions into Black Hills in 1873 with General Custer. "So I had that character of improbable integrity [to build the fiction on]." Speaks of the mythological power of hero's journey. In seeking suitable levels of consciousness, "the journey . . . is the story. The question marks are always larger than the answers."

57. "Quote Bag." By Bob Hartley. *Detroit Free Press* 13 March 1994: 4F.

    Quotes from Harrison's comments (published in Peter Biskind, "Who's Afraid of the Bad *Wolf*," *Premiere*, March 1994, 58) on episode of lycanthropy that led the producer Douglas Wick to encourage Harrison to write a screenplay based on the experience. "Where I live is extremely remote. There are wolves up there. I dreamed that one of them had been hit by a car. When I picked it up, it went into my mouth and into my body, which is uncomfortable. . . . One night, I thought someone was coming into the yard, so I hopped out of bed, tore off the doors to get to whoever was out there, and my face was covered with hair . . . it meant the dog wouldn't have anything to do with me for about a day and a half. I don't care for that kind of thing; I'm a very ordinary person."

58. Interview. "A Storyteller's Story." By Burr Snider. *San Francisco Examiner Magazine* 17 April 1994: 12, 14–15.

    Telephone interview that begins with talk about barbecue and proceeds to Hemingway. "Oh, that Hemingway stuff, that's an early lumpage," he sighs. "I never cared for Hemingway at all, even when I was young. Remember, I'm from upper Michigan, and up there he's just considered a tourist from Chicago. I liked Faulkner and James Joyce, just wore out *Finnegans Wake*, and this macho thing . . . it's such a dreadful word." Explains *macho* with rhetorical question: "What does going fishing have to do with your weenie?" Explains his ideas on sexuality: "I never really thought of sexuality as anything more than a spectrum that you go along . . . we're supposed to find our true character. . . . It's only because we're a nontraditional culture where sexual eroticism is such an explosive symbol that violence inevitably becomes a substitute for eroticism." Recalls the excesses of his younger years; he says he is "the pitiful weeping writer character" in *Julip*. "That germinated a long time. All our paths are not so gladsome, and the victim is very often the survivor. It's a nation of whiners, my friend. Do I weep much myself? No, not anymore, not since what I call the Leon Spinks years, when I had the first really discretionary capital of my life." Talks about Hollywood and film experiences, then addresses the San Francisco readers, mentioning his admiration for Gary Snyder.

59. Interview. "Will Write for Food." By Nick Ravo. *New York Times* 17 April 1994: sec. 9, p. 8. Reprinted in the *International Herald-Tribune*.

    Harrison interviewed for this profile in Sonoita AZ in his favorite local dining spot, the El Pastaro, a small Italian restaurant. Talk is all about food and more food. Introductory paragraph gives a hint into interviewer's take on Harrison and his life at the time of his publicity tour for *Julip*: "The dark days of reckless pharmaceutical excess are embarrassing to recall for Jim Harrison, poet, novelist, screenwriter, semiprofessional food critic and self-described pig." Interviewer focuses on his perception of Harrison's "Balzacian" excesses: "Too many courses [at dinner]. Too much wine. Too many cigarettes." This interview takes place just before the films *Wolf* and *Legends of the Fall* are released. The meal is coming to an end, as is the interview: "The cheeks get a little redder, the talk a little more convoluted. Somebody—guess who—belches. Mr. Harrison, the pain of his past apparently anesthetized by the meal, tells a few tales. . . . The behavior gets a little more raucous. The cigarette smoke even thicker. Mr. Harrison reaches over and hacks at a guest's dessert. 'Try some of my tiramisu,' he says."

60. "Jim Harrison and Terry Tempest Williams." Hosted by Maya Angelou.

27 April 1994. City Arts of San Francisco Audiotape. San Francisco: Pacific Vista Productions, 1994. Untranscribed. 55 minutes.

Recording of live public conversation at the Herbst Theater, San Francisco, between Harrison and Williams on environmental and related issues. Their appearance inaugurates first annual Wallace Stegner Memorial Program, sponsored by the California Academy of Sciences.

61. Interview. "For Harrison, Writing a Matter of Shifting Gears." By Rebecca Newth. *Arkansas Democrat-Gazette* 15 May 1994: 8J.

Harrison calls his seventeen books "a testament to an unhappy childhood" and expresses his dissatisfaction with the current MFA explosion he sees taking place in this country. The interviewer (Harrison's sister-in-law) asks about his writing of food essays and wonders whether "first-rate ideas" come from there. Harrison responds: "Everything is suggestive of everything else. That's almost by definition what metaphor is about. You get to jump through the cosmos like a kangaroo wherever you like." Calls the novella "sort of a halfway genre, the absolute compression of the form." The interviewer then poses a series of quotations made by Harrison in past publications—"Imagination is superior to memory," "What is prayer if you cannot pray for everyone?" "Newspapers are the true surrealists"—and asks him to respond or explain them. Ends with Harrison discussing the "Blakean notion that everything that lives is holy" and his understanding of how that philosophy informs his work.

62. Interview. "Untamed Characters: Jim Harrison's World Gets Hollywood's Attention." By John Blades. *Chicago Tribune* 16 May 1994: sec. 5, p. 2.

Harrison describes a plane crash he was involved in as "a kid" at Chicago's Meigs Field, his eye injury, and the source of a recent back strain, caused when, in "a playful but misguided attempt at old-fashioned chivalry," he tried to lift a female bookstore employee over a desk. Interviewer notes that "feral types figure prominently in Harrison's fiction, significantly enriching the family treasury." Harrison tells the interviewer that he'll "welcome the ferns and other wild things that grow in Michigan when the book junket is over," and notes: "Sony's got $110 million in two movies (*Legends of the Fall* and *Wolf*). If they don't pan out, they're going to be pointing the finger at me. But I know thickets that are so big, they'll never find me."

63. Interview. "When the Wolf Howls." By Michael Walker. *Los Angeles Times/Calendar* 12 June 1994: 8, 30, 31, 34.

Begins with background on Harrison and his publications. "I only seem to be able to write a book every 2½ years," Harrison notes, "and when I get done I have a considerable amount of overflow energy that other people use in teaching, but I don't teach. Usually, that's when I do my good work." Regarding the movie *Wolf*, about to be released this week, the interviewer asks Harrison about the novel and the screenplay, which is "unrelated" to the novel. Harrison tells Walker: "People keep misquoting Thoreau: 'In wilderness is the preservation of the world.' . . . But it's wildness—he never said wilderness. All of our reality is shaped to get us to work on time. Wolves aren't involved in that." Includes a quotation from one of Harrison's *Esquire* columns: "The idea is to eat well and not die from it—for the simple reason that that would be the end of my eating." Harrison drinks wine at lunch and feels that this is a kind of crime in the bottled-water atmosphere of Los Angeles. He says of that city: "You have to treat it like you're in the woods and there actually are grizzlies. Because you don't do well out here if you [expletive] up. It's an extraordinarily unforgiving town." Much discussion of the process of writing and producing screenplays. Includes Harrison talking about Jung, who "says depression comes from trying to live too high in the mind. . . . You get up there and you almost don't have an exit, like a bird caught in a granary. He doesn't know the way out is down." The publisher Seymour Lawrence has just died unexpectedly, and Harrison states: "He was grand to me." Harrison calls success in America "deeply irrational," a "shuddering elevator."

64. Interview. "Writer's Wild Dream Comes Alive on Film." By Frank Bruni. *Detroit Free Press* 14 June 1994: 1D.

Harrison interviewed by *Free Press* movie critic regarding release of *Wolf*, directed by Mike Nichols, and starring Jack Nicholson and Michelle Pfeiffer. Idea for movie came from an episode nearly two decades earlier at his cabin in Upper Peninsula when Harrison, wakened sharply from dream and in semiconscious state, thought he had become a wolf. "In many ways it's a fantasy—that freedom and power," he says. "We live in an improbably complicated zoo. It's just that we built it ourselves. . . . Everyone's trying to put legalistic parameters around their hearts and their fears. This political correctness thing is going crazy, it's like mass hysteria." Reports Harrison also wrote first draft of screenplay for *Legends of the Fall*, slated for September release. Registers "shock" at the director, Tony Scott's, "overblown" movie version of *Revenge*. Provides background on film version of *Wolf*, which initially Harrison hoped would be "an extremely adult version of *Romeo and Juliet*," but by the fifth draft Harrison grew bored and signed off (though he retained right of approval and screenwriting credit).

65. Interview. "Man of the Moment Jim Harrison: Season of the Wolf." By Anthony Brandt. *Men's Journal* June–July 1994: 96–98, 137. Reprinted in *Conversations*

with *Jim Harrison*. Ed. Robert DeMott. Jackson: University Press of Mississippi, 2002. 144–50.

    Takes place just after the publication of *Julip* and a discomforting encounter with insistent birdwatchers who had gathered at Harrison's Arizona winter home in Patagonia. Harrison describes the experience that generated *Wolf*. "I was having a bad time mentally and about 2 a.m., I thought somebody was coming into the yard in Grand Marais . . . which is isolated. I saw car lights—it was really just lightning, it was in summer—and I woke instantly and threw myself out of bed. I was obviously in the middle of a dream, because I shot up in the air so high that I caught my head on a deer-antler chandelier . . . and I ran out into the yard screaming and howling. I stopped, and I don't know which part is dream, which is real, though I have the scar on my head from the chandelier, but my face was covered with hair, my arms, everything. It scared the living shit out of me." Discusses his resignation from the *Wolf* film project, citing differences with the director, Mike Nichols. Interviewer says of Harrison that he is "probably closer, inside, to true wildness and more at home in it than any American writer since Melville took up with cannibals." Harrison describes his 7 depressions, the deaths of his father and sister [in 1962], and the photos he saw of their bodies after death; he says that they still appear to him in dreams and describes these "memory knots" as "tiny claymores that blow up on contact." Notes that psychological healing is "often a theme in his work now," such as in the novella "The Beige Dolorosa." Harrison states: "Writers err on the side of making people either smaller than life or larger. . . . I'd rather err on the side of making them larger."

66. "The Modern Legends of Wolf." By Chuck Crusafulli. *Fangoria* July 1994: 28–32. no. 134.

    Article deals with the movie *Wolf* and the writing of the screenplay.

67. "Botsford Inn's Owner Loves the Place." By Bob Talbert. *Detroit Free Press* 10 July 1994: 7H.

    In subsection entitled "Harrison on Hemingway," Harrison apologizes for his recent assessment of Hemingway in the *Traverse City MI Northern Express* biweekly as a "cruel and implacable man" whose suicide was "the nicest thing he ever did." What he meant to say was: "It's too bad he had to shoot himself, but given the mess he was at the time it was an act of grace."

68. "Jim Harrison for Bookshow." By Tom Smith. Writer's Institute, State University of New York at Albany, 12 July 1994. Online transcript.

69. Interview. "Crying Wolf." By Stephen McGinty. *The Herald* (Glasgow, Scotland) 24 August 1994: 12.

Transatlantic telephone interview with Harrison, who reveals background on the film *Wolf* and source of artistic differences with the director, Mike Nichols. "Among the Native Americans if you are sick in your body and mind then you have to go into the body of an animal where you either get well and come out and change your name, or you stay and become a bear, a wolf or coyote. I think it's not a bad thing to stay. But Nichols did. That was the problem." High praise for Jack Nicholson as an actor. "He is a different type of actor. I think he becomes the part to a degree that nobody else does."

## 1995

70. Interview. "Jim Harrison's 'Legends' Goes to Hollywood." By Tom BeVier. *Traverse* 14.9 (February 1995): 20–21.

    A telephone interview with Harrison in Patagonia AZ. On the film version of *Legends of the Fall*, Harrison is said to think that "it's the best film treatment any of his works has received." Harrison himself says: "It's an epic. . . . I think of it as *Gone with the Wind* goes west." On the difference between this film and that of *Wolf*, Harrison states: "It hurts when they don't have faith in the essential material. . . . In the case of *Legends*, it was an enormous relief that they cared for the material." Compared to other film versions of his novels, Harrison seems pleased with *Legends*, giving it "a nine on a scale of one to ten." *Revenge* gets only a 5 from him and *Wolf* a 4. At a prerelease screening: "I liked seeing people with red eyes after seeing the movie because characters I made up had died." Director of *Legends* is Edward Zwick, the and screenwriter is Bill Wittliff, who also did television adaptation of Larry McMurtry's *Lonesome Dove*.

71. Interview. "A Conversation with Jim Harrison." By Joseph Bednarik. *Northwest Review* 33.2 (May 1995): 106–18. Reprinted in *Conversations with Jim Harrison*. Ed. Robert DeMott. Jackson: University Press of Mississippi, 2002. 133–43.

    This informative question-and-answer interview takes place in Harrison's San Francisco hotel room after a promotional reading tour. Some discussion of *Julip* in which Harrison says of the title character: "It seems Julip survives these men and survives everything because she has this very specific skill in relationship with animals. It's a tremendous focus for her life, like in our darkest times we always have our poetry." Harrison describes writing the poem "Sonoran Radio" and says that he had avoided the teaching profession because it makes him into "a walking blood bank for students." He explains his experience of lycanthropy and writing the screenplay for

*Wolf*, and of his time in Hollywood he notes: "I should've stayed back on the farm like Bob Frost." Detailing a reference he had made previously, where he called bears his "dharma gate," Harrison remarks: "Everything can be a dharma gate but there's this enormous specificity in bears. And you know, one's animal changes. When I finally got to see a wolf where I lived, that meant an enormous amount to me." When asked if, in terms of his writing, he considers anything to be "out of bounds," Harrison answers, "somebody else's religious rituals," and adds, "the most disgusting thing you see now is the new age 'appropriation' of what's Native American. That just terrifies me." Talks approvingly about Terry Tempest Williams and her "pan-erotics of nature." Harrison responds to the query, "Do different parts of your suites emerge at different times and in different places?" answering: "Oh, absolutely. The suite form I like is when all these little wedges are intended to suggest; then, finally, a whole—almost topographically. It's a map, the sacred." Harrison comments on "Bobo," the name of a "religion" he shares with Gary Snyder; he says that "Bobo knows all modernity is just a flaky paint job." Ends with comments on Zen and feminism.

## 1996

72. Interview. "Lake Effect: Talking with Jim Harrison." By Edward C. Reilly. *Jim Harrison*. New York: Twayne Publishing, 1996. 2–5, 8–11, 13, 17–18, 22–23.

    Material from Reilly's December 1991 interview with Harrison in Lake Leelanau appears throughout his 1996 monograph (the first critical book on Harrison) but is especially abundant in the opening chapter, where it is quoted for biographical background on pp. 2–5, 8–11, 13, 17–18, and 22–23.

73. "A Few Questions If You Please." By Bob Talbert. *Detroit Free Press* 18 February 1996: 6F.

    Column with interview comments for Harrison.

74. "Jim Harrison: L'Ours du Michigan" (Jim Harrison: The Bear of Michigan). By Andre Clavel. *L'Express* 20 July 1995: 90–91.

    Profile of Harrison in Michigan. Clavel sees his work as a kind of exorcism for past depressions and suffering.

75. "Showbiz Slant Skewed Olympic Coverage." By Bob Talbert. *Detroit Free Press* 13 August 1996: 7D.

    Column with interview comments from Harrison. First half of column devoted to Harrison's "sage and peppery observations" on NBC's coverage of Summer Olympics: "It appears to me the core of the mud bath is NBC's treatment of the Olympics as a peer offshoot of show business rather than a sporting event of grand proportions." Laments emphasis on events that cater to "PC Yuppies," including "California frenzies [such] as water polo and beach volleyball," plus "hopeless portrayals of athletes using skewed and misty camera angles and no real content." Ends by plugging his daughter Jamie's new novel, *Going Local*.

## 1997

76. "Art and Literature and Food and Hollywood." Question-and-answer session with audience following Seattle Arts and Lectures Series reading/talk on 3 March 1997. Not transcribed; unpublished. Approximately 23 minutes long. Part of the "Voices and Visions" program.

    Audience members wrote their questions on cards; then Harrison shuffled through the pile and chose which ones to answer. Some of the questions are more personal than professional, more trivial than substantive—"What is your favorite salad dressing," "Why do you slam Ivy League colleges?"—yet Harrison's answers were candid, often thoughtful, and always entertaining. Audience applause for his observation: "The idea in America that every question has an answer is specious, you know, it seems to me." Reveals he invented quote ("Eat *or* die") by (Mikhail) Lermontov when he was writing "The Raw and the Cooked" column for *Esquire*: "That's a philosophical base for ranting about food." Calls film a "director's medium." Daughter Jamie has been his only editor since she was 18. "I won't let anyone on the East Coast touch my prose." To the final question, "What are your plans for the millennium?" Harrison responds: "I believe it's a hoax."

77. Question-and-answer session with audience following Portland Arts and Lectures Series reading/talk on 5 March 1997. Not transcribed; unpublished. Approximately 13 minutes long.

    Once again audience members wrote their questions on cards, and then Harrison shuffled through the pile and chose which ones to answer. Wide range of questions on variety of topics and somewhat gossipy and desultory responses. What part of the country do you like best? "I like thickets." Favorite restaurants? What are you reading? Praises Mary Karr's *The Liar's Club*'s "excellent prose, visceral, lively." Writing *Letters to Yesenin* was an "upheaval," as opposed to *After Ikkyu and Other Poems*, poems "recollected in tranquility." Tells horrifying story he was told of Idi Amin's atrocities. Strang (in *Sundog*) not a real person but based on dam construction people Harrison had met. Can't exactly answer why his and Jack Nicholson's voices sound the same. He "was embarrassed to admit to some very rational people that [he] had dreamed [*Dalva*] first" rather than base his portrait on an actual person.

78. Interview. "Jim Harrison: 'What I'm Thinking about for Two Hours.'" By Casey Walker. *Wild Duck Review* 3 (April 1997): 3–6. Reprinted in *Conversations with Jim Harrison*. Ed. Robert DeMott. Jackson: University Press of Mississippi, 2002. 151–63.

Speaks thoughtfully on his perceptions of "nature writing" and nature itself. "I remember when I first saw a wolf in the Upper Peninsula it was doubted by a professor. I didn't mind because he sat in an office and I sat in my cabin in a forest on the river and had seen things from my window that were astonishing—male and female loons taking turns on the nest, each going crazy waiting for relief, making all kinds of noise, responding to coyotes and whippoorwills, back and forth. I think our sense of fieldwork can best be approached through what Thoreau called 'sauntering.'" Talks about the self in nature and the problems that result when you bring too many expectations or too much equipment. He criticizes the Robinson Jeffers sort of elitism and separation, "the view, 'I alone overlook the rock and 'the Pacific,'" and also the overzealous need to save the environment: "We say we're going to help nature but then forget how to let natural processes proceed." Talks about the need for unification in fighting for the environment: "Things with enormous moral force are often completely ignored in Washington. You can't be like a big muffin going to Washington, you have to unify and go in there like a big axe. It's the only way things are perceived there . . . it's a Machiavellian world and there's no sense going in there like Gandhi." Converses on the role of poet: "The duty of the poet is not to shit out of his mouth like a politician. Poets should be out there on the borderland saying this kind of thing." Talks about morality of "New Puritanism" and political correctness. Talks about poetry and nature: "It's hard to get up in the morning and look in the mirror and say, I am part of nature too. But you are, what the fuck do you think you are? We're just the most dangerous form of nature and we better be aware of it with all our brilliant little ideas." Explains Rene Char quote that "Lucidity is the wound closest to the sun." Talks about "transcend[ing] being a victim." He says the spirit of his work is "Otherness": "Otherness to remind ourselves of the bedrock of life, and death, and love, and suffering. . . . Early on, my inability to face certain horrors as directly as I should have contributed to that. But, then I'm always looking for the song I could make out of it, too." Says "juice" is lacking in creative writing programs: "Juice can't be taught in a creative writing program. . . . But, I think an ideal MFA writing program would require one year of manual labor in the country, one year of life in the city, one year spent alone reading; and only then would anyone return and begin writing. How else would anyone know anything?"

79. Interview. "Interview with Jim Harrison." By Robert DeMott and Patrick Smith. Lake Leelanau MI, 28–29 August 1997. Published in *Conversations with Jim Harrison*. Ed. Robert DeMott. Jackson: University Press of Mississippi, 2002. 193–220.

A wide-ranging talk with Harrison. Covers numerous topics, including the expected material on his hobbies (hunting, fishing, cooking) and literary friendships (with Russell Chatham, Thomas McGuane, Peter Matthiessen, William Styron, and others) and early career as a poet. Explains choices involved in establishing a career as a writer outside the sphere of the university, and considers dangers of being an "academic" novelist, which can lead to writing that is "of interest only to other academic novelists or his peers." Also converses on his interest in psychology, his preoccupation with Native American history (which figures prominently in the novel *Dalva* and its sequel, *The Road Home*), his relationship with Hollywood as a scriptwriter, and his reactions to movies made from his books: movie version of *Legends of the Fall* "was not gritty enough." Discusses notion of maintaining integrity as a writer: "The arts are fabulously undemocratic." Says that as a novelist, in order to survive, he must "reconstitute reality" as a way of "creating a habitat for [his] soul." Warns about difficulties and seductions of public acclaim, and cautions about vicissitudes of changing literary tastes. Claims that "to write an accessible, popular novel that would actually make a living would shatter everything I believed in as an artist." Gives reasons for switching fiction publisher to Grove/Atlantic and poetry publisher to Copper Canyon Press, and states preferences for independent publishers and bookstores. Explains attractions of novella form: "Some ideas you have just simply aren't long enough for a novel. You try to write the kind of prose that you admire and I like density." Discusses difficulties and challenges of establishing a distinctive "voice" for his characters in *Dalva* and *The Road Home*. States categorically that a novelist needs Keatsian "negative capability . . . more than anything else."

80. Interview. "Q&A: Interview with Jim Harrison." Anonymous. *Glen Arbor* MI *Sun* 15 October 1997: 1, 2.

A short interview mostly dealing with issues relating to Leelanau County, where Harrison lived at the time.

# 1998

81. Interview. "Lord Jim: Jim Harrison, a Sense of Place." By Terry W. Phipps. *Grand Rapids Magazine* May 1998: 19–25. Reprinted in *Conversations with Jim Harrison*. Ed. Robert DeMott. Jackson: University Press of Mississippi, 2002. 164–74.

Phipps writes: "From the stuff that made Steinbeck, Hemingway and Faulkner, Harrison convincingly carved his niche, not by formula writing, but by his formidable literary depth, his sheer intelligence and experimental tenacity with the literature itself." Discusses the influence of his literary parents and childhood in Michigan. At 16 Harrison gives up dreams of the clergy to become a writer: "It was a combination of my romantic convictions and my profound boredom with the middle-class way of life which gave me the urge to become a writer." On the comparison to Hemingway Harrison responds, "It doesn't exist," and says: "You know what that is? It's just a convenience. I don't think the average reviewers have read very much. There's no remote comparison." Discussion of *Dalva* and the writing process reveals that Harrison writes longhand, is surrounded by totems, and thinks that everybody has to use the reality they know. Describes the essay "Dream as a Metaphor of Survival" (see items D87 and D139). He notes: "Many artists are permanently dislocated. In this world, it probably makes them more functional." Harrison himself sometimes prefers "place anonymity," desires dislocation and long drives, like the character of Brown Dog who is "free" in the sense that "he has no papers. His only mail is every four years; he gets a notice to renew his driver's license—that is all." Ownership prevents "freedom of the road and freedom of movement." Lengthy discussions of potential film versions of Harrison's works and potential actors to play in them. On a discussion of foreign filmmaking, Harrison states: "I'm most concerned with consensual reality: it's what you get from photography, and literature when it's somewhat visually oriented like painting is. You realize it back when Erik Erikson said, 'Reality is mankind's' greatest illusion. So what you get from good photography or good painter [sic] is, you remove habitual and conditioned responses from reality, and then you get to see it again." Writing for Harrison involves "a combination of images that have a distinct emotional equivalent," and he says: "I see a scene like a master." Later, Harrison says he writes like a "failed painter" and states that he has always "made framed reality." On the subject of place he remarks: "The location. I think character so often arises out of location. You know the media keeps trying to tell us we're all the same, maybe we're all the same if you don't get off the freeway, but if you take . . . the time to talk to anybody, more than an hour, you're just convulsed again by the mystery of personality. That's what keeps you going."

82. Interview. "Interview with Jim Harrison." By Robert DeMott and Patrick Smith. Lake Leelanau MI, 30–31 July 1998. Published in *Conversations with Jim Harrison*. Ed. Robert DeMott. Jackson: University Press of Mississippi, 2002. 193–220.

Another wide-ranging, informal conversation at Harrison's summer home. Talks about releasing *The Road Home* and *The Shape of the Journey* within about a month of each other, the former appearing in French before its publication in English. Discusses poetry versus prose and his affinity for poetry. Discusses characters in *The Road Home* and how he is frustrated with reviewers who want to identify him with each of his characters: "These are people of their own." Talks about upcoming publication of his children's book, *The Boy Who Ran to the Woods*, in relation to his psychological urge to find hiding places, thickets—a theme he says a French interviewer picked up on. Talks about the "obsessive" researching he does for his novels. Discusses linked characters in *The Road Home* and *Dalva*. Compares Hemingway and Faulkner and the self-consciousness of some literature. Reminiscences on hunting. Discusses plans for writing a novella called "I Forgot to Go to Spain." Talks about Robert Duncan, sports, foreign reception of his work, the book business (including his experience working for a book distributor), his dislike of the academic life (especially MFA programs), and various writers and poets, especially friendships with McGuane, Doug Peacock, and others.

83. Interview. "Vogre Sentimental du Michigan" (The Sentimental Ogre from Michigan). By Jean-Phillipe Bernard. *Le Temps* 12 September 1998: 13.

    "The Sentimental Ogre from Michigan" discusses *The Road Home* and views of America as a "colonialist people" responsible for Native Americans' Holocaust. Espouses helping exceptionally talented younger writers, such as Colum McCann: "In today's literary world, you have to help these kind of people, allow them to fight against purely venal publishers. Because all you have to do is peruse the displays in a library to see that those people do not like books. They prefer shit."

84. "Vours Qui Aimait les Hommes" (The Bear That Loved Men). By Martine Laval. *Telerama* 23 September 1998: 56–57. no. 2541.

    Harrison still popularly considered a macho writer, but beneath that legend is a great writer whose *The Road Home* is pure lyricism. In his descriptions of characters Harrison is in the tradition of Turgenev and Dostoevsky, whom, Laval, claims, he discusses as if they were old friends. Regarding his obsession with certain characters, especially Dalva, Harrison says: "The writer is a horse. The characters put a halter on him and take him for a gallop. But you don't expect them to do that for years!"

85. "Les Coups de Guele de 'Big Jim'" (The Outbursts of "Big Jim"). By Alexis Liebaert. *L'Edj* 24–30 September 1998: 74–76.

    Collection of Harrison's quotable statements on array of topics, including

God, Hemingway, Monica Lewinsky, Indians, literature, death, music, etc. Calls Gabriel Garcia Marquez the greatest living writer.

86. "Qu'on Cesse de Me Comparer a Hemingway!" (If Only They'd Stop Comparing Me to Hemingway!). By Cedric Fabre. *Politis* 28 September 1998: 18–19.

    Touches on a number of topics, including importance of great spaces, the role of nature as inspiration, the tragedy of separating ourselves from nature. Considers Hemingway a "European" writer, and ranks Melville and Faulkner as the best American writers.

87. Interview. "A Stranger in His Own Land." By Ted Roelofs. *Grand Rapids* MI *Press* 11 October 1998: A1, A19.

    Interview takes place in Lake Leelanau. Talks about upcoming multicity book tour for *The Road Home*. "I look at it like a 40-day root canal." Tells about paying back the loan Jack Nicholson made him when he was struggling and other money matters. "But as he talks, you begin to realize you will not find the essential Jim Harrison in this room, in the scrub flats of the UP [Michigan's Upper Peninsula], or the bar at the Bluebird Inn in Leland where he holds forth . . . the other Harrison lives, elusively, in a large body of work."

88. Interview. "A Natural Writer." By Tom BeVier. *Detroit Free Press* 20 October 1998: 1C–2C.

    Harrison, interviewed at home in Lake Leelanau during an extended book publicity tour, thinks *The Road Home* is his "best book" and probably his "last biggie." Literary success has not changed him. Explains enormous sale of his books in France: "The French . . . like their literature as they like their food, herbal and full-bodied." Explains his interest in Zen studies and zazen (meditation) and the influence of Gary Snyder, "the only writer I'd met who knew how to live. He taught me that you need a life to go along with writing."

89. Interview. "Interview: *The Road Home*." Borders. Online posting. http://www.borders.com/features/mmk98097.html (accessed 14 December 1998; site discontinued).

    Harrison discusses the difficulties of inhabiting five voices for *The Road Home*. Talks about what he's been reading: *One Thousand White Women* by Jim Fergus, Merrill Gilfillan's work, *Go by Go* by Jon Jackson, *Independent People* by the, Icelandic author Halldor Laxness. Talks about practicing Zen with a Christian background: "The obvious influence of Zen is the level of attention that you apply to your life." Also talks about critical response in France: "I don't have a full comprehension of the reviews. This is sort of pleasant, like a child hearing adults talking happily and not quite knowing what they are saying." Ends with reminiscence of his favorite meal, "a couple of chickens stuffed with about $1,000 worth of truffles," prepared by his friend the French gourmand Gerard Oberle.

90. "The Road Home." By Judith Moore. *San Diego Weekly Reader* 22 October 1998. "Reading" section.

    Short synopsis of Harrison's career and plot of *The Road Home*, followed by brief conversation with Harrison: "I don't get my pats on the back in New York; I get them in France. . . . In America . . . people think if the action of fiction takes place outside, it's about violence, and if the action takes place inside, it's about the life of the mind. But the French understand that while my characters are often outside, they also have a life of the mind." Discusses necessity of appetites in his fiction—food and sex. Appalled by "free-floating anger" on rereading his first novel, *Wolf*. "You can make everything you write cold and hard and bitter and stupid. I think it's important, though, for the writer to write characters he wants to come back to, situations like those with *Dalva* are the kinds of situations I have been attracted to as opposed to just irony, which scratches its tired ass."

91. Interview. "Image Matters to Jim Harrison." By Terry W. Phipps. *Book* October–November 1998: 19–25.

    Harrison claims his first image of Dalva was of her naked. Biographical synopsis of his life and work by interviewer, including favorite haunts—Dick's Pour House in Lake Leelanau, Art's Tavern in Glen Arbor, the Blue Bird in Leland, the Dunes Saloon in Grand Marais, and Hattie's Grill in Sutton's Bay. Says: "I think character so often arises out of location." Says he's never stopped writing poetry, and explains what a force it is in his life: "You can put off a novel for a while but, you can't not write a poem because that particular muse is not very cooperative." Disavows link with Hemingway: "It doesn't exist," he says. Mentions that he cowrote the 1989 movie *Cold Feet* with Keith Carradine, Tom Waits, and Rip Torn. Says *The Road Home* is "just the novel I intended to write when I wrote *Dalva*." His curiosity to find out, "What would Dalva and Duane's child [Nelse] be like?" led him to the book. "What I was trying to get is that whole concept of otherness with the basic life rituals of love and death, marriage, and your location: What's the soul history of where you live? . . . I was trying to get at the soul of the landscape in that sense, and the otherness of these people who are viewed as eccentric."

92. "Road Trip." By Gregory McNamee. *Literature and Fiction @ Amazon.com*, November 1998.

    Harrison remarks that returning to Dalva's story in *The Road Home* was "really quite grueling and frightening." Says he thought about continuing *Dalva* even back when he was writing it, but said he doesn't feel a sense of comfort or control over such ideas. Talks about writing in a female voice in terms of Flaubert's *Madame Bovary* and in reading Jung at age 19. Ease in other voices he says comes from being an artist and having "our feet planted in at least three worlds." Talks about the difficulty of weaving *The Road Home* with *Dalva*. Discusses his solo car trips as invigorating: "I think it's partly the gift of inaccessibility. In our daily lives we dig such deep ruts that the ground closes over our heads. But an artist can't afford to let his perceptions die, and a car trip can bring them back to life—the sensation can be similar to walking in a new wild area without a map." Claims to be "fooling with another book of three novellas (although I have to write a screenplay first in order to afford it)." Praises poetry of Joseph Stroud, prose of Merrill Gilfillan, and work of Gerald Vizenor.

93. Radio interview with Jim Harrison. By Mel Waggoner. *Profiles*, Oregon Public Radio, 18 November 1998. Untranscribed.

    Harrison interviewed during book tour for *The Road Home* and *The Shape of the Journey*. Begins by reading early poems "Horse" and "Young Bull." Harrison discusses teenage interest in Keats and Byron as models and inspirations for a writer's life. "If you are a farm boy and you're making a buck a day picking potato bugs that sounds like an interesting life." Remembers wanting to be a painter like Modigliani, but had no gift for it. Poetry represents "dense" experience, "closest to the bone"; claims *Letters to Yesenin* was an "anti-suicide note" and "still really can't bear to look at it." Reads poem 6—"the only ardently political poem"—from "Geo-Bestiary" (concluding section of *The Shape of the Journey*). *Wolf* called "a false memoir" to "throw people off the track because it is basically 98% true." Tells story of Jack Nicholson loaning money at crucial time in his career. Wrote *Legends of the Fall* in 9 days, something that "has never happened before or since." It was "like taking dictation, though indeed I had thought about it for several years." But it's "a fable," "an old fashioned once-upon-a-time story." Recommends *Carried Away* as the film made from his work (*Farmer*) that he most recommends. Speaks of background of *Dalva*: calls Nebraska Sandhills area the "last collision of cultures in America," ending with Wounded Knee in 1890. His favorite county in America is Cherry County, which stretches 100 by 50 miles and has only 4,000 people. The landscape is "unbearably gorgeous . . . a gorgeous habitat for the human soul." Praises Sherman Alexie's film *Smoke Signals*.

94. Interview. "Jim Harrison: A Master Craftsman, Taking the Long Road Home." *Inside Borders* December 1998: 6–7.

95. Interview. "The SALON Interview: Jim Harrison." By Jonathan Miles. *SALON Magazine* 2 December 1998. Online posting. 1 January 2000. http://www.salon.com/books/int/1998/12/cov_02intb.html.

   Talks about possible reasons for French enthusiasm for his work: "It's the landscape and the setting that they've long been interested in. They don't have that there—that enormous space—and they have a much more homogeneous social life. They like the stew that America is." Also interviewer refers to Barry Hannah's popularity in France, and Harrison agrees that the French are "not so grotesquely plot-oriented.": "In my fiction you have the life of relative action but also the life of the mind." Talks about dreaming of *Dalva*, also of the Jungian "twin sister" connection with her. Talks about his dream life, of being "a bird with a bear's body, a bear with a vast wingspan. The bear and the bird is what helped me survive." Moves this into a discussion of his connection to animals. Discusses the different voices in *The Road Home*. Elucidates his frustration with the misperception of his "macho" characters: "[The misuse of the term *macho*] is one of the unfortunate things about feminism but I certainly understand it. A lot of men are just assholes. You think, where did they get it? You always wonder if they're feeling a little ambivalent to insist on the preeminence of their weenie in the world. Something's gone haywire in there."

96. Interview. "Wild at Heart." By Sylvain Bourmeau. *Les Inrockuptibles* 2–8 December 1998: 20–21.

   A rarity among Harrison's interviews: a two-person dialogue between Jim Harrison and the Irish novelist Colum McCann, who considers Harrison his master in the art. Harrison considers McCann one of the best young writers on the scene today (McCann lives in New York City). Harrison admits that he intended to make his readers cry at the end of *The Road Home* and that "one can be sentimental without falling into sentimentalism": "Novels need these human emotions. Without feelings we are just pieces of meat on the floor." He continues: "Do you know this singer, Césaria Évora? Every time I hear her song 'Saudade,' I melt. I know that's the point of this musical style, the saudade, whose theme is a sort of nostalgia for things we'll never find again—a woman or a place."

97. Interview. "Author Clings to Rural Roots, Independence." By John Flesher. *Philadelphia Tribune* 11 December 1998: 2. Also printed as "Author Clings to His Rural Roots in Books and Life." *Cleveland Plain Dealer* 12 December 1998.

   Interviewer describes Harrison's no-trespassing sign in his driveway as a symbol for his disdainful attitude toward the literary establishment: "Do Not Enter This Driveway Unless You Have Called First. This Means You."

Describes Harrison's contradictions of subject matter and style. Includes a quote from the owner of Dick's Pour House, Dick Plamondon: "His fame, fortune haven't changed him one iota. A lot of people, it would go to their head. Not Jim."

98. Interview. "Just Desserts." By David Streitfeld. *Washington Post Book World* 13 December 1998: 15. "Book Report" page.

    Streitfeld begins by describing Harrison's eating habits and reveals the effects of such habits with Harrison's self-description: "The polite word for what my body looks like is burly." *The Road Home* is in its fourth printing and has 50,000 copies in print, yet "national coverage of Harrison has been scant." Charles Frazier, the author of *Cold Mountain*, doesn't understand the neglect: "He's one of a very small number of writers whom I immediately buy." Harrison talks about how he "feels free and pleasant," "a little autumnal," but not troubled by his old age. "I have a little unused life yet." Discusses his thickets, his "really great hiding places." Praises northern Nebraska's Niobrara River area: "Reminds me of what America was supposed to look like before it became something else." Tells of his lycanthropy experience at his cabin in Upper Peninsula. Talks about being so obsessed while writing *Dalva* and *The Road Home* that he got physically ill from exhaustion. Interviewer describes him as "a minor deity" in France: "Thanks to his previous novel, he said, there's a dozen baby girls in France named Dalva." In true Harrison form the author makes friends with the waitress during their meal, offering up a few choice quotes for the interviewer, including what he says to the waitress at the end of the meal: "No dessert for me. I'm trying to be a male model."

## 1999

99. Interview. "Interview with Jim Harrison." By Eleanor Wachtel. *Brick* 63 (Fall 1999): 18–26. Reprinted in *Conversations with Jim Harrison*. Ed. Robert DeMott. Jackson: University Press of Mississippi, 2002. 175–92.

    An edited and rearranged interview in traditional question-and-answer format, created by Wachtel from two different Canadian Broadcasting Company *Writers and Company* broadcasts on 25 September 1994 and 15 November 1998. Print version sacrifices numerous observations by Harrison, for instance, on importance of "solace thickets" where he can hide and see out but not be seen, a good deal of commentary about landscapes and wilderness ("Jesus did a solid forty days, which is a long camping trip"), elucidation of Dogen's statement on the "ten thousand things," etc. Print version begins with Harrison explaining how his totemic objects provide "continuity" against "the dislocation that we ordinarily feel." Admits that the view of nature in his work is "not very romantic." Discusses main characters "wondering what they actually are" in novellas "The Beige Dolorosa" and "A Woman Lit by Fireflies." Criticizes "predatory aspects of sex. That's the fun of writing *Julip,* when you see these men, who were just like friends of mine, chasing around this younger woman, it's wonderfully comic." Believes "life is sentimental. Why should I be cold and hard about it? That's the main content. The biggest thing in people's lives is their loves and dreams and visions." Explains quotation that serves as epigraph for *Julip*—"When the wine is bitter, become the wine"—by claiming: "Rilke's meaning here is if you are ill, you have to go through the whole thing, you have to cure the whole body at once, even if it takes years. You can't continue just simply putting another patch on the tire." Admits that he needs "to keep telling large stories to resolve my own demons." Explains importance of dream life for one's own enrichment. Elaborates on his lycanthropic experience years earlier—"that was caused by anger." Ends on "a grace note, to have found a form that you can express yourself totally in. So we should think of ourselves as inordinately lucky that this happened."

100. Interview. "Guest Author Chat with Jim Harrison." MSN *Microsoft Network's Books and Reading Community Chat Room* 25 February 1999.

    Harrison in his first online chat room. Talks about his poems in *The Shape of the Journey.* "I try to locate myself on earth, and I get the most value cooking the stew a bit longer." He called Jack Nicholson for advice on getting out of Northridge's voice in *The Road Home.* "He told me, 'You just do something different. Any odd thing.' I went pan fishing. I dragged a 200-lb boat around, something I hadn't done since I was a kid. I became a child again and got that old man out of my head." Claims interest in shape-shifting stories. Says he's not sure where his roots are: "As an American writer, I'm peculiar." Says he doesn't revise: "I tend to think about a book for 34 years before beginning to write it. I brood about it. When I sit down to write, the image pool is overflowing." Regarding interviews, he says: "Most interviews are lethargic because it's hard to think on your toes and have any teeth in what you say." Says he is currently reading the *Sports Illustrated* Swimsuit Issue and Mike Davis's *Ecology of Fear,* also *The Log from the Sea of Cortez* by Steinbeck and some cookbooks. Says: "Talking in a chat room isn't that painful. I don't do TV interviews anymore. Being here talking from home is better than traveling and being where you can't smoke." Some philosophical talk about longing, perception, otherness. "I don't think of myself as a thinker. I'm just a storyteller, or, as my mother says, a 'fibber.'"

101. Interview. "An Interview with Jim Harrison: Thoughts on Independence in Publishing and Bookselling." By David Darling. *Independent Publisher* 17 (March–April 1999): 8–11, 17.

Harrison discusses his "affinity for independent presses and independent bookstores." Says he thinks most people prefer books even in this age of computers. Discusses his independence in regard to living outside the mainstream literary world. Gives names of two independently published books: *Go by Go*, a mystery by Jon Jackson, and *Chokecherry Places* by Merrill Gilfillan. Sidebar articles on Sam Hamill's Copper Canyon Press, the publisher of Harrison's collected poems, *The Shape of the Journey*, and Morgan Entrekin's Grove/Atlantic, the publisher of *The Road Home* and Harrison's fiction.

102. "Zest for the West: Jim Harrison Calls Evil Companions Honor an Award He Couldn't Refuse." By Alan Dumas. *Denver Rocky Mountain News* 1 April 1999. 1 page.

Evil Companions Literary Award given on 8 April 1999 is an annual award that "goes to a writer who lives in, writes about or has ties to the West." Says he had to accept this award: "It has the right resonance." Discusses how writing in a female voice is mysterious but also essential to him: "So much of it is utterly strange and private. I didn't want to limit my writing, and I realized if I wrote from a man's point of view, I'd give up too much." Talks about disappointment with TV movie version of *Dalva*, starring Farrah Fawcett: "I couldn't watch it. I spent that evening under the bed throwing up hairballs like a terminally ill cat." Also mentions that the movie *Carried Away*, with Dennis Hopper, was based on his novel *Farmer*. Talks about hating book tours: "It's like a school carnival where you stick your head through a hole and people throw things at you." Says he's working on a novella "about an Indian going postal [*sic*; coastal] in Hollywood" as well as "something called *The Beast God Forgot to Invent*."

103. "Road Trips a Must for Jim Harrison: Writer Recharges His Psychic Batteries." By William Porter. *Denver Post* 4 April 1999: 1, 6.

Harrison talks about his connection to Colorado: "When I was 14, I'd gotten saved at a revival service, and had notions of becoming a Baptist preacher. That all fell apart two years later when I hitchhiked to Colorado and discovered the world." Interviewer says "solace is a big theme for Harrison." Talks about female voice in his work: "I thought it would be easy. It wasn't. I really thought I knew the answer. People forget that writers aren't intellectuals. Poets and writers don't really know what they're writing." Current favorite writers are Dagoberto Gilb, Linda Hogan, Merrill

Gilfillan, and Colum McCann. "The most important thing to remember is, 'Eat or die.'"

104. "Collecting Jim Harrison, 'Untrammeled Renegade Genius.'" By Beef Torrey. *Firsts: The Book Collector's Magazine* 9.5 (May 1999): 38–47.

Torrey's love affair with Harrison's books has remained undiminished since 1981, when he read *Farmer* while visiting Richard Brautigan in Pine Creek MT. (Brautigan had provided Harrison with novel's title.) Profile of Harrison's writing career interspersed with comments by Harrison from Torrey's interview (in late 1998 in Patagonia AZ). Recalls ninth-grade teacher, Bernice Smith, who "started giving me books that I couldn't ordinarily have gotten," fueling his interest in becoming a writer. Recalls *Farmer* "only sold a couple of thousand copies and it was a terrible disappointment. I thought, if this is the best I can do, and it's utterly and totally rejected, then I don't know where I'm even supposed to be. There didn't seem to be any room for what I wanted to do; what I valued most, no one in the literary community valued." Currently working on "another book of three novellas." The first continues the story of Brown Dog, "who's on the lam in L.A. The second will be centered in Mexico. . . . It's a bit ambitious. . . . I'm not sure about the third novella. Just yesterday I had the idea of writing about Dalva's son [Nelse] and his lover, and what their marriage is like in 1999. In other words, I don't have a great deal of control over what kind of fiction I am going to write."

## 2000

105. Interview. "Interview with Jim Harrison." By Carrie Preston and Michel Anthony. *Red Cedar Review* 35 (Winter–Spring 2000): 24–44. Reprinted in *Conversations with Jim Harrison*. Ed. Robert DeMott. Jackson: University Press of Mississippi, 2002. 221–40.

A traditionally formatted question-and-answer session in which Harrison talks about the influence of Herbert Weisinger, a Michigan State professor and mentor to Harrison who got him his teaching job at the State University of New York at Stony Brook. Discusses whether he is a feminist and his recent essay in the *New York Times Magazine* on using female narrators in his fiction ("First Person Female" [see item D167]). Discusses his poem "Counting Birds" and how the poem relates to his sense of keeping time. Discusses money; says he's glad to be out of the screenplay-writing world of Hollywood. Prefers writing and living in Michigan to anything else he could be doing. Explains how history is sometimes mediated through film, including films of his own work, such as *Legends of the Fall*. Talks about

Carl Jung and James Hillman and concepts of masculinity and femininity. Claims cooking is one of the ways he reenters the world after finishing a novel. Talks about a current work in progress, a novella called "I Forgot to Go to Spain." Gives advice: "You can avoid a lot of problems associated with success with sufficient alertness. Only there are some situations where you are trapped." Dislikes book tours. Sees himself outside mainstream society, and discusses what this means for him as a writer: "Somebody's got to stay outside. That is what Outlyer means. I can't say that they are the sane ones because they are transparently not. But it gives you a way of looking at your own culture if you are on the outside."

106. Interview. "Interview with Jim Harrison." By Robert DeMott. Lake Leelanau MI, 2 September 2000. Published in *Conversations with Jim Harrison*. Ed. Robert DeMott. Jackson: University Press of Mississippi, 2002. 193–220.

   Wide-ranging interview regarding details of Harrison's life and career and previous interviews.

107. "Honest Reflection, Uncommon Perception." By Nancy Sundstrom. *Bay Area Times Magazine* (Traverse City MI) October 2000: 7–8.

108. Interview. "A Look Back, a Look Ahead." By Marta Hepler Drahos. *Traverse City MI Record-Eagle* 8 October 2000: 2F.

   Harrison, interviewed in Grand Marais for this profile prior to an extended book tour to promote two new works, explains that he wrote his children's "recovery story," *The Boy Who Ran to the Woods*, to explain to his grandson, Will, "how I hurt my eye." He provides background on his novella collection *The Beast God Forgot to Invent*. Of characters in the title piece, he says, some are based on "compilations" of Upper Peninsula people he knows; of Brown Dog in "Westward Ho," he says the character feeds his survival mechanism and gives him a sense of freedom. Speaks of his liking for the novella form, "halfway between short and long." Also speaks of his necessity to hike every day: "My therapy is walking." Mentions that he is working on a memoir and a full-length "biggie"—a novel about timber and mining in northern Michigan.

109. Interview with Jim Harrison for radio program. By Joseph Bednarik. *Writing on Air*, Seattle WA, 24 October 2000. Unpublished.

   Interview primarily about Harrison's poetry, with reading of several poems. Begins with implications of being "called" to a life in poetry "most definitively" at age 19. Besides marriage of forty years, "that's your primary fidelity in life, and it's important not to dissipate it in any other human activities." Provides some background on a new poem, "In Vera Cruz in 1941," that is "partly a grief poem" (his mother had died a month earlier), but also realizes it can't be explained fully: "We don't know where anything comes from like that." Poetry, he claims, is a "nonharmonic resonance," and the largest "force" in an artist is "restlessness for the work that's just over the lip of consciousness." Speaks of his new incarnation as "Jaime Harrison Walgren," a "Mexican poet" who eschews the United States as a "vast, horny Empire subduing the Earth." Concludes with familiar refrain: "The work is what matters, not . . . personality."

110. Interview. "Jim Harrison." By Jonathan Shipley. 3 November 2000. book reporter.com. 4 pp.

Interview occasioned by release of book of novellas *The Beast God Forgot to Invent*. Joe, in title novella, is "a metaphor for our incomprehension of the artist." The attitudes of Brown Dog in "Westward Ho" "are my survival mechanism in a world in which I most often feel out of place." Third novella, "I Forgot to Go to Spain," is a "fable about the truly awful aspects of success in our culture." Prefers writing novellas because of their "density"— "I don't like loose sprawling prose." His advice to aspiring writers: "Don't do it unless you're willing to give your whole life to it. Red wine and garlic also helps."

**2002**

111. Interviews. *Conversations with Jim Harrison*. Ed. Robert DeMott. Jackson: University Press of Mississippi, 2002. A collection of interviews with Harrison from 1971 to 2000. Part of the ongoing University Press of Mississippi "Conversation" series.

The second full-length scholarly look at Harrison's life and writing. A collection of the best and most informative interviews with Harrison over his long career. This book also contains the most comprehensive chronology of Harrison's life available to date.

112. Interview. By Joseph Bednarik. *Five Points* 6.2 (2002): 45–66. This is the literary journal for the Georgia State University Press edited by David Bottoms.

113. Interview. "Jim Harrison: The Interview." By Robert L. Nicholas. *Oxford Town* 14–20 November 2002: 10, 11.

A short and insightful interview concerning Harrison's just-published memoir *Off to the Side*.

**2003**

114. "Good Food, Loyal Dogs and a Good Smoke." By Bill Kohlhaase. *Tributary* February 2003: 10–11.

115. "Out to Lunch." By Richard Grant. *Telegraph Magazine* 7 June 2003: 66–69.

Portraits of Harrison by Michael Kelly. *Telegraph Magazine* is the weekly general-interest magazine published by the *London Daily Telegraph*.

**2004**

116. "Dogs in Modern Lit: Interview with Jim Harrison." By Robert Birnbaum. *The Bark* 29 (Winter 2004): 99.

117. Interview. "Birnbaum v. Jim Harrison." By Robert Birnbaum. *Dallas Morning News* June 2004.

    An online interview with Harrison to discuss his newest novel, *True North*.

    A short question-and-answer session between Harrison and Birnbaum concerning dogs in literature.

118. Interview. "Fame and Fortune: Jim Harrison Learns His Money Lessons." By Jay MacDonald. *USA Today* 23 June 2004.

    An interview dealing mainly with financial issues relating to writing and the pitfalls of not having a sound financial plan.

**2005**

119. Interview. "Repair Work: An Interview with Jim Harrison." By Angela Elam. *New Letters* 71.3 (Summer–Fall 2005): 81–104. *New Letters* is the literary magazine for the University of Missouri–Kansas City. Interview was actually conducted in 2004.

120. Interview. "'Legends of the Fall' Author Jim Harrison: Loves Home, Hates School." By Kimberly Maul. *Book Standard* 21 December 2005. Online interview with Harrison.

**2006**

121. Interview. "Jim Harrison—Just a Writer." By Lindsay Ahl. *Bliss Santa Fe* 5 (Summer 2006): 47–51. This is the first published appearance of this interview and was released in May 2006. This issue also contains poetry from Harrison.

**2007**

122. Interview. "Jim Harrison: A Prolific Author Catalogs His Work and Life." By Mary Isca Pirkola. *Grand Valley Magazine* 5.3 (Winter 2007): 13–16. This is the first published appearance of this interview.

    An interesting look at Harrison's career and his archive, which is housed at Grand Valley State University.

123. Interview. "Pleasures of the Hard-Worn Life: Jim Harrison Hunts, Cooks,

Eats and Writes with Abandon." By Charles McGrath. *New York Times* 25 January 2007: E1, E5. Photographs by Jeff Topping. This was the first published appearance of this interview conducted at Harrison's winter casita in Patagonia AZ.

A long piece on Harrison in "The Arts" section. It contains two recipes from Harrison and his wife, Linda.

124. Interview. "Brother's Death Inspires Novel." By Ashley Simpson Shires. *Denver Rocky Mountain News* 2 March 2007: 35.

Harrison discusses his novel *Returning to Earth*, among other things.

125. Interview. "Appetite for Life." By Andrew Smart. *Hour Detroit* April 2007: 48. This is the first published appearance of this interview. Interview in "The Insider/Arts and Leisure" section.

A relatively short question-and-answer interview mostly dealing with food, wine, and Michigan.

126. Interview. "Novelist, Poet Is a Legend at Large." By Kathleen Johnson. *Kansas City Star* 12 October 2008: H11.

**See Also**

Collins, Nancy. "Wolf, Man, Jack." *Vanity Fair* April 1994: 118–24, 166–70. This interview is principally concerned with Jack Nicholson and the film adaptation of *Wolf*, but it also includes some comments by Harrison.

McDonell, Terry. "Russell Chatham: A Complicated Sense of Place." *Smart* 11 (July–August 1990): 58–60. Includes some references to Harrison with regard to the relationship between him and Chatham.

# Section I
## *Critical Articles, Essays, and Studies concerning Jim Harrison's Works*

**1968**

1. Quasha, George. "Impure Americana, Fixtures of Place—Part One of an Essay to Welcome New Work: On the Occasion of Jim Harrison's *Locations*." *Stony Brook* 1.2 (Fall 1968): 224–35.

**1969**

2. Simpson, Louis. "Poetry in the Sixties—Long Live Blake! Down with Donne!" *New York Times Book Review* 28 December 1969: 1, 2, 18. A long essay concerning the poetry of Allen Ginsberg, George Oppen, Denise Levertov, LeRoi Jones, Robert Duncan, Jim Harrison, Robert Bly, and Diane Wakoski.

**1971**

3. Knickerbocker, D. C. "Jim Harrison: A New Voice from Hemingway's Hills." *Grand Rapids MI Press* 26 December 1971: 6, 7. A long essay on Harrison with early photos of Harrison and his young family. Also reprints the poems "Sketch for a Job Application Blank" and "Northern Michigan."

**1972**

4. Amanuddin, Syed. "Poets from East and West: Jim Harrison, Mirza Ghalib, John Millett, D. C. Berry, Sarakumar Mukherjee." *Creative Moment* 1.2 (1972): 35–40.

**1973**

5. Margolis, Susan. "100 Seducers on Their Craft." *Rolling Stone* 16 August 1973: 43–44. Also contains a short quote from Harrison and a photo.

## 1974

6. Noverr, Douglas A. "New Dimensions in Recent Michigan Fiction." *Midwestern Miscellany* 1 (1974): 9–14. A scholarly essay that deals with Harrison's first novel, *Wolf*.

## 1977

7. Averill, David. "Writer Discounts Complaints of Hollywood, Success." *Traverse City MI Record-Eagle* 4 March 1977: 15.

## 1979

8. Prescott, Peter S. "The Macho Mystique." *Newsweek* 9 July 1979: 72. no. 94.
9. Magnusson, Paul. "The Wolves Are Howling at Jim Harrison's Door." *Detroit Free Press* 16 September 1979: 1-E, 4-E, 5-E.

## 1980

10. Wilson, John. "*Legends of the Fall*." *Magill's Literary Annual: Books of 1979*. Ed. Frank N. Magill. Englewood Cliffs NJ: Salem Press, 1980. 462–66.
11. Chaplin, Gordon. "More Mad Dogs and Fewer Street Lamps." *Washington Post* 2 March 1980: F-1, F-3–F-4.
12. Burger, Frederick. "Macho Writer, He Despises the Term, This Man They Call the New Hemingway." *Philadelphia Inquirer* 23 July 1980: 1D, 2D.

## 1981

13. Golden, Michael. "The Next Great American Writer." *Smoke Signals* 2.2–3 (1981): 14–21. "The White Line Issue."
14. Wood, Guy. *Bibliography of Leelanauiana*. Empire MI, 1981. 15. Small bibliography self-published by Guy Wood covering the published work of authors of Leelanau County, Michigan. Includes Harrison's early books.

## 1982

16. Rohrkemper, John. "'Natty Bumppo Wants Tobacco': Jim Harrison's Wilderness." *Great Lakes Review: A Journal of Midwest Life* 8.2–9.1 (Fall 1982–Spring 1983): 20–28.
17. Roberson, William H. "A Good Day to Live: The Prose Works of Jim Harrison." *Great Lakes Review: A Journal of Midwest Life* 8.2–9.1 (Fall 1982–Spring 1983): 29–37.
18. Burger, Frederick. "Why I Hate TV by John D. MacDonald, Stephen King, Arthur Miller, Erskine Caldwell and Other Folks Who Like to Write." *Miami*

*Herald* 13–19 June 1982: 4, 5. An article from writers, including Harrison, on the state of American television.

19. Colonnese, Tom. "Jim Harrison: A Checklist." *Bulletin of Bibliography* 39.3 (September 1982): 132–35.

**1983**

20. Burkholder, Robert E. "Jim Harrison." *Dictionary of Literary Biography Yearbook 1982*. Ed. Richard Ziegfeld. Detroit: Gale Research/Bruccoli Clark, 1983. 266–76.
21. Munro, C. Lynn. "Jim Harrison." *Critical Survey of Long Fiction 4*. Ed. Frank N. Magill. La Canada CA: Salem Press, 1983. 1286–95.
22. Anonymous. "Jim Harrison." *Michigan: The Magazine of the Detroit News* 9 January 1983: 18. Under the broader essay "Michigans of the Year Award."

**1984**

23. Iyer, Pico. "Searching for America." *The Recovery of Innocence: Literary Glimpses of the American Dream*. London: Concord Grove Press, 1984. 97–103.
24. Gilligan, Thomas Mahler. "Myth and Reality in Jim Harrison's *Warlock*." *Critique: Studies in Modern Fiction* 25.3 (Spring 1984): 147–53.
25. Newer, Hank. "Out of the Woods." *Ozark* April 1984: 29, 30, 82, 86, 87. A lengthy and insightful essay on Harrison.
26. Iyer, Pico. "Romancing the Home." *Nation* 238 (23 June 1984): 767–70.

**1985**

27. Marowski, Daniel G., and Jean C. Stine. "Jim Harrison." *Contemporary Literary Criticism*. Vol. 33 Detroit: Gale Research, 1985. 196–201.
28. Iyer, Pico. "Searching for America." *London Magazine* February 1985: 67–72.
29. Fergus, Jim. "Jim Harrison: Today's Hemingway?" *MD* May 1985: 116–18, 244–46.
30. Reilly, Edward C. "Cervantes' *Quixote* and Harrison's *Warlock*: Some Similarities and Differences." *Notes on Contemporary Literature* 15.3 (May 1985): 3.
31. Jenks, Tom. "How Writer's [sic] Live Today." *Esquire* August 1985: 123–27. Short piece on Harrison under the heading "Local Color."

**1986**

32. Reilly, Edward C. "The Tragedy and the Folly: Harrison's *A Good Day to Die*—an Earlier Vision." *Publications of the Mississippi Philological Association* 1986: 23–33.
33. Eckstein, Barbara J. "On Being Male in America; or, The Dancer in the

Dance." *Southern Review: Literary and Interdisciplinary Essays* 19.1 (March 1986): 76–88.

**1988**
34. Roberson, William H. "'Macho Mistake': The Misrepresentation of Jim Harrison's Fiction." *Critique: Studies in Modern Fiction* 29.4 (Summer 1988): 233–44.
35. BeVier, Tom. "The Softer Side of a Macho Man." *Michigan: The Magazine of the Detroit News* 6 March 1988: 15–19.
36. BeVier, Tom. "A Hint of Harrison." *Traverse* April 1988: 17.
37. Love, Keith. "Literary Voice in the Wilderness." *Los Angeles Times* 12 April 1988: 1, 4, 5.
38. Stocking, Kathleen. "Heart and Soul." *Detroit Monthly* September 1988: 178, 180.
39. Sipchen, Bob. "The Falsetto Novelists." *Los Angeles Times* 29 December 1988: 1, 8. An essay concerning contemporary male authors writing in a female voice. The authors noted are Reynolds Price, Jay McInerney, John Updike, and Harrison.

**1989**
40. Aubrey, Bryan. "*Dalva*." *Magill's Literary Annual 1989*. Ed. Frank N. Magill. Englewood Cliffs NJ: Salem Press, 1989. 212–15.
41. Gruzinska, Aleksandra. "E. M. Cioran and 'The Man Who Gave up His Name' by Jim Harrison." *Journal of the American Romanian Society of Arts and Sciences* 12 (1989): 83–93.
42. Bass, Rick. "Shyness." *Black Warrior Review* 15.2 (Spring 1989): 155–59.
43. Lorenz, Paul H. "Rethinking Machismo: Jim Harrison's *Legends of the Fall*." *Publications of the Arkansas Philological Association* 15.1 (Spring 1989): 41–51.
44. Reed, Julia. "Books." *Vogue* September 1989: 502, 506, 510.

**1990**
45. Barillas, William. "To Sustain the Bio-Region: Michigan Poets of Place." *MidAmerica* 17 (1990): 10–33. A scholarly look at Michigan poets in which Harrison is included. Many examples of Harrison's poetry are included in this essay.
46. Barron, John. "The Write Brothers." *Detroit Monthly* August 1990: 24–26. An essay dealing with the Michigan writers Elmore Leonard and Harrison in the "Book" section of the magazine.
47. Auer, Tom. "A Man Lit by Passion." *Bloomsbury Review* 10.6 (November–December 1990): 1, 16.

48. Knickerbocker, Dennis. "A Novelist's Call for the Wild: Jim Harrison Hunts for a Sacramental Code." *Lansing MI State Journal* 2 December 1990: 1E, 6E. In the "Sports" section.

## 1991

49. Munro, C. Lynn. "Jim Harrison." *Critical Survey of Long Fiction*. Ed. Frank N. Magill. rev. ed. Englewood Cliffs NJ: Salem Press, 1991. 1534–49.
50. Smyntek, John. "Michigan Author Will Do an Eat Column." *Detroit Free Press* 15 January 1991: 8F.
51. Guequierre, Nathan. "A Story of His Life: Jim Harrison Comes to Town." *Art Muscle* 15 January 1991: 16, 17.

## 1992

52. Munro, C. Lynn. "Jim Harrison." *Critical Survey of Poetry*. Ed. Frank N. Magill. Englewood Cliffs NJ: Salem Press, 1992.
53. Wieneke, Connie. "Jim Harrison Writes and Cooks with Passion." *Headwaters Review* June 1992: 2. A newsletter from the Valley Bookstore in Jackson, Wyoming.
54. Anonymous. "Jim Harrison." *Current Biography* 53.1 (July 1992): 20–23. Ed. Charles Moritz.
55. Cross, Robert. "Siren Song: Will Success Lure Poet-Novelist Jim Harrison out of His Midwestern Lair?" *Chicago Tribune Magazine* 30 August 1992: sec. 10, pp. 14–18, 24.

## 1993

56. Irwin, T. W. "Bullyboys: Jim Harrison Looks for America . . ." *Spy* March 1993: 70–71.
57. Granon, Francois. "Cigarettes, Whiskey et P'tites Pepees." *Telerama* 28 July 1993: 12–17. no. 2272.

## 1994

58. Biskin, Peter. "Who's Afraid of the Big Bad Wolf?" *Premiere* March 1994: 56–63. Generally concerned with movie adaptation of *Wolf*.
59. Bancroft, Colette M. "A Fine Visit with Jim Harrison." *Arizona Daily Star* (Tucson) 23 March 1994: 3B.
60. Sander, Amy. "A Few Words with Jim Harrison." *Northern Express* 16–30 May 1994: 1, 3, 4.
61. Schwager, Jeff. "Wolfman Jim." *LA Village View* 27 May 1994: 29, 30.
62. Morice, Laura. "Drama: *Wolf*." *US* June 1994: 75. Generally concerned with movie adaptation of *Wolf*.

## 1995

63. Sundstrom, Nancy. "Harrison Pleased with 'Legends.'" *Traverse City MI Record-Eagle* 12 January 1995: 1D.
64. BeVier, Tom. "Author Falls for the Film Version of Legends." *Detroit News* 30 January 1995: 1C, 8C.

## 1996

65. Bly, Carol. "The Psychological and Moral Habitats of American Children and Adults." *Changing the Bully Who Rules the World*. Minneapolis: Milkweed Editions, 1996. 289–318.
66. Reilly, Edward C. *Jim Harrison*. New York: Twayne Publishing, 1996. First full-length critical study of Harrison's writing. Dust-jacket photo by Gary Issacs.
67. Thorne, John. *Serious Pig: An American Cook in Search of His Roots*. New York: North Point Press, 1996. 411–14. A short chapter titled "Walking the Wild Side" about Harrison's relation with hunting, fishing, eating, and death.
68. Harvey, Miles. "The Outside Canon: A Few Good Books." *Outside* May 1996: 80. A brief mention of the poetry collection *The Theory and Practice of Rivers* is included in this essay on the editor's favorite outdoor-related books. Also mentioned in this paragraph are *Wolf*, *Dalva*, and *Legends of the Fall*.
69. Lynch, Thomas. "Jim Harrison, Splendid Poet, Goes on a Spiritual Pilgrimage." *Detroit Free Press* 20 October 1996.

## 1997

70. Johnson, Robert. "Brown Dog's Insight: The Fiction of Jim Harrison." *Notes on Contemporary Literature* 27.1 (January 1997): 2–4.

## 1998

71. McClintock, James I. "Dalva: Jim Harrison's 'Twin Sister.'" *Journal of Men's Studies* 6.3 (Spring 1998): 319–30.
72. Phipps, Terry W. "The Sounds of Silence." *Lakeland Boating* September 1998: 50–54. An essay that deals mostly with the Grand Marais region of Michigan.
73. Anonymous. "Two Old Friends Return to the Drum." *Shaman Drum Newsletter* September–October 1998: 1. The newsletter for the Shaman Drum Bookstore in Ann Arbor, Michigan.
74. Barrett, Dan. "Road Rules." *Boston Phoenix* 13 November 1998.
75. Streitfeld, David. "Just Deserts." *Washington Post Book Report* 13 December 1998.

## 1999

76. Barillas, William. "Jim Harrison, Willa Cather, and the Revision of Midwestern Pastoral." *MidAmerica* 26 (1999): 171–84. Ed. David D. Anderson.
77. Boa, Robert. "Jim Harrison: Novelist and Poet." MSU *Alumni Magazine* Winter 1999: 11. Short piece about Harrison with photo.
78. Rubel, David, ed. "Jim Harrison." *The Reading List's Contemporary Fiction: A Critical Guide to the Complete Works of 110 Authors*. New York: Henry Holt & Co., 1999. 151–54.
79. Kooser, Ted. "Early Morning Walks: Postcards to Jim Harrison." *Shenandoah* 49.3 (Fall 1999): 36–43. A collection of postcard poems shared between Kooser and Harrison.
80. Smith, Patrick. "'In My Own Memory, Time Has Never Stopped': Essays on Jim Harrison's Fiction." Unpublished dissertation. Ohio University, August 1999. 327 pp.

## 2000

81. Brandt, Anthony. "The 50 Best Books, Music, and Movies of the Century." *Men's Journal: The Great Life*. New York: Penguin Books, 2000. 253. The author has included *Legends of the Fall* as no. 22 in his list of best fiction books of the century.
82. Smith, Patrick. *The Facts on File Companion to the American Short Story*. Ed. Abby H. P. Werlock. New York: Checkmark Books, 2000. 204, 243, 258, 450. A short biography of Harrison and short outlines of *Legends of the Fall*, *Julip*, and *The Woman Lit by Fireflies*.
83. Davis, Todd F. "A Spiritual Topography: Northern Michigan in the Poetry of Jim Harrison." *Midwest Quarterly* 42.1 (Fall 2000): 94–104.
84. McClintock, James. "Jim Harrison: Soul-Maker." *Midwest Quarterly* 41.2 (November 2000): 191–207.
85. Miles, Jonathan. *The Salon.com Reader's Guide to Contemporary Authors*. Ed. Laura Miller. New York: Penguin Group, 2000. 179–80.
86. Smith, Patrick. "A Man's Man's World." *January Magazine* November 2000. Online magazine. 5 pp.

## 2001

87. Smith, Patrick. *American Writers: A Collection of Literary Biographies, Supplement VIII*. Ed. Jay Parini. New York: Charles Scribner's Sons, 2001. 37–57.
88. Vickers, Jean. "Jim Harrison: Literary Shape-Shifter." *Novel and Short Story Writer's Market 2002*. Ed. Ann Bowling. Cincinnati: Writers Digest Books, 2001. 10–14.

89. Preston, Carrie. "Meeting Jim Harrison, NYC." *The Anthologist* Fall 2001. A poem written in commemoration of meeting Mr. Harrison.
90. Hammond, Ruth. "Help a Poet Go Fishing." *Carnegie Mellon Magazine* Fall 2001: 10.

## 2002

91. Smith, Patrick. *The True Bones of My Life: Essays on the Fiction of Jim Harrison.* East Lansing: Michigan State University Press, 2002. A full-length study of Harrison's fiction.
92. Smith, Patrick. *Thematic Guide to Popular Short Stories.* Westport CT: Greenwood Press, 2002. 119, 120. This annotated anthology of short stories contains a brief plot summary and critical statement on Harrison's novella "Legends of the Fall."
93. LeMay, Konnie. "Harrison and Harrison: Two World-Class Writers and Their U.P. Inspirations." *Lake Superior Magazine* February 2002.
94. Collins, Tom. "Jim Harrison." *Albuquerque Journal* 20 February 2002.
95. Rentilly, J. "Jim Harrison." *Razor* May 2002: 44–45. vols. 3–5. In the "Edge Profile" section. Also included is a full-page color photograph of Harrison.
96. Freeze, Eric. "Jim Harrison: Into the Woods." *Quarter After Eight* May 2002. This is the student literary quarterly from Ohio University.
97. Mudge, Alden. "Jim Harrison's Wild Ride, 'Legends of the Fall' Author Overcomes His Obsessions." *BookPage* November 2002.
98. Fuljum, Bob. "Seven Lively Sins." *Pages* November–December 2002: 52.
99. Salter Reynolds, Susan. "A Writer at Life's Banquet." *Los Angeles Times* 24 November 2002: E1, E4.

## 2003

100. Davis, Todd F., and Kenneth Womack. "Embracing the Fall: Reconfiguring Redemption in Jim Harrison's *The Woman Lit by Fireflies, Dalva* and *The Road Home.*" *Western American Literature* 38.2 (Summer 2003): 132–52.
101. Kohlhaase, Bill. "Good Food, Loyal Dogs and a Good Smoke." *Tributary* February 2003: 10–11. A short piece about Harrison and his memoir *Off to the Side.*

## 2004

102. Ahearn, Allen, and Carl Hahn. *Jim Harrison: Author Price Guide.* Dickerson MD: Quill & Brush, 2004. A price guide to the value of Harrison's books and broadsides on the secondary market. Helpful bibliographic information mostly intended for book collectors and book dealers. First published

in 1992, revised in 1997 and again in 2004, with this being the most recent version with updated values and material added.

103. Chachere, Richard. *Jungian Reflections on Literary and Film Classics: Opus 2, Legends of the Fall*. Lafayette LA: Cypremort Point Press, 2004. An in-depth look at the film *Legends of the Fall*, but also discusses Harrison's novella of the same name.
104. Tschida, Ron. "An Original Voice." *This Week: Southwest Montana's Arts and Entertainment Magazine* 14–20 May 2004.

## 2005

105. Barillas, William. *The Midwestern Pastoral: Place and Landscape in Literature of the American Heartland*. Athens: Ohio University Press, 2005. 169–205. Entire chapter on Harrison's poetry, fiction, and essays. Also numerous other mentions of Harrison's work throughout the book.
106. Bunge, Nancy. "Influencing Each Other through the Mail: William Stafford's and Marvin Bell's *Segues* and Jim Harrison's and Ted Kooser's *Braided Creek*." *Midwestern Miscellany* 33 (Fall 2005): 48–56.
107. Konsmo, Natalie. "Jim Harrison and *The Summer He Didn't Die*." *Tributary* October 2005: 18.

## 2006

108. Pichaske, David R. *Rooted: Seven Midwest Writers of Place*. Iowa City: University of Iowa Press, 2006. 263–96. Chapter 8 is titled "Jim Harrison—Reluctant Postmodernist."
109. Hemingway, Valerie. "Jim Harrison's Earthy Prose, Award-winning Novels, and Gourmet Cooking." *Distinctly Montana* Winter 2006–07: 118–25. A short, informative piece on Harrison and his Montana home.
110. Boucq, Isabelle. "Jim Harrison: A Modern-Day Rabelais." *France Today* November 2006: 16, 17.
111. Nelson, Sara. "A Legend, in the Fall." *PW Publishers Weekly* 6 November 2006: 31, 32. A short piece on Harrison and the release of advance reading copies of his forthcoming novel *Returning to Earth*.

## 2007

112. Castanier, Bill. "MSU's Three Literary Lions of the 21st Century." *MSU Alumni Magazine* 24.4 (Summer 2007): 20–24. An essay dealing with Harrison, Richard Ford, and Thomas McGuane, all alumni of Michigan State University.
113. Ryan, Michael C. "A Sportsman's Ethos: Jim Harrison's Environmental Ideals." *Aethlon: The Journal of Sport Literature* 24.1 (Fall 2006–Winter 2007): 87–93.

# Section J
## *Reviews of Jim Harrison's Works*

In chronological order:
- *Plain Song* (1965; poetry)
- *Walking* (1967; poetry)
- *Locations* (1968; poetry)
- *Wolf* (1971; fiction)
- *Outlyer and Ghazals* (1971; poetry)
- *A Good Day to Die* (1973; fiction)
- *Letters to Yesenin* (1973; poetry)
- *Farmer* (1976; fiction)
- *Returning to Earth* (1977; poetry)
- *Legends of the Fall* (1979; fiction)
- *Letters to Yesenin and Returning to Earth* (1979; poetry)
- *Warlock* (1981; fiction)
- *Selected and New Poems 1961–1981* (1981; poetry)
- *Natural World: A Bestiary* (1982; poetry)
- *Sundog* (1984; fiction)
- *The Theory and Practice of Rivers* (1986; poetry)
- *The Woman Lit by Fireflies* (1990; fiction)
- *Just Before Dark* (1991; nonfiction)
- *Julip* (1994; fiction)
- *After Ikkyu and Other Poems* (1996; poetry)
- *The Road Home* (1998; fiction)
- *The Shape of the Journey: New and Collected Poems* (1998; poetry)
- *The Boy Who Ran to the Woods* (2000; children's fiction)
- *The Beast God Forgot to Invent* (2000; fiction)
- *The Raw and the Cooked: Adventure of a Roving Gourmand* (2001; nonfiction)
- *Off to the Side* (2002; nonfiction)

*A Conversation* (2002; poetry)
*Braided Creek* (2003; poetry)
*True North* (2004; fiction)
*Livingston Suite* (2005; poetry)
*The Summer He Didn't Die* (2005; fiction)
*Saving Daylight* (2006; poetry)
*Returning to Earth* (2007; fiction)
*Letters to Yesenin* (2007; poetry)
*The English Major* (2008; fiction)

### *Plain Song*

1. Untitled and anonymous Rev. of *Plain Song*. *Poet Lore* Winter 1965: 376.
2. Andrew, John Williams. Rev. of *Plain Song*. *Poet Lore* 60.4 (Winter 1965): 36. In the "New Books" column.
3. Quasha, George. Untitled Rev. of *Plain Song*. *Library Journal* 1 December 1965: 5286.
4. Willingham, John R. Untitled Rev. of *Plain Song*. *Library Journal* 1 December 1965: 5286.
5. Dickey, William. "The Thing Itself." Rev. of *Plain Song*. *Hudson Review* Spring 1966: 147, 149–51.
6. Untitled and anonymous Rev. of *Plain Song*. *Southern Review* Spring 1966: 569–70.
7. Jones, Donald. "Numinous Surds." Rev. of *Plain Song*. *Prairie Schooner* Winter 1966–67: 227.
8. Corbett, William. "One Redskin." Rev. of *Plain Song*. *Harvard Advocate* March 1966: 34.
9. McCloskey, Mark. "Five Poets." Rev. of *Plain Song*. *Poetry* 108.4 (July 1966): 272–73. In the "Poetry" column.

### *Locations*

10. Quasha, George. "Impure Americana, Fixtures of Place—Part One of an Essay to Welcome New Work: On the Occasion of Jim Harrison's *Locations*." Rev. of *Locations*. *Stony Brook* 1.2 (Fall 1968): 224–35.
11. Simpson, Louis. "Poetry in the Sixties: Long Live Blake! Down with Donne!" Rev. of *Locations*. *New York Times Book Review* 28 December 1969: 18.
12. Bucholtz, Mel. "A Review." Rev. of *Locations*. *Lillabulero* 8 (Winter 1970): 84–88. Many excerpts of Harrison's poetry are included in this review.
13. Untitled and anonymous Rev. of *Locations*. *Kirkus Reviews* February 1971: 322–23.

14. Mueller, Lisel. "Versions of Reality." Rev. of *Locations*. *Poetry* 117.5 (February 1971): 322, 323. Part of a long review that includes eight other books.

## *Wolf*

15. Lehmann-Haupt, Christopher. "The Woods Are Ugly, Cold, Wet." Rev. of *Wolf*. *New York Times* 24 November 1971: 33.
16. Oates, Joyce Carol. Untitled Rev. of *Wolf*. *SR* 25 (December 1971): 29–31.
17. Yardley, Jonathan. "Also Extravagantly Free-Male." Rev. of *Wolf*. *New York Times Book Review* 12 December 1971: 4, 38.
18. Oates, Joyce Carol. "Going Places." Rev. of *Wolf*. *Partisan Review* 39.3 (Summer 1972): 462–63.
19. "Michigan in Fiction." Anonymous Rev. of *Wolf*. *Michigan Department of Education* 1976: 12.

## *Outlyer and Ghazals*

20. Rankin, Rush. "*Outlyer and Ghazals*." Rev. of *Outlyer and Ghazals*. *Survey of Contemporary Literature* 1971: 5688–91.
21. Young, Vernon. "Lines Written in Rouen." Rev. of *Outlyer and Ghazals*. *Hudson Review* Winter 1971–72: 670–71.
22. Untitled and anonymous Rev. of *Outlyer and Ghazals*. *Kirkus Reviews* 15 (February 1971): 213.
23. Rosenberg, Kenyon C. Untitled Rev. of *Outlyer and Ghazals*. *Library Journal* 1 June 1971: 1986.
24. Rosenthal, M. L. "*Outlyer and Ghazals*." Rev. of *Outlyer and Ghazals*. *New York Times Book Review* 18 July 1971: 7, 18.
25. "1971: A Selection of Noteworthy Titles." Anonymous Rev. of *Outlyer and Ghazals*. *New York Times Book Review* 5 December 1971: 86.
26. Whitehead, James. "Leaping Ghazals and Inside Jokes Concealed in Tropes." Rev. of *Outlyer and Ghazals*. *Saturday Review of Literature* 18 December 1971: 37.
27. "A Gathering of Poets." Anonymous Rev. of *Outlyer and Ghazals*. *Western Humanities Review* Spring 1972: 193–94.
28. Netta, Lou. Rev. of *Outlyer and Ghazals*. *NEW: American and Canadian Poetry* 18 (April 1972): 45.

## *A Good Day to Die*

29. Untitled and anonymous Rev. of *A Good Day to Die*. *Publishers Weekly* 16 July 1973: 108.
30. Untitled and anonymous Rev. of *A Good Day to Die*. *New York Times Book Review* 9 September 1973: 4.

31. Woods, William Crawford. "What a Strange Accomplishment." Rev. of *A Good Day to Die*. *Washington Post* 9 September 1973: 4.
32. Lehmann-Haupt, Christopher. "Old Monsters Never Die." Rev. of *A Good Day to Die*. *New York Times Book Review* 13 September 1973.
33. Fanning, Patrick. Untitled Rev. of *A Good Day to Die*. *Library Journal* 15 September 1973: 2570.
34. Selander, Glenn E. Untitled Rev. of *A Good Day to Die*. *Western American Literature* 17 (1982): 276–77.

### *Letters to Yesenin*

35. Hubert, Jim. "Jim Hubert Reviews Jim Harrison." Rev. of *Letters to Yesenin*. *Aisling* 7–8 (Summer 1976): 12. A literary journal from LaMarque TX.
36. Reed, J. D. "One of the Beasts." Rev. of *Letters to Yesenin*. *American Poetry Review* 5.4 (July–August 1976): 36–38.

### *Farmer*

37. "Michigan in Books." Untitled and anonymous Rev. of *Farmer*. *Michigan Department of Education* 13.3 (Fall 1976): 6, 7.
38. Untitled and anonymous Rev. of *Farmer*. *Publishers Weekly* 31 May 1976: 191.
39. Untitled and anonymous Rev. of *Farmer*. *Library Journal* 15 June 1976: 1446.
40. Lehmann-Haupt, Christopher. "Celebrations of the Natural." Rev. of *Farmer*. *New York Times* 26 July 1976: 21.
41. Sololov, Raymond. Untitled Rev. of *Farmer*. *Newsweek* 30 August 1976: 70.
42. Untitled and anonymous Rev. of *Farmer*. *New Yorker* 30 August 1976: 90.
43. Schott, Webster. "Farmer." Rev. of *Farmer*. *New York Times Book Review* 10 October 1976: 32.
44. Howe, Parkman. "Two Novels Accent Self-Discovery." Rev. of *Farmer*. *Christian Science Monitor* 27 January 1977: 23.

### *Returning to Earth*

45. Carruth, Hayden. "The Passionate Few." Rev. of *Returning to Earth*. *Harper's* June 1978: 86–88.

### *Legends of the Fall*

46. Grinnell, James W. "Legends of the Fall." Rev. of *Legends of the Fall*. *Studies in Short Fiction* 1979: 504–06.
47. Carver, Ray. Untitled Rev. of *Legends of the Fall*. *San Francisco Review of Books* March 1979: 23–24. Reprinted as "Rousing Tales" in *No Heroics, Please: Uncollected Writings*. London: Harvill, 1991. 171–75.

48. Untitled and anonymous Rev. of *Legends of the Fall*. *Publishers Weekly* 19 March 1979: 87.
49. Bourjaily, Vance. "Three Novellas: Violent Means." Rev. of *Legends of the Fall*. *New York Times Book Review* 17 June 1979: 14, 27.
50. Opdahl, Keith. "Junk Food." Rev. of *Legends of the Fall*. *Nation* 7 July 1979: 23–34.
51. Prescott, Peter. "The Macho Mystique." Rev. of *Legends of the Fall*. *Newsweek* 9 July 1979: 72.
52. Untitled and anonymous Rev. of *Legends of the Fall*. *Atlantic Monthly* September 1979: 92.
53. Lutholtz, M. William. "Tough Guy in Tender Times." Rev. of *Legends of the Fall*. *Christian Science Monitor* 5 September 1979: 19.
54. Wolff, Tobias. "Legends of the Fall, Jim Harrison." Rev. of *Legends of the Fall*. *Porch* 3.2 (Spring 1980): 53.
55. Scannell, Verson. "Willfully Waffling." Rev. of *Legends of the Fall*. *Times Literary Supplement* 12 March 1980: 326.
56. Wolcott, James. "Title." Rev. of *Legends of the Fall*. *Esquire* October 1981: 23.
57. Bruni, Frank. "'Legends' Falls under the Weight of Its Pretensions." Rev. of *Legends of the Fall*. *Detroit Free Press* 13 June 1995: 4D. Primarily concerned with film version of *Legends of the Fall*.

## *Warlock*

58. Kogan, Rick. "Alas, *Warlock* Casts No Spell to Hold Reader." Rev. of *Warlock*. *Chicago Sun-Times* 18 October 1981.
59. Casey, John D. "American Settings." Rev. of *Warlock*. *New York Times* 22 November 1981: sec. 7, pp. 14, 45.
60. Beasecker, Robert. Untitled Rev. of *Warlock*. *Chronicle* 19.1 (Spring 1983): 41. Publication of the Historical Society of Michigan.

## *Selected and New Poems 1961–1981*

61. Carruth, Hayden. Untitled Rev. of *Selected and New Poems 1961–1981*. *Sulfur* no. 7 (1982): 157–60.
62. Lipari, Joseph A. Untitled Rev. of *Selected and New Poems 1961–1981*. *Library Journal* 15 June 1982.
63. Untitled and anonymous Rev. of *Selected and New Poems 1961–1981*. *Publishers Weekly* 25 June 1982: 114.
64. Taylor, Keith. "Star-Crossed Jock Ego." Rev. of *Selected and New Poems 1961–1981*. *In Print: A Book Review* September 1982. 2 pp. Borders Book Shop, Ann Arbor MI.

65. Tillinghast, Richard. "From Michigan and Tennessee." Rev. of *Selected and New Poems 1961–1981*. *New York Times* 12 December 1982: sec. 7, pp. 14, 31.
66. Hotch, Ripley. "Two He-Man Poets and Jim Harrison Is Stronger." Rev. of *Selected and New Poems 1961–1981*. *Detroit News* 1983.
67. Harmon, William. "Animism and Kindred Delight." Rev. of *Selected and New Poems 1961–1981*. *Parnassus* Spring–Summer 1983: 129, 138–44.
68. "Books for Vacation Reading." Anonymous Rev. of *Selected and New Poems 1961–1981*. *New York Times Book Review* 12 June 1983.

## *Sundog*

69. Greene, A. C. "The Man-God of the Michigan Jungles." Rev. of *Sundog*. *New York Times* 15 July 1983: sec. 7, p. 14.
70. Untitled and anonymous Rev. of *Sundog*. *Publishers Weekly* 13 April 1984: 52.
71. Kakutani, Michiko. "Books of the Times." Rev. of *Sundog*. *New York Times* 21 May 1984: C14.
72. Iyer, Pico. "Romancing the Home." Rev. of *Sundog*. *Nation* 23 June 1984: 767, 768. This review was also reprinted as "Searching for America" in *Tropical Classical*. By Pico Iyer. New York: Alfred A. Knopf, 1997. 212–17.
73. Stielstra, Julie. "Real Men Get Struck by Lightning." Rev. of *Sundog*. *Michigan Voice* July–August 1984: 17.
74. Shack, Neville. "The Biographical Entails." Rev. of *Sundog*. *Times Literary Supplement* 16 August 1985: 907.
75. Deveson, Richards. "Call of the Wild." Rev. of *Sundog*. NS 23 August 1985: 28.

## *The Theory and Practice of Rivers*

76. Rohrkemper, John. Untitled Rev. of *The Theory and Practice of Rivers*. *Centennial Review* 30.4 (1986): 535–36.
77. Torgersen, Eric. "The Murmur of Gods." Rev. of *The Theory and Practice of Rivers*. *Borders Review* July 1986: 2. Borders Book Shop, Ann Arbor MI.
78. Muratori, Fred. Untitled Rev. of *The Theory and Practice of Rivers*. *Library Journal* August 1986.
79. Dischell, Stuart. Untitled Rev. of *The Theory and Practice of Rivers*. *Partisan Review* 2 (1987): 345–46. "Books" section.
80. Quammen, David. "The Lessons of Rivers." Rev. of *The Theory and Practice of Rivers*. *Outside* March 1989: 89, 118.
81. Hillringhouse, Mark. "Jim Harrison, *The Theory and Practice of Rivers*." Rev. of *The Theory and Practice of Rivers*. *Literary Review* Fall 1991: 157–58.

### Dalva

82. Yardley, Jonathan. "A Lonely Heart in the Heartland." Rev. of *Dalva*. *Washington Post Book World* 6 March 1988.
83. Kakutani, Michiko. "Epic America in a Woman's Quest." Rev. of *Dalva*. *New York Times* 9 March 1988: C25.
84. Clute, John. "Elegiac Heirs." Rev. of *Dalva*. *Times Literary Supplement* 14 March 1988: 299.
85. Erdrich, Louise. "*Dalva*: An Elegant Chorus of Passionate Voices Riding the Winds of Change." Rev. of *Dalva*. *Chicago Tribune* 20 March 1988: sec. 14, p. 1.
86. Jones-Davis, Georgia. "The Literary Seductions of a Macho Woman." Rev. of *Dalva*. *Los Angeles Times* 10 April 1988: 12.
87. Abbott, Raymond. "Savages and Sioux." Rev. of *Dalva*. *New York Times* 12 June 1988: sec. 7, p. 28.
88. Huey, Michael C. "Writing and Telling in Harrison's Latest." Rev. of *Dalva*. *Christian Science Monitor* 13 June 1988: 19.

### The Theory and Practice of Rivers and New Poems

89. Untitled and anonymous Rev. of *The Theory and Practice of Rivers and New Poems*. *Publishers Weekly* 25 August 1989.
90. Grinnell, James. "*The Theory and Practice of Rivers and New Poems*." Rev. of *The Theory and Practice of Rivers and New Poems*. *Bloomsbury Review* 10.3 (May–June 1990): 27.

### The Woman Lit by Fireflies

91. Horton, Diane. "Versatile, Vivacious, Vivid, Individual: Jim Harrison Shows Characteristic Talents in Three New Novellas." Rev. of *The Woman Lit by Fireflies*. *Kansas City Star* 1990.
92. Coates, Joseph. "Bedrock Americana: Jim Harrison Speaks of Worlds Where Nature and Spirit Are One." Rev. of *The Woman Lit by Fireflies*. *Chicago Tribune* 12 August 1990: sec. 14, pp. 1, 4.
93. Delbanco, Nicholas. "A Perfect Union: Varied Novellas Are Connected by Harrison's Voice." Rev. of *The Woman Lit by Fireflies*. *Detroit Free Press* 12 August 1990: 7Q.
94. Pintarich, Paul. "Swell Storytelling: Jim Harrison, Who Lives on Michigan's Remote Upper Peninsula Has Gone Too Long Unrecognized, Spins a Varied Web of Yarns." Rev. of *The Woman Lit by Fireflies*. *Sunday Portland Oregonian* 12 August 1990: C2.
95. Gerstel, Judy. "A Vulnerable Predator: Jim Harrison Writes with a Keen, Compassionate Eye." Rev. of *The Woman Lit by Fireflies*. *Detroit Free Press* 15 August 1990: 1D.

96. Freeman, Judith. "Women's Intimations." Rev. of *The Woman Lit by Fireflies*. *Los Angeles Times Book Review* 19 August 1990: 1, 5.
97. Buettler, Bill. "Sensitive Look at Midlife Fuels Harrison's 'Fireflies.'" Rev. of *The Woman Lit by Fireflies*. *Atlanta Journal-Constitution* 26 August 1990: N8.
98. Kakutani, Michiko. "The Shapes and Textures of 3 Lives." Rev. of *The Woman Lit by Fireflies*. *New York Times* 28 August 1990: C16.
99. Krystal, Arthur. "Jim Harrison: Three for the Road." Rev. of *The Woman Lit by Fireflies*. *Washington Post* 2 September 1990: 7.
100. Liebrum, Martha. "A Man of the Woods Writing about Women." Rev. of *The Woman Lit by Fireflies*. *Houston Post* 2 September 1990: C6.
101. Prichard, Peter S. "Grace and Grit in Harrison's *Fireflies*." Rev. of *The Woman Lit by Fireflies*. *USA Today* 7 September 1990: D4.
102. Harrington, Maureen. "A Man's Man Has Knack for Sounding Woman's Voice." Rev. of *A Woman Lit by Fireflies*. *Denver Post* 9 September 1990: E8.
103. Houston, Robert. "Love for the Proper Outlaw." Rev. of *The Woman Lit by Fireflies*. *New York Times* 16 September 1990: sec. 7, p. 13.
104. Rozen, Leah. "The Woman Lit by Fireflies." Rev. of *The Woman Lit by Fireflies*. *People* 29 October 1990: 36–37.
105. Shapiro, Nancy. "Words Macho, Magical." Rev. of *The Woman Lit by Fireflies*. *St. Louis Post-Dispatch* 4 November 1990: C5.
106. Beasecker, Robert. Untitled Rev. of *The Woman Lit by Fireflies*. *Chronicle* 27.1–2 (October 1993): 40, 41. Publication of the Historical Society of Michigan.
107. Hillebrand, Robert. "The Woman Lit by Fireflies." Rev. of *The Woman Lit by Fireflies*. *Booklovers* 5.3 (August–October 1997): 7, 9.

## *Just Before Dark*

108. McNamee, Gregory. Untitled Rev. of *Just Before Dark*. *Outside* July 1991: 102–103.
109. Jerome, John. "Caution: Men Writing." Rev. of *Just Before Dark*. *Book World* 28 July 1991. This review also appeared in the 2 July 1991 *Washington Post*.
110. Guy, David. "Visiting Inner Worlds *Just Before Dark*." Rev. of *Just Before Dark*. *USA Today* 25 July 1991: D8.
111. Bohaska, Chris. "Living Hard: Jim Harrison Devours Life." Rev. of *Just Before Dark*. *City Paper* 6 September 1991: 16–17.

## *Julip*

112. Cheuse, Alan. "Jim Harrison's Misfits: A Fatherless Woman, an Upper Peninsula Rogue and Victimized Academic." Rev. of *Julip*. *Chicago Tribune* 8 May 1994: sec. 14, p. 5.

113. Agee, Jonis. "The Macho Chronicles." Rev. of *Julip. New York Times* 22 May 1994: sec. 7, p. 41.
114. Mills, Jerry Leath. "Three Novellas, Three Lessons in Life." Rev. of *Julip. Atlanta Journal-Constitution* 22 May 1994: N12.
115. Long, Timothy. "Chronicler of Macho Angst Takes a New Direction." Rev. of *Julip. Boston Globe* 5 August 1994: B49.
116. Harrison, Alexander. "Seeking New Frontiers." Rev. of *Julip. Times Literary Supplement* 25 November 1994: 20.
117. Lyons, Daniel. "Author Returns to Short Stories, but with Less Power Than Before." Rev. of *Julip. Detroit Free Press* 20 March 1995: 3C.
118. Grinnell, James W. "*Julip.*" Rev. of *Julip. Bloomsbury Review* 15.3 (May–June 1995): 17.

## *The Road Home*

119. Minzesheimer, Bob. "Harrison's 'Road' Ends with Honors." Rev. of *The Road Home. USA Today* 1998.
120. "Two Old Friends Return to the Drum." Anonymous Rev. of *The Road Home. Shaman Drum Newsletter* September–October 1998: 1.
121. Cheuse, Alan. "An American Saga." Rev. of *The Road Home. BookPage* (Nashville TN) October 1998.
122. Clifford, Frank. "The Road Home." Rev. of *The Road Home. BookPage* (Nashville TN) October 1998.
123. Ferrari-Adler, Jofie. "Lives Deeply Connected." Rev. of *The Road Home. St. Petersburg FL Times* 4 October 1998: 5D.
124. Roelofs, Ted. "Harrison Unravels Family Mysteries on Nebraska Plains." Rev. of *The Road Home. Grand Rapids MI Press* 11 October 1998.
125. Dykes, Steve. "Harrison Heads 'Home.'" Rev. of *The Road Home. Boston Sunday Herald* 18 October 1998: 53.
126. Kissel, Howard. "American Heritage: Jim Harrison Tells One Family's Story through Generations of Journal Entries." Rev. of *The Road Home. New York Daily News* 18 October 1998. Also printed in the 1 November 1998 *St. Paul MN Pioneer Press* as "'Road' Work Ahead" and in the 30 November 1998 *Jacksonville FL Journal-Courier* as "Jim Harrison a Largely Unknown Great American Novelist."
127. Jones, Malcolm, Jr. "Book Marks." Rev. of *The Road Home. Newsweek* 19 October 1998:85.
128. BeVier, Tom. "A Natural Writer." Rev. of *The Road Home. Detroit Free Press* 20 October 1998: 1C–2C. Also published in *Atlantic City NJ Press* 1 November 1998. (See item J160 as well.)

129. Gallagher, John. "Harrison's 'Road Home': A Sad Tale of a Bitter Man." Rev. of *The Road Home*. *Detroit Free Press* 20 October 1998.
130. Moore, Judith. "The Road Home." Rev. of *The Road Home*. *San Diego Reader* 22 October 1998.
131. Goodykoontz, Bill. "Jim Harrison Caters to Fans' Appetites: 'Road Home' Takes Tantalizing Turns." Rev. of *The Road Home*. *Arizona Republic* 25 October 1998.
132. Phipps, Terry W. "Image Matters to Jim Harrison." Rev. of *The Road Home*. *Book* October–November 1998: 42–49.
133. Vogel, Traci. "Ah, Humanity." Rev. of *The Road Home*. *The Stranger* November 1998. In the "Readings" column. (See item J164 as well.)
134. Quackenbush, Rich. "'The Road Home' Is Well-Traveled." Rev. of *The Road Home*. *Houston Chronicle* 1 November 1998.
135. McNamee, Thomas. "O Pioneers!" Rev. of *The Road Home*. *New York Times* 8 November 1998: 11.
136. Egner, Diane. Rev. of *The Road Home*. *Tampa Tribune and Times* 15 November 1998. In the "New in Fiction" column.
137. Smith, Wendy. "Returning to the Earth." Rev. of *The Road Home*. *Washington Post* 15 November 1998.
138. Gwinn, Mary Ann. "Voices of Home: Jim Harrison's Powerful Novel Echoes through Four Generations of a Western Nebraska Family." Rev. of *The Road Home*. *Seattle Times and Post-Intelligencer* 15 November 1998.
139. Horvath, Brooke. "Getting a Soul to Clap Its Hands." Rev. of *The Road Home*. *Cleveland Plain Dealer* 22 November 1998.
140. Mort, Mona. "Evolutionary Journeys." Rev. of *The Road Home*. *Tucson Weekly* 26 November, 2 December 1998: 30, 33. (See item J174 as well.)
141. Untitled and anonymous Rev. of *The Road Home*. *Detroit Free Press* 28 November 1998.
142. Liebs, Scott. "O Nebraska." Rev. of *The Road Home*. *San Diego Union-Tribune* 29 November 1998: 11.
143. Untitled and anonymous Rev. of *The Road Home*. Amazon.com, 4 December 1998. Online source: http://amazon.com.
144. Johnson, Dennis Loy. "Throwback Harrison Crafts Something New." Rev. of *The Road Home*. *Sunday Greensburg PA Tribune Review* 6 December 1998.
145. Streitfeld, David. Rev. of *The Road Home*. *Washington Post* 13 December 1998. In the "Book Report" column. (See item J179 as well.)
146. Feeley, George. "10 Years Later, Author Picks Up Tale of Nebraska's Northridges." Rev. of *The Road Home*. *Philadelphia Inquirer* 3 January 1999.
147. Kunerth, Jeff. "Coasting on Life's Cycle." Rev. of *The Road Home*. *Riverside CA Press Enterprise* 10 January 1999. Also printed in the *Orlando Sentinel*.

148. Corcoran, Tom. "A Trip through Time and Nature." Rev. of *The Road Home*. *Los Angeles Times* 12 January 1999.
149. BeVier, Tom. "Harrison Cements His Literary Reputation." Rev. of *The Road Home*. *Chicago Tribune* 17 January 1999.
150. Grinnell, James. "Defined and Refined." Rev. of *The Road Home*. *Bloomsbury Review* 19.1 (January–February 1999). (See item J186 as well.)
151. Untitled and anonymous Rev. of *The Road Home*. *Bloomsbury Review* 19.1 (January–February 1999): 1, 5. (See item J187 as well.)
152. Kilgore, Richard. "Works Convey Copious Talents." Rev. of *The Road Home*. *Dallas Morning News* 14 February 1999. (See item J188 as well.)
153. Dumas, Alan. "Zest for the West: Jim Harrison Calls Evil Companions Honor an Award He Couldn't Refuse." Rev. of *The Road Home*. *Denver Rocky Mountain News* 1 April 1999.
154. Erion, Chuck. "Millennial List of Titles Traces a Life of Reading." Rev. of *The Road Home*. *Kitchener ON Record* 31 December 1999. Brief note.

### *The Shape of the Journey*

155. Untitled and anonymous Rev. of *The Shape of the Journey: New and Collected Poems*. *Minneapolis-St. Paul Star Tribune* 27 September 1998.
156. "The Poets of Our Age." Anonymous Rev. of *The Shape of the Journey: New and Collected Poems*. *Men's Journal* October 1998.
157. Seaman, Donna. Untitled Rev. of *The Shape of the Journey: New and Collected Poems*. *Booklist* 1 October 1998.
158. "Native Son: Harrison to Sign His Latest Books." Anonymous Rev. of *The Shape of the Journey: New and Collected Poems*. *Detroit Free Press* 12 October 1998.
159. Ratner, Rochelle. Untitled Rev. of *The Shape of the Journey: New and Collected Poems*. *Library Journal* 15 October 1998: 74.
160. BeVier, Tom. "A Natural Writer." Rev. of *The Shape of the Journey: New and Collected Poems*. *Detroit Free Press* 20 October 1998: 1C–2C. Also published in *Atlantic City NJ Press* 1 November 1998. (See item J128 as well.)
161. Moore, Judith. "Reading." Rev. of *The Shape of the Journey: New and Collected Poems*. *San Diego Reader* 22 October 1998.
162. "Author Profile: Jim Harrison." Anonymous Rev. of *The Shape of the Journey: New and Collected Poems*. *Prime* November 1998.
163. Untitled and anonymous Rev. of *The Shape of the Journey: New and Collected Poems*. *Shambhala Sun* November 1998.
164. Vogel, Traci. "Ah, Humanity." Rev. of *The Shape of the Journey: New and Collected Poems*. *The Stranger* November 1998. In the "Readings" column. (See item J133 as well.)

165. Untitled and anonymous Rev. of *The Shape of the Journey: New and Collected Poems*. *Publishers Weekly* 2 November 1998.
166. Flesher, John. "Poet of the Natural World." Rev. of *The Shape of the Journey: New and Collected Poems*. *Toledo OH Blade* 11 November 1998: 39. Also published as the Associated Press review "Famed Author Clings to Rural Roots in His Books and Life" in the 11 December 1998 *Philadelphia Tribune* and as "Author Clings to Rural Roots, Independence" in the 27 December 1998 *Ocala FL Star-Banner*.
167. Shea, Dennis. "Jim Harrison Bares His Poet's Mettle in a Collection from 'Up North.'" Rev. of *The Shape of the Journey: New and Collected Poems*. *Leelanau MI Metro Times* 11–17 November 1998.
168. Henry, Larry. Untitled Rev. of *The Shape of the Journey: New and Collected Poems*. *News and Revue* (Reno NV) 12 November 1998.
169. McNamee, Thomas. "'Road Home' Is Lined with Love." Rev. of *The Shape of the Journey: New and Collected Poems*. *Seattle Post-Intelligencer* 13 November 1998.
170. Skloot, Floyd. "Harrison's Poems Are Elegies for the Rural Life." Rev. of *The Shape of the Journey: New and Collected Poems*. *Sunday Portland Oregonian* 15 November 1998.
171. Johnson, Charles. "Harrison: Hitting a Sweet High C in Poetry." Rev. of *The Shape of the Journey: New and Collected Poems*. *Port Townsend WA Leader* 18 November 1998: B4.
172. Worth, January. "Poets Pack Their Prose with the Power of Passion, Death and Great Outdoors." Rev. of *The Shape of the Journey: New and Collected Poems*. *Detroit Free Press* 18 November 1998.
173. Lyke, M. L. "Writer Harrison Takes His Own Road: And the Ride Can Be Rough." Rev. of *The Shape of the Journey: New and Collected Poems*. *Seattle Post-Intelligencer* 23 November 1998: D1, D3.
174. Mort, Mona. "Evolutionary Journeys." Rev. of *The Shape of the Journey: New and Collected Poems*. *Tucson Weekly* 26 November, 2 December 1998: 30, 33. (See item J140 as well.)
175. Buzzelli, Elizabeth Kane. Untitled Rev. of *The Shape of the Journey: New and Collected Poems*. *Traverse City MI Record-Eagle* 29 November 1998.
176. Cassell, Faris. Untitled Rev. of *The Shape of the Journey: New and Collected Poems*. *Eugene OR Register-Guard* 29 November 1998. In the "Northwest Bound" column.
177. Swan, Alison. Untitled Rev. of *The Shape of the Journey: New and Collected Poems*. *Current* (Ann Arbor MI) December 1998.
178. Untitled and anonymous Rev. of *The Shape of the Journey: New and Collected Poems*. *Seattle Times and Post-Intelligencer* 6 December 1998.

179. Streitfeld, David. Rev. of *The Shape of the Journey: New and Collected Poems*. *Washington Post* 13 December 1998. In the "Book Report" column. (See item J145 as well.)
180. Untitled and anonymous Rev. of *The Shape of the Journey: New and Collected Poems*. *Providence RI Sunday Journal* 20 December 1998.
181. Untitled and anonymous review of *The Shape of the Journey: New and Collected Poems*. *American Poet* Winter 1998–99.
182. Oser, Lee. Untitled Rev. of *The Shape of the Journey: New and Collected Poems*. *World Literature Today* Autumn 1999. Literary quarterly of the University of Oklahoma.
183. Untitled and anonymous Rev. of *The Shape of the Journey: New and Collected Poems*. *Biblio* January 1999.
184. Davenport, Arlice. "Nature, Mind Converge in Harrison's 'Journey.'" Rev. of *The Shape of the Journey: New and Collected Poems*. *Wichita Eagle* 3 January 1999: 4D–5D.
185. Veale, Scott. "Eat Drink Man Woman." Rev. of *The Shape of the Journey: New and Collected Poems*. *New York Times* 3 January 1999: 15.
186. Grinnell, James. "Defined and Refined." Rev. of *The Shape of the Journey: New and Collected Poems*. *Bloomsbury Review* 19.1 (January–February 1999). (See item J150 as well.)
187. Untitled and anonymous Rev. of *The Shape of the Journey: New and Collected Poems*. *Bloomsbury Review* 19.1 (January–February 1999): 1, 5. (See item J151 as well.)
188. Kilgore, Richard. "Works Convey Copious Talents." Rev. of *The Shape of the Journey: New and Collected Poems*. *Dallas Morning News* 14 February 1999. (See item J152 as well.)
189. Untitled and anonymous Rev. of *The Shape of the Journey: New and Collected Poems*. *Oakland Press* (Pontiac MI) 24 February 1999.
190. Untitled and anonymous Rev. of *The Shape of the Journey: New and Collected Poems*. *Booklist* 15 March 1999: 1276. In the "Spotlight on Poetry" column.
191. Walker, Kevin. "Library Review of Poetry Books Receives the 'Thumbs Up' Sign." Rev. of *The Shape of the Journey: New and Collected Poems*. *Brighton MI Argus* 24 March 1999.
192. Porter, William. "Road Trips a Must for Jim Harrison." Rev. of *The Shape of the Journey: New and Collected Poems*. *Denver Post* 4 April 1999: 1, 6.
193. Thorpe, Peter. Untitled Rev. of *The Shape of the Journey: New and Collected Poems*. *Denver Rocky Mountain News* 11 April 1999.
194. Waddington, Chris. "Harrison: Fans of His Prose Will Find Much Familiar in His Poetry." Rev. of *The Shape of the Journey: New and Collected Poems*. *Minneapolis-St. Paul Star Tribune* 11 April 1999.

195. "Harrison 'Journey' Finds Truth in Poetry." Anonymous Rev. of *The Shape of the Journey: New and Collected Poems*. Traverse City MI *Record-Eagle* 23 May 1999.
196. Graber, Michael. "Poet's Collected 'Journey' Stretches for Too Many Miles." Rev. of *The Shape of the Journey: New and Collected Poems*. *Memphis Commercial Appeal* 6 June 1999.
197. Archibeque, Carlyle. Untitled Rev. of *The Shape of the Journey: New and Collected Poems*. (SIC) *VICE and VERSE* 7 (June–July 1999).
198. Hatch, James. "Moments of Glad Grace." Rev. of *The Shape of the Journey: New and Collected Poems*. *American Book Review* November–December 1999: 20–21.
199. Gifford, Barry. Untitled Rev. of *The Shape of the Journey: New and Collected Poems*. *First Intensity* (Berkeley CA) 14 (Spring 2000).
200. Taylor, Henry. "Next-to-Last Things." Rev. of *The Shape of the Journey: New and Collected Poems*. *Poetry* May 2000: 96, 99–102.

### *The Boy Who Ran to the Woods*

201. Untitled and anonymous Rev. of *The Boy Who Ran to the Woods*. *Publishers Weekly* 17 July 2000: 120.
202. Green, Lynn. "Boyz 'n the Woods: My Little Runaway." Rev. of *The Boy Who Ran to the Woods*. *BookPage* (Nashville TN) October 2000: 33.
203. Sundstrom, Nancy. "Honest Reflection, Uncommon Perception." Rev. of *The Boy Who Ran to the Woods*. *Bay Area Times Magazine* (Traverse City MI) October 2000: 7–8. (See item J231 as well.)
204. Untitled and anonymous Rev. of *The Boy Who Ran to the Woods*. *Publishers Weekly* 2 October 2000: 82.
205. Eberhart, John Mark. "Novella Ideas." Rev. of *The Boy Who Ran to the Woods*. *Kansas City Star* 15 October 2000. (See item J238 as well.)
206. "Nurtured by Nature." Anonymous Rev. of *The Boy Who Ran to the Woods*. *Austin American-Statesman* 19 October 2000.
207. McNulty, Tim. "Two New Books Show Harrison's Very Wide Range." Rev. of *The Boy Who Ran to the Woods*. *Seattle Times* 22 October 2000. (See item J243 as well.)
208. Burke, Lynne. "Renowned Authors Turn Their Efforts to the Early-to-Bed Set." Rev. of *The Boy Who Ran to the Woods*. *Minneapolis-St. Paul Star Tribune* 23 October 2000.
209. Patterson, J. C. "Legend Times Four: Literary Great Jim Harrison Returns with Three Novellas and a Children's Book." Anonymous Rev. of *The Boy Who Ran to the Woods*. *Planet Weekly* 26 October, 1 November 2000. (See item J245 as well.)

210. McMahon, Regan. "Harrison Heads to the Woods." Rev. of *The Boy Who Ran to the Woods*. *San Francisco Chronicle* 29 October 2000.

211. Harrelson, Barbara. "A Bad Boy Takes Refuge in the Forest." Rev. of *The Boy Who Ran to the Woods*. *Santa Fe New Mexican* 5 November 2000.

212. Kilgore, Richard. "The Beast Within: Harrison's Short Stories Examine Shifting Personalities of His Characters and Himself." Rev. of *The Boy Who Ran to the Woods*. *Dallas Morning News* 24 January 2001. (See item J279 as well.)

213. Perry, Susan. "Bringing Literature to Life: Recommended Books." Rev. of *The Boy Who Ran to the Woods*. *Bay Area Parent* November 2002: 25. In the "Playing Smart" column.

214. Diaz, Vicki. "These Books Make Perfect Holiday Gifts for Children." Rev. of *The Boy Who Ran to the Woods*. *Livonia MI Observer* 24 November 2002.

## *The Beast God Forgot to Invent*

215. Bing, Jonathan. "Fiction Forecast." Rev. of *The Beast God Forgot to Invent*. *BookForum* 2000: 28.

216. French, Kate. "When the Egg Cracks: Three Protagonists See It Again for the First Time." Rev. of *The Beast God Forgot to Invent*. *Yale Review of Books* Winter 2000: 7.

217. Feld, Ross. "Lone Wolves." Rev. of *The Beast God Forgot to Invent*. *Ruminator Review* Winter 2000–2001: 27.

218. Hoffert, Barbara. "PrePub Alert." Rev. of *The Beast God Forgot to Invent*. *Library Journal* 15 June 2000: 58.

219. Morris, Anna. "New Fall Books Will Knock Your Sandals Off." Rev. of *The Beast God Forgot to Invent*. *Austin American-Statesman* 22 June 2000: E2.

220. Caso, Frank. Untitled Rev. of *The Beast God Forgot to Invent*. *Booklist* July 2000. Starred review in the "Upfront" section.

221. Kloszewski, Marc. Untitled Rev. of *The Beast God Forgot to Invent*. *Library Journal* August 2000: 164.

222. Untitled and anonymous Rev. of *The Beast God Forgot to Invent*. *Kirkus Reviews* 1 August 2000.

223. Coe, Richard. "New Novella Triptych Is Vintage Harrison." Rev. of *The Beast God Forgot to Invent*. *Anniston AL Star* 6 August 2000.

224. Anonymous and untitled Rev. of *The Beast God Forgot to Invent*. *Publishers Weekly* 7 August 2000: 72. In the "Forecasts" section.

225. Anonymous and untitled Rev. of *The Beast God Forgot to Invent*. *Publishers Weekly* 4 September 2000: 63.

226. "Fall 2000 Special Preview Issue." Anonymous Rev. of *The Beast God Forgot to Invent*. *KOEN25* 8 September 2000. From Koen Book Distributors.

227. Waddington, Chris. "Bookmarks: Fall Arts Preview." Rev. of *The Beast God Forgot to Invent. Minneapolis-St. Paul Star Tribune* 10 September 2000.
228. McKee, Jenn. Untitled Rev. of *The Beast God Forgot to Invent. BookPage* (Nashville TN) October 2000: 33.
229. Moss, Peyton. Untitled Rev. of *The Beast God Forgot to Invent. ForeWord* 3.10 (October 2000): 51–52.
230. "Pen Names." Anonymous Rev. of *The Beast God Forgot to Invent. Lemuria Literary Type* 26.1 (October 2000). Monthly newsletter from Lemuria Books in Jackson MS.
231. Sundstrom, Nancy. "Honest Reflection, Uncommon Perception." Rev. of *The Beast God Forgot to Invent. Bay Area Times Magazine* (Traverse City MI) October 2000: 7–8. (See item J203 as well.)
232. Franscell, Ron. "Jim Harrison and His Primal Men." Rev. of *The Beast God Forgot to Invent. Chicago Sun-Times* 1 October 2000: 17E, 20E.
233. Antonucci, Ron. "Trio of Novellas Written by a Master." Rev. of *The Beast God Forgot to Invent. Cleveland Plain Dealer* 8 October 2000.
234. Berthel, Ron. Untitled Rev. of *The Beast God Forgot to Invent. Pittsburgh Tribune-Review* 8 October 2000.
235. Drahos, Marta Hepler. "A Look Back, a Look Ahead." Rev. of *The Beast God Forgot to Invent. Traverse City MI Record-Eagle* 8 October 2000: 2F. (See item H108 as well.)
236. Salter Reynolds, Susan. Untitled Rev. of *The Beast God Forgot to Invent. Los Angeles Times Book Review* 8 October 2000: 11.
237. Patterson, J. C. "Beast Is Harrison's Wisest, Slyest." Rev. of *The Beast God Forgot to Invent. Jackson MS Clarion Ledger* 9 October 2000: 3G.
238. Eberhart, John Mark. "Novella Ideas." Rev. of *The Beast God Forgot to Invent. Kansas City Star* 15 October 2000. (See item J205 as well.)
239. Lange, Pam. "The Man Show." Rev. of *The Beast God Forgot to Invent. Austin American-Statesman* 19 October 2000: L6-L-7.
240. Miles, Jonathan. Untitled Rev. of *The Beast God Forgot to Invent. Salon.com.* http://www.salon.com/book/review/2000/10/19/harrison/index.html (accessed 19 October 2000; site discontinued).
241. Garner, Dwight. "Sauternes and Spaghetti: Jim Harrison's Life Affirmers Will Swallow Anything." Rev. of *The Beast God Forgot to Invent. New York Times Book Review* 20 October 2000: 9.
242. Franscell, Ron. "Jim Harrison Strips Away Layers of Men in New Collection." Rev. of *The Beast God Forgot to Invent. Milwaukee Journal Sentinel* 22 October 2000.
243. McNulty, Tim. "Two New Books Show Harrison's Very Wide Range." Rev.

of *The Beast God Forgot to Invent*. *Seattle Times* 22 October 2000. (See item J207 as well.)

244. Eberhart, John Mark. "Harrison's Novellas Fill the Bill When You're Short on Time." Rev. of *The Beast God Forgot to Invent*. *Chicago Tribune* 23 October 2000.

245. Patterson, J. C. "Legend Times Four: Literary Great Jim Harrison Returns with Three Novellas and a Children's Book." Rev. of *The Beast God Forgot to Invent*. *Planet Weekly* 26 October–1 November 2000. (See item J209 as well.)

246. MacMillan, Alissa. "Pages." Rev. of *The Beast God Forgot to Invent*. *New York Daily News* 29 October 2000.

247. Mesler, Corey. "A Trio of Unlikely Heroes Seek out Meaning in Vulgar Preoccupations." Rev. of *The Beast God Forgot to Invent*. *Memphis Commercial Appeal* 29 October 2000.

248. Barcott, Bruce. Untitled Rev. of *The Beast God Forgot to Invent*. *Outside* November 2000: 182.

249. Smith, Patrick. "A Man's Man's World." Rev. of *The Beast God Forgot to Invent*. *January Magazine* November 2000. Online magazine.

250. Carvalho, Jim. "Old Dudes and Derriere." Rev. of *The Beast God Forgot to Invent*. *Tucson Weekly* 2 November 2000: 44.

251. Shipley, Jonathan. Untitled Rev. of *The Beast God Forgot to Invent*. Bookreporter.com 3 November 2000. Online review on Bookreporter.com.

252. "And Bear in Mind." Anonymous Rev. of *The Beast God Forgot to Invent*, *New York Times Book Review* 5 November 2000.

253. Byrne, Steve. "Back in Form." Rev. of *The Beast God Forgot to Invent*. *Detroit Free Press* 5 November 2000.

254. Fiedler, Terry. "Call of the Mild: Three Novellas Are Two-Thirds Classic Harrison." Rev. of *The Beast God Forgot to Invent*. *Minneapolis-St. Paul Star Tribune* 5 November 2000.

255. Franscell, Ron. "Animal Magnetism and the Myths of Masculinity." Rev. of *The Beast God Forgot to Invent*. *San Francisco Chronicle* 5 November 2000.

256. Buzzelli, Elizabeth Kane. "Harrison's 'Beast' Leads to Edge of Despair: Natural Man Is Pitted against Plastic Life in Stirring Novella." Rev. of *The Beast God Forgot to Invent*. *Traverse City MI Record-Eagle* 12 November 2000.

257. MacDonald, Jay. "Harrison Shuns Spotlight." Rev. of *The Beast God Forgot to Invent*. *Fort Myers FL News-Press* 12 November 2000.

258. MacDonald, Jay. "Beastly Novella Trilogy Brilliant." Rev. of *The Beast God Forgot to Invent*. *Fort Myers FL News-Press* 12 November 2000.

259. Salij, Marta. "The Beast." Rev. of *The Beast God Forgot to Invent*. *Detroit Free Press* 15 November 2000: 3.

260. Eberhart, John Mark. "The Busy Writer Tells His Stories." Rev. of *The Beast God Forgot to Invent*. Fredericksburg VA *Free Lance–Star* 19 November 2000: F6.
261. Kilby, Damian. "Jim Harrison on the Male Animal." Rev. of *The Beast God Forgot to Invent*. Portland *Oregonian* 19 November 2000: G-9, G-11.
262. "Fiction: A Feast of New Voices, Old Favorites." Anonymous Rev. of *The Beast God Forgot to Invent*. *Atlanta Journal-Constitution* 26 November 2000.
263. Bancroft, Colette. "Novella Collection Hits the Mark." Rev. of *The Beast God Forgot to Invent*. St. Petersburg FL *Times* 26 November 2000: 4D.
264. Schneider, Wolf. "The Rejuvenation of the Middle-Aged Man." Rev. of *The Beast God Forgot to Invent*. *Santa Fe New Mexican* 26 November 2000.
265. Grinnell, Jim. "Searching for Suitable Habitat and Contentment." Rev. of *The Beast God Forgot to Invent*. *Bloomsbury Review* November–December 2000.
266. Lawrence, Russ. Untitled Rev. of *The Beast God Forgot to Invent*. *Book Sense* 76 November–December 2000: 2.
267. Anonymous and untitled Rev. of *The Beast God Forgot to Invent*. *Tampa Tribune* December 2000. In the "New in Fiction" section.
268. "The Best Fiction of 2000." Anonymous Rev. of *The Beast God Forgot to Invent*. *Los Angeles Times Book Review* 3 December 2000: 2.
269. Cryer, Dan. "From Hunter to Connoisseur." Rev. of *The Beast God Forgot to Invent*. *Newsday* 3 December 2000.
270. Anonymous and untitled Rev. of *The Beast God Forgot to Invent*. *New York Times Book Review* 3 December 2000: 166. In the "Notable Books" section.
271. Jones, Malcolm. "Critical Moment." Rev. of *The Beast God Forgot to Invent*. *Newsweek* 4 December 2000: 69.
272. Anonymous and untitled Rev. of *The Beast God Forgot to Invent*. *Publishers Weekly Daily* 6 December 2000.
273. Houston, Pam. "Hideous Men." Rev. of *The Beast God Forgot to Invent*. *Washington Post* 17 December 2000: 9.
274. Porter, William. "Jim Harrison Older, Smarter, Delving Deeper." Rev. of *The Beast God Forgot to Invent*. *Denver Post* 17 December 2000.
275. Murphy, Eileen. "A Man's World: What Lies beneath Jim Harrison's Macho Bluster." Rev. of *The Beast God Forgot to Invent*. *Baltimore City Paper* 27 December 2000.
276. Prozak, Christian. "The Beast God Forgot to Invent." Rev. of *The Beast God Forgot to Invent*. *Exquisite Corpse: A Journal of Letters and Life* Online Issue 8 (Spring 2001). Online journal www.corpse.org.
277. Franscell, Ron. "Stopping to Ponder the Nature of the 'Beast.'" Rev. of *The Beast God Forgot to Invent*. *Atlanta Journal-Constitution* 14 January 2001.
278. Florio, Gwen. "Aging Characters from an Aging Pen." Rev. of *The Beast God Forgot to Invent*. *Philadelphia Inquirer* 21 January 2001.

279. Kilgore, Richard. "The Beast Within: Harrison's Short Stories Examine Shifting Personalities of His Characters and Himself." Rev. of *The Beast God Forgot to Invent*. *Dallas Morning News* 24 January 2001. (See item J212 as well.)
280. Weiss, Philip. "As I Grow Middle-Aged, I Like the Old Broads." Rev. of *The Beast God Forgot to Invent*. *New York Observer* 5 February 2001: 1, 13.
281. Shreve, Porter. "Where Human Meets Nature." Rev. of *The Beast God Forgot to Invent*. *Boston Globe* 8 April 2001: 2.
282. Waddington, Chris. Untitled Rev. of *The Raw and the Cooked*. *Minneapolis-St. Paul Star Tribune* 5 October 2001.
283. Veale, Scott. Untitled Rev. of *The Beast God Forgot to Invent*. *New York Times Book Review* 28 October 2001: 32. In the "New and Noteworthy Paperbacks" section.
284. Waddington, Chris. "Come and Get It! Food Essays Are the Cherry atop Harrison's Literary Career." Rev. of *The Raw and the Cooked*. *Minneapolis-St. Paul Star Tribune* 28 October 2001.
285. Anonymous and untitled Rev. of *The Beast God Forgot to Invent*. *Denver Rocky Mountain News* 2 November 2001. In the "Paperback Picks" section.

**The Raw and the Cooked: Adventures of a Roving Gourmand**

286. Anonymous and untitled Rev. of *The Raw and the Cooked*. *Publishers Weekly* 13 August 2001: 188.
287. Miller, Wendy. Untitled Rev. of *The Raw and the Cooked*. *Library Journal* 1 September 2001.
288. Untitled and anonymous Rev. of *The Raw and the Cooked*. *Kirkus Reviews* 15 September 2001: 1338. In the "Nonfiction" section.
289. Anonymous and untitled Rev. of *The Raw and the Cooked*. *Publishers Weekly* 17 September 2001: 63.
290. Trachtenberg, Jeffrey A. "Bookmarks." Rev. of *The Raw and the Cooked*. *Wall Street Journal* 26 October 2001.
291. Anonymous and untitled Rev. of *The Raw and the Cooked*. *Minneapolis-St. Paul Star Tribune* 28 October 2001.
292. Anonymous and untitled Rev. of *The Raw and the Cooked*. *Salon.com* 8 November 2001. An online review in the "New in Paperback" section.
293. Berthel, Ron. "Kennedy Family in the Spotlight Again in November's New Books." Rev. of *The Raw and the Cooked*. *Pittsburgh Tribune-Review* 11 November 2001.
294. Farkus, David. "Food Essays Are Hard to Digest." Rev. of *The Raw and the Cooked*. *Cleveland Plain Dealer* 11 November 2001. Also available online at Cleveland.com.

295. Stephenson, Anne. Untitled Rev. of *The Raw and the Cooked*. *Arizona Republic* 11 November 2001. In the "New and Notable" section.
296. Byrne, Steve. "Harrison Outlines Culinary Journey." Rev. of *The Raw and the Cooked*. *Detroit Free Press* 25 November 2001.
297. Stern, Jane, and Michael Stern. "Pass the Bicarb." Rev. of *The Raw and the Cooked*. *New York Times Book Review* 25 November 2001: 8.
298. Rosati, Arianna Pavia. "The Holy Grail: A Perfect Meal." Rev. of *The Raw and the Cooked*. *Hartford CT Courant* 25 November 2001.
299. Keeler, Janet. "Tasty Holiday Treats." Rev. of *The Raw and the Cooked*. *St. Petersburg FL Times* 2 December 2001.
300. Stephenson, Anne. "Tasty Essays." Rev. of *The Raw and the Cooked*. *Denver Post* 7 December 2001.
301. Stephenson, Anne. "Tasty Essays." Rev. of *The Raw and the Cooked*. *Denver Rocky Mountain News* 7 December 2001.
302. Anonymous and untitled Rev. of *The Raw and the Cooked*. *Houston Chronicle* 8 December 2002. In the "New in Paperback" section.
303. Gamino, John. "Collection Makes for a Delicious Stew." Rev. of *The Raw and the Cooked*. *Dallas Morning News* 9 December 2001. Also available online at DallasNews.com.
304. Untitled and anonymous Rev. of *The Raw and the Cooked*. *Parsippany NJ Daily Record* 9 December 2001.
305. Skowles, John. "Nonfiction in Brief." Rev. of *The Raw and the Cooked*. *Atlanta Journal-Constitution* 9 December 2001.
306. "Food Writing from the Edge." Anonymous Rev. of *The Raw and the Cooked*. *Fort Worth Star-Telegram* 10 December 2001.
307. "Essay Collection." Anonymous Rev. of *The Raw and the Cooked*. *Santa Fe New Mexican* 23 December 2001.
308. Skowles, John. "Well Done." Rev. of *The Raw and the Cooked*. *San Diego Union-Tribune* 23 December 2001.
309. Byrne, Steve. "Food for Thought." Rev. of *The Raw and the Cooked*. *San Antonio Express-News—Morning Edition* 30 December 2001.
310. Porter, William. "Harrison Sates His Appetites." Rev. of *The Raw and the Cooked*. *Denver Post* 30 December 2001.
311. Anonymous and untitled Rev. of *The Raw and the Cooked*. *Hour Detroit* (Royal Oak MI) January 2002.
312. Torrey, Beef. "A Feast of Words." Rev. of *The Raw and the Cooked*. *Lincoln NE Journal Star* 6 January 2002: 8x.
313. Graham, Barry. "Harrison's Musings on Cooking and Eating Are Far-Reaching." Rev. of *The Raw and the Cooked*. *Chattanooga TN Times Free Press* 13 January 2002.

314. Lindsey, Craig D. "Jim Harrison Serves a Filling Meal That's Unfulfilling." Rev. of *The Raw and the Cooked*. *Houston Chronicle* 22 February 2002. Available online at HoustonChronicle.com
315. Carvalho, Jim. "Gut Buster." Rev. of *The Raw and the Cooked*. *Tucson Weekly* 26 February–6 March 2002: 48.
316. Baldwin, Robert. Untitled Rev. of *The Raw and the Cooked*. *Bloomsbury Review* 22.3 (May–June 2002): 8–9. In the "Cookbooks" section.
317. Veale, Scott. "New and Noteworthy Paperbacks." Rev. of *The Raw and the Cooked*. *New York Times Book Review* 2 December 2002: 28.
318. Anonymous and untitled Rev. of *The Raw and the Cooked*. *Saveur* February 2007. In the same issue, there is a brief mention of this title in the feature "The Saveur 100."

## *Off to the Side*

319. Anonymous and untitled Rev. of *Off to the Side*. *Publishers Weekly* 12 August 2002: 166.
320. Anonymous and untitled Rev. of *Off to the Side*. *Publishers Weekly* 26 August 2002: 51.
321. Anonymous and untitled Rev. of *Off to the Side*. *Kirkus Reviews* 1 September 2002.
322. Anonymous and untitled Rev. of *Off to the Side*. *Washington Post Book World* 15 September 2002. Fall preview.
323. "New and Noteworthy Paperbacks." Anonymous Rev. of *Off to the Side*. *New York Times Book Review* 5 October 2003: 28.
324. Yardley, Jonathan. "A Plainspoken Writer Recalls His Old-Fashioned Ascent." Rev. of *Off to the Side*. *Washington Post* 11 October 2002: BW02.
325. Rowen, John. "Author's Memoir Is Tale of Overcoming Adversity." Rev. of *Off to the Side*. *Schenectady NY Gazette* 27 October 2002: G6.
326. Mudge, Alden. "Jim Harrison's Wild Ride." Rev. of *Off to the Side*. *BookPage* (Nashville TN) November 2002: 11.
327. Miles, Jonathan. "A Life, in Excess." Rev. of *Off to the Side*. *Men's Journal* November 2002: 54.
328. Dyer, Daniel. "You Might Not Like Him, but You'll Enjoy His Story." Rev. of *Off to the Side*. *Cleveland Plain Dealer* 3 November 2002.
329. Cryer, Dan. "From the Farm to Hollywood, and Back." Rev. of *Off to the Side*. *Newsday* 7 November 2002.
330. McNulty, Tim. "Jim Harrison's Best Character May Just Be Jim Harrison." Rev. of *Off to the Side*. *Seattle Times* 8 November 2002.
331. Nicholas, Robert L. "Jim Harrison: The Interview." Rev. of *Off to the Side*. *Oxford Town* 14 November 2002: 10, 11. (See item H113 as well.)

332. Ensslin, John. "Side Lines." Rev. of *Off to the Side*. *Denver Post* 15 November 2002.

333. Ensslin, John. "Side Lines." Rev. of *Off to the Side*. *Denver Rocky Mountain News* 15 November 2002: 23D, 29D. Also available online at http://www.rockymountainnews.com.

334. Westrum, Dex. "A Literary Life." Rev. of *Off to the Side*. *Milwaukee Journal Sentinel* 17 November 2002: 6.

335. "Harrison Signs Memoirs at Lemuria." Anonymous Rev. of *Off to the Side*. *Planet Weekly* 20 November 2002.

336. Van Wyngarden, Bruce. Untitled Rev. of *Off to the Side*. *Memphis Flyer* 21 November 2002: 30–31.

337. Marshall, John. "*Off to the Side* Is an Enticing Ramble, Detours and All." Rev. of *Off to the Side*. *Seattle Post-Intelligencer* 22 November 2002. Also available online at http://seattlepi.nwsource.com.

338. Baker, Jeff. "Jim Harrison: A Raw, Cooked Life." Rev. of *Off to the Side*. *Portland Oregonian* 24 November 2002: E7, E10.

339. Barcott, Bruce. "Living Large." Rev. of *Off to the Side*. *New York Times Book Review* 24 November 2002: 22.

340. MacDonald, Jay. "From Pauper to Hollywood, Harrison's Written through it." Rev. of *Off to the Side*. *Ft. Myers News-Press* 24 November 2002. Also available online at news-press.com.

341. MacDonald, Jay. "*Off to the Side* Aptly Describes Novelist." Rev. of *Off to the Side*. *Ft. Myers FL News-Press* 24 November 2002. Also available online at news-press.com.

342. Salter Reynolds, Susan. "A Writer at Life's Banquet." Rev. of *Off to the Side*. *Los Angeles Times* 24 November 2002. In the "Style and Culture" section.

343. Sallis, James. "Convey the Physical and the Cerebral." Rev. of *Off to the Side*. *Boston Globe* 24 November 2002.

344. "The Star's 100 Noteworthy Books of 2002." Anonymous Rev. of *Off to the Side*. *Kansas City Star* 24 November 2002: 21. Not a review in the classic sense, it simply cites 100 noteworthy books of 2002: "Forthright memoir is no surprise, coming from this large-spirited literary rebel."

345. Pohrt, Karl. "76 Independent Bookseller Recommendations." Rev. of *Off to the Side*. *Book Sense* November–December 2002: 12.

346. Buchanan, Rob. "The Manly Diaries." Rev. of *Off to the Side*. *Outside* December 2002: 34.

347. Gargan, William. Untitled Rev. of *Off to the Side*. *Library Journal* December 2002.

348. Torrey, Beef. "On Being a Big Deal." Rev. of *Off to the Side*. *Independent Publisher* December 2002. Available only online: www.independentpublisher.com.
349. Byrne, Steve. "The Writer Who Ran to the Woods." Rev. of *Off to the Side*. *Detroit Free Press* 1 December 2002.
350. Yardley, Jonathan. Untitled Rev. of *Off to the Side*. *Washington Post* 1 December 2002: 2.
351. "And Bear in Mind." Anonymous Rev. of *Off to the Side*. *New York Times Book Review* 1 December 2002: 26. Editor's choices of other recent books of particular interest.
352. Idema, James. "A Big Man Writes about the Big Life Outdoors." Rev. of *Off to the Side*. *Santa Fe New Mexican* 1 December 2002: 6.
353. "Notable Nonfiction." Anonymous Rev. of *Off to the Side*. *New York Times Book Review* 8 December 2002: 70.
354. Pohrt, Karl. "The Book Sense Best Recent Titles Overall." Rev. of *Off to the Side*. *White Plains NY Central Journal News* 8 December 2002.
355. Geier, Thom. "Off to the Side." Rev. of *Off to the Side*. *Entertainment Weekly* 13 December 2002: 89.
356. Torrey, Beef. "A Life Well Lived." Rev. of *Off to the Side*. *Lincoln NE Journal Star* 15 December 2002: 8x.
357. Corbett, William. "Sidelines: Jim Harrison's Storied Career." Rev. of *Off to the Side*. *Phoenix Sun* 16 December 2002.
358. Murphy, Bernadette. "Memoir Is Author's Hideaway." Rev. of *Off to the Side*. *Los Angeles Times* 17 December 2002: 5. In the "Style and Culture/Book Review" section.
359. Diaz, Victoria. "Former Michigan Author's Memoir Makes You Cry, Laugh." Rev. of *Off to the Side*. *Livonia MI Observer* 22 December 2002: 23.
360. Waddington, Chris. "In the Flesh." Rev. of *Off to the Side*. *Minneapolis-St. Paul Star Tribune* 22 December 2002: F16.
361. Nicholas, Robert L. "*Off to the Side*: A Memoir by Jim Harrison." Rev. of *Off to the Side*. *Magnolia MS Gazette* 26 December 2002: B1.
362. Kilgore, Richard. "An Artist Embraces Life, Regrets and All." Rev. of *Off to the Side*. *Dallas Morning News* 29 December 2002: 2.
363. Dombrowski, Christophe. Untitled Rev. of *Off to the Side*. *Big Sky Journal* 5.3 (Spring 2003): 134. An untitled review in the "Books" section.
364. Beck, Judith Neuman. "Harrison Memoir Has Heart." Rev. of *Off to the Side*. *San Jose Mercury News* 12 January 2003.
365. Bass, Rick. "Memoir of a Gifted Geezer." Rev. of *Off to the Side*. *Shambhala Sun* March 2003: 91–94.

366. Parrett, Aaron. "Harrison's *Off to the Side* Is Right on Target as Memoirs Go." Rev. of *Off to the Side*. *Great Falls* MT *Tribune* 23 March 2003: 1P, 5P.
367. Graham, Barry. "Alcohol, Testosterone and Lithium." Rev. of *Off to the Side*. *Detroit Metro Times* 4 April 2003: 46.
368. Grant, Richard. "Out to Lunch." Rev. of *Off to the Side*. *Telegraph Magazine* 7 June 2003: 86–89. Photographs by Michael Kelley.
369. Vice, Brad. "Harrison Tells Great Stories in Blustering Memoir." Rev. of *Off to the Side*. *San Francisco Chronicle* 5 December 2003: 2.
370. Cronin, Justin. "In His Manly Memoir, Harrison Offers Candor and Chaos." Rev. of *Off to the Side*. *Boston Globe* 29 December 2003.

## *Braided Creek*

371. Untitled and anonymous Rev. of *Braided Creek*. *Lincoln* NE *Journal Star* 2003.
372. Grinnell, Jim. Untitled Rev. of *Braided Creek*. *Bloomsbury Review* 23.2 (March–April 2003).
373. Olson, Ray. Untitled Rev. of *Braided Creek*. *Houston Chronicle* 1 April 2003.
374. Untitled and anonymous Rev. of *Braided Creek*. *Booklist* 1 April 2003.
375. Eberhart, John Mark. "A Plaint Not So Plaintive." Rev. of *Braided Creek*. *Kansas City Star* 11 May 2003.
376. Reese, Jim. "Harrison and Kooser Remind Us of What We May Be Missing." Rev. of *Braided Creek*. *Lincoln* NE *Journal Star* 25 May 2003: 3K.
377. DeMott, Robert. Untitled Rev. of *Braided Creek*. *Quarter After Eight* 11.12 (2004–05): 251–54.

## *True North*

378. MacDonald, Jay. "Author Explores Dark Side of Immense Wealth." Rev. of *True North*. *Ft. Myers* FL *News-Press* 9 May 2004.
379. Tschida, Ron. "An Original Voice: Savor the Writings of Jim Harrison, One of America's Best, in His New Book, *True North*." Rev. of *True North*. *Bozeman* MT *Daily Chronicle* 14–20 May 2004: 16–17. In the "This Week" section.
380. Quinn, Anthony. "*True North*: The Family Trees." Rev. of *True North*. *New York Times Book Review* 23 May 2004: 18. Also a follow-up review in the *New York Times Book Review* (30 May 2004: 14) in the "And Bear in Mind" section.
381. Lyons, Stephen. "A Son's Life Clear-Cut by Decades of Guilt." Rev. of *True North*. *San Francisco Chronicle* 30 May 2004: M3.
382. Winslow, Art. "A Guilt Ridden Man Must Face Up to His Troubling Legacy." Rev. of *True North*. *Chicago Tribune* 30 May 2004.
383. Lamberti, Patty. "'True North' by Jim Harrison." Rev. of *True North*. *Playboy* June 2004: 40. *Playboy* has named *True North* the "book of the month" in its review section.

384. Shipley, Leanne, and Faith Harty. "Jim Harrison *True North*." Rev. of *True North*. *Elle* June 2004: 128. In the "Elle Lettres" section listed as Readers' Prize 2004.
385. Byrne, Steve. "True Harrison." Rev. of *True North*. *Detroit Free Press* 2 June 2004: 1C, 3C.
386. Eberhart, John Mark. "Gentleman Jim?" Rev. of *True North*. *Kansas City Star* 6 June 2004.
387. Curwen, Thomas. "Love's Powerful Pull." Rev. of *True North*. *Los Angeles Times Book Review* 6 June 2004: R3.
388. Gwinn, Mary Ann. "Harrison's *True North* Delves into Battle between Father, Son." Rev. of *True North*. *Lincoln NE Journal Star* 27 June 2004: 2K. In the "Books" section.
389. Arlin, Nick. "*True North*." Rev. of *True North*. *Bloomsbury Review* 25.2 (March–April 2005): 31.

## *The Summer He Didn't Die*
390. Winegar, Karin. "Fiction Review: *The Summer He Didn't Die* by Jim Harrison." Rev. of *The Summer He Didn't Die*. *Minneapolis-St. Paul Star Tribune* 17 July 2005.
391. Barnes, Harper. "*The Summer He Didn't Die*." Rev. of *The Summer He Didn't Die*. *St. Louis Post-Dispatch* 31 July 2005.
392. Hauptfleisch, Gordon. "Jim Harrison Combines Two Character-Rich Works with a Memoir in *The Summer He Didn't Die*." Rev. of *The Summer He Didn't Die*. *San Diego Union-Tribune* 31 July 2005.
393. Thompson, Jean. "*The Summer He Didn't Die*: The Return of Brown Dog and Other Tales." Rev. of *The Summer He Didn't Die*. *New York Times Book Review* 7 August 2005.
394. Sabo, Mary Ann. "Harrison's Stories Give Michigan Its Due." Rev. of *The Summer He Didn't Die*. *Grand Rapids MI Press* 21 August 2005.
395. Byrne, Steve. "Harrison Revisits His Character and Himself." Rev. of *The Summer He Didn't Die*. *Detroit Free Press* 21 August 2005.
396. Johnson, Kathleen. "Three Cheers for Jim Harrison." Rev. of *The Summer He Didn't Die*. *Kansas City Star* 21 August 2005.
397. Baker, Jeff. "Jim Harrison: Big Two-Hearted Writer." Rev. of *The Summer He Didn't Die*. *Portland Oregonian* 28 August 2005.
398. Greenya, John. "*The Summer He Didn't Die*." Rev. of *The Summer He Didn't Die*. *Washington Times* 28 August 2005.
399. O'Neal, Glenn. "'Summer' Waters Run Deep." Rev. of *The Summer He Didn't Die*. *USA Today* 31 August 2005.

400. Grimm, Fred. "Harrison Revives a Beloved Character in *Summer He Didn't Die*." Rev. of *The Summer He Didn't Die*. Lincoln NE *Journal Star* 18 September 2005: 3K.
401. "*The Summer He Didn't Die*." Anonymous Rev. of *The Summer He Didn't Die*. *Bookmarks* November–December 2005: 50.
402. Murray, John A. "The Summer He Didn't Die." Rev. of *The Summer He Didn't Die*. *Bloomsbury Review* 25.5 (November–December 2005): 22.

## *Saving Daylight*

403. Kirby, David. "Moonlighting." Rev. of *Saving Daylight*. *New York Times Book Review* 30 April 2006: 17.
404. Johnson, Kathleen. "A Metaphor Runs through It." Rev. of *Saving Daylight*. *Kansas City Star* 30 April 2006.
405. Shumaker, Jon. "Jim Harrison Ponders Existence in His Fantastic New Book of Poetry." Rev. of *Saving Daylight*. *Tucson Weekly* 8 June 2006.
406. Gundy, Jeff. Untitled Rev. of *Saving Daylight*. *ForeWord* 9.5 (September–October 2006): 52.
407. Baldwin, Robert Milo. "Saving Daylight." Rev. of *Saving Daylight*. *Bloomsbury Review* 27.2 (March–April 2007): 10.

## *Returning to Earth*

408. Rungren, Lawrence. Untitled Rev. of *Returning to Earth*. *Library Journal* 15 November 2006.
409. Brandt, Anthony. "Skeletons in the Closet." Rev. of *Returning to Earth*. *National Geographic Adventure* December 2006–January 2007: 42. In the "Books, Media and Culture" section.
410. Matthews, Charles. "Death in a Dysfunctional Family." Rev. of *Returning to Earth*. *San Francisco Chronicle* 2 January 2007: D2.
411. McNulty, Tim. "*Returning to Earth*, in Grief, Giving Family Wings." Rev. of *Returning to Earth*. *Seattle Times* 5 January 2007.
412. Lenfestey, Jim. "The Burdens We Bear." Rev. of *Returning to Earth*. *Minneapolis-St. Paul Star Tribune* 7 January 2007: F12.
413. Dyer, Daniel. "A Touch of Faulkner in Harrison's Latest." Rev. of *Returning to Earth*. *Cleveland Plain Dealer* 7 January 2007.
414. Roelofs, Ted. "Harrison's Latest Wholly Rewarding." Rev. of *Returning to Earth*. *Grand Rapids MI Press* 14 January 2007.
415. Thurber, Bart. "Root System." Rev. of *Returning to Earth*. *San Diego Union Tribune* 14 January 2007.
416. Salter Reynolds, Susan. "Returning to Earth by Jim Harrison." Rev. of *Returning to Earth*. *Los Angeles Times Book Review* 28 January 2007.

417. Johnson, Kathleen. "Death in the North Woods." Rev. of *Returning to Earth*. *Kansas City Star* 4 February 2007: G11.
418. Shechner, Mark. "New Take on an Old-Fashioned Melting Pot Tale." Rev. of *Returning to Earth*. *Buffalo News* 4 February 2007.
419. Blythe, Will. "Food for the Soul." Rev. of *Returning to Earth*. *New York Times Book Review* 11 February 2007: 1, 8. Photo of Harrison on the cover by Anderson Ulf.
420. Gwartney, Debra. "Returning to 'True North,' and Still Looking In." Rev. of *Returning to Earth*. *Portland Oregonian* 11 February 2007.
421. McAlpin, Heller. "Redeeming the Past, and Preparing for Death." Rev. of *Returning to Earth*. *Boston Globe* 11 February 2007.
422. "Returning to Earth." Anonymous Rev. of *Returning to Earth*. *Bookmarks* March–April 2007: 32.
423. Murray, John A. "Returning to Earth." Rev. of *Returning to Earth*. *Bloomsbury Review* 27.3 (May–June 2007): 6.

### *Letters to Yesenin*
424. Gonzalez, Ray. "Letters to Yesenin." Rev. of *Letters to Yesenin*. *Bloomsbury Review* 27.6 (November–December 2007): 19.

### *The English Major*
425. Wagamese, Richard. "Funny, Gutsy, Brimming with Wisdom." Rev. of *The English Major*. *Edmonton Journal* September 2008.
426. Shellenbarger, Pat. "Jim Harrison's 'English Major' in State of Change." Rev. of *The English Major*. *Grand Rapids Press* 28 September 2008.
427. Varno, David. "Fiction: Better Off without a Wife." Rev. of *The English Major*. *Brooklyn Rail* October 2008.
428. Brandt, Anthony. "Two for the Road: The Wide-Open Space at the End of a Marriage." Rev. of *The English Major*. *National Geographic Adventure* October 2008: 23.
429. McNulty, Tim. "The English Major: Cathartic Cross-Country Trek Finds Novelist Back on Track." Rev. of *The English Major*. *Seattle Times* 2 October 2008.
430. Cheuse, Alan. "The English Major by Jim Harrison: A Road Novel for Aging Guys." Rev. of *The English Major*. *Chicago Tribune* 4 October 2008.
431. Pevere, Geoff. "A Real Guy's Novel with Genuine Bite." Rev. of *The English Major*. *Toronto Star* 5 October 2008.
432. Shires, Ashley Simpson. "The English Major." Rev. of *The English Major*. *Rocky Mountain News* 9 October 2008.

433. Johnson, Kathleen. "Author Jim Harrison Finds Inspiration in the Wide Open Spaces of the West." Rev. of *The English Major*. *Kansas City Star* 11 October 2008.
434. Mickunas, Vick. "A Pleasant Cross-Country Journey in Search of Self." Rev. of *The English Major*. *Dayton Daily News* 12 October 2008.
435. Broening, John. "Middle-Age Ramble." Rev. of *The English Major*. *Denver Post* 12 October 2008: 11E, 14E.
436. Johnson, Kathleen. "Life Lessons on the Road." Review of *The English Major*. *Kansas City Star* 12 October 2008: H11.
437. Broening, John. "Middle-Age Ramble." Review of *The English Major*. *Denver Post* 12 October 2008: 11E, 14E.
438. Antonucci, Ron. "Jim Harrison's Fictional English Major Is a Fun Road Trip." Rev. of *The English Major*. *Cleveland Plain Dealer* 19 October 2008.
439. Egan, Jennifer. "Go West, Old Man." Rev. of *The English Major*. *New York Times Book Review* 19 October 2008: 12.
440. Salter Reynolds, Susan. "The English Major: A Novel by Jim Harrison." Rev. of *The English Major*. *Los Angeles Times* 19 October 2008.
441. Perry, Roy E. "The English Major by Jim Harrison." Rev. of *The English Major*. *The Tennessean* 19 October 2008:
442. "Briefly Noted." Anonymous Rev. of *The English Major*. *New Yorker* 20 October 2008: 93.
443. Giardina, Anthony. "Fiction Review: Jim Harrison's *The English Major*." Rev. of *The English Major*. *San Francisco Chronicle* 21 October 2008: E-2.
444. Beuttler, Bill. "Jim Harrison's Road Trip." Rev. of *The English Major*. *The Phoenix* 28 October 2008:
445. Tyer, Brad. "*The English Major* by Jim Harrison." Rev. of *The English Major*. *Houston Chronicle* 31 October 2008.
446. Tillotson, Kristin. "With 25th Book, Jim Harrison Takes a Leisurely Road Trip." Rev. of *The English Major*. *Minneapolis–St. Paul Star-Tribune* 31 October 2008:
447. Brice, Charles W. "Bumpy Road for an Old Satyr." Review of *The English Major*. *Pittsburgh Post-Gazette* 2 November 2008: E5.
448. Schudel, Matt. "Teacher's Pet." Rev. of *The English Major*. *The Washington Post* 16 November 2008:
449. Salter Reynolds, Susan. "Jim Harrison's *The English Major* Gets a Passing Grade." Rev. of *The English Major*. *Lincoln Journal Star* 23 November 2008.

# Index

This index contains the titles of Harrison's poems (sections A and B), fiction (sections A and C), essays (section D), and screenplays (section F). Untitled introductions, contributions to print symposiums, criticism, reviews, and encomiums (sections D, E, and G) are indexed under the author and title of the work in which they appeared. The publisher or journal in which Harrison's works appear is indexed for sections A–G. Publishers for works of criticism about Harrison and reviews of Harrison are omitted. Reviews and criticisms of Harrison's works (sections I and J) are indexed under the name of the reviewer and the publication in which the review appeared. Interviews (section H) are indexed under the interviewer and the venue or publication in which the interview appeared.

*31 New American Poets* (Schreiber, ed.), B21
*50 Modern American and British Poetry, 1920–1970* (Untermeyer, ed.), B38
*1929* (Turner) (encomium), G239
*The 1990 Western Wilderness Calendar* (Sanders, ed.), G25
"The 10,000 Calorie Diet" (essay), D117; excerpt, D182
"10,000 Successive Octobers" (criticism by JH), E23

Abbey, Edward: review by JH, E21
Abbott, Raymond (reviewer), J87
"About a Poem" (essay), D270
*The Abstract Wild* (Turner) (encomium), G141
The Academy of American Poets (audiotape), G3
Academy of American Poets Audio Archive, H5
*The Accidental Connoisseur* (Osborne) (encomium), G250

Ackerman, Jennifer (encomium), G147
Adams, Christina (encomium), G214
Adamson, Gil (encomium), G289
"Adding It Up" (poem), B142
Addison Wesley Longman, D172
Adler, John Morel (encomium), G91
*The Adventure of Food* (Sterling), D163
*Adventures in Wine* (Elkjer, ed.), D195
*Adventures on the Wine Route* (Lynch): introduction, D223, D227
"Advertisements" (letter to editor) (essay), D37
*Aethlon: The Journal of Sport Literature*, I113
*After Experience* (Snodgrass): JH review of, E5
"After Ikkyu" (poem): audiotape, G10; excerpts, B96, B101, B138
*After Ikkyu and Other Poems* (poetry), A29, A29.a (dust jacket p. 58)
*Afterimages: Zen Poems* (Takahashi): review by JH, E13
"After Reading Takahashi" (poem), B44, B51, B61, B78
"After the Anonymous Swedish" (poem), B19, B28, B100
"After the War" (poem), B140
*After You've Gone* (Lent) (encomium), G294
*Against the Silences to Come* (Loewinshon): JH review of, E3
Agee, Jonis (reviewer), J113
*Agenda* magazine, B52
Ahearn, Allen (critic), I102
Ahl, Lindsay (interviewer), H121
*Airman Mortensen* (Blake) (encomium), G107
*Aisling* magazine, B51, J35
*Albuquerque Journal*, I94
"Alcohol" (poem), B149, B151, D245
Alexander, Robert (encomium), G121, G230
*Alice Waters and Chez Panisse* (McNamee) (encomium), G280

"Alien" (poem), B188
*All My Friends Are Going to Be Strangers* (McMurtry): encomium, G45; review by JH, E10
*All the Finest Girls* (Styron) (encomium), G210
*All the Pretty Horses* (McCarthy) (encomium), G117
*All Things Considered* (radio broadcast), H24
Alternative Press, A27
Amanuddin, Syed (critic), I4
Amazon.com, J143
*America* (Setterberg, ed.), D165
*American Atlas* (Gerber) (encomium), G47
American Audio Prose Library, G4, G5, H15
*American Book Review*, J198
"American Girl" (poem), B13
*The American Literary Anthology 2* (Plimpton and Ardery, eds.), B25
*The American Literary Anthology 3* (Plimpton and Ardery, eds.), B29
*American Literary History* magazine, D166
*American Poet*, J181
*The American Poetry Anthology* (Halpern, ed.), B47
*American Poetry Review* magazine, B42, B53, B61, B164, D26, J36; review by JH, E13
*American Poets Say Goodbye to the 20th Century* (Codrescu and Rosenthal, eds.), B95
*American Protest Literature* (Trodd), B153
*American Way* magazine, B77, C15, H37
*Amicus Journal* magazine, B75
Ammons, A. R.: JH review of, E2
*Among the Elephants* (Douglas-Hamilton and Douglas-Hamilton): review by JH, E17
*Amulet* (Rakosi): JH review of, E4
Andrew, John Williams (reviewer), J2
*An Angler's Album* (Traub, ed.), D69
"Angry Women" (poem), B151
*Annex* magazine, D34
*Annie's Soup Kitchen* (Smith) (encomium), G232
*Anniston AL Star*, J223
*Another Attempt at Rescue* (Smoker) (encomium), G254
"Another Old Mariachi" (poem), B173
*Antaeus* magazine, B89, D45, D55, D74
*The Anthologist*, I89
Anthony, Michel (interviewer), H105
*Antioch Review* magazine, B33
Antonucci, Ron (reviewer), J233, J438
*Any Small Thing Can Save You* (Adams) (encomium), G214
"An Appreciation" (essay on Russell Chatham), D41

*Aqua Prieta* (film treatment), F9
Aralia Press, A42
Archibeque, Carlyle (reviewer), J197
Arctos Press, B109
Ardinger, Richard (encomium), G68
*Arise and Walk* (Gifford) (encomium), G130
*Arizona Daily Star* (Tucson), I59
"Arizona II": excerpt from *The English Major*, C31, C33
*Arizona Republic*, J131, J295
*Arkansas Democrat-Gazette*, H61
Arlin, Nick (reviewer), J389
Artisan, D251
*Art Muscle*, I51
Ashbrook, Tom (interviewer), G18
*As She Climbed across the Table* (Lethem) (encomium), G155
Athenaeum, B27
*Atlanta Journal-Constitution*, J97, J114, J262, J277, J305
*Atlantic Monthly*, J52
Atlantic Monthly Press, A30, A36, A38, A39.a, A48, A49, D125, D140, D142
Aubrey, Bryan (critic), I40
*Audubon Animals* (Elman): review by JH, E22
*The Audubon Society Book of Wild Birds* (Line and Russell): review by JH, E22
*The Audubon Wildlife Treasury* (Line): review by JH, E22
Auer, Tom: critic, I47; interviewer, H40
*Austin American-Statesman*, J206, J219, J239
Author Trading Card, no. 404 (Booksmith), G31
Author Trading Card, no. 899 (Booksmith), G40
*Automobile Magazine*, D47, D57, D75, D79, D123
Averill, David (critic), I7
"Awake" (poem), B33, B38, B41, B73

*The Babbo Cookbook* (Batali) (encomium), G222
Baca, Jimmy Santiago (encomium), G111, G201
"Back Home" (essay), D120
Baker, Jeff (reviewer), J338, J397
Baldwin, Robert Milo (reviewer), J316, J407
*Baltimore City Paper*, J275
Bancroft, Colette M.: critic, I59; reviewer, J263
Bantam Books, B28
Barcott, Bruce (reviewer), J248, J339
Barich, Bill (encomium), G60, G71, G176
Barillas, William (critic), I45, I76, I105

"Barking" (poem), B163, B187
*The Bark* magazine, H116
Barnes, Harper (reviewer), J391
Barnstone, Willis (encomium), G268
"Bar Pool" (essay), D83, note following D278
Barrett Dan (critic), I74
Barron, John (critic), I46
"Bars: A Poem" (poem), B122
Basic Books, D254
Bass, Rick: critic, I42; encomium, G82, G86, G100, G168; reviewer, J365
Batali, Mario (encomium), G222
"Battenkill Magnum Rolladuffle" (advertisement), G32
Baxter, Charles (encomium), G79
*Bay Area Parent*, J213
*Bay Area Times Magazine (Traverse City MI)*, H107, J203, J231
Bayless, Rick (encomium), G198
"Bear" (poem), B109
"The Bear" (poem), B121, B171
"Bear Posole" (essay), D241
Beasecker, Robert (reviewer), J60, J106
*The Beast God Forgot to Invent* (fiction—novellas), A36, A36.b (dust jacket p. 69); reviews, J215–J285; trading card, G31
"The Beast God Forgot to Invent" (novella): edited version of the novella that appeared in the fall of 2000, C22; excerpt, C29
*The Beast God Forgot to Invent* (treatment), F39
*Beast of Never, Cat of God* (Butz) (encomium), G258
"The Beauty of the Jump" (essay), D180
*Beaux Arts* magazine, D171
*Because a Fire Was in My Head* (Stegner) (encomium), G283
Beck, Judith Neuman (reviewer), J364
"Becoming" (poem), B164; *Saving Daylight*, B176
Bedford/St. Martin's Press, B134
Bednarik, Joseph: interviewer, H41, H71, H109, H112; JH introduction for, D153
"Beef, Bread and Iron" (essay), D123
"The Beginner's Mind" (essay), D137, D193
Belknap Press of Harvard University Press, B153
*Below Cold Mountain* (Stroud) (encomium), G162
*Bending the Bow* (Duncan): review by JH, E8
*Beneath a Single Moon* (Johnson and Paulenich, eds.), B78, D96
Berlitz, Charles: review by JH, E16

*The Bermuda Triangle* (Berlitz): review by JH, E16
Bernard, Jean-Phillipe (interviewer), H83
Berthel, Ron (reviewer), J234, J293
*The Best American Poetry 2006* (Collins and Lehman, eds.), B154
*The Best American Sports Writing 2001* (Collins, ed.), D183
*The Best American Travel Writing 2002* (Mayes, ed.), D198
*The Best American Travel Writing 2005* (Kincaid, ed.), D240
*Best Life* magazine, C34
*The Best of Outside*, D52
*The Best of Sports Afield* (Cassell, ed.), D140
*The Best of the West 2* (Thomas and Thomas), C12
*Between Wars* (screenplay), F28
Beuttler, Bill: interviewer, H37; reviewer, J444
BeVier, Tom: critic, I35, I36, I64; interviewer, H23, H70, H88; reviewer, J128, J149, J160
*Biblio*, J183
*Bibliography of Leelanauiana* (Wood), I14
Big Bridge Press, B76
*Big Sky Cooking* (Brokaw and Wright), D251
*Big Sky Journal* magazine, B105, D157, J363
*Big Small Plates* (Pawlcyn) (encomium), G270
"Big Women" (essay), D73
*Billy Watson's Croker Sack* (Burroughs) (encomium), G109
Bing, Jonathan (reviewer), J215
"Bird Hunting" (essay), D84, D125, note following D278
"Birds Again" (poem), B179
*Birds in the Hand* (Nelson and Nelson, eds.), C27
*Birds of the West Coast* (Lansdowne): review by JH, E22
Birnbaum, Robert (interviewer), H116, H117
"Birthday" (poem), B120
*Birthday Poems* (Shinder, ed.), B120
Biskin, Peter (critic), I58
Blackstone Audiobooks, G14, G16
*Black Warrior Review*, I42
Blades, John (interviewer), H62
Blake, Michael (encomium), G107
*The Blind See Only This World* (Corbett et al., eds.), B110
*Bliss Jumps the Gun* (Sloan) (encomium), G179
*Bliss Santa Fe* magazine, B162, H121
Block, Ron (encomium), G93
*Blood Orchid* (Bowden) (encomium), G136

*Blood Sport: A Journey Up the Hassayampa* (Jones) (encomium), G49
*Bloomsbury Review*, D59, H40, I47, J90, J118, J150, J151, J186, J187, J265, J316, J372, J389, J402, J407, J423, J424
*Blue Bossa* (Schneider) (encomium), G166
*Blue Moon in Kentucky* (screenplay), F19
*Blues for Cannibals* (Bowden) (encomium), G213
Blumenfield, Samuel (interviewer), H51
Bly, Carol (critic), I65
Blythe, Will (reviewer), J419
Boa, Robert (critic), I77
*The Body Electric* (Berg et al., eds.), B108
Bohaska, Chris (reviewer), J111
Bohy, Ric (interviewer), H20
*The Boilerplate Rhino* (Quammen), B111
Bonetti, Kay (interviewer), G4, H15, H16
*Book for Sensei*, B76
*BookForum*, J215
*Booklist*, J157, J190, J220, J374
*Booklovers*, J107
*Book* magazine, H91, J132
[bookmark], G41
*Bookmarks*, J401, J422
*A Book of Animal Poems* (Cole, ed.), B39
*The Book of Fictional Days* (calendar), G35
*The Book of Sharks* (Ellis): review by JH, E22
Book of the Road, G6
*BookPage* (Nashville TN), I97, J121, J122, J202, J228, J326
bookreporter.com, H110, J251
*Book Sense*, J266, J345
"Books for Young Adults: Writer's Recommendations" (criticism by JH), E25
Booksmith, G31, G40
*Book Standard* (Web site), H120
*Bookstore* (Tillman): quotations in, D162
*Book World*, J109
*Border Beat* magazine, B99, D174
"Borderlands" (essay), D134
Borders (Web site), H89
*Borders Review* (Borders Book Shop, Ann Arbor MI) (reviewer), J77
*Boston Globe*, J115, J281, J343, J370, J421
*Boston Phoenix*, I74
*Boston Sunday Herald*, J125
Boucq, Isabelle (critic), I110
Bourjaily, Vance (reviewer), J49
Bourmeau, Sylvain (interviewer), H96
Bowden, Charles (encomium), G85, G136, G213, G257, G286
Boyden, Joseph (encomium), G260
*The Boy Who Ran to the Woods* (children's fiction), A38, A38.b (dust jacket p. 72); reviews, J201–J214

*Bozeman MT Daily Chronicle*, J379
Bradbury Press, B88
*Braided Creek: A Conversation in Poetry* (poetry), A43, A43.c (cover p. 84); excerpts, B102, B124, B125, B126, B127, B136, B145, B146, B147, B155, B159, B162, B165, B169, B171, B172, B179; reviews, J370–J376
"The Brand New Statue of Liberty" (poem), B64
Brandt, Anthony: critic, I81; interviewer, H65; reviewer, J409, J428
Brautigan, Ianthe (encomium), G183
Brautigan, Richard (encomium), G53, G182
*Breaking and Entering* (Williams) (encomium), G78
"Breakthrough" (poem), B19
Brewer, Jo: review by JH, E22
Brice, Charles W. (reviewer), J447
*Brick* magazine, B116, B141, B149, B163, B174, B182, D186, D187; "Eat or Die" column, D217, D220, D230, D231, D245, D246, D255, D256, D266, D267, D275, D278
*The Bride Wore the Traditional Gold* (Spivak): review by JH, E11
*Brighton MI Argus*, J191
Bringhurst, Robert, J265
Broening, John (reviewer), J435, J437
*Broken Country* (Rawlins) (encomium), G145
*Brooklyn Rail*, J427
"Brothers and Sisters" (poem), B150, B177
Brown, Larry (encomium), G277
"Brown Dog" (novella), A22; excerpt as "The Woman Lit by Fireflies," C15; excerpts, B77, C32
*Brown Dog of the Yaak* (Bass, ed.), D164
Bruni, Frank: interviewer, H64; reviewer, J57
Buchanan, Rob (reviewer), J346
Bucholtz, Mel (reviewer), J12
*The Buddhist Third Class Junkmail Oracle* (Golden) (encomium), G173
Buettler, Bill (reviewer), J97
*Buffalo for the Broken Heart* (O'Brien) (encomium), G207
*Buffalo News*, J418
Buffett, Jimmy (album notes for), D40
*Building the Cold from Memory* (Driscoll) (encomium), G80
Bukowski, Charles: review by JH, E27
*Bulletin of Bibliography*, I19
Bunge, Nancy: critic, I106; interviewer, H49
Burger, Frederick (critic), I12, I18
Burke, James Lee (encomium), G149

Burke, Lynne (reviewer), J208
Burkholder, Robert E. (critic), I20
"Burning the Ditches" (poem), B175
*Burning the Prairie* (Reinhard) (encomium), G74
Burroughs, Franklin (encomium), G109
Butson, Denver (encomium), G195
*Butterflies* (Sandman and Brewer): review by JH, E22
Butz, Bob (encomium), G258
Buzzelli, Elizabeth Kane (reviewer), J175, J256
Byler, Stephen Raleigh (encomium), G216
Byrne, Steve (reviewer), J253, J296, J309, J349, J385, J395

"Cabbage" (poem), B151, B155, B172
*Cabbage* (poetry broadside), A50, A50.a (facsimile p. 102)
Cabin Bookshelf, D29
"Cabin Poem" (poem), B70, B118, B137
Caddy, John (encomium), G67
*Cahiers du Cinema*, H54
*Caliban* magazine, B74, C8, D60
"California Hybrid" (criticism by JH), E3
*Call of the Wild* (Reece) (encomium), G219
"Canada" (essay), D85
Canty, Kevin (encomium), G180
*Captive* (screenplay), F30
Caputo, Philip (encomium), G212
"Cardinal" (poem), B27, B106
Carl Fischer, B45
Carlisle, Olga: JH review of, E6
*Carnegie Mellon Magazine*, I90
*Carried Away* (screenplay), F5
Carrington, Raye (quotes in collection of), D160
Carroll, E. (encomium), G62
Carruth, Hayden: encomium for, G42; JH review of, E1; reviewer, J45, J61
Carvalho, Jim (reviewer), J250, J315
Carver, Ray (reviewer), J47
Casey, John D. (reviewer), J59
Caso, Frank (reviewer), J220
Cassell, Faris (reviewer), J176
Castanier, Bill (critic), I112
*Catledge* (screenplay), F28
*Centennial Review*, J76
Center for Book Arts, A23
Center Publications, A13
Chachere, Richard (critic), I103
Chaco Press, G27
"The Changing Face of Northern Michigan" (essay), D51
*Changing the Bully Who Rules the World* (Bly, ed.), C18, I65

Chaplin, Gordon (critic), I11
"Charles Cleland . . . on the occasion of his retirement" (essay), D226
"Charles Olson" (obituary) (essay), D4
Charles Scribner's Sons, B58, B111, B154, D169, I87
*Charlie Boy* (screenplay), F13
Chatham, Russell: encomium, G94; essay by JH in collection, D30
"The Chatham Ghazal" (poem), B52, B53
*Chattanooga TN Times Free Press*, J313
*Chatter and Feathers* (Harrison and Oberle), D171
"A Chat with a Novelist" (interview with Thomas McGuane) (essay), D7
Chaudhuri, Amit (encomium), G227
Chavez, Denise (encomium), G272
*Checkmark Books*, I82
Cheuse, Alan (reviewer), J112, J121, J430
Chicago Review Press, D54
*Chicago Sun-Times*, J58, J232
*Chicago Tribune*, H62, J85, J92, J112, J149, J244, J382, J430
*Chicago Tribune Magazine*, H48, I55
*Chokecherry Places* (Gilfillan) (encomium), G170
Christian Bourgois, A30.b
*Christian Science Monitor*, J44, J53, J88
*Chronicle* (Historical Society of Michigan), J60, J106
Chronicle Books, C16
*Cicada* (Nickels) (encomium), G187
*Cimarron Rose* (Burke) (encomium), G149
*The Circle of Hahn* (Weigl) (encomium), G191
City Arts of San Francisco, H60
*City Paper*, J111
Clark, LaVerne Harrell (interviewer), H6
Clark, Patricia (encomium), G255
Clark, Robert (encomium), G140
Clark City Press, A21, A24, B84, D8, D22, D29, D30, D70, D96, D126, G38
Clavel, Andre (interviewer), H74
"Clear Water 3" (poem), B51
"Clear Water 4" (poem), B51
Cleary, Thomas (encomium), G116
*Cleveland Plain Dealer*, H97, J139, J233, J294, J328, J413, J438
Clewes, Richard (encomium), G267
Clifford, Frank (reviewer), J122
"Close to the Bone" (essay), D276
Clute, John (reviewer), J84
Coates, Joseph (reviewer), J92
"Cobra" (poem), B111
Codrescu, Andrei (encomium), G241
Coe, Richard (reviewer), J223

*Cold* (Smolens) (encomium), G203
*Cold Feet* (screenplay), F1
Collins, Nancy (interviewer), note following H126
Collins, Tom (critic), I94
Colonnese, Tom (critic), I19
*Coming Home to Eat* (Nabhan) (encomium), G211
"Coming to Our Senses" (essay), D116
"Complaint" (poem), B3; "audiotape," G1
*Condé Nast Traveler*, D61
*Conjunctions* magazine, B183
"Consciousness Dining" (essay), D66
"Contact" (essay), D115
*Contact* magazine, D1
*Contemporary Authors: New Revision Series* (Evory and Straub, ed.), H11
*Contemporary Literary Criticism* (Gale Research), H21, I27
*Contemporary Michigan Poetry* (Delp et al., eds.), B67
*The Contract Surgeon* (O'Brien) (encomium), G177
"Controllers' Strike as Seen from Up North" (essay), D32
*A Conversation* (poetry), A42, A42 (covers p. 82)
*Conversations with American Novelists* (Bonetti et al., eds.), H16
*Conversations with Jim Harrison* (DeMott, ed.), H79, H111
*Conversations with Thomas McGuane* (Torrey, ed.), D7
"Cooking Your Life" (essay), D103
Coolidge Hall at the Library of Congress (poetry reading), G2
Copper Canyon Press, A31, A32, A41, A43, A51, A53, B101, B126
*Copper Canyon Press, Report to Friends, Fall 2003*, B125
*Copper Canyon Press Catalog*, B101, B113, B124, B127, B136, B145, B147, B155, B159, B171, B179, B180; encomium, G236
Corbett, Jim (encomium), G104
Corbett, William: encomium, G153; reviewer, J8, J357
Corcoran, Tom: encomium, G165, G237; reviewer, J148
"Correspondence from Jim Harrison" (essay), D174
*Corson's Inlet* (Ammons): JH review of, E2
Coughlin, Ruth Pollack (interviewer), H34
Counterpoint Press, D265
"Counting Birds" (poem), B71, B78, B111
Court Street Chapbook Series, A12

Cowan, James (encomium), G142
*The Cowboy Way* (McCumber) (encomium), G175
"Cowgirl" (poem), B34, B40
"Coyote No. 1" (poem), B86
*Coyote No. 1* (poetry broadside), A27, A27.a (facsimile p. 54)
Crawford, Max (encomium), G215
*Crawling out the Window* (Hennen) (encomium), G154
*Crazy for Rivers* (Barich) (encomium), G176
*Creative Moment*, I4
*Critical Survey of Long Fiction* (Magill, ed.), I49
*Critical Survey of Long Fiction 4* (Magill, ed.), I21
*Critical Survey of Poetry* (Magill, ed.), I52
*Critique: Studies in Modern Fiction*, I24, I34
*Crockett* (treatment), F33
Cronin, Justin (reviewer), J370
Cross, Robert: critic, I55; interviewer, H48
*Crossing the Yellow River* (Hamill) (encomium), G188
Crown Publishers, B91
*Cruising World* magazine, D48
Crusafulli, Chuck (interviewer), H66
Cryer, Dan (reviewer), J269, J329
*The Crying Heart Tattoo* (Martin) (encomium), G56
*Current* (Ann Arbor M1), J177
*Current Biography*, I54
Currey, Richard (encomium), G77
Curwen, Thomas (reviewer), J387
*Cutbank* magazine, B86
Cutthroat Press, B137
Cypremort Point Press, I103

*Dad's Own Cook Book* (Sloan) (encomium), G127
*Dallas Morning News*, H117, J152, J188, J212, J279, J303, J362
*Dalva* (audiotape), G7
*Dalva* (novel), A20, A20.b (dust jacket p. 40); essay: "From the Dalva Notebooks: 1985–1987," D55, D68, D141, D154; excerpts, C9, C10, C12, C30; reviews, J82–J88
*Dalva* (treatment), F29
"*Dalva*: How It Happened to Me," C9; as "How It Happened to Me," C12
D'Ambrosio, Charles (encomium), G138
*Dancer* (McCann), B130
"Dancing" (poem): excerpt, B130
"Dan Lahren" (essay), D157
Darling, David (interviewer), H101

*A Dash of Style* (Lukeman), B158
Davenport, Arlice (reviewer), J184
"The Davenport Lunar Eclipse, August 16, 1989" (poem), B74
*The Davenport Lunar Eclipse* (poetry broadside), A46, A46.a (facsimile, deluxe edition p. 92), diner edition p. 94)
"David" (poem), B3; audiotape, G1
David McKay Co., B38
*David Milch Project* (screenplay), F25
Davis, Lloyd (JH Introduction to poems by), D34
Davis, Todd F.: critic, I83, I100; encomium, G218, G275
"A Day in May" ("Salvation in the Keys") (essay), D23, D86, D149
"The Days of Wine and Pig Hocks" (essay), D99
*Dayton Daily News*, J434
D. B. (Reid) (encomium), G242
*Dead Calm* (screenplay), F13
"Dead Doe" (poem), B3; audiotape, G1
*Dear American Airlines* (Miles) (encomium), G290
"Dear Caliban" (essay), D60
"Dear George Hitchcock" (essay), D3
"Dear J. D. Salinger" (essay), D194
*The Death of Jim Loney* (Welch) (introduction), D273
Delacorte Press/Seymour Lawrence, A14, A15, A16
de la Valdene, Guy: encomium, G88, G137, G231; JH introduction to, D142
Delbanco, Nicholas (reviewer), J93
Dell, D154
Delp, Michael (encomium), G75, G235
DeMott, Robert: interviewer, H82, H106; reviewer, J377
*Denver Post*, J102, J192, J274, J300, J310, J332, J435, J437
*Denver Rocky Mountain News*, H102, H124, J153, J193, J285, J301, J333
"Despond" (poem), B132
*Detroit Free Press*, D32, D35, D36, D58, H2, H4, H7, H22, H32, H35, H43, H45, H46, H52, H57, H64, H67, H73, H75, H88, I9, I50, I69, J57, J93, J95, J117, J128, J129, J141, J158, J160, J172, J253, J259, J296, J349, J385, J395
*Detroit* magazine, H14
*Detroit Metro Times*, J367
*Detroit Monthly*, H26, I38, I46
*Detroit News*, D65, H34, I64, J66
Dettman, Marc (interviewer), H10
Deveson, Richards (reviewer), J75

*Dharma Family Treasures* (Eastoak, ed.), B98
*Diana Guest, Stonecarver* (Guest): encomium, G124; introduction and essay, D126
Diaz, Victoria (reviewer), J214, J359
Dickey, William (reviewer), J5
*Dictionary of Literary Biography Yearbook* (Ziegfeld, ed.), H12, I20
*Diddy Wah Diddy* magazine, H39
*Diggin' in and Piggin' Out* (Welsch), D155
Dim Gray Bar Press, A23, A26
Dischell, Stuart (reviewer), J79
*Discovery '65* (The Poetry Center), B2
*Dismal River* (Block) (encomium), G93
*Distinctly Montana*, I109
*Divided Light* (Shinder, ed.), B62
"Dogen's Dream" (poem), B78, B98
"Dog Hunter" (excerpt from *Farmer*), C6
"Dog Years" (essay), D236
Dombrowski, Christophe (reviewer), J363
"A Domestic Poem for Portia" (poem), B112
"Don't Feed the Poets" (essay), D268
"Don't Fence Me In" (essay), D61, D274
"Don't Go out over Your Head" (essay), D267
Dorn, Ed: JH review of, E6
Douglas-Hamilton, Iain and Oria: review by JH, E17
Drahos, Marta Hepler: interviewer, H108; reviewer, J235
*The Drake* magazine, D202
*The Dreadful Lemon Sky* (MacDonald): review by JH, E14
"Dream as a Metaphor of Survival" (essay), D87, D139, note following D278; excerpt, D164
Dream Garden Press, 1989, G25
"Dream Love" (poem), B162, B164
*Dreams* (poetry broadside), A3, A3.a (facsimile p. 8)
*Dress Her in Indigo* (screenplay), F12
"Drinking Song" (poem), B38, B41, B60, B68
Driscoll, Jack (encomium), G80
"Ducks" (essay), D239
Duerden, Richard: JH review of: E3, E3
Dumas, Alan: interviewer, H102; reviewer, J153
Duncan, David James (encomium), G200
Duncan, Robert: JH review of, E8
*Dunes Review*, B143
"Dusk" (poem), B65
*Dwellers in the Sea* (Faulkner and Fell): review by JH, E22
*Dwellings* (Hogan) (encomium), G139
Dyer, Daniel (reviewer), J328, J413

*Dying: An Introduction* (Sissman): JH review of, E5
Dykes, Steve (reviewer), J125

"Early Fishing" (poem), B181
*Earth First Journal*, B188
"Easter 2008" (poem), B183
"Easter Morning" (poem), B142, B144, B148, B185
*Easy Meat* (Harvey) (encomium), G144
"Eating Close to the Ground" (essay), D105
"Eating French" (essay), D168
*Eating the Sting.* (Caddy) (encomium), G67
"Eat or Die" (essay), D217, D260
"Eat Your Heart Out" (essay) [The Jam Issue], D33
"Eat Your Heart Out" (essay) [The White Line Issue], D31
Eberhart, John Mark (reviewer), J205, J238, J244, J260, J375, J386
Ecco Press, D143, D151, D239
Eckstein, Barbara J. (critic), I33
"Editorial Note" [on *Sumac* magazine], D2
*L'Edj*, H85
*Edmonton Journal*, J425
*Edward Curtis Project* (screenplay), F22
"Effluvia" (poem), B152
Egan, Jennifer (reviewer), J439
Egner, Diane (reviewer), J136
*Eight Dogs Named Jack* (Borri), D261
"Eight Ghazals" (poem), B32
Elam, Angela (interviewer), G15, H119
Elderberry Press, C29
*Elements of the Writing Craft* (Olmstead, ed.), C20
"Eleven Dawns with Su Tung-p'o" (poem), B182
Eliott, Ira (interviewer), H3
*Elle*, J384
Ellis, Jerry (encomium), G99
Ellis, Richard: review by JH, E22
Elman, Robert: review by JH, E22
*Emergences and Spinner Falls* (Haight) (encomium), G224
"Endgames" (poem), B142
"The End of Nature" (essay), D210
*End of the Earth* (Matthiessen) (encomium), G234
Enger, Leif (encomium), G206
*The English Major* (novel), A55, A55.b (dust jacket p. 113); excerpt as "Arizona II," C31, C33; reviews, J424–J448
*Ennui to Go* (Winokur), D243
Ensslin, John (reviewer), J332, J333
*The Enterprise*, D81

*Entertainment Weekly*, J355
"L'Envoi" (poem), B151
E. P. Dutton, D8, D22, D29, D30
E. P. Dutton/Seymour Lawrence, A18a, A20
"Epithalamium" (poem), B61
*Equinox* (O'Brien) (encomium), G156
Equinox Books, B47
Erdrich, Heide (encomium), G150
Erdrich, Lise (encomium), G285
Erdrich, Louise (reviewer), J85
Erion, Chuck (reviewer), J154
*Eros and Equus* (Chester, ed.), D252
*Escapes* (Williams) (encomium), G95
Eshleman, Clayton: review by JH, E9
"Eshleman's Indiana" (criticism by JH), E9
*Esquire* magazine, C2, C3, C9, C17, D23, D24, D27, D39, D43, D53, D119, D135, H19, I31, J56; essays reprinted from *The Raw and the Cooked*, A26; "The Raw and the Cooked" column, D98, D99, D102, D103, D105, D106, D107, D108, D113, D114, D115, D116, D117, D118, D120, D121, D122, D124, D132, D133, D134, D136
*Esquire Sportsman* magazine column, D112, D127, D130
"Essays on Home" (essay in larger piece), D128
*The Essential Chuang Tzu* (Hamill and Seaton) (encomium), G164
"Eternity and Food" (essay), D256
*Ethiopia* (Torgersen) (encomium), G58
*Eugene* OR *Register-Guard*, J176
"Everyday Life: The Question of Zen" (essay), B78, D96, D186; as "The Question of Zen," D169
*The Evil Companions Literary Award* (fiction broadside), A34, A34 (facsimile p. 67)
"Exercise" (poem), B1, B45; audiotape, G1
*Exercise for Chorus and Tape*, B45
*Exodus/Exodo* (Bowden) (encomium), G286
*Exposure* (Reed) (encomium), G70
*L'Express*, H74
*Expressways* (Reed): JH review of, E7
*Exquisite Corpse: A Journal of Letters and Life Online*, B131, B140, J276
*Exquisite Corpse* magazine, B64

Fabre, Cedric (interviewer), H86
*The Face of Poetry* (Clark and MacArthur, eds.), B49
"Fair/Boy Christian Takes a Break" (poem), B37; excerpt, B104
Falconer, Delia (encomium), G264
*Falling off the Map* (Iyer) (encomium), G122

*Fangoria* magazine, H66
Fanning, Patrick (reviewer), J33
Farcountry Press, D241
Farkus, David (reviewer), J294
*Farmer* (novel), A11, A11.a (unrevised proofs p. 22), A11.b (dust jacket p. 24); excerpt as "Dog Hunter," C6; excerpts, C23, C27, C30; excerpts on audiotape, G5; reviews, J37–J44; screenplay as *Carried Away*, F5
*Far Tortuga* (television series treatment), F11
"The Fast" (essay), D82
*Fatal Light* (Currey) (encomium), G77
"Father Daughter" (short story), C26
"Father-in-Law" (essay), D148, D227
Faulkner, Douglas: review by JH, E22
Fawcett Columbine, D73
Fawcett Publications, B36
Feeley, George (reviewer), J146
Feibleman, Peter: screenplay for *Charlie Boy*, F13
Feld, Ross (reviewer), J217
Fell, Barry: review by JH, E22
Fergus, Jim: critic, I29; encomium, G161, G253; interviewer, H18, H21, H27
Ferrari-Adler, Jofie (reviewer), J123
"Fibber" (poem), B181
*Fidelity* (Redhill) (encomium), G248
Fiedler, Terry (reviewer), J254
*Field and Stream* magazine, D221, D233, D236, D277
"Field Days: A Lifetime of Hunting, Fishing, and Dogs" (essay), D221
*Field Folly Snow* (Parks) (encomium), G288
"Fifty Days on the Water" (essay), D233
*Figure in the Door* (Gregor): JH review of, E5
*Finding Lily* (Clewes), B157; encomium, G267
"Finding Sister" (essay): as "First Person Female," D167
*Finding the Lamb* (Newth) (encomium), G57
Finkelstein, Dave (encomium), G98
*Fire Exit* magazine, B13, B14
*First Intensity* (Berkeley CA), J199
"First Person Female" (essay), D167
*Firsts: The Book Collector's Magazine*, H104
"The Fisherman Gourmand" (essay), D251
*Fishing for Myth* (Erdrich) (encomium), G150
*Fishing Idaho* (Evancho), B137
"Fishing is the most wonderful thing I do . . ." (quotation), D202
Fiskin, Jeffrey (co-author of *Revenge*), F2
*Five Blind Men*, B20
*Five Forks* (Alexander) (encomium), G230
*Five Points* magazine, B102, B121, B161, B181, H112

Flesher, John: interviewer, H97; reviewer, J166
*The Flight of the Iguana* (Quammen) (encomium), G76
"Floating Is Better Than Sinking" (essay), D48
*Flora Montagu* (treatment), F37
Florio, Gwen (reviewer), J278
*Focus 101* (Clark), H6
"Followers" (poem), B61, B93
"Food, Finance, and Spirit" (essay), D278
"Food, Fitness, and Death" (essay), D246
"Food, Sex and Death" (essay), D230
"Food and Mood" (essay), D254
*Fools Crow* (Welch) (encomium), G64
*For a Handful of Feathers* (de la Valdene) (encomium), G137
*For a Handful of Feathers* (de la Valdene) (JH introduction to), D142
"Fording and Dread" (essay), D42
"Ford's Better Idea" (signature to letter of protest), G24
*ForeWord*, J229, J406
*The Forgotten Language* (Merrill, ed.), B79
*The Fork* (Duerden): JH review of, E3
*Forrest Gump* (Groom) (encomium), G69
*For the Love of Music* (Steinberg and Rothe) (encomium), G271
*Fort Myers FL News-Press*, J257, J258, J340, J341, J378
*Fort Worth Star-Telegram*, J306
Foster, Nelson (encomium), G158
"Four Matrices" (poem): version of Matrix 1 and Matrix 2, B35
Four Walls Eight Windows, B95
Fox Run Press, A46
*France Today*, I110
Franscell, Ron (reviewer), J232, J242, J255, J277
*Fredericksburg VA Free Lance-Star*, J260
*Freefall* (Reed) (encomium), G54
Freeman, Judith (reviewer), J96
Freeze, Eric (critic), I96
French, Kate (reviewer), J216
*Fresh Air* (radio broadcast), H36
"Fresh Southern Air" (essay), D133
"Fresh Usual Words" (criticism by JH), E5
"Frog" (poem), B88
*From Geo-Bestiary* (poetry broadside), A31, A31.a (facsimile p. 62)
"From the Dalva Notebooks: 1985–1987" (essay), D55, D68, D141, D154
"From the Notebooks" (poem), B8
Fuljum, Bob (critic), I98
*Funeral and Memorial Service Readings* (Baum, ed.), B103

*Furthering My Education* (Corbett) (encomium), G153
*Futures* magazine, B81

Gallagher, John (reviewer), J129
Gallagher, Winifred (encomium), G129
Gallimaufry Press, B49
Galvin, James (encomium), G113
Gamino, John (reviewer), J303
*A Garden of Forking Paths* (Anstandig and Killough), B168, D260
Garfunkel, Art (encomium), G83
Gargan, William (reviewer), J347
Garner, Dwight (reviewer), J241
Gaston, Bill (encomium), G205
"Gathering April" (poem), B55, B105
Geier, Thom (reviewer), J355
"Gentle Reader" (essay), D174
"Geo-Bestiary" (poem): excerpts, B107, B125, B127
Geraud, Saint (Bill Knott): JH review of, E6
Gerber, Dan (encomium), G43, G47, G48, G66, G84, G87, G110, G171, G204
"Germinating Work" (essay), D154
*Geronimo Rex* (Hannah): encomium, G44; review by JH, E11
Gerstel, Judy: interviewer, H35; reviewer, J95
"Ghazal for Christmas"(poem), A5.a (portfolio and poem p. 11), B34
*Ghazal for Christmas* (poetry broadside), A5
"Ghazal V" (poem), B40
"Ghazal VIII" (poem), B40
"Ghazal XXX" (poem), B40
"Ghazal XXXIX" (poem), B128
"Ghazals XXI and XLIX" (poem), B37
*Ghosts of Tsavo* (Caputo) (encomium), G212
Giardina, Anthony (reviewer), J443
Gifford, Barry: encomium, G55, G90, G130, G190; reviewer, J199
*Gigantic* (Nesbitt), C25
*Gila: The Life and Death of an American River* (McNamee) (encomium), G131
Gilb, Dagoberto (encomium), G133
Gilfillan, Merrill (encomium), G170, G229
Gilligan, Thomas Mahler (critic), I24
*Glen Arbor (MI) Sun*, H80
"Gnomic Verse" (criticism by JH), E4
*Goatwalking* (Corbett) (encomium), G104
"Going Places" (essay), D52, D165, D172, D222; quotes from, G29
Golden, Mike: critic, I13; encomium, G173
*Gone* (Roper) (encomium), G228
"Gone to Sanctuary, from the Sins of Confusion," G29

Gonzalez, Ray (reviewer), J424
"Good Art Does Not Specialize in Cheap Solutions" (essay), D219
*The Good Body* (Gaston) (encomium), G205
*A Good Day to Die* (novel), A9, A9.a (advance uncorrected proofs p. 16), A9.b (dust jacket p. 18); excerpts, B73, C11, C25; reviews, J29–J34; screenplay, F7
*Good Poems for Hard Times* (Keillor), B148
Goodykoontz, Bill (reviewer), J131
G. P. Putnam's Sons, D244
Graber, Michael (reviewer), J196
Graham, Barry (reviewer), J313, J367
Granary Books, B110
"Grand Marais: A Rare Refuge for Anglers" (essay), D36
*Grand Rapids* magazine, H10
*Grand Rapids MI Press*, H1, H81, H87, I3, J124, J394, J414, J426
"Grand Raptures" (essay), D262
*Grand Valley Magazine*, G39, H122
Granon, Francois: critic, I57; interviewer, H53
Grant, Richard: interviewer, H115; reviewer, J368
*Grass Fires* (Gerber) (encomium), G84
Graves, John (encomium), G249, G278
*Greater Nowheres* (Finkelstein) (encomium), G98
*Great Falls MT Tribune*, J366
*Great Fiction from the New Esquire Fortnightly*, C2
*Great Lakes Review* magazine, B46, I16, I17
"A Great Novelist Howls at Hollywood Scripts" (essay), D212
"Great Poems Make Good Prayers" (essay), D135
Green, Lynn (reviewer), J202
Greene, A. C. (reviewer), J69
*Greensburg PA Tribune Review*, J144
Greenya, John (reviewer), J398
Gregor, Arthur: JH review of, E5
Grey Spider Press, A37
*Grieving God's Way* (Brownley), B139
Grimm, Fred (reviewer), J400
"Grim Reapers of the Land's Bounty" (essay), D9, D213; as "The Violators," D93
Grinnell, James W. (reviewer), J46, J90, J118, J150, J186, J265, J372
*Grizzly Years* (Peacock) (encomium), G92
Groom, Winston (encomium), G69
*Grove Atlantic Catalog*, C21
Grove Press, A44, A52, C25, D184, D185, D228

*Grove Press, Atlantic Press and Canongate Books Catalog*, D182
*Grrrr: A Collection of Poems about Bears* (Corbett et al., eds.), B109
"Grumpy Old Men (I grow older. I still like women, but mostly I like Mexican food)" (poem): *Braided Creek*, B133
Gruzinska, Aleksandra (critic), I41
Guequierre, Nathan (critic), I51
Guest, Diana: encomium, G124; introduction and essay, D126
"Guiding Light in the Keys" (essay), D16
Gundy, Jeff (reviewer), J406
*Gunslinger* (Dorn): review by JH, E6
Guy, David (reviewer), J110
Gwartney, Debra (reviewer), J420
Gwinn, Mary Ann (reviewer), J138, J388

Hacker, David (interviewer), H22
Hadley, Drum (encomium), G259
Hahn, Carl (critic), I102
Haight, Robert (encomium), G224
"Hakuin and Welch" (poem), B164
*Halflives* (Williams), B104; encomium, G174
Hall, James (encomium), G96
Hamill, Sam (encomium), G164, G188
Hammond, Ruth (critic), I90
Hamper, Ben (encomium), G101
*Hanging Loose* magazine, B15
Hannah, Barry: encomium, G44; review by JH, E11
*Hannah and the Mountain* (Johnson) (encomium), G252
Harcourt Brace & Co., B85, D162
Harcourt Brace Jovanovich, B57
"Hard Times" (poem), B183
*Hard to Be Good* (Barich) (encomium), G71
Harmon, William (reviewer), J67
*In Harm's Way* (Stanton) (encomium), G225
HarperCollins, B84, C28
*Harper's* magazine, D76, J45
Harrelson, Barbara (reviewer), J211
Harrington, Maureen (reviewer), J102
Harrison, Alexander (reviewer), J116
Harrison, Jamie (co-author of treatments), F36–F39
*Hartford CT Courant*, J298
Hartley, Aidan (encomium), G238
Hartley, Bob (interviewer), H57
Harty, Faith (reviewer), J384
*Harvard Advocate*, J8
*The Harvester's Vase* (O'Gorman): JH review of, E5
"A Harvest of Riches" (contribution to), D59
Harvey, John (encomium), G144

Harvey, Miles (critic), I68
Hatch, James (reviewer), J198
Hauptfleisch, Gordon (reviewer), J392
*Headwaters Review*, I53
"Heart Food in L. A." (essay), D132
*Heartland II: Poets of the Midwest* (Stryck, ed.), B44
*The Heart of the Beast* (Weatherford) (encomium), G208
*Heart of the Land* (Barbato and Weinerman, eds.), D137
*Heartsblood, Hunting, Spirituality and Wildness in America* (Peterson, ed.), D173
*Hearts of the Tattooed: Poems* (Hubert) (encomium), G52
*The Heartsong of Charging Elk* (Welch) (encomium), G192
*Heaven Is under Our Feet* (Henley and Marsh), D97
Heidelberg Graphics, H6
*The Heirs of Columbus* (Vizenor) (encomium), G106
"Hello Walls" (poem), B51
Hemingway, Ernest: review by JH, E12
Hemingway, Valerie: critic, I109; encomium, G245
"Hemingway Fished Here" (essay), D27; as "The Last Good Country," D88
Henderson, Fergus (encomium), G240
Hennen, Tom (encomium), G154
Henry, Larry (reviewer), J168
Henry Holt & Co., D150
*The Herald* (Glasgow, Scotland), H55, H69
"Here I Stand for a Few Minutes" (essay), D266
*Hermit Poems* (Welch): JH review of, E3
*Heron Dance* magazine, B118
"Hideouts, Dream Towns and Great Escapes" (introduction) (essay), D235
"High on the Hog" (foreword) (essay), D155
*High Water Mark* (Shumate) (encomium), G243
*Hika* magazine, B5
Hill & Wang, B21
Hillebrand, Robert (reviewer), J107
Hillringhouse, Mark (reviewer), J81
"Hitchhiking" (poem): audiotape, G1
*Hit on the House* (Jackson) (encomium), G123
Hjortsberg, William (encomium), G46
Hochman, Will (encomium), G221
Hoffert, Barbara (reviewer), J218
Hogan, Linda (encomium), G115, G139, G167, G293
*Hole in the Sky* (Kittredge) (encomium), G112
*Hooked* (Carrington, ed.), D160; quotes in, D160

*Hooked* (Edgerton), C32
Hopkins, John: review by JH, E11
"Horse" (poem), B27, B39, B57, B58
Horton, Diane (reviewer), J91
Horvath, Brooke (reviewer), J139
"Hospital" (poem), B34
Hotch, Ripley (reviewer), J66
*Hotline Healers* (Vizenor) (encomium), G151
Houghton Mifflin Co., A25, D183, D240
Houghton Mifflin/Seymour Lawrence, A22, A28
*Hour Detroit* (Royal Oak MI), H125, J311
Houston, Pam (reviewer), J273
Houston, Robert (reviewer), J103
*Houston Chronicle*, J134, J302, J314, J373, J445
*Houston Post*, J100
Howe, Parkman (reviewer), J44
"How It Happened to Me": excerpt from *Dalva*, C12; excerpt from *Dalva*, as "Dalva: How It Happened to Me," C9
"How Men Pray" (essay), D205
*Hua Hu Ching* (Walker), B84
Hubert, Jim: encomium, G52; reviewer, B51, J35
*Hudson Review*, J5, J21
Huey, Michael C. (reviewer), J88
"A Huge Hunger in Paris" (essay), D136
"Hunger, Real and Unreal" (essay), D63; excerpt, D138
*Hungry Mind Review*, D128, E25
*A Hunter's Heart* (Peterson, ed.), D150
"Hunter's Journal" (essay), D144
*The Hunting Animal* (Russell) (encomium), G59
"A Hunting Pal" (essay), D147; as "Hunting with a Friend," D142
"Hunting with a Friend" (Introduction to *For a Handful of Feathers*), D142; as "A Hunting Pal," D147; excerpt, D173
*The Hunt out of the Thicket* (Adler) (encomium), G91
Hurst, Jack: review by JH, E18

"Ice Fishing: The Moronic Sport" ("To Each His Own Chills and Thrills") (essay), D10, D29; excerpt, D69
"The Idea of Balance Is to Be Found in Herons and Loons" (poem), B75, B78, B118
Idema, James (reviewer), J352
"Ignoring Columbus" (essay), D104
"I'll Take the Top Half—Cloudy Side Up" (essay), D35
*Images from the Great West* (Gaede): Photograph of JH, G27
*Imaginary Paintings and Other Poems* (Baxter) (encomium), G79

*Imagining Worlds* (Ford and Ford), D141
"The Importance of Being Young—and Ernest" (criticism by JH), E12
*Independent Publisher*, H101, J348
*Indiana* (Eshleman): review by JH, E9
Indiana University Press, B23
*An Inheritance of Horses* (Kilgo) (encomium), G132
"In Interims: Outlyer" (poem), B20, B24
"In Key West: Safety without Portfolio" (essay): excerpt from "Safety without Portfolio in Key West," D28
*In Print: A Book Review 1982*, J64
*Les Inrockuptibles*, H51, H96
*Inside Borders* magazine, D179, H94
*Inspiring Thirst* (Kermit Lynch), D227
*International Herald-Tribune*, H59
*In the Beginning* (Bauer, ed.), C16
*In the Center of the Nation* (O'Brien) (encomium), G108
*In the Fall* (Lent) (encomium), G189
*In the Land of the Temple Caves* (Turner) (encomium), G247
*An Introduction to Poetry* (Knorr, ed.), B135
*I Prefer the Skyline of a Shelf of Books* (poetry broadside), A45, A45.a (facsimile p. 90)
*The Irish Thing* (treatment), F31
*Iron Locusts* (film treatment), F8
Irwin, T. (critic), I56
Island Press, D173
*The Island Within* (Nelson) (encomium), G81, G105
"Is Winemaking an Art?" (essay), D206
Ithaca House, A12
Ivan R. Dee, D253
"I Was Proud" (poem), B44
Iyer, Pico: critic, I23, I26, I28; encomium, G122; reviewer, J72

Jackson, Jon (encomium), G123, G244
*Jackson MS Clarion Ledger*, J237
*January Magazine*, I86, J249
*Jeanne* (Carroll) (encomium), G62
Jenks, Tom: critic, I31; interviewer, H19
Jerome, John (reviewer), J109
"Jim—Age 38, 5'10" W. 196 Strapping Goggle-Eyed Nordic Bankrupt" (poem), B49
*Jim Harrison* (Chatham) (poster), G38
*Jim Harrison* (Reilly), H72, I66
"Jim Harrison, Writer" (essay), D200
"Jim Harrison: A Conversation" (audiotape), G3
*Jim Harrison: Author Price Guide* (Ahearn), I102

*Jim Harrison: Half Dog and Half Wolf* (*Jim Harrison: Entre Chien et Loup*) (Video Documentary), G20, H50
"Jim Harrison on D. T. Suzuki" (essay), D182
"Jim Harrison on the Orvis T3" (advertisement), G36
"Jim Harrison's First Car" (essay), D201
"Jim Harrison to Henry Rago" (essay), D253
"Joe's Poem" (poem), B121
*John Keats's Porridge* (McCabe, ed.), D20
Johnson, Charles (reviewer), J171
Johnson, Dennis Loy (reviewer), J144
Johnson, Jonathan (encomium), G199, G252
Johnson, Kathleen: interviewer, H126; reviewer, J396, J404, J417, J433, J436
Johnson, Robert (critic), I70
*John Steinbeck* (Shillinglaw, ed.) (essay in), D197
Jones, Donald (reviewer), J7
Jones, Malcolm, Jr. (reviewer), J127, J271
Jones, Robert F. (encomium), G49
Jones-Davis, Georgia (reviewer), J86
*Journal of Men's Studies*, I71
*Journal of the American Romanian Society of Arts and Sciences*, I41
*Journeyman's Wages* (Starck) (encomium), G134
Jousse, Thierry (interviewer), H54
*Julip* (fiction—novellas), A28, A28.b (dust jacket p. 56); reviews, J112–J118
"Julip" (novella), C17; excerpt, C30; excerpt on audiotape, G9
*Julip* (treatment), F35
*June 30th, June 30th.* (Brautigan) (encomium), G53
"Just Before Dark" (essay), D102, D209; excerpt, D228
*Just Before Dark: Collected Nonfiction* (essays), A24, A24.b (dust jacket p. 48); advertising piece for, A25; contents, D83-D96; excerpt from introduction, D164; excerpts, D199, G30; previously unpublished essays in, note following, D278; quotations from, G29; reviews, J108–J111

Kain, John (encomium), G273
Kakutani, Michiko (reviewer), J71, J83, J98
Kalish, Mildred Armstrong (encomium), G282
*Kansas City Star*, H126, J91, J205, J238, J344, J375, J386, J396, J404, J417, J433, J436
*Kayak* magazine, D3
Keeler, Janet (reviewer), J299

*Kentucky Straight* (Offutt) (encomium), G120
*Kermit Lynch Wine Merchant Newsletter* magazine, D148, D178, D204, D206, D207, D211, D223, D232, D234, D247, D250, D259, D269, D272, E26
"Key Porter Books" (poem), B157
Key West Literary Seminar, G11
The Key West Literary Seminar (audiotape), G11
*The Key West Reader* (Murphy, ed.), B73, C11
Kilby, Damian (reviewer), J261
Kilgo, James (encomium), G132
Kilgore, Richard (reviewer), J152, J188, J212, J279, J362
*Killing Mister Watson.* (Matthiessen) (encomium), G89
"King of Pain" (criticism by JH), E27
"Kinship" (poem): audiotape, G1
Kirby, David (reviewer), J403
*Kirkus Reviews*, J13, J22, J222, J288, J321
Kissel, Howard (reviewer), J126
*Kitchener ON Record*, J154
Kittredge, William (encomium), G112
Kloszewski, Marc (reviewer), J221
Knickerbocker, Dennis (critic), I48
Knickerbocker, Dennis C.: critic, I3; interviewer, H1
Knott, Bill (Saint Geraud): JH review of, E6
"Kobun" (poem), B78
*Kobun* (poetry broadside), A23, A23.a (facsimile p. 46)
KOEN, J226
Kogan, Rick (reviewer), J58
Kohlhaase, Bill: critic, I101; interviewer, H114
Konsmo, Natalie (critic), I107
Kooser, Ted: critic, I79; encomium, G217. See also *Braided Creek: A Conversation in Poetry* (poetry)
Kray, Elizabeth (interviewer), H5
Krystal, Arthur (reviewer), J99
Kubica, Chris (encomium), G221
Kunerth, Jeff (reviewer), J147

La Farge, Oliver (encomium), G251
*Lakeland Boating*, I72
*Lake Superior Magazine*, I93
Lamberti, Patty (reviewer), J383
"Land Divers" (poem), B175
Lange, Pam (reviewer), J239
*Lannan Readings and Conversations*, B165
Lansdowne, J. F.: review by JH, E22
*Lansing MI Capital Times*, H38
*Lansing MI State Journal*, I48

"Larson's Holstein Bull" (poem), B170, B174, B183
"The Last Best Place?" (essay), D113
*A Last Bridge Home* (Gerber) (encomium), G110
"The Last Good Country" ("Hemingway Fished Here") (essay), D27, D88
*The Last Good Water* (Delp) (encomium), G235
*The Last Posse* (screenplay), F28
*Later in Life* (treatment), F24
*Laughing Boy* (La Farge) (encomium), G251
"Lauren Hutton's ABC's" (essay), D271
Laval, Martine (interviewer), H84
LA *Village View*, I61
Lawrence, Russ (reviewer), J266
Lawrence Erlbaum Associates, B112
"Leave Us Alone" (letter) (essay), D65
"Leaving Home" (essay), D203
*Leelanau Cellars Vis à Vis White Table Wine*, B80
*Leelanau MI Metro Times*, J167
*Legends of the Fall* (audiotape), G8; interview with JH, H56
*Legends of the Fall* (DVD): liner notes, D242
*Legends of the Fall* (fiction—novellas), A14, A14.a (proof copies p. 30), A14.c (dust jacket p. 32); reviews, J46–J57
"Legends of the Fall" (novella), A14, C2; excerpts, B102, C16, C20, C29, D252; excerpts on audiotape, G5; screenplay, F4
*Legends of the Fall* (screenplay), F4
Lehmann-Haupt, Christopher (reviewer), J15, J32, J40
LeMay, Konnie (critic), I93
*Lemuria Literary Type*, J230
Lenfestey, Jim (reviewer), J412
Lent, Jeffrey (encomium), G189, G223, G276, G294
Le Querrec, Guy (introduction), D196
*Lessons in Essence* (Standridge) (encomium), G266
Lethem, Jonathan (encomium), G155
"Let's Get Lost" (essay), D107
letter [on Tom Wolfe essay], D76
letter [on William Carlos Williams], D1
"Letter Poem to Sam Hamill and Dan Gerber" (poem), B116
*Letters between the Lines* (Parisi and Young, eds.), D253
*Letters from the Leelanau* (Stocking, ed.), H31
letters to Gerard Oberle (essay): as "Wild Creatures," D185
*Letters to J. D. Salinger* (Kubica and Hochman, eds.), D194; encomium, G221

"Letters to Yesenin" (poem), B42, B73, B108; excerpts, B46, B50, B59, B91, B172, B179, B180
*Letters to Yesenin* (poetry), A10, A10.c (dust jacket p. 20), A53, A53.a (uncorrected proof p. 110), A53.b (trade edition cover p. 110); excerpts on audiotape, G2; reviews, J35–J36, J423
*Letters to Yesenin and Returning to Earth* (poetry), A13 (cover p. 28)
"Letters to Yesenin/Jim Harrison" (advertising piece) (essay), D17
"A Letter to Ted and Dan" (poem), B143
"Letter to the Editor" [on Charles Fair review of Paul Zweig] (essay), D26
*Libby, Montana: Asbestos and the Deadly Silence of an American Corporation* (Peacock) (encomium), G233
*Library Journal*, J3, J4, J23, J33, J39, J62, J78, J159, J218, J221, J287, J347, J408
Liebart, Alexis (interviewer), H85
Liebrum, Martha (reviewer), J100
Liebs, Scott (reviewer), J142
"Life on the Border" (essay), D190
*A Light from Within* (Smith) (gallery program), D111
*Lillabulero*, B31, J12
Limberlost Press, D44
*Lincoln NE Journal Star*, J312, J356, J371, J376, J388, J400, J449
Lindsay, Charles (encomium), G185
Lindsey, Craig D. (reviewer), J314
Line, Les: review by JH, E22
Lipari, Joseph A. (reviewer), J62
*Literary Cavalcade* magazine, D222
*A Literary Feast* (Golden, ed.), D125
Literary Guild of America, C1
*Literary Michigan—a Sense of Place, a Sense of Time*, B69
*Literary Outtakes* (Dark, ed.), D73
*Literary Review*, J81
Literature and Fiction @ Amazon.com (Web site), H92
*Literature and Its Writers*, 3rd ed. (Charters and Charters, eds.), B134
Little, Brown & Co., D159
*Little Heathens* (Kalish) (encomium), G282
*Livingston Suite* (poetry), A47, A47.a (cover p. 96)
*Livonia MI*, J214, J359
*Local Wonders* (Kooser) (encomium), G217
"Locations" (poem), B14, B18, B22, B47
*Locations* (poetry), A4, A4.a (dust jacket p. 10); excerpts on audiotape, G2; reviews, J10–J14

Loewinshon, Ron: JH review of, E3
"Log of the Earthtoy Drifthumper" (essay), D47
*London Magazine*, I28
Long, Timothy (reviewer), J115
*The Longest Silence* (McGuane) (encomium), G209
"Look at Keys" (letter) (essay), D81
"Look for Real Issues in This Campaign" (letter) (essay), D58
"Looking forward to Age" (poem): excerpt, B155
Lord John Press, G26
Lord John Signatures (autograph), G26
*Lord John Ten* (Etchison, ed.), B70
Lorenz, Paul H. (critic), I43
*Los Angeles Times*, H25, I37, I39, I99, J86, J148, J342, J358, J440
*Los Angeles Times Book Review*, J96, J236, J268, J387, J416
*Los Angeles Times/Calendar*, H63
*Lost Man's River* (Matthiessen) (encomium), G152
*Lost Nation* (Lent) (encomium), G223
*The Lost Thoughts of Soldiers* (Falconer) (encomium), G264
Love, Keith: critic, I37; interviewer, H25
*Loveletter* magazine, B11
"Lullaby for a Daughter" (poem), B13, B85, B112, B138
"Lunch Chez Lulu" (essay), D248
Lutholtz, M. William (reviewer), J53
Lyke, M. L. (reviewer), J173
Lynch, Kermit (introduction to), D196
Lynch, Thomas (critic), I69
Lyons, Daniel (reviewer), J117
Lyons, Stephen (reviewer), J381
Lyons Press, C23, D224

MacDonald, Jay: interviewer, H118; reviewer, J257, J258, J340, J341, J378
MacDonald, John D.: review by JH, E14; screenplay for *Dress Her in Indigo*, F12
MacFarlane, Robert (encomium), G292
"A Machine with Two Pistons" (essay), D15
MacMillan, Alissa (reviewer), J246
"The Mad Marlin of Punta Carnero" (essay), D14
*The Magic of Blood* (Gilb) (encomium), G133
*Magill's Literary Annual* (Magill, ed.), I10, I40
*Magnolia* MS *Gazette*, J361
Magnusson, Paul: critic, I9; interviewer, H7
"The Main Character is the Cold and the Snow" (criticism by JH), E20

*Making Game: An Essay on Woodcock* (de la Valdene) (encomium), G88
Malan, Rian (encomium), G97
"Malediction" (poem): audiotape, G1
*Manchester Guardian Weekly* magazine, H47
*The Mango Opera* (Corcoran) (encomium), G165
"The Man in the Back Row Has a Question II" (essay), D152
"The Man in the Back Row Has a Question VII" (essay), D188
*Man in the Green Suit* (treatment), F18
Manior de Pron, D171
*Manitou* (film treatment), F10
"A Man's Guide to Drinking" (essay), D191
*A Man's Journey to Simple Abundance* (Breathnach), D169
"The Man Who Gave Up His Name" (novella), A14.c.; excerpt, C20
*The Man Who Loved Music* (treatment), F34
Many Voice Press of Flathead Valley Community College, B170
*Mapmaker's Dream* (Cowan) A (encomium), G142
"Mapman" (poem), B181
*The Map of Who We Are* (Smith) (encomium), G148
"Marching to a Different Drummer" (essay), D19
"March Walk" (poem), B115, B135
Margolis, Susan (critic), I5
*Mark of the Grizzly—True Stories of Bear Attacks and the Hard Lessons Learned* (McMillion) (encomium), G163
Marowski, Daniel G. (critic), I27
"Marquette Beach to Larry Sullivan" (poem), B121
"Marriage Ghazal" (poem), B56
Marshall, John (reviewer), J337
*Martha Stewart Living* magazine, D276
Martin, David (encomium), G56
*Mastadon: 80% Complete* (Johnson) (encomium), G199
*Master Class* (Bunge), H49
"Matrix 1: Home" (poem), B35
"Matrix 3: Home" (poem), B35
Matthews, Charles (reviewer), J410
Matthiessen, Peter: encomium, G89, G152, G234; essay in tribute to, D43; review by JH, E23, E24; television series treatment for *Far Tortuga*, F11
Matthieussent, Brice (interviewer), G20, H50
Maul, Kimberly (interviewer), H120
McAlpin, Heller (reviewer), J421

MCA Records, D40
McCann, Colum (interviewer), H96
McCarthy, Cormac (encomium), G117
McClintock, James I. (critic), I71, I85
McCloskey, Mark (reviewer), J9
McCumber, David (encomium), G135, G175
McDonald, Roger (encomium), G169
McDonell, Terry (interviewer), note following H126
McFarland & Co., B103
McGinty, Stephen (interviewer), H55, H69
McGookey, Kathleen (encomium), G202
McGrath, Charles (interviewer), H123
McGraw-Hill, D141
McGuane, Thomas: co-author of *Cold Feet*, F2; encomium, G181, G185, G209
McIntyre, Joan: encomium, G51; review by JH, E15
McKee, Jenn (reviewer), J228
McMahon, Regan (reviewer), J210
McMillion, Scott (encomium), G163
McMurtry, Larry: encomium, G45; review by JH, E10
McNamee, Gregory: encomium, G131; interviewer, H92; reviewer, J108
McNamee, Thomas: encomium, G280; reviewer, J135, J169
McNamer, Deidre (encomium), G284
McNulty, Tim (reviewer), J207, J243, J330, J411, J429
*MD magazine*, H18, I29
*The Meadow* (Galvin) (encomium), G113
Meadow Run Press, D149
"Meals of Peace and Restoration" (essay), D62
*The Meaning of Life* (Moorhead, ed.), D54
*Mean Spirit* (Hogan) (encomium), G115
"Meatballs" (essay), D187
*Mechanical Birds* (Butson) (encomium), G195
*Meditations on the Chase* (Jones, ed.), C23
Meek, James (encomium), G265
Meltzer, David: JH review of, E3
*Mem-ka-Weh* (Weeks): introduction, D110
"A Memoir of Horse Pulling" (essay), D94, note following D278; earlier version as "The Real Fun of the Fair Was the Horse Pulling," D6
"Memorial Day" (poem), B152
"Memories of Meals with Lulu" (essay), D248
*Memphis Commercial Appeal*, J196, J247
*Memphis Flyer*, J336
*Men on the Moon* (Ortiz) (encomium), G172
*Men's Journal* magazine, B122, B133, C22, D168, D177, D180, D189, D190, D191, D192, D205, D208, D210, D235, H65, J156, J327
*Men's Journal: The Great Life* (Brandt), I81
Mephistophles Publications, B26
Mesler, Corey (reviewer), J247
Metropolitan Books, B130
*Mexico: One Plate at a Time* (Bayless) (encomium), G198
*Miami Herald*, I18
*Miami Vice TV Project* (screenplay), F27
Michigan Council for the Humanities, B69
*Michigan Department of Education*, J19, J37
*Michigan Living*, D51
"Michigan: Not Quite Leaving Michigan" (essay), D215
*Michigan Quarterly Review* magazine, D175
*Michigan Seasons* (Rulseh, ed.), D29
*Michigan Signatures* (Drake, ed.), B22
Michigan State University Press, B97, D153
*Michigan: The Magazine of the Detroit News*, C7, H8, H20, H23, I22, I35
*Michigan Voice*, J73
Mickunas, Vick (reviewer), J434
*MidAmerica*, I45, I76
Middleton, Harry (encomium), G125
*Midnight Mind Magazine*, D201
"Midrange Road Kill" (essay), D76
*Midwestern Miscellany*, I6, I106
*The Midwestern Pastoral* (Barillas), I105
*Midwest Quarterly*, B150, I83, I85
Miles, Jonathan: critic, I84; encomium, G290; interviewer, H95; reviewer, J240, J327
Milkweed Editions, C18, D164
Miller, Tom (encomium), G146
Miller, Wendy (reviewer), J287
Millman, Lawrence (encomium), G194
Mills, Jerry Leath (reviewer), J114
Milne, Lorus and Margery: review by JH, E19
*Milwaukee Journal Sentinel*, J242, J334
*Mind in the Water* (McIntyre) (encomium), G51
Mindy, Judith (encomium), G186
*Mine in the Waters* (McIntyre): review by JH, E15
*Minneapolis-St. Paul Star Tribune*, H13, J155, J194, J208, J227, J254, J282, J284, J291, J360, J390, J412, J446
Minzesheimer, Bob (reviewer), J119
*A Miracle of Catfish* (Brown)(encomium), G277
"The Misadventure Journals" (essay), D277
*Missouri Review* magazine, H16
"Missy 1966–1971" (poem), B103

*Mistletoe* magazine, B26
Mitchell, Stephen (encomium), G102
*Modern Poems* (Ellman and O'Clair, eds.), B37
"Modern Times" (poem), B164
*Molto Italiano* (Batali), D239
"Mom and Dad" (poem), B159
Momentum Books, D261
*The Monkey Wrench Gang* (Abbey): review by JH, E21
"The Montana Suite Convenes: Richard Ford, Annick Smith, Jim Harrison, Beverly Lowry, William Kittredge, and Tom McGuane. Absent: Rick Bass" (painting), G28
*Montana Writer's Cookbook* (Montana Center for the Book), D241
Moore, Judith: interviewer, H90; reviewer, J130, J161
Moore, Susanna (encomium), G128
"The Morality of Food" (essay), D114
*More Light* (Shinder, ed.), B85
Morice, Laura (critic), I62
"Morning" (poem), B27, B90
Morris, Anna (reviewer), J219
Mort, Mona (reviewer), J140, J174
Moss, Peyton (reviewer), J229
"Mother Night" (poem), B167, B185; excerpt, B156
*Move 4* magazine, B4
Mowat, Farley: review by JH, E20
*Mr. Darwin's Shooter* (McDonald) (encomium), G169
MSN *Microsoft Network's Books and Reading Community Chat Room*, H100
MSU *Alumni Magazine*, I77, I112
Mudge, Alden: critic, I97; reviewer, J326
Mueller, Lisel (reviewer), J14
Munro, C. Lynn: critic, I21, I49, I52
Muratori, Fred (reviewer), J78
Murphy, Bernadette (reviewer), J358
Murphy, Eileen (reviewer), J275
Murray, John A. (reviewer), J402, J423
"Muse and Hearth" (criticism by JH), E2
Muskegon Museum of Art, D111
*My Dogs and Guns* (Graves) (encomium), G278
*My Father on a Bicycle* (Clark) (encomium), G255
"My Friend the Bear" (poem), B109
"My Leader" (poem), B181
*My Mane Catches the Wind* (Hopkins, ed.), B57
"My Problems with White Wines" (essay), D211, D227

*Myself and Strangers* (Graves) (encomium), G249
*My Story as Told by Water* (Duncan) (encomium), G200
*My Traitor's Heart* (Malan) (encomium), G97

Nabhan, Gary Paul (encomium), G211
Nabokov, Peter (encomium), G262
"Naked Women Dancing" (essay), D192
*The Naomi Poems: Corpse and Beans* (Saint Geraud [Bill Knott]): JH review of, E6
*Narrative Magazine*, B175, C33
*Nashville's Grand Old Opry* (Hurst): review by JH, E18
*National Geographic Adventure*, J409, J428
National Public Radio, H24, H36
*Nation* magazine, B1, E1, E23, I26, J50, J72
"A Natural History of Some Poems" (essay), D95, note following D278
"Natural World" (poem), B7, B15, B22
*Natural World: A Bestiary* (poetry), A17, A17.a. (cover p. 36)
"Nature" (criticism by JH), E22
*The Nature Reader* (Halpern and Frank, eds.), D151
*Nature Writing* (Finch and Elder, eds.), D193
Neary, Lynn (interviewer), H24
N. E. Corp, C2
Nelson, Richard (encomium), G81, G105
Nelson, Sara (critic), I111
*Neon: Artcetera* magazine, D161
*Neon* magazine, D219
Neruda, Pablo (introduction to), D225
"Nesting in Air" (essay), D131
Netta, Lou (reviewer), J28
NEW: *American and Canadian Poetry* magazine, B6, J28
New Directions, D225
Newer, Hank (critic), I25
*The New Great American Writers Cookbook* (Wells, ed.), D214
*New Letters* magazine, B63, B151, H119
*New Letters on the Air* (audiotape and CD), G15
"New Liturgy" (poem), B1; audiotape, G1
"New Map of the Sacred Territory" (essay), D112
New Michigan Press, A50, A54
*New Poems from the Third Coast* (Berg et al., eds.), B107
New Rivers Press, B94
*News and Revue*, J168
*Newsday*, J269, J329
*Newsweek*, I8, J41, J51, J127, J271
Newth, Rebecca: encomium, G57; interviewer, H61

*New University Thought* magazine, B10
*The New Wolves* (Bass) (encomium), G168
"New World" (poem), B189
New World Library, D158
*New York Daily News*, J126, J246
*New Yorker*, C14, C26, D237, G28, J42, J442
*New York Observer*, J280
*New York Review of Books*, G23, G24
*New York Times*, H59, H123, J15, J40, J59, J65, J69, J71, J83, J87, J98, J103, J113, J135, J185
*New York Times Book Review*, B117, D37, D238, D257, D268, E4, E5, E8, E10, E11, E14, E18, E20, E21, E22, E24, E27, I2, J11, J17, J24, J25, J30, J32, J43, J49, J68, J241, J252, J270, J283, J297, J317, J323, J339, J351, J353, J380, J393, J403, J419, J439
*New York Times Magazine*, D167
Nicholas, Robert L.: interviewer, H113; reviewer, J331, J361
*The Nick Adams Stories* (Hemingway): review by JH, E12
Nickels, Mark (encomium), G187
*Night Dharma* (poetry broadside), A41, A41.a. (facsimile p. 80)
"Night Games" ("A River Never Sleeps") (essay), D24, D90
"Night in Boston" (poem), B5, B6, B21
"Nightmare" (poem): audiotape, G1
*Night Train* (Erdrich) (encomium), G285
"Night Walking" (essay), D50, D158, D170
*Nine Below Zero* (Canty) (encomium), G180
*Noise Number 4* (McLelland, ed.), B48
"No Man Is in Iceland" (short story), C8
*No Man's Dog* (Jackson) (encomium), G244
"North" (poem): excerpt, B102
"North at Fifty-Three" (poem), B82
North Atlantic Books, B98
*Northern Express*, I60
Northern Illinois University Press, B44
*Northern Latitudes* (Millman) (encomium), G194
*Northern Lights* magazine, D131
"Northern Michigan" (poem), B69, B77, B134, I3
"The Northness of North" (criticism by JH), E1
North Point Press, C27, D49
*Northwest Review* magazine, B92, H71
*North Winter* (Carruth): JH review of, E1
Norton, Mike (interviewer), H29
*The Norton Anthology of Modern Poetry* (Ellman and O'Clair, eds.), B37
*The Norton Book of Nature Writing* (Finch and Elder, eds.), D193
Norton, B100

"Not at All Like Up Home in Michigan" (essay), D25; as "Okeechobee," D91
"A Note" (editorial in *Sumac*), D5
"A Note on J. D. Reed's Expressways" (criticism by JH), E7
"Note on Shinkichi Takahashi" (criticism by JH), E13
*Notes from the Shore* (Ackerman) (encomium), G147
*Notes on Contemporary Literature*, I30, I70
"Not Writing My Name" (poem), B61
*Novel and Short Story Writer's Market 2002* (Bowling, ed.), I88
"November" (poem), B121
Noverr, Douglas A. (critic), I6
NS, J75
Nunn, Kem (encomium), G114
Nuwer, Hank (interviewer), H17

*Oakland Press* (Pontiac MI), J189
Oates, Joyce Carol (reviewer), J16, J18
O'Brien, Dan (encomium), G73, G108, G156, G177, G207
*October Chronicle*, H3
*Octopus Alibi* (Corcoran) (encomium), G237
"Odious Comparisons" (essay), D232
"Of Arms, the Man and the Whale They Sing" (criticism by JH), E15
*Off to the Side: A Memoir* (memoir), A40, A40.a. (proof copies p. 76), A40.d. (dust jacket p. 78); excerpt: "Painting with a Turtle Hair Paintbrush," D216; excerpts, C30, D249, D254, D261; quotation from, D224; reviews, J319–J369
Offutt, Chris (encomium), G120
O'Gorman, Ned: JH review of, E5
*Ohio University unpublished disseratation*, I80
*Oil Notes* (Bass) (encomium), G82
"Okeechobee" ("Not at All Like Up Home in Michigan") (essay), D25, D91
*Old Bird Boy* (poetry broadside), A54, A54.a. (facsimile p. 112)
"Old Days" (poem), B117
"Older Love" (poem), B116, B119, B121, B162
*Older Love* (poetry broadside), A33 (facsimile p. 66)
"Old Faithful and Mysterious" (essay), D11
"An Old Man" (poem), B150
Olney, Richard: review by JH, D227, E26
Olson, Ray (reviewer), J373
O'Neal, Glenn (reviewer), J399
"One Foot in the Grave" (essay), D101
"One Good Thing Leads to Another" (essay), D272
*One Hundred Paintings* (Chatham): encomium, G94; preface, D70, D109

*One Thousand White Women* (Fergus) (encomium), G161
"On Horseback in China" (poem), B181
"Only 100 Pounds? Turn Him Loose" (essay), D13
*On Nature* (Halpern, ed.), D49
*On Out* (Welch): JH review of, E3
*On Point—WBUR Boston* (Interview), G18
*On the Trail to Wounded Knee* (Le Querrec) (introduction to), D196; Excerpt in Video Documentary, G21
"On the Way to the Doctor's" (poem), B151, B154
Opdahl, Keith (reviewer), J50
Open Book Press, A17
*Open City* magazine, B142, B173, C31
*Open Poems: Four Anthologies of Expanded Poems* (Gross and Quasha, eds.), B41
Orchard Books, B65, B90
Oregon Public Radio, H93
*Orion* magazine, B189
Ortiz, Simon J. (encomium), G119, G172
*Orvis Catalog*, G33
*Orvis Catalog—Fly Fishing*, G32, G36
*Orvis Catalog—the Sporting Tradition*, G30
*The Orvis Fly-Fishing Guide 2007* (Rosenbauer) (encomium), G281
*The Orvis Pocket Guide to Nymphing Techniques* (Rosenbauer) (encomium), G220
Osborne, Lawrence (encomium), G250
Oser, Lee (reviewer), J182
Ostria, Vincent (interviewer), H54
Otterbacher, John (encomium), G279
*Our Private Lives* (Halpern, ed.), D68
"Our Roving Poet/Novelist/Sybarite Almost Buys a Subaru Legacy" (essay), D79
"Outcast" (short story), C34
*The Outlander* (Adamson) (encomium), G289
"Outlaw Cook" (essay), D122
"Outlyer and Ghazals" (poem): excerpt, B41
*Outlyer and Ghazals* (poetry), A6, A6.b. (dust jacket p. 12); excerpts on audiotape, G2; reviews, J20–J28
*Out of Control* (Gerber) (encomium), G48
*Out of Range* (Box), D244
*Out of the Noosphere*, D52
*Out of the War Shadow* (Levertov, ed.), B7
*Outside Bozeman*, D202
*Outside* magazine, D28, D52, H27, I68, J80, J108, J248, J346
*Out Your Backdoor* magazine, H42
*Over the Graves of Horses* (Delp) (encomium), G75

*Oxford Town* magazine, H113, J331
*Ozark*, I25

*Pacific Dream* (Illig), C29
Pacific Vista Productions, H60
*Pages*, I98
"Painting with a Turtle Hair Paintbrush" (essay), D216
"The Panic Hole" (essay), D78
Pantheon Books, C24
*Paper Products* (Hall) (encomium), G96
*Parables and Portraits* (Mitchell) (encomium), G102
"Paris Rebellion" (essay), D220
*Paris Review*, D145, D152, D188, D218, H21
"Park at Night" (poem), B4; audiotape, G1
Parks, Cecily (encomium), G288
*Parnassus*, J67
Parrett, Aaron (reviewer), J366
*Parsippany NJ Daily Record*, J304
*Partisan Review* magazine, B30, J18, J79
*The Party Train* (Alexander et al., eds.), B94
"Passacaglia on Getting Lost" (essay), D45, D49, D151, D158
*Patterns of Exposition, 16th ed.* (Schwegler, ed.), D172
Patterson, J. C. (reviewer), J209, J237, J245
*Paul Strand* (Strange, ed.), D71
Pawlcyn, Cindy (encomium), G270
*Peace Like a River* (Enger) (encomium), G206
Peacock, Andrea (encomium), G233
Peacock, Doug (encomium), G92, G256
Pearson Education, B168, D260
*A Peculiar Grace* (Lent) (encomium), G276
Penguin Books, D273
*Peninsula* (Steinberg, ed.), D170
Pennyroyal Press, G37
*People*, J104
*The People's Act of Love* (Meek) (encomium), G265
Peregrine Smith Books, B79
Perry, Roy E. (reviewer), J441
Perry, Susan (reviewer), J213
Pevere, Geoff (reviewer), J431
*Philadelphia Inquirer*, I12, J146, J278
*Philadelphia Tribune*, H97
Phipps, Terry W.: critic, I72; interviewer, H81, H91; reviewer, J132
*The Phoenix*, J444
*Phoenix Sun*, J357
Pichaske, David R. (critic), I108
*Piece of Resistance*, F13
"Pie in the Sky" (essay), D130
"Piggies Come to Market" (essay), D80

Pintarich, Paul (reviewer), J94
Pirkola, Mary Isca (interviewer), H122
*Pittsburgh Post-Gazette*, J447
*Pittsburgh Tribune-Review*, J234, J293
*A Place to Stand: The Making of a Poet* (Baca) (encomium), G201
*Plain Song* (poetry), A1; excerpts on audiotape, G1, G2; reviews, J1–J9
*Planet Weekly*, J209, J245, J335
Plante Cable/Cine Cinema Cable/Gedeon, G20, H50
"A Plaster Trout in Worm Heaven" (essay), D8
*Playboy* magazine, D22, D46, D271, J383
*Playing off the Rail* (McCumber) (encomium), G135
*The Pleasures of the Damned* (Bukowski): review by JH, E27
Ploughshares books, B66
*Ploughshares* magazine, B54
*The Ploughshares Poetry Reader* (Peseroff, ed.), B66
Pocket Books, B40, G9
"Poem" (poem), B2, B3, B28, B79
"Poem of War" (poem), B129, B153; excerpt, B180
*Poems across the Big Sky* (Jaeger, ed.), B170
*Poetic Medicine* (Fox), D156
*Poet Lore*, J1, J2, J200
"Poet Power" (signature to letter of protest), G23
"Poetry as Survival" (essay), D74, D164
Poetry Center at the 92nd Street Y (poetry reading), G1
*Poetry from A to Z* (Janeczko), B88
*Poetry* magazine, B3, B12, B187, E2, E3, J9, J14
*Poetry Now* magazine, B55, B56
*The Poetry of Horses* (Cole, ed.), B58
"The Poetry Symposium" (contribution to larger piece), D238
*Poets against the War* (Hamill, ed.), B129
*Poets on Street Corners* (Carlisle): JH review of, E6
Pohrt, Karl (reviewer), J345, J354
*The Point* (D'Ambrosio) (encomium), G138
"Political Intervention" (letter) (essay), D100
"The Political Scene" (essay), D176
*Politis* magazine, H86
*Pomona Queen* (Nunn) (encomium), G114
*Pony Tail: A Magazine for Always*, B19, G22
*Porch*, J54
"Porpoise" (poem), B73
"Portal, Arizona" (poem), B110

*Portal, Arizona* (poetry broadside), A35
Porter, Bill (encomium), G126
Porter, William: interviewer, H103; reviewer, J192, J274, J310
Portland Arts and Lectures Series (audiotape), G13; question- and-answer session, H77
*Portland Oregonian*, J94, J170, J261, J338, J397, J420
*Port Townsend wa Leader*, J171
*Port Tropique* (Gifford) (encomium), G55
"Posole from Sonora" (recipe) (essay), D214
*Pot on the Fire* (Thorne) (encomium), G197
Potter, Jeff (interviewer), H42
*Power: A Novel* (Hogan) (encomium), G167
*The Power of Place* (Gallagher) (encomium), G129
*Practice of the Wild* (Snyder): review by JH, E25
*Prairie Schooner*, J7
"Preface" (to *One Hundred Paintings*): edited version, D109
*Premiere*, I58
Prentice-Hall, B115, B135
"The Preparation of Thomas Hearns" (essay), D92, note following D278
Prescott, Peter S.: critic, I8; reviewer, J51
Pressed Wafer and Granary Books, A35
*The Pressed Wafer Broadsides for John Wieners*: "Portal, Arizona" in, A35, A35 (colophon, poem p. 68)
Pressed Wafer, B110
Preston, Carrie: critic, I89; interviewer, H105
Prichard, Peter S. (reviewer), J101
*Prime 1998*, J162
*Prince of Los Angeles* (screenplay), F6
"Principles" (essay), D108
*The Process* (Meltzer): JH review of, E3
*Profiles* (radio broadcast), H93
*Providence ri Sunday Journal*, J180
Prozak, Christian (reviewer), J276
*Psychoanalytic Review*, D87, D139
*Publications of the Arkansas Philological Association*, I43
*Publications of the Mississippi Philological Association*, I32
*Publishers Weekly Daily*, J272
*Publishers Weekly* magazine, H33, I111, J29, J38, J48, J63, J70, J89, J165, J201, J204, J224, J225, J286, J289, J319, J320
"Pure Poetry" (criticism by JH), E8
Pushcart, H33
Pym Randall Press, A2.a., A2.b.

Quackenbush, Rich (reviewer), J134
Quality Paperback Book Club, B100
Quammen, David: encomium, G76, G143; reviewer, J80
Quarrington, Paul (encomium), G196
"The Quarter" (poem), B184
*Quarter After Eight*, I96, J377
Quasha, George: critic, I1; reviewer, J3, J10
Queffelec, Yann (encomium), G72
"The Question of Zen" (essay), D169; as "Everyday Life: A Question of Zen," B78, D96, D186
Quinn, Anthony (reviewer), J380
Quixote Press, B22
*The Quotable Writer* (Underwood, ed.) (quotations in), D224
*Quotes and Reflections for 365 Days* (Cock), B156

"Rage and Appetite" (essay), D275
Rakosi, Carl: JH review of, E4
Random House, B25, D264
Rankin, Rush (reviewer), J20
*A Rare and Precious Thing* (Kain) (encomium), G273
*Rational Zen* (Cleary) (encomium), G116
Ratner, Rochelle (reviewer), J159
Ravo, Nick (interviewer), H59
"The Raw and the Cooked" (essay), D163; excerpt, D244
*The Raw and the Cooked* (essays), A26, A26.a. (title page p. 52)
*The Raw and the Cooked* (treatment), F36
*The Raw and the Cooked: Adventures of a Roving Gourmand* (essays), A39, A39.b. (dust jacket p. 74), D184, D185; excerpt, D241; previously unpublished essays in, note following D278; reviews, J286–J318
Rawlins, C. L. (encomium), G145
Raynal, Patrick (interviewer), H28, H47
*Razor*, I95
"Reading Calasso" (poem), B161
*The Reading List's Contemporary Fiction* (Rubel, ed.), I78
"Real Big Brown Truck" (essay), D75
"The Real Fun of the Fair Was the Horse Pulling" (essay), note following D278; as "A Memoir of Horse Pulling," D94; basis for "A Memoir of Horse Pulling," D6
"A Really Big Lunch" (essay), D237, D240, D264; excerpt, D243
*Real Time* (Chaudhuri) (encomium), G227
Recorded Books, G7
*The Recovery of Innocence* (Iyer), I23
*Red Cedar Review*, B43, B114, H105

*Redemption* (Turner) (encomium), G274
Redhill, Michael (encomium), G248
Red Hydra Press, A45
*Red Line* (Bowden) (encomium), G85
Red Pine, trans (encomium), G178
*Red Rover* (McNamer) (encomium), G284
*Red Stag* (de la Valdene) (encomium), G231
*Red Streak* magazine, D212
Reece, Parks (encomium), G219
Reed, Christine (encomium), G70
Reed, J. D.: encomium, G54, G70; JH review of, E7; reviewer, J36
Reed, Julia: critic, I44; interviewer, H30
Reese, Jim (reviewer), J376
*Reflexions* (Olney): review by JH, D227, E26
*Refuge* (Williams) (encomium), G103
Reid, Elwood (encomium), G242
Reilly, Edward C.: critic, I30, I32, I66; interviewer, H72
Reinhard, John (encomium), G74
"Re: life, philosophically—no comment" (essay), D54
*Rendezvousing with Contemporary Writers* (interview), H17
*Rendezvous* magazine, H17
Rentilly, J. (critic), I95
"Republican Wives" (novella), A49
*Republican Wives: A Novella* (novella), A48, A48 (cover p. 98)
"Repulsion and Grace" (essay), D121
*Rescuers* (Winegar) (encomium), G261
*Residence on Earth* (Neruda) (introduction), D225
"Resuming the Pleasure" (essay), D250
*The Retreat* (Rambaud), D228
"Return" (poem), B3
"Returning at Night" (poem), B28
*Returning to Earth* (author trading card), G40
*Returning to Earth* (novel), A52, A52.a., A52.b. (proof and advance copies p. 106), A52.c. (dust jacket); audiotape and CD, G17; reviews, J407–J422
"Returning to Earth" (poem), A14; excerpts, B54, B66
*Returning to Earth* (poetry), A12.a. (cover p. 26); reviews, J45
"Return of the Native; or Lighten Up" (essay), D106
"Return to Yesenin" (poem), B94
*The Revenant* (Gerber) (encomium), G43
*Revenant* (treatment), F16
*Revenge* (audiotape), G6
"Revenge" (novella), A14; edited version, C3; excerpts, C16, C28; excerpts on audiotape, G5

*Revenge* (screenplay), F2
"The Revenge Symposium" (essay in), D39
"Revenge: The American Way of Revenge and How It Compares to the Real Thing" (essay), D46
"A Revisionist's Walden" (essay), D97
*Revue des Deux Mondes* magazine, D178, E26
Reynolds, Susan Salter. *See* Salter Reynolds, Susan
Ricci, Jim (interviewer), H45, H46
"Richard Olney's Final Book, *Reflexions*": criticism by JH, D227, E26
*Riddles in the Sand* (Buffett) (album notes for), D40
Rinella, Steven (encomium), G263
*Ripe: Poems* (Davis) (encomium), G218
*The Rites of Autumn* (O'Brien) (encomium), G73
"A River Never Sleeps" (essay), D24; as "Night Games," D90
*River of the West* (Clark) (encomium), G140
*Rivers and Birds* (Gilfillan) (encomium), G229
*Riverside CA Press Enterprise*, J147
*Rivers of Memory* (Middleton) (encomium), G125
*The Riverwatch* magazine, B87
*Rivethead* (Hamper) (encomium), G101
Rizzoli, D69
"The Road: A Love Story" (essay), D208
*The Road Home* (novel), A30, A30.b. (dust jacket p. 60); excerpts, C21, C24, C30; reviews, J119–J154
*Road to Heaven* (Porter) (encomium), G126
*Road Trips, Head Trips and Other Car Crazed Writings* (Lindamood, ed.), B93
*The Roaring Stream* (Foster) (encomium), G158
Roberson, William H. (critic), I17, I34
*Rocky Mountain News*, J432
Roelofs, Ted: interviewer, H87; reviewer, J124, J414
Rohrkemper, John: critic, I16; reviewer, J76
*Rolling Stone* magazine, D50, I5
"Rooster" (poem), B61, B168
*Rooted* (Pichaske, ed.), C30, I108
Roper, Martin (encomium), G228
Rosati, Arianna Pavia (reviewer), J298
Rosenbauer, Tom (encomium), G220, G281
Rosenberg, Kenyon C. (reviewer), J23
Rosenthal, M. L. (reviewer), J24
Ross, Jean W. (interviewer), H11, H12
*Rounding the Human Corners* (Hogan) (encomium), G293
Roundtable Conversation series, Academy of American Poets Audio Archive, H5

*La Route du Retour (The Road Home)*, A30.b.
"Roving" (essay), D57
Rowen, John (reviewer), J325
Rozen, Leah (reviewer), J104
Rubel, David, ed (critic), I78
*Ruminator Review*, D176, J217
Rungren, Lawrence (reviewer), J408
*Running with the Bulls* (Hemingway) (encomium), G245
Russell, Franklin: encomium, G59; review by JH, E19, E22
*Russell Chatham—Deep Creek* (Winn Publishing), D41
Ryan, Michael C. (critic), I113

Sabo, Mary Ann (reviewer), J394
*The Sacred Earth* (Gardner, ed.), D158
"Sacred Territory" (essay), D146
"Safety without Portfolio in Key West" (essay), D28
*Sailing Grace* (Otterbacher) (encomium), G279
Saint Geraud (Bill Knott): JH review of, E6
*Saints of Hysteria* (Duhamel et al., eds.), B169
Salij, Marta (reviewer), J259
Sallis, James (reviewer), J343
*Salon.com*, J240, J292
*The Salon.com Reader's Guide to Contemporary Authors* (Miller, ed.), I84
SALON *Magazine*, H95
Salter, John (encomium), G269
Salter Reynolds, Susan: critic, I99; reviewer, J236, J342, J416, J440, J449
"Salvation in the Keys" (essay), D23; as "A Day in May," D86
*Samba (Brazil)* (screenplay), F21
"The Same Goose Moon" (poem), B76
*The Same Goose Moon* (poetry broadside), A37, A37 (facsimile p. 70)
Samson, John G.: review by JH, E22
*San Antonio Express-News—Morning Edition*, J309
Sander, Amy (critic), I60
*San Diego Reader*, H90, J130, J161
*San Diego Union Tribune*, J142, J308, J392, J415
Sandman, Kjell: review by JH, E22
*Sand Rivers* (Matthiessen): review by JH, E24
*San Francisco Chronicle*, J210, J255, J369, J381, J410, J443
*San Francisco Examiner Magazine*, H58
*San Francisco Review of Books*, J47
*San Jose Mercury News*, J364
*Santa Fean* magazine, D209

*Santa Fe New Mexican*, J211, J264, J307, J352
Sasquatch Books, D243
*Saturday Review of Literature*, J26
*Saudade* (See) (encomium), G291
"Save These Books" (contribution to larger piece), D257
*Saveur* magazine, D248, J318
*Saving Daylight* (poetry), A51, A51.b. (dust jacket p. 104); reviews, J402–J406
"Saving the Daylight" (poem), B140
Scannell, Verson (reviewer), J55
*The Scavenger's Guide to Haute Cuisine* (Rinella) (encomium), G263
*Schenectady NY Gazette*, J325
Schneider, Bart (encomium), G166
Schneider, Wolf (reviewer), J264
Schott, Webster (reviewer), J43
Schudel, Matt (reviewer), J448
Schwager, Jeff (critic), I61
Schwenk, Theodor: review by JH, E22
"Science" (poem), B166
"Scrubbing the Floor the Night a Great Lady Died" (poem), D252
*Scythian Women* (treatment), F38
Seaman, Donna (reviewer), J157
*Searching for Intruders* (Byler) (encomium), G216
*Season of the Angler* (Seybold, ed.), B68
Seaton, J. P.: encomium, G164
Seattle Arts and Lectures Series (audiotape), G12; question- and-answer session, H76
*Seattle Post-Intelligencer*, J138, J169, J173, J178, J337
*Seattle Times*, J207, J243, J330, J411, J429
*A Second Life* (Gerber)(encomium), G204
*Secret Ingredients* (Remnick, ed.), D264
*The Secret Life of Animals* (Milne et al.): review by JH, E19
*Secret Spaces of Childhood* (Goodenough, ed.), D175
See, Anik (encomium), G291
*Seeds from a Birch Tree* (Strand) (encomium), G157
Selander, Glenn E. (reviewer), J34
*Selected and New Poems* (poetry), A16, A16.b. (dust jacket p. 35); reviews, J61–J68
*Sensitive Chaos* (Schwenk): review by JH, E22
"Sequence" (poem), B19
"Sequence (stanza 3)" (poem), B26
"Sequence of Women" (poem): audiotape, G1
"Sergei Yesenin" (essay), D145
"Sergei Yesenin 1895–1925" (poem), B43, B114

*Sergei Yesenin 1895–1925* (poetry broadside), A8, A8.a. (facsimiles p. 14)
*Serious Pig* (Thorne), I67
"Seven Ghazals" (poem), B30
Seymour Lawrence, D72; with Delacorte Press, A14, A15, A16; with E. P. Dutton, A18.a., A20; with Houghton Mifflin, A22, A28
Seymour Lawrence Publisher (Seymour Lawrence) (contribution to), D72
Shack, Neville (reviewer), J74
*Shadow and Light* (Moser) (portrait), G37
*A Shadow in the City* (Bowden) (encomium), G257
*Shake the Kaleidoscope: A New Anthology of Modern Poetry* (Klonsky, ed.), B40
*Shaman Drum Newsletter*, I73, J120
Shambhala Publications, A29, B78, G10
*Shambhala Sun* magazine, D270, J163, J365
*The Shape of the Journey* (poetry), A32, A32.b. (dust jacket p. 64); reviews, J155–J200; "The Same Goose Moon" in, A37
Shapiro, Nancy (reviewer), J105
"She" (poem): audiotape, G1
Shea, Dennis (reviewer), J167
Shechner, Mark (reviewer), J418
Sheehan, Marc J. (interviewer), H38
Sheep Meadow Press, B62
Shellenbarger, Pat (reviewer), J426
*Shenandoah*, I79
Shillinglaw, Susan, ed. (contribution to essay collection), D197
Shipley, Jonathan: interviewer, H110; reviewer, J251
Shipley, Leanne (reviewer), J384
Shires, Ashley Simpson: interviewer, H124; reviewer, J432
Shreve, Porter (reviewer), J281
Shumaker, Jon (reviewer), J405
Shumate, David (encomium), G243
(SIC) VICE and VERSE, J197
Siegel, Eric (interviewer), H2
"The Sign" (poem), B19
*Silent Seasons* (Chatham, ed.), D8, D22, D29, D202; untitled essay, D30
*Silverfish Review*, H41
Simon and Schuster, A6, A7.a., A7.b., A9, B41, D52, D200
*Simple Cooking* magazine, D144
Simpson, Louis: critic, I2; reviewer, J11
"The Singular Excitement of Water Sports" (essay), D21
Sipchen, Bob (critic), I39
Sissman, L. E.: JH review of, E5
Sisyphus, Aloysius (interviewer), H39

"Sitting Around" (essay), D129
"The Situation of American Writing 1999" (essay), D166
"Sketch for a Job Application Blank" (poem), B37, B47, G1, I3; audiotape, G1; excerpt, B158
*Sketch for a Job Application Blank* (poetry broadside), A25, A25.a. (facsimile p. 50)
Skloot, Floyd (reviewer), J170
Skowles, John (reviewer), J305, J308
Skwira, Gregory (interviewer), H14
*Sleeping Beauties* (Moore) (encomium), G128
Sloan, Bob (encomium), G127, G179
Smart, Andrew (interviewer), H125
*Smart* magazine, C13, note following H126; "Sporting Food" column, D56, D62, D63, D64, D66, D67, D77, D78, D80, D82
Smith, Jack R. (program notes for exhibition by), D111
Smith, Lawrence R. (encomium), G148, G232
Smith, Patrick: critic, I80, I82, I86, I87, I91, I92; interviewer, H82; reviewer, J249
Smith, Tom (interviewer), H68
Smith, Wendy: interviewer, H33; reviewer, J137
Smoker, Mandy (encomium), G254
"The Smoker Knocked My Socks Off" (advertisement), G33
*Smoke Signals* magazine, B59, C4, C5, D31, D33, D38, D42, I13
Smolens, John (encomium), G203
Smyntek, John (critic), I50
"Snake-Eating" (essay), D245
Snider, Burr (interviewer), H58
Snodgrass, W. D.: JH review of, E5
*The Snow Catcher* (Twichell) (encomium), G159
*The Snow Leopard* (Matthiessen): review by JH, E23
*Snow on the Backs of Animals.* (Gerber) (encomium), G66
*The Snow Walker* (Mowat): review by JH, E20
Snyder, Gary: review by JH, E25
Sololov, Raymond (reviewer), J41
*So Long at the Fair* (Williams): JH review of, E5
"Some Ghazals" (poem), B31
*Some Heaven* (Davis) (encomium), G275
*Some Horses* (McGuane) (encomium), G181
"Some Recent Books" (criticism by JH), E6
Sommerness, Marty (interviewer), H3
*The Song of the Dodo* (Quammen) (encomium), G143

"Sonoran Radio" (poem), B89, B99
Sony, D242
"A Sort of Purist-Type Chili" (recipe) (essay), D20
"Soul Food" ("American Food Journal") (essay), D189, D198
"Sound" (poem), B28
Soundelux Audio Publishing, G8, H56
*Soundings* magazine, B8, B16
*Southern Review*, I33, J6
*Spectrum* magazine, B35
*The Spirit Cabinet* (Quarrington) (encomium), G196
"The Spirit of Wine" (essay), D269
Spivak, Talbot: review by JH, E11
"Sporting Food" (essay), D56
"A Sporting Life" (essay), D22
"Sporting Life Recaptured" (essay), D18; as "Canada," D85
*Sports Afield* magazine, D140, D146, D147
*Sports Afloat* (Constable, ed.), D21
Sports Illustrated Books, D213
*Sports Illustrated: Fifty Years of Great Writing*, D213
*Sports Illustrated* magazine, D6, D8, D9, D10, D11, D12, D16, D18, D19, D25, E15, E16, E17, E19
Spragg, Mark (encomium), G246
"Spring Coda" (essay), D127
"A Spring Sermon . . . or Siberia" (essay), D140
*Spy*, I56
Square Books, A45
"Squaw Gulch" (essay), D143
SR, J16
Stackpole Books, D149
Standridge, Dana (encomium), G266
*Stanley Jaffee Project* (screenplay), F23
Stanton, Doug (encomium), G225
Starck, Clemens (encomium), G134
"Starting Over" (essay), D177, D183; excerpt, D229
State University of New York at Albany, H68
Stegner, Lynn (encomium), G283
Steinberg, Michael, and Larry Rothe (encomium), G271
Stephenson, Anne (reviewer), J295, J300, J301
Stern, Jane and Michael (reviewer), J297
Stielstra, Julie (reviewer), J73
*Still Water* (Garfunkel) (encomium), G83
Stine, Jean C. (critic), I27
*St. Louis Post-Dispatch*, J105, J391
Stocking, Kathleen: critic, I38; interviewer, H4, H8, H26, H31

*Stony Brook Holographs*, A3.a. (portfolio p. 6); "Dreams" in, A3
*Stony Brook* magazine, B18, B24, I1, J10
Stony Brook Poetics Foundation, A3
"Stony Brook Poets' Prophesy—June 23, 1968" (signature to letter of protest), G22
*The Story Factor* (Simmons), D254
Story Press, C20
*St. Petersburg FL Times*, J123, J263, J299
Strand, Clark (encomium), G157
*The Stranger*, J133, J164
Streitfeld, David: critic, I75; interviewer, H44, H98; reviewer, J145, J179
Strick, Wesley (co-author of *Wolf*), F3
Stroud, Joseph (encomium), G162
*Studies in Short Fiction*, J46
Styron, Alexandra (encomium), G210
"Suite to Appleness" (poem), B9, B23
"Suite to Fathers" (poem), B12, B47, B62
*Sulfur*, J61
*Sumac* magazine, B17, B32, B34, D2, D4, D5, D7, E6, E7, E9
Sumac Poetry Series, Center Publication, A13
Sumac Press, A5, A8, A10, B20, D17
*The Sumac Reader* (Bednarik, ed.), B97; introduction, D153
*The Summer He Didn't Die* (audiotape and CD), G16
*The Summer He Didn't Die* (fiction—novellas), A49, A49 (dust jacket p. 100); reviews, J389–J401
"The Summer He Didn't Die" (novella), A49
*Sunbeams: A Book of Quotations* (Safransky), C10
"Sunday Discordancies" (poem), B181
*Sundog* (novel), A18, A18.b. (dust jacket p. 37); excerpt as "Sundog," C7; excerpts on audiotape, G5; reviews, J69–J75
"Sundog: A Leelanau Peninsula Author Begins the Long, Painful Journey Back toward Earth": excerpt from *Sundog*, C7
Sundstrom, Nancy: critic, I63; interviewer, H107; reviewer, J203, J231
Sunee, Kim (encomium), G287
*The Sun* magazine, B82, C10
"Sunset Limited" (novella), A22
"The Sunset Limited" (novella): shorter version of the novella that appears in *The Woman Lit by Fireflies*, C13
*Sur la Piste de Bigfoot* (Le Querrec), D196
Survey of Contemporary Literature, J20
"Susan Thompson, Cape Split, Maine, 1945" (essay), D71
*The Swamp* (Thomas): review by JH, E22

Swan, Alison (reviewer), J177
*Sweetbitter Love: Poems of Shappo* (Barnstone) (encomium), G268
*Sydney Pollack Project* (screenplay), F26
*Symbiography* (Hjortsberg) (encomium), G46
"A Symposium on Secret Places" (contribution to larger piece), D175; as "Through Thicket and Thin," D181

*A Taco Testimony* (Chavez) (encomium), G272
Takahashi, Shinkichi: encomium, G65; review by JH, E13
*Take My Advice* (Harmon, ed.), D200
*Taking Care* (Williams) (encomium), G63
Talbert, Bob (interviewer), H32, H43, H52, H67, H73, H75
Tamarack Editions, B60
Tamori & Chang, C19
*Tampa Tribune*, J267
*Tampa Tribune and Times*, J136
*A Tan and Sandy Silence* (MacDonald), B36
*Tangier Buzzless Flies* (Hopkins): review by JH, E11
*Tape for the Turn of the Year* (Ammons): JH review of, E2
"Tape One of the First Thirty-Three: The Dead Food Scrolls" (essay), D38
Tarcher/Putnam, D156
*Tarpon* (Video Documentary), G19
Taylor, Henry (reviewer), J200
Taylor, Keith (reviewer), J64
*Teaching the Art of Poetry* (Wormser and Cappella), B112
*Teewinot: A Year in the Teton Range* (Turner) (encomium), G184
*Telegraph Magazine*, H115, J368
*Telerama* magazine, H28, H53, H84, I57
*Le Temps*, H83
*The Tennessean*, J441
Ten Speed Press, D227
*Thematic Guide to Popular Short Stories* (Smith), I92
"Then and Now" (essay), D64
"The Theory and Practice of Rivers" (poem), B63, B124; excerpts, B67, B72, B80, B81, B83, B84, B87, B113, B139, B157, B160
*The Theory and Practice of Rivers* (poetry), A19, A19.b. (dust jacket p. 38); reviews, J76–J81
*The Theory and Practice of Rivers and New Poems* (poetry), A21, A21.a. (dust jacket p. 42); reviews, J89–J90

*These United States* (Leonard, ed.), D215
"Thin Ice" (poem), B15, B28
*Thin Ice* (Van Til and Olson), D262
*The Third Coast: Contemporary Michigan Fiction* (Tipton and Wegner, eds.), C6
*The Third Coast: Contemporary Michigan Poetry* (Hilberry, ed.), B50
"Thirty-three Angles on Eating French" (essay): as "Eating French," D168
*This Art: Poetry about Poetry* (Weigers, ed.), B126
*This Delicious Day* (Janeczko, ed.), B65
*This Week: Southwest Montana's Arts and Entertainment Magazine*, I104
Thomas, Bill: review by JH, E22
Thompson, Jean (reviewer), J393
Thompson, Sedge (interviewer), H36
Thorne, John: critic, I67; encomium, G197
Thorpe, Peter (reviewer), J193
*Three Day Road* (Boyden) (encomium), G260
*Three Junes* (Glass), C24
"Three Novels: Comic, Cute, Cool" (criticism by JH), E11
"Three Poems in Search of Small Gods" (poem), B183
*Through Lakota Eyes: A Film about Human Rights* (Video Documentary), G21
"Through Thicket and Thin" (essay), D181; as untitled essay, D175
Thunder's Mouth Press, B120
Thunder's Mouth Press/Nation Books, B129, D215
Thurber, Bart (reviewer), J415
Tide-Mark Press, G35
Tillinghast, Richard (reviewer), J65
Tillotson, Kristin (reviewer), J446
"Time" (poem) (essay), B141, D230
Time-Life Books, D21
*Times Literary Supplement*, J55, J74, J84, J116
"Time Suite" (poem), B92, B95; excerpts, B102, B138
*Time Suite: Poems by Jim Harrison*, B138
"To a Meadowlark" (poem), B161, B178, D274
"Today We Moved" (poem), B44
"To Each His Own Chills and Thrills" (essay), D10, D29; excerpt, D69
*Toledo OH Blade*, J166
"Tongue" (essay), D231
*The Top Ten* (Zane, ed.) (contribution to larger piece), D263
Torgersen, Eric: encomium, G58; reviewer, J77
*Toronto Star*, J431
"To Rose" (poem), B179
Torrey, Beef: interviewer, H104; reviewer, J312, J348, J356
Tortugas, B73
*Touching the Fire* (Welsch) (encomium), G118
Trachtenberg, J. A. (interviewer), H9
Trachtenberg, Jeffrey A. (reviewer), J290
"Tracking" (autobiographical essay), A49; excerpt, D258
"Trader" (poem), B37
*Trading with the Enemy* (Miller) (encomium), G146
*Trail of Crumbs* (Sunee) (encomium), G287
"Transcribe Books" (poem), B156
*Travelers' Tales France* (O'Reilly et al., eds.), D199
*Travelers' Tales Mexico* (O'Reilly and Habegger), D138
Travelers' Tales, D138, D163, D165, D195, D199
*Traveling Light* (Barich) (encomium), G60
*Traverse City MI Record-Eagle*, D100, H29, H108, I7, I63, J175, J195, J235, J256
"Traverse City Zoo" (poem), B39
*Traverse* magazine, B72, B123, D203, H70, I36
*The Tree of Meaning* (Bringhurst) (foreword by JH), D265
*Tributary* magazine, H114, I101, I107
*Tricycle: The Buddhist Review* magazine, B96, D129, D216
*Triquarterly* magazine, B9, B152
*The Triumph of the Sparrow* (Takahashi) (encomium), G65
*A Trout in the Sea of Cortez* (Salter) (encomium), G269
*The True Bones of My Life: Essays on the Fiction of Jim Harrison* (Smith), I91
*True* magazine, D13, D14, D15
*True North* (audiotape and CD), G14
*True North* (novel), A44, A44.a. (proof p. 86), A44.b. (cover p. 86), A44.c. (dust jacket p. 88); reviews, J377–J388
*The Truth of the Trees* (Bennett, ed.), B106
*Trying to Catch the Horses* (Gerber) (encomium), G171
Tschida, Ron: critic, I104; reviewer, J379
*Tucson Weekly*, J140, J174, J250, J315, J405
"The Tugboats of Costa Rica" (essay), D67
Turner, Frederick (encomium), G239, G247, G274
Turner, Jack (encomium), G141, G184
Twayne Publishing, H72
Twichell, Chase (encomium), G159
"Twilight" (poem), B123
"Two Girls" (poem), B151
Tyer, Brad (reviewer), J445

*Under 30* (Newman and Henkin, eds.), B23
Underwood, Lamar (quotations in), D224
*An Unfinished Life* (Spragg) (encomium), G246
*An Unfortunate Woman* (Brautigan) (encomium), G182
"University Acquires Harrison's Manuscripts, Materials" (news report), G39
University of Iowa Press, B128, D20
University of Michigan Press, D175, H31
University of Nebraska Press, B178, D274
University Press of Mississippi, D214, H111
"Unmentionable Cuisine" (essay), D124
*An Upper Great Lakes Archaeological Odyssey* (Lovis, ed.), D226
*Upstream* (Lindsay and McGuane) (encomium), G185
*USA Today*, H118, J101, J110, J119, J399
*US* magazine, I62
*Utne Reader*, D181

*Vanity Fair* magazine, note following H126
Van Wyngarden, Bruce (reviewer), J336
Varno, David (reviewer), J427
Veale, Scott (reviewer), J185, J283, J317
"La Venerie Francaise" ("Where the Chase Is the Song of Hound and Horn") (essay), D12, D89
"Versions of Childhood" (essay), D179
"Versions of Reality" (essay), D184, note following D278
Vice, Brad (reviewer), J369
Vickers, Jean (critic), I88
Viking Press, A11, B29, B39
Village Press, D110
Villard Books, D52
"Vin Blanc" (essay), D259
Vintage Books, D68
"The Violators" ("Grim Reapers of the Land's Bounty") (essay), D9, D93, D150
*Visiting Walt* (Coghill and Tammaro, ed.), B128
Vizenor, Gerald (encomium), G106, G151
Vogel, Traci (reviewer), J133, J164
*Vogue* magazine, H30, I44
*A Voice from the River* (Gerber) (encomium), G87
*Voice of the Borderlands* (Hadley) (encomium), G259
"Voice of the Wilderness" (criticism by JH), E24
*The Voice That Is Great within Us* (Carruth), B28

Wachtel, Eleanor (interviewer), H99
Waddington, Chris (reviewer), J194, J227, J282, J284, J360

Wagamese, Richard (reviewer), J425
Waggoner, Mel (interviewer), H93
"Waiting" (poem), B61
*Wakefield* (Codrescu) (encomium), G241
Waking Owl Books, G41
Walker, Casey (interviewer), H78
Walker, Kevin (reviewer), J191
Walker, Michael (interviewer), H63
"Walking" (poem), A2.a., A2.b., B52, B78, B79
*Walking* (poetry), A2, A2 (cover p. 4)
*Walking It Off* (Peacock) (encomium), G256
"Walking the San Pedro" (essay), D118
*Walking the Trail* (Ellis) (encomium), G99
*Walking with the Bear* (Mindy) (encomium), G186
*Wall Street Journal*, J290
"Walter of Battersea" (poem), B61
*Wamba* (Crawford) (encomium), G215
*Warlock* (novel), A15, A15.b. (dust jacket p. 34); excerpt, C5, C16; reviews, J58–J60
*Warlock* (treatment), F20
"War Suite" (poem), B10, B11, B16, B21, B25
*Washington Post*, E12, I11, J31, J99, J137, J145, J179, J273, J324, J350, J398, J448
*Washington Post Book Report*, I75
*Washington Post Book World*, H44, H98, J82, J322
Washington Square Press, A30.b.
*The Watch* (Bass) (encomium), G86
Wayne State University Press, B50, B67, B107, D226
*The Way We Are* (treatment), F32
Weatherford, Joyce (encomium), G208
*The Wedding.* (Queffelec) (encomium), G72
Weeks, George (JH introduction to), G164
"Weeping" (poem), B51
Weidenfeld & Nicholson, B68
Weigl, Bruce (encomium), G191
Weinzwieg, Ari (encomium), G226
Weiss, Philip (reviewer), J280
Welch, James: encomium, G50, G64, G192; introduction to, D225
Welch, Lew: JH review of, E3
Welsch, Roger (encomium), G118
*Wendigo* (film treatment), F10
*Western American Literature*, I100, J34
*Western Humanities Review*, J27
*Western Wings* (Williams) (encomium), G160
*West of Key West* (Cole and Pollard, eds.), D149
Westrum, Dex (reviewer), J334
*The West's New Writers* magazine, H9
"Westward Ho": excerpt, C29
*Wetting Our Lines Together* (Hoey, ed.), B60

*Whatever Shines: Volume I* (McGookey) (encomium), G202

"What Have We Done with the Thighs" (essay), D98

"What Is It about Anjelica Houston? We Asked Nine Men to Comment" (essay), D53

"*What Thou Lovest Well Remains*" (Ardinger, ed.): encomium, G68; preface by JH, D44

"Where the Chase Is the Song of Hound and Horn" (essay), D12; as "La Venerie Francaise," D89

*Where the Lightning Strikes* (Nabokov) (encomium), G262

*Wherever Home Begins* (Janeczko, ed.), B90

"White" (poem), B19

Whitehead, James (reviewer), J26

*White Pine Sucker River* (Alexander) (encomium), G121

*White Plains NY Central Journal News*, J354

*The Whole Beast* (Henderson) (encomium), G240

*Who's Writing This* (Halpern, ed.), D143

*Why I Write* (Blythe, ed.), D159

"Why I Write, or Not" (essay), D159, D161

"Why I Write: Thoughts on the Craft of Fiction" (essay): quotation from, D224

*Wichita Eagle*, J184

*The Wide Open* (Smith and O'Conner), B178, D274

Wieneke, Connie (critic), I53

*Wild at Heart* (Gifford) (encomium), G90

"Wild Creatures: A Correspondence with Gerard Oberle" (essay), D185, note following D278; as letters, D171

*Wild Duck Review*, H78

*The Wild Girl: The Notebooks of Ned Giles, 1932* (Fergus) (encomium), G253

*Wild on the Fly* magazine, D229

*The Wild Places* (MacFarlane) (encomium), G292

*Wild Stories* (Evans, ed.), D177

William B. Eerdmans Publishing, D262

Williams, Ben o. (encomium), G160

Williams, Brooke (encomium), G174

Williams, Joy (encomium), G63, G78, G95

Williams, Miller: JH review of, E5

Williams, Terry Tempest: encomium, G103; interviewer, H60

Willingham, John R. (reviewer), J4

Willow Creek Press, D252

Wilson, John (critic), I10

*The Wind Is Round* (Hannum and Chase, eds.), B27

"Wine" (essay), D178, D195

"Wine Criticism and Literary Criticism (Part II)" (essay), D234

"Wine from the Heart" (essay), D207

Winegar, Karin: encomium, G261; interviewer, H13; reviewer, J390

"Wine Notes" (essay), D204

Winepress Publishing, B139

"Wine Strategies" (essay), D247

Winn Books, A19

Winn Publishing, D41

Winslow, Art (reviewer), J382

*Winter in the Blood* (Welch) (encomium), G50

*Winter: Notes from Montana* (Bass) (encomium), G100

Wolcott, James (reviewer), J56

*Wolf* (novel), A7, A7.b. (dust jacket p. 13); excerpts, C1, C4, C19, D51; excerpts on audiotape, G5; quote from, G25; reviews, J15–J19

*Wolf* (screenplay), F3

Wolff, Tobias (reviewer), J54

*Wolf Walking* (Daniels, ed.), C19

Womack, Kenneth (critic), I100

"The Woman from Spiritwood" (poem), B55, B61

*The Woman Lit by Fireflies* (fiction—novellas), A22, A22.b. (dust jacket p. 44); reviews, J91–J107

"The Woman Lit by Fireflies" (novella), C18; excerpt, C30; shorter version of final novella published under the same name, C14

"The Woman Lit by Fireflies" [excerpt from "Brown Dog"], C15

"(Woman Reading) by Balthus, 1996" (contribution to larger piece), D218

"Women Impossible Not to Love and Impossible to Love Right" (criticism by JH), E10

"Women We Love: Madeleine Stowe" (essay), D119

Wood, Guy (critic), I14

Woods, William Crawford (reviewer), J31

"Word Drunk" (poem), B125, B146

*Working Horses* (treatment), F17

*Working in the Dark* (Baca) (encomium), G111

*Works in Progress Number 4*, C1

*World Literature Today* magazine, J182

*World Poetry* (Washburn and Major), B100

*The Worlds of Ernest Thompson Seton* (Samsom): review by JH, E22

Worth, January (reviewer), J172

*Woven Stone* (Ortiz) (encomium), G119

*Write Away* (George), C28

"A Writer Loses His Way in Clouds of Theory about the Bermuda Triangle" (criticism by JH), E16
*The Writer's Almanac* (Web site), B119, B132, B144, B166, B167, B176, B177, B184, B185, B186
*The Writer's Chapbook* (Plimpton, ed.), H21
*Writer's Chronicle* magazine, D258, H49
*A Writer's Country* (Knorr and Schell, eds.), B115
Writer's Digest Books, C32
*The Writer's Journal* (Bender), D154
*Writing for Your Life* (Steinberg, ed.), H33
*Writing on Air* (radio broadcast), H109
W. W. Norton & Company, A1, A4, B37, B108, B158, D193, D263
*Wyoming* (Gifford) (encomium), G190

*Yale Review of Books*, J216
Yardley, Jonathan (reviewer), J17, J82, J324, J350
*A Year in Poetry* (Foster and Guthrie, eds.), B91
"A Year's Changes" (poem), B17, B97; excerpt, B36
*You Can't Catch Death* (Brautigan) (encomium), G183
Young, Vernon (reviewer), J21
"Young Love" (poem), B131
*You: Poems by Hayden Carruth* (Carruth) For (encomium), G42

*The Zanzibar Chest* (Hartley) (encomium), G238
*The Zen Works of Stonehouse* (Red Pine) (encomium), G178
*Zingerman's Guide to Good Parmigiano-Reggiano* (Weinzwieg) (encomium), G226
"Zingerman's is the ne plus ultra of delicatessens" (advertisement), G34
*Zingerman's Thanksgiving Catalog*, G34
*Zoetrope* magazine, D161
"A Zoologist Shares the Joys and Woes of Life among the Elephants" (criticism by JH), E17